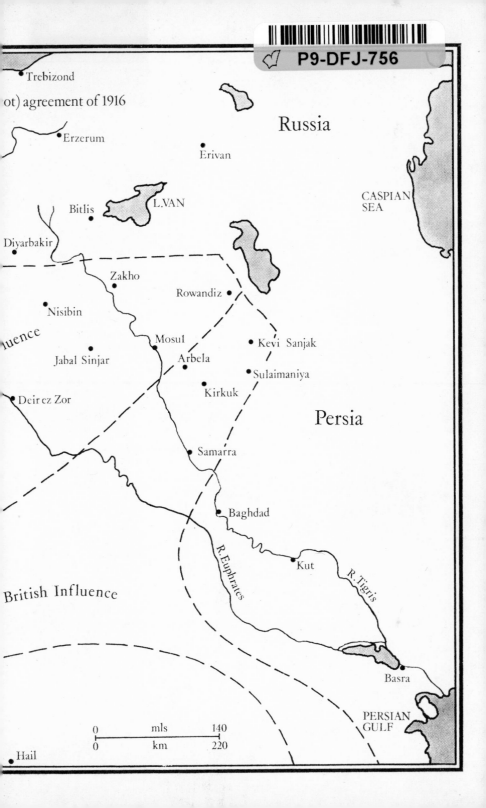

ot) agreement of 1916

Trebizond

Russia

Erzerum

Erivan

CASPIAN
SEA

Bitlis   L.VAN

Diyarbakir

Zakho

Rowandiz

Nisibin

uence   Mosul   Kevi Sanjak

Jabal Sinjar   Arbela

Deir ez Zor   Kirkuk   Sulaimaniya

Persia

Samarra

Baghdad

R. Euphrates

Kut   R. Tigris

British Influence

Basra

PERSIAN
GULF

0	mls	140
0	km	220

Hail

Gertrude Bell

H V F Winstone

Gertrude Bell

JONATHAN CAPE
THIRTY BEDFORD SQUARE LONDON

First published 1978
© 1978 by H. V. F. Winstone

Jonathan Cape Ltd, 30 Bedford Square, London WC1

British Library Cataloguing in Publication Data

Winstone, Harry Victor Frederick
Gertrude Bell.
1. Bell, Gertrude   2. Travellers—East—
Biography
915'.04'41   G463.B423
ISBN 0 224 01432 3

Printed in Great Britain by The Anchor Press Ltd
and bound by Wm Brendon & Son Ltd
both of Tiptree, Essex

Contents

To Joan and Neil
who helped and endured

Illustrations

Between pages 226 and 227

Between pages 242 and 243

Facsimiles

Maps

Introduction

No life could ever have been better documented than that of Gertrude Bell. From early childhood to the end of her days she recorded every step, every significant event, in letters to her family and friends. That rich vein of source material has been well and truly mined. There have been several studies based on the letters, most of them written by women, and one of them has been widely and deservedly praised, Miss Elizabeth Burgoyne's *Gertrude Bell: from her Personal Papers*, a two-volume work covering the years 1889–1914 and 1914–26, the first part of which was published in 1958.

When Lady Bell, Gertrude's stepmother, published the selected *Letters of Gertrude Bell* in 1927 there was an immediate complaint that important correspondence had been omitted, and the same accusation was levelled at Miss Burgoyne's work when it appeared. It must be supposed that reviewers were referring to the letters exchanged between Gertrude and the man who came into her life just before the First World War, Lt-Colonel Doughty-Wylie, but if that were the case they must have known that Mrs Doughty-Wylie was still alive and that the Bell family had quite properly concealed the correspondence from public view in order to protect her from the embarrassment and distress which would have been caused by its publication. Apart from that batch of letters I can find no evidence among the papers kept by Gertrude's parents and sisters, now in the keeping of the University Library at Newcastle upon Tyne, to suggest that there has ever been sinful omission of salient facts or documents, apart from a somewhat incomplete account of her death.

Nevertheless we are presented with a one-sided account. It is in relation to her most important work, her roles in the war-time politics of Arabia and the post-war settlement in Iraq, that there is a significant gap in the existing record of her life, but again the official documents needed to amplify her own accounts of these matters were not available to earlier writers. On the other hand, unofficial and semi-official documents were available and might have been used to give balance and contrast to a story which suffers from a lack of that most charming of human qualities, the ability to be wrong. I refer particularly to the letters to Sir Valentine Chirol and Colonel Frank Balfour, now in the University Library of Durham, and the papers of Sir Arnold Wilson in the British Museum, some of which have been used by Sir Arnold's own biographer.

The need for a biography which relies on testimony other than that contained in Gertrude's own letters has long been evident. I have necessarily started where others have started, at the beginning, and I must hope that readers already familiar with the earlier biographies, and with the Lady Bell selected *Letters* and *Earlier Letters* (edited by Lady Richmond), will forgive the repetition. Where I have quoted extensively from the correspondence I have tried to use the unpublished letters as much as possible, or those from which Miss Burgoyne chose so well, though inevitably with brevity.

Perhaps the most difficult decision facing anyone who tries to write about Gertrude Bell is whether or not to use footnotes. Almost every moment of her life is attested and affirmed by a document of one sort or another and to enumerate them all would be to turn the work into something resembling an exercise in higher mathematics. I have therefore relied on extensive notes to chapters at the end of the book, thus I hope satisfying those with a craving for archival information without bothering the reader who prefers an unbroken narrative.

I have deliberately refrained from seeking the sanction or approval of the Bell family in writing this work. I did not expect to find any very remarkable skeletons in the cupboard, neither did I find any. But formal approval, at whatever remove of time, is always slightly inhibiting. All the same I have needed help from several branches of the family and I am especially indebted to Mrs Pauline Dower, Gertrude's niece, and to the Hon. Mrs Sylvia Henley, a cousin on the Stanley side, who are closer than anyone to the facts about the life of my subject. I would like to express my thanks also to the present Lady Bell for loaning me a portrait of Gertrude's mother; to Lady Plowden, another of Gertrude's nieces, Lady Arthur, Mrs Geoffrey Dixon, and Mrs Daphne Owen; and to Mr John Bell Dixon whose patient search through his grandmother's diaries enabled me to fill a number of gaps in my knowledge of the family background. In the same context Mr John Dorman Bolckow provided me with extremely useful background on the people and the structure of the steel industry in the north-east of England in the days when his own forbears and the Bells were its leading figures.

Particular acknowledgment must also be made to Mr Seton Dearden, author and authority on Iraq and the Middle East, who kindly found for me a letter from Captain Shakespear to Gertrude which he rescued from the old Baghdad chancery, and who was the first to publish a selection of the Doughty-Wylie letters, in the *Cornhill Magazine*. Although I went back to the original letters I have referred to his well-ordered presentation of the story and have quoted him in connection with it. As for the later chapters which deal primarily with the Iraq period, I am greatly indebted to Mr C. J. Edmonds and Brigadier S. H. Longrigg, incomparable authorities on the Kurdish question and Iraq respectively. In that connection too, my thanks to Mr Lionel Jardine who responded generously to my frequent and importunate calls on his time and patience. Also in regard to the Iraq period I would like to thank Dr John Clayton, son of Sir Gilbert Clayton, and Mrs Margaret Gosling for their help. Of those who remembered Gertrude Bell in the later years of her life and who were able to give me personal accounts of her, none stands higher in the esteem of those who know Arabia than Dame Violet Dickson, who still wanders among her friends of the desert, and I wish to express my gratitude to her for allowing me to quote her impressions, especially those contained in her book *Forty Years in Kuwait*; and to her daughter Mrs Zahra Freeth, my constant guide in the Arabian peninsula. I am also grateful to Lt-Colonel Gerald de Gaury for his knowledgeable observations.

The official and academic institutions on which I have relied heavily are acknowledged elsewhere. I would, however, like to thank in particular Mrs Penelope Tuson of the India Office, whose guidance through the files of what might broadly be called the 'Gulf' region has saved me, and many other researchers, much time and effort; her expert help was tantamount to encouragement of my project. Mrs Anne Cullen researched for me in the library of the University of Newcastle upon Tyne, where the majority of the Gertrude Bell records are now kept, and she saved me many a time-consuming journey, as did my daughter Ruth who similarly delved into the files of the University Library at Durham. I thank them both.

Finally a note on spellings. For the sake of clarity and readability minor changes to spelling and punctuation have been made to some quotations from Gertrude's letters. As for Arabic transliteration it is quite impossible to achieve absolute conformity in narrative and quotations, but in the case of common words like *amir*, *badawin*, *sharif* and place names, I have sometimes changed the spelling in an attempt to save the reader from the most irritating inconsistencies.

London 1978   H.V.F.W.

Acknowledgments

The author wishes to thank the following for their help in making available the letters and documents on which this book is based: the Librarian and Keeper of the Pybus Collection, the University of Newcastle upon Tyne, and the Assistant Librarian, Special Collections; the Librarian, University Library, Durham, and the Keeper of Oriental Books; the Controller, HMSO and the Keeper of the Public Record Office, for access to the files of the Foreign and Colonial Offices, and the Director of the India Office Library and Records for access to documents relating to the India Office and the Government of India; the Ministry of Defence, Army and Naval intelligence records; the British Museum and the British Library in connection with the papers of Sir Arnold Wilson and books in general; the Director and Secretary of the Royal Geographical Society for access to Gertrude Bell's letters, photographs, note books and other documents in the Society's keeping, and for the loan of books.

He also thanks the following for permission to reproduce illustrations: the present Lady Bell for nos 1, 2 and 5; Newcastle University Library for nos 3, 4, 10–13, 15, 18 and 37; *Country Life* for no. 6; the National Trust for no. 7; the Royal Geographical Society for nos 8, 14, 16, 17 and 19–34; the Radio Times Hulton Picture Library for nos 9, 35 and 36.

The endpaper maps showing the secret Sykes–Picot agreement are derived from a War Office map (WO 106/1415) in the Public Record Office, to which certain place names have been added for the convenience of the reader. The remaining maps are reproduced with permission of the Royal Geographical Society. The line drawing on the title page is based on a bust of Gertrude Bell in the possession of the Royal Geographical Society.

The author has made every effort to trace all copyright material which has been used here, but apologises to any publisher or author whom he has been unable to contact.

1

Early Days

Fifty years after her death the Victorian mansion in which Gertrude Bell was born, the Hall at Washington in England's northern county of Durham, is a training centre for the National Coal Board. Visitors arrive at the village from many parts of the world but they usually come to see another house, the Old Hall, which was built in the thirteenth century and became the home of the de Wessingtons, George Washington's ancestors. Few make the journey of a hundred yards or so to the redbrick establishment which was the home of three generations of the Bell family and whose first owner, Sir Isaac Lowthian Bell (usually called Lowthian), may be said to have done as much as any man to create the industries that have sustained and tormented the north-east of England to this day, and to foster the technical advances of the late nineteenth century which made Britain rich beyond the dreams of the pioneers of the Industrial Revolution. Those who take the trouble to call at the other Hall may, by peering through its stained-glass and leaded windows, just make out a wall plaque and its legend which neatly sets out the essential facts of the life of the industrialist's grand-daughter:

GERTRUDE BELL
Scholar, historian, archaeologist, explorer,
poet, mountaineer, gardener,
distinguished servant of the state.
She was born here on 14 July 1868
and died in Baghdad 12 July 1926

It is necessary to go to the back of the house to find a tall, slender tower with windows from bottom to top, each surmounted by a rather ugly gargoyle head, and topped by a copper vane pointing an accusing finger to heaven, to discover that this monument to the neo-Gothic ideal was the inspiration of one of England's great scientists and foremost ironmasters. 'This tower,' says a barely decipherable inscription, 'was erected by I. Lowthian Bell in the years 1854 and 1857.' If Gertrude was the most famous daughter of a remarkable family he was its finest son and he is denied a proper regard in history only for the fact that his private and business papers were lost, or perhaps destroyed, after his death. To him Gertrude owed her vital qualities of mind and and will, and the vast fortune that was her sheet-anchor.

Gertrude Margaret Lowthian Bell, to give her all her names, has been called a 'child of fortune', and it may be that if any of us could choose the time and place of our birth, midsummer in the year 1868 in the compact and beautiful county of Durham, within one of England's richest and most enlightened families, would be a popular set of circumstances. But wealth and security are no guarantees of protection from nature's shocks.

Her father, Hugh Bell, with his good looks and intelligence, his impeccable manners, tousled red hair and carefully trimmed beard, must have been regarded as an eligible catch by many a mother and daughter beyond his native heath. At the age of twenty-three, however, he married a local girl, Maria, the daughter of John Shield, a prominent merchant of Newcastle upon Tyne. The wedding took place on April 23rd, 1867 at the Parish church of Rothesay on the island of Bute in the Clyde, where the Shield family maintained a summer residence. She was twenty-three years old, delicate in health and, it is said, of frail beauty. Gertrude was born in the July of the following year. Relatives were numerous on both sides of the family and they descended on the Hall at Washington in droves to admire the baby and embrace her mother and father. Maria soon came to be known as Mary, sometimes as Mary Hugh, and at weekends she would stroll proudly in the surrounding country or into the village with the infant Gertrude, accompanied by aunts, uncles, nephews and nieces; at other times they would take a carriage or train to Northallerton, some twenty miles to the south across the north Yorkshire moors, where grandfather Lowthian was building a new home, or to Redcar on the coast where Hugh was also building a house for his family, both establishments being designed by Philip Webb, the friend and collaborator of William Morris who had himself undertaken to look after the interior decoration of Lowthian's residence, Rounton Grange.

Although Washington Hall was a spacious house, with attic rooms for ten or more domestic servants and an inner courtyard, there were usually several friends or relatives in residence; the wooded outskirts and high walls were poor barriers against the busy world of the ironmaster's making. Hugh and Mary must have looked forward to the relative seclusion of their own home, especially when they learnt that another child was expected. 'Red Barns', as they called the new house at Redcar, was ready for occupation in the autumn of 1870. Gertrude's brother was born there on March 29th, 1871. Mary, exhausted by her second pregnancy and the effort of childbirth, never arose from her bed. She contracted a fatal pneumonia and died on April 19th at the age of twenty-seven. Her son, a healthy but not particularly robust child, was named Maurice Hugh Lowthian.

Hugh led a lonely life at Redcar in the desolate years that followed his wife's death. A wet-nurse had to be found to rear Maurice, and Gertrude, now four years old and a high-spirited handful by all accounts, was put in the care of a governess, Miss Ogle, but that lady does not seem to have been able to dampen the child's spirit. She and her brother as he got older were inevitably drawn to the sea, which lapped almost to their garden gate at high tide, and the unfortunate Miss Ogle spent much of her time rescuing them from the beach and the boats moored on it. She eventually gave way to a middle-aged German lady, Miss Klug, who appears to have had more success in handling Gertrude and her young brother. The earliest surviving letters speak well of Miss Klug's instruction in handwriting and composition. In March 1874 when the children were staying at the family's London home, 10 Belgrave Terrace, the five-year-old Gertrude wrote to her grandmother Margaret in a large, competent and confident hand: 'My dear Grandmama, My dolls have given me great amusement you were very good to get them done for me. We are very happy here. We like our riding lessons very much. We went to a Circus yesterday we saw a horse march in time to the music it was very pretty. I shall like to be with you in London ... Maurice and I send love to G\ud\upapa and Auntie Ada, from your affectionate grandchild, Gertrude M. L. Bell.'

There were fleeting memories of Gertrude's mother in the

B

10 Belgrave Terrace
March 26

My dear Grandmama

My dolls have

given me great amuse=

=ment you were very

good to get them done

for me. We are very happy

An extract from Gertrude's first recorded letter

years that followed her death. In April 1871 Lowthian's brother John and his second wife Margaret Elizabeth ('Lizzie' to the family) were on holiday in Italy when the news came to them from Hugh's sister Florence. Lizzie made a cryptic entry in her diary: 'Hear from Fanny Bell's letter that we shall see Mary Hugh no more.' The influence of the Bell family in those days may be judged from the fact that a Royal Navy warship was made available to them to speed their journey home, though they do not, in fact, seem to have hurried unduly. On June 20th Lizzie noted: 'Start by train for Rounton. Find Isaac and the girls well and after lunch walk to Mary's grave and talk to Isaac about her.' It seems that Gertrude's grandfather had moved to Rounton Grange, his new home near Northallerton, by then, which perhaps explains why Mary was buried there. Ada Bell, Hugh's unmarried sister, was living with him at Red Barns at that time and playing a large part in the upbringing of Gertrude and Maurice. Lizzie visited her often and they would take the children over to Rounton to put flowers on the grave. But Gertrude's fondest reminder of her mother was in her constant childhood companion and life-long friend Horace Marshall, who was the son of Mary's sister Kate, Mrs Thomas Marshall. Horace was almost exactly her own age and he shared her adventurous spirit. Maurice had some difficulty in keeping up with her tomboyish behaviour – she was seldom unequal to the challenge of a tree or building – but her cousin, with whom she spent countless holidays at his home in Leeds and Scotland, was a companion after her own heart.

The clear and painstaking handwriting which Gertrude cultivated as a child endured until she was nine or ten years old. Afterwards it degenerated quickly into the impetuous scrawl that was to cause many a headache among recipients of her letters and those who came to read them in later years. She had not yet taken to writing on trains and boats, though she was already a seasoned traveller for her tender years. In 1876 she was in London again and in April wrote to her father: 'Dear Papa, I like the riding very much I see the primroses in the hedges and I am learning to ride in my stirrups. Today we went for a drive with the maids and gathered lots of primroses.' Her abiding love of flowers was another of the qualities which showed themselves in childhood.

There is an affectionate portrait of father and daughter at this time, painted by Sir Edward Poynter. Gertrude is shown as a pretty child with an oval face, curly shoulder-length hair and a

wide-eyed expression, seated on Hugh's knee and holding his
hand. The artist has captured both the underlying unhappiness of
the time and the devotion between father and daughter which
was to prevail throughout their lives.

Two years earlier Gertrude had written her first letter to Miss
Olliffe, the daughter of the distinguished Irish physician and a
friend of Hugh's sisters Maisie and Ada. The letter was sent after
a holiday in Scotland where her father had met Miss Olliffe for
the first time. It contained news of the family's Persian cat.

My dear Florence,
Mopsa has been very naughty this morning. She has been
scampering all over the dining-room Cilla says. I had a great
chase all over the hall and dining room to catch her and bring
her to Papa. She bit and made one little red mark on my hand.
During breakfast she hissed at Kitty Scott ... I forgot to say
Kitty was very frightened ...
       Your affectionate little friend Gertrude Bell

The friendship between Hugh and Florence flourished despite
some initial hesitation on his part. Florence described their first
encounter: ' ... he was standing in profile at the end of a path half
roofed over with climbing roses. He had thick curling hair and
his beard was a bright auburn colour. He looked beautiful but
very sad.'

Hugh's sisters repeatedly told Florence that they wished she
would marry their brother, but his first impulse was to 'fly from
danger'. He had vowed never to marry again after Mary's death
but he would not be the first widower to reconsider such a
decision. One of the sisters in question, Mary Katherine, or
Maisie as she was called by the family, was married to Edward
Lyulph Stanley, the son of Baron Stanley of Alderley and heir to
the baronies of Alderley and Sheffield. Lyulph was the favourite
uncle of Bertrand Russell, who was four years Gertrude's junior,
and it was after a gathering at the home of the formidable Lady
Stanley – so 'keen on enlightenment' and so 'contemptuous of
Victorian goody-goody priggery' – that the marital die was cast
for the second time in Hugh Bell's life, at the age of thirty-two.
Florence Eveleen Eleanore Olliffe was an artist of considerable
virtuosity and the gathering at the Stanley household on June
4th, 1876 was arranged in order to stage an opera she had written
and produced. After the performance Hugh escorted her to her

home in Sloane Street in a hansom cab and they arrived an engaged couple. 'Lady Olliffe, I have brought your daughter home, and I have come to ask if I may take her away again,' was said to be Hugh's urbane proposal. Lady Olliffe burst into tears.

The couple were married on August 10th at the little Trinity church which then stood in Sloane Street. For the first time in her life Gertrude became aware of a mother. She and Florence had already formed a bond of friendship and soon a happy and dutiful stepdaughter began to address letters to 'My dear Mamy' and 'Dearest Mother'. In September 1877 she went on holiday to Dulverton with Maurice and the Marshalls.

My dear Mamy,
We are having such fun here. Yesterday we caught an alive eel. Horace caught it. Yesterday evening Horace and Maurice caught two fish in the harbour and Horace caught such a big one. Every morning we go to the rocks in our wading suits, our game is to jump off the rocks into the pool, we call it taking headers, it is such fun. Give my love to Papa. From your loving child, *Gertrude*. Horace sends his love to you and Papa.

In the following year she spent a great deal of time with her grandparents at Rounton Grange, a tall stone house built according to that principle of a softer, early-English style which Morris and his followers advocated in response to some of the harsher architectural experiments of the time. Interior decoration was the combined work of Morris and Burne-Jones. While there, in August 1878, she wrote again to Florence in the innocent vein of childhood:

My dear mother,
You have sent me all the things I wanted. I liked my letter so much. I had a lovely ride, Prince had not forgotten me. It is a nasty raw day. Auntie Masie comes up to us in the evenings, she is so kind. Grandmamma wants you to send my best dress she gave me. Dear Mother I have not forgotten the promise I made to you and all the sugar I give to Prince. Give my love to Papa. From your loving child, Gertrude.

But the enchantment of childhood was slowly ebbing and a young lady began to emerge from the letters she continued to write, lovingly and dutifully, to her parents and her friends.

By about 1879 her neat and careful script and her ingenuous

words and phrases had given way to the dashed-off, sometimes scrawled writing of later years, and to more serious matters such as examinations. An undated and unaddressed letter of the period bridges the gap between the child and the young woman. It was written from 'Highfield', the Marshalls' home in Leeds:

> Dearest Mother, Thank-you very much for letting me stay here ... I shall be able to go on with my chaticism very easily after I have gone through it with Aunty Katie, for I am learning it very throughly and going thorough all the notes. I got my sum-book and am working at my holiday tasks every day. I do so want to pass the Cambridge Exam ... I climb all the trees and walls I can lay hold of here ... I remain your very loving daughter, Gertrude. PS (à la Maurice) How are Don and Prince and Fay and Tom and the Canary and Benedicts and Hugo and Elsa and Abby and Mrs Abby and you and Papa and the rabbits. P.S. Aunty Katie sends you much love and says she is rather fond of me on the hole.

The inquiries after domestic pets and servants ceased from then on, as did her role in the mandatory funeral processions at Red Barns when one of the cats or other animals died and had to be buried. Only two factors remained constant in her letters – the spelling, which improved little in her lifetime so that the reader is often mystified by untranslatable words, and the deep and genuine affection.

Dearest Mother,

Thank-you very much for letting me stay here till the 3d Have you got your dressing-room furnished yet? I shall be able to go on with my chatidsin very easily after I have gone through it with aunty Katie, for I am learning it very throughly and going through all the notes. I got my sum-book and am working at my holiday-tasks every day. I do so want to pass the Cambridge Exam.

An extract from one of Gertrude's letters to her stepmother, Florence

2
Society and Oxford

With the appearance of Florence, who was twenty-five when she married Gertrude's father, there was a perceptible change in the life-style of the family. In 1875 Lowthian Bell had been elected a Fellow of the Royal Society and Liberal Member of Parliament for Hartlepool. The prestige of the Bells stood high and it was common enough to see the family gathered in force aboard uncle John's yacht on a celebratory voyage from Saltburn, just south of Redcar where it was moored, to Scarborough or some other resort. On one occasion the Bells and other families of means in the district gathered at the Yorkshire home of a prominent manufacturing family. As they left the hostess was overheard asking a relative sympathetically, 'I wonder what they feel like going back to their poky little homes?' The phrase was used from then on to describe the several estates in Durham and Northumberland which the Bells owned. Hugh's favourite pastimes were those of the country gentleman, hunting, shooting, riding, and Gertrude often accompanied him on one of her ponies. Discussion at Red Barns and Rounton Grange usually centred on industry and politics and, of course, matters of science and technology. Florence brought a new set of friends and precepts with her. Reared in Paris in the days of the Second Empire, her earliest recollections were of the illustrious men and women who sought the companionship of her Irish father and her fascinating mother, Laura, as they passed through the French capital.

Sir Joseph Olliffe was honorary physician to the British Embassy. A man of learning and pronounced Irish wit, he had devised an elaborate plan to redevelop the town of Deauville, in collaboration with Count de Morny, when he and his family were forced to flee Paris by the advance of the Prussian army in 1870.

Charles Dickens was a regular caller at the Olliffes' home when he was in France and he found special delight in the company of the young Florence, begging her father to allow her to attend his play-readings when she was between seven and ten years old. It was on Sir Joseph's orders that the novelist and his family were sent back to England when the 'Boulogne sore-throat' struck in 1856; and it was to Lady Olliffe that Dickens divulged his youthful love of Maria Beadnell, Dora of *David Copperfield*. Florence was multi-lingual and was reared on the Paris Opéra and the Théâtre français. Her real passion, though, was music and she wanted to study at the Royal College in London as a child but her parents would not hear of it, and so she settled for writing as a pastime, though even that art had to be practised in some secrecy. She reacted to the constraints of her time by making a friend of Coquelin, who produced one of her plays anonymously, and by becoming one of the leading lights of the realist school of drama which, in later years, centred on Ibsen and Shaw. She had endless patience with children, for whom she wrote a string of one-act plays in English, French and German, and she had decided views on their upbringing. She believed that 'urbanity should be persistently taught and practised in the home'. Good manners were her yardstick in judging people, and it was said of her that she belonged to a generation which held that 'people might not talk about their health or their means'. She upheld the principle religiously as she held court at the Yorkshire home of the Bells, almost always dressed in black, and always at the centre of a scene which was warm in its domesticity and scintillating in its companionship.

Florence Bell's sister Mary was married to Frank Lascelles, then a secretary at the embassy in Washington, and she and Hugh spent their honeymoon with them in America. When they arrived back at Red Barns she began to take a close interest in the educational progress of her 'affectionate little friend'. By the age of eleven Gertrude was reading Green's *History* before breakfast and devouring books with immense enthusiasm. Her bubbling enjoyment of holidays with her favourite aunts — Katie at Highfield, where Horace remained her constant companion, and her father's sister Florence, now Mrs Walter Johnson, in Inverness-shire — still flowed from her letters, but now there was more of books and history. 'I have finished my days of Bruce. On Thursday Ivor and I took off our shoes and stockings and padeled up a beautiful little burn. Aunty Florence is learning galic, she says that it is very difficult.' The redoubtable Miss Klug still gave Gertrude instruction and fought a losing battle with her spelling and her high spirits: 'The other day when I was playing with Arthur and Bunting [Aunt Ada's children] in the garden, Arthur was swinging the swing, and, before I could catch him, Bunting rushed across and the swing knocked him on the eyelid and made it swell very much.' By the summer of 1881 her antics were becoming alarming. To Florence she writes: 'Dearest Mother, when are you coming home? We shall be so glad to see you. I throw Fay [the dog] into the pool every day, he does hate it so much.' Again: 'I'm having such fun with the dirt ... I am learning Euclid with Horace.'

By now two children of Hugh's second marriage had been born, a son Hugh Lowthian who, in the family tradition, was known by another name altogether, Hugo; and Florence Elsa who was known by her second name. It was with Elsa and Hugo, two and three years old respectively, that Gertrude was 'having such fun with the dirt'. In the summer of 1881 the third and last child of the marriage, Mary Katherine (Molly), was on the way. In 1882 Horace Marshall went away to Eton while Maurice was at preparatory school. Gertrude kept in touch with them, telling them of her own boisterous activities which in that year consisted mainly of leading her young brother and sister, Hugo and Elsa, in climbing expeditions up and over the scaffolding at Red Barns where Hugh was making additions to the building. She spent much of the summer with aunt Katie at Leeds and she went to her first political meeting at which the Liberal Prime Minister and his son Herbert were the chief speakers. She wrote to her mother:

I saw Mr Gladstone as he was driving away from the Great Mass Meeting. Of course he was very tired when I saw him, but he struck me as looking so very old and grey. Aunty Katie went 3 times to hear him speak and he only spoke 4 times. She said she had never heard anything like it. At the great mass meeting there were 30,000 people. Gladstone was very tired so they tried to put on some other people to speak for half an hour, but the people would hear nobody but Gladstone. At last Herbert Gladstone rose, the people were delighted and listened to him for half an hour. Every time he said he was going to stop they said 'go it 'Erbert'. Auntie Katie said he spoke very well and very like his father ...

In the same year she passed her first local Cambridge examination. In May 1882 she wrote to her 'Most dear cousin', Horace. ' ... Have you seen Browning's new book? I suppose not. There is only one thing in it that we poor mortals can understand.'

She listed her week's reading for Horace's approval: 'Monday (evening) Mrs Carlisle's Letters 1st volume; Tuesday Mrs C's letters finished, began Life of Macaulay; Wednesday 1 Vol. Life of M finished, began 11 vol; Thursday 11 Vol. of Life of M. finished, I Vol. Mozart's Letters began; Friday 11 Vol. M's Letters finished. That is not bad is it? as all these books are great fat ones ... Our collection of eggs is getting on splendidly.' She was fourteen years of age. It was almost time for her to begin her formal education.

Gertrude continued to live at Red Barns and to receive the tuition of Florence and Miss Klug until the spring of 1884 when she was sent to live at the Olliffe home at 95 Sloane Street. She went as a day scholar to Queen's College in Harley Street, where a school friend of her mother, Camilla Croudace, was Lady President. She cannot have been disappointed in Gertrude to whom learning came so easily and who was to declare in later years, 'I believe I can learn anything'. In her first year she came first in a class of some forty girls in English history with marks of 88 out of 88. She was second in English grammar, third in geography and fourth in French and ancient history. Only in Scripture, a subject she could never cope with because, as she told her teachers, she 'simply didn't believe it', and in German, did she do 'badly'; she came sixth and seventh in them. Her history master at Queen's, where she became a boarder in her second year, was Mr Cramb, whose unfortunate name did nothing to conceal his outstanding ability as a teacher. To him Gertrude owed her early enthusiasm for history and the encouragement to pursue that subject at university.

Maurice had now joined his cousin at Eton and Gertrude made frequent journeys from London to Windsor to be with them. In June 1884 she was planning to visit them along with Florence and she wrote asking for cotton dresses — 'I am dreadfully hot' — and protesting that her masters had had 'another fit of giving papers, a very bad attack this time, and I really don't see at the present time how I shall ever get them all done'. Another of her mother's school friends, Carrie Coxhead, invited her to spend part of her summer holiday in 1884 at her home in Northumberland, and so another family tie was re-established.

Her letters show a quickening sense of purpose and a developing critical faculty. 'I was very much disappointed with Uncle Hugh's books,' she told her father after staying with Mary's brother, Hugh Shield. 'I don't think they are at all interesting. Also I don't think much of his pictures. Of course I don't know but that's what I think. Am I right? On the other hand he has five Turner engravings, very large ones, they're very beautiful. One I recognized to be from a picture Ruskin talks about, because of a peculiar shadow ... '

She began to find her feet socially during her second year at Queen's College. 'It's a very disagreeable process finding out that one is no better than the common run of people,' she wrote after staying with Mrs Richmond Ritchie, Thackeray's daughter Anne, and discovering through her that modesty was not without attraction. She added with commendable candour: 'I've gone through rather a hard course of it since I came to College and I don't like it at all; still I am afraid there is a good deal more to come yet.' She went with Anne Ritchie to the National Portrait Gallery to see a picture of Anne's father. She met Fanny Kemble, Mrs Siddons's niece, who was well known to her step-mother, and spent some time with her uncle Hugh Shield, whose books she disapproved of, at his rooms in the Temple.

She had two history lecturers at Queen's College, Mr de Soyres and Mr Rankine, and her attitude to them showed signs of the outspoken relationship that she was to have with authority for the rest of her life. She sent her father an essay she had written on Cromwell, together with Mr de Soyres's comments. Her master wrote:

There is an abundance of ability in this essay but it is rather a brilliant piece of advocacy for Cromwell, like a clever Barrister's address to the jury, calmly assuming some things really in doubt, pressing on all the adversary's weak points and ignoring his strong points. It is this drawback which makes me hesitate to affix 'Excellent' though I have given it to one or two essays distinctly inferior in talent.

In a note of self-appraisal she commented: 'The fault of my essay is that I tried to prove that Cromwell was *right* when I need only have proved that he was *not wrong* which is a very different thing.' She also enclosed for her father's interest an old essay marked by the other master. 'I don't think it is at all good myself, but Mr Rankine told me that he liked it very much. I don't believe much in Mr Rankine ... He's got a sort of delusion that he always has to give me Exc.' She was about to take more examinations. 'I'm in despair about my modern history; it's so difficult or else I am so stupid, but at any rate that horrid history won't go into my head. I can't keep the German Protestants and the French Protestants and the Moravian Protestants distinct and the Swiss and the Hungarians distinct ... I'm rather quaking at the exams. I hope I shall pull through not too disgracefully somehow ... Bother! – what a smudge!'

Before leaving school at the end of term she heard that her grandfather had been made a baronet. 'I know about Grandpapa,' she told her father. 'I have written to congratulate him. I mayn't say to anyone else but I may say to you I suppose that I am very sorry indeed, it's a great pity. I think he quite deserves to have it only I wish it could have been offered and refused.'

Her father had mixed feelings about a university education for his daughter but he acceded to Mr Cramb's advice and she was enrolled at Lady Margaret Hall, Oxford, in 1886.

'I've done Milton most of today. I always feel I could stand on my head for want of a better outlet for my delight after Lycidas or Comus. It's very difficult to keep the knowledge of all that exquisite beauty to myself without discussing it with anyone.' The joy of learning expressed in letters to her mother and father during the two years at Queen's College was to last all her life and Oxford was but another stage in a long and loving pursuit. Only the piano ever really defeated her – she pleaded with her parents to let her give it up – though singing and other forms of music gave her pleasure in her earlier years: 'I am singing Lascia ch'io pianga and Verdi Prati (are they right spelt).'

She was just eighteen when she arrived at Lady Margaret Hall. There were only two colleges at the university which women could attend in her time, Somerville and L.M.H., and ladies were forbidden to walk beyond the confines of the college unchaperoned. At lectures they were separated from the men, usually being placed

on the stage or in some corner of the room where they could be
kept under observation. Her earliest companions were Mary
Talbot, the gentle daughter of John Talbot, the distinguished
Burgess of the University, and niece of the Warden of Keble;
Edith Langridge, who had been at Queen's College before her
and had been asked by Miss Croudace to look after her; and
Janet Hogarth, sister of the archaeologist and Arabist David
Hogarth, the first link in a chain of events that was to lead her
inexorably to an eastern stage of which she as yet knew nothing.
Her tutor was the 'decidedly clever' Arthur Hassall, and the first
impression of Gertrude at Oxford is provided by his wife, who
after entertaining the new girl to tea, said that she found her 'prim'.

It is to Janet Hogarth, however, that we owe the most intimate
glimpse of Gertrude in her two years at university.

> ... she came up ... I think, partly to work off the 'awkward
> years' before being launched fully into London Society, but
> also because of her obvious aptitude for historical study. She
> was, I think, the most brilliant creature who ever came
> amongst us, the most alive at every point, with her timeless
> energy, her splendid vitality, her unlimited capacity for work,
> for talk, for play. She was always an odd mixture of maturity
> and childishness, grown up in her judgement of men and
> affairs, child-like in her certainties, and most engaging in her
> entire belief in her father and the vivid intellectual world in
> which she had been brought up.

According to her aunt Florence, she was somewhat podgy at
this time and given to stooping, which caused her to have rounded
shoulders. Photographs of the period bear out the impression,
which is not a surprising one in a girl of her age. In any case the
puppy fat and the stoop soon disappeared. Gertrude, like her
half-sisters then growing to womanhood at Red Barns, was
renowned for her erect carriage and for the deportment which
her stepmother insisted on with the authority of her close association with the stage and the leading actresses of her day. Janet
Hogarth spoke of this 'half child, half woman' as being 'rather
untidy, with vivid auburn hair, greenish eyes, brilliant complexion, curiously long and pointed nose, and a most confiding
assurance of being welcome in our society'. Gertrude's family,
especially her stepmother and, in later years, her sister Elsa,
always took care to stress her essential regard for the conventions

of Victorian society; to insist that though she might privately question the opinion of a teacher, she would never overstep the mark in her public attitude to him, any more than she would go beyond a clearly defined line in disputes with her parents. In fact, there was always a streak of ambivalence in her attitude to authority. Like most well-brought-up people in Victorian England, Gertrude believed firmly in the conventions and manners of the age. But she was not unwilling to flout the accepted rules of conduct when her temper was roused or her sense of rightness was violated. She soon discovered for instance that she was not allowed to use the Radcliffe Camera since she was not yet an honours student. She was outraged when the librarian refused her a ticket and whenever she passed him in the street she wanted to shake her fist at him. That he was merely obeying the rules never occurred to her. She was not accustomed to obstacles. Her period at Lady Margaret Hall in the time of its famous principal Dame Elizabeth Wordsworth was nevertheless happy and productive. She read regularly for seven hours a day and yet found time for every kind of sport and leisure activity that was permitted her. Swimming, fencing, rowing, tennis and hockey all attracted her, as did the Union debates and the simple pleasure of 'swinging' across the Parks to watch a cricket match or to attend St Mary's where the university sermon was often delivered by the eloquent Bishop Boyd Carpenter.

There were times when, even for her, work became difficult and oppressive. 'The amount of work is hopeless. Slave as one may, one never gets through the due quota every week. This last week for instance, I ought to have read the life of Richard III, another in two volumes of Henry VIII, the continuous history of Hallam and Green from Edward IV to Ed. VI, the third volume of Stubbs, 6 or 7 lectures of Mr Lodge, to have looked up a few of Mr Campion's last term lectures, and some of Mr Bright's, and lastly to have written 6 essays for Mr Hassall. Now I ask you, is that possible?' Occasionally the effects of overwork told on her. 'Do you know I'm rather a poor thing this term; I haven't felt well ever since I came up, and yesterday I woke in the middle of the night to find myself fainting ... Wasn't it a very odd thing to do? After a time I got up and went to Edith Langridge who gave me some brandy and then I went to sleep again.' But such moments were rare. She generally sailed through her undergraduate years.

Her financial independence and early environment of brilliant
and free-thinking debate placed her in a category which both
friends and teachers found unusual. Mary Talbot, brought up in
an atmosphere of High Anglicanism, took some time to come to
terms with Gertrude's animated and unreserved manner and her
'unequivocal atheism'. Janet Hogarth, reared on less confining
beliefs, often disagreed with her but was seldom shocked by her
outspoken opinions. 'I had a charming lesson with Mr Hassall
yesterday,' Gertrude wrote to her father. 'He came in late from
riding – kept me waiting a minute or two – and we sat down in
armchairs on either side of the fire and talked hard for the first
half hour before we got to business at all. We talked politics
mostly in the intervals. He is what he is pleased to call a Democratic Tory! but I find that admits of being in thorough sympathy
with the Liberals, an admirer of Mr Gladstone and a Home
Ruler!'

Her own somewhat discriminating brand of Liberalism was
portrayed in another letter to him, written early in her second
year and showing, also, some of the social frustration of her sex
in the Oxford of the 1880s.

I had such a good evening last Thursday. Three of us went to
the Union to hear a debate in which T. P. O'Connor was going
to speak. The proposer – a little Tory who evidently thought
himself like Beaconsfield, he wore the same sort of hair and
sat in the same sort of way! – delivered a speech against Home
Rule which was not very good. Then the opposer spoke on
the other side. He was an Irishman and evidently very keen
about it ... Then Mr O'Connor got up and spoke for over an
hour. His speech was of course rather more of bluster than of
fact – that was natural in addressing an audience of Under-
graduates – but it was good all round and sometimes excellent
... Dear me, he *was* funny. He had a rather humorous appearance to begin with and a humorous Irish voice and accent. At
one point in his speech he was so irresistibly funny that the
whole room subsided into peals and peals of laughter ... He
heartily supported the plan of Campagne [*sic*], and I don't
think he will leave off trying for Home Rule until he gets it ...
Have you ordered my spoons? I am going to a teaparty of
Mary's today to meet some sort of relation of hers who
married a Miss Gladstone and is Headmaster of Wellington.

She is so unhappy because Miss Wordsworth has pronounced that she had better entertain him in the drawing room! It isn't half the same thing giving a teaparty not in one's own room ...

She made her first journey abroad during the year, taking her summer holiday with 'a suitable family' at Weilheim in Germany. By her second year it was clear that she would be ready to take her degree before most of her fellow students, even though she had gone up a year younger than most of them. Her finals in June 1888 demanded little exertion on her part. She was well prepared for them. Only when it came to her viva voce was there cause for concern. According to a commonly accepted account of the proceedings, which were witnessed by her parents, she was asked by one examiner about a German town on the left bank of the Rhine. Gertrude, who had visited the town the year before, is alleged to have told him: 'I am sorry, but it is on the right. I know, I have been there.' But according to her tutor it was the distinguished historian Professor S. R. Gardiner who provoked the response, 'I am afraid I must differ from your estimate of Charles I.' He was said to have been so taken aback that he handed her over to another examiner without further word. Whichever version is correct it is a faithful comment on Gertrude's life-long inability to resist the honest retort, whether she faced her peers or, in terms of age and experience if not of social position, her superiors.

The lapse made no difference to her results. She took a brilliant 'first', the earliest of her sex to achieve that distinction in her subject. Her joy when she learnt the results was only diminished when she read further down the list to discover that Mary Talbot, who had worked so hard in company with her, had been awarded a 'second'.

As Gertude and her friends arrived for the last of four com-memoration balls which marked the end of the academic year, they heard of the death of Wilhelm I of Prussia. She was wearing a gown of exotic green that had been delivered by her couturier that day. She immediately returned to her room and changed into sombre black.

While Gertrude was at Oxford there were three deaths in the family which brought sadness and a note of dissension to a united clan. Early in 1887 her stepmother's only surviving brother, Tommy Olliffe, was hit by a bus in the King's Road, Chelsea, and died soon afterwards as the result of the injuries he sustained. A year earlier her grandmother, Margaret, had died after a long illness. She was the daughter of another outstanding scientist and industrialist of the North-east, Hugh Lee Pattinson, whom Lowthian Bell met soon after joining his father's ironworks at Walker-on-Tyne in 1836. Pattinson was the son of a Quaker shop-keeper and taught himself physics and chemistry. He discovered an economic method of removing silver from lead ores and thus gave rise to a profitable local industry. He met Lowthian at the Newcastle Literary and Philosophical Society where, coinciden-tally, Lowthian's father Thomas had met his partner James Losh at the beginning of the century. Though Pattinson was twenty years Bell's senior the two men became close companions and opened a chemical works together at Washington, but Pattinson retired shortly after to devote himself to astronomy. Lowthian married Pattinson's daughter in 1842 and she presided over the domestic affairs of the Hall at Washington with kindly but firm authority, in token of which the place became known to local people as 'Dame Margaret's Hall'.

Also in 1887 news came of another family death; John Bell, Lowthian's brother and senior partner, died of a heart-attack at his home in Algiers. John was a substantial shareholder in the Bell enterprises. He and his second wife Lizzie had four daughters the eldest of whom, Evelyn, married John Edward Courtenay Bodley the historian and, according to his own testimony, 'Founder's Kin of the King of all Libraries'. Naturally John Bell left his shares to his wife. But over the years a family row ensued as to the interpretation of the company's articles of association which, according to Hugh Bell, held that all such shares should be made available to existing directors of the firm at a price agreed by the board. Courtenay Bodley insisted that any such arrangement would deprive his own wife, and therefore him too, of a rightful inheritance. Hugh eventually won the battle – he almost certainly had the letter of the law on his side, for Bodley was not a man to shirk litigation if he had a leg to stand on – and the shares were eventually purchased at a price he considered to be greatly below their market value. A fierce verbal onslaught developed and nobody was better qualified to wage a war of words than Bodley, sometime secretary to Charles Dilke, author of the standard

English history of France and, in later years, public adversary of
King Edward VII who neglected to confer a knighthood on him
in expected reward for writing the official version of the coronation. The sovereign and Hugh Bell became the favourite targets
of his vitriolic tongue.

After university came a long-awaited holiday, walking in her
beloved Yorkshire, helping her young sisters Elsa and Molly
with their studies, and flirting with that inner circle of social life
in London to which admission was far fom being indiscriminately
open. The house in Sloane Street became Gertrude's London
address again, as it had been in her first year at Queen's College,
and she soon became a welcome and admired member of a circle
at the centre of which was her aunt Maisie's mother-in-law, the
forthright Lady Stanley of Dover Street. She had been instrumental in founding Girton College at Cambridge, and Gertrude
entertained slight misgivings at having gone to the other place.
The matriarch had visited her at Lady Margaret Hall during her
first term. 'I felt rather guilty when I shook hands with her —
rather as if *I'm not going to Girton* were written on my forehead,
but she didn't say anything.' In fact, Gertrude seems to have had
a relatively easy relationship with the tiresome old lady, which is
more than can be said for her grandson Bertrand Russell, who
found sanctuary from her worst conversational excesses in
Gertrude's aunt Maisie and the witty Lyulph. 'So long as I live
there shall be no chapel at Girton,' she would announce with all
the force of her commanding personality. One of her favourite
sayings was that she always thought it not so bad to break the
seventh commandment as the sixth, 'at any rate it requires the
consent of the other party'. If anyone left the room she could be
relied on to say 'fools are so fatiguin' '. Her birthday dinner
parties were always thirteen in number and she considered herself
very broadminded because she had allowed her son to marry into
'trade'. 'As Sir Hugh was a multi-millionaire I was not very
impressed,' observed Bertrand Russell in later years.

3
Europe and London

In November and the first few days of December 1888 tea and dinner engagements occupy much of Gertrude's diary and letters. At the age of twenty she was a confident and welcome figure in society and she was often in the company of the Russells and Stanleys, the impulsive and learned Mrs J. R. Green who completed her husband's *Short History of the English People* after his death, and the Norman Grosvenors – the son of Lord Ebury and daughter of James Stuart Worsley. Meanwhile there were daily visits from her 'fitter' as she assembled her wardrobe for the first big journey abroad. In the often quoted words of her aunt Lady Mary Lascelles, whose husband was now Minister at Bucharest, a European tour would help 'to get rid of her Oxfordy manner'. There was certainly something of the blue-stocking about her at this time, though she was saved from the more insufferable aspects of that condition by her natural ebullience and vivacity.

She left London with her father in the second week of December carrying in her luggage eleven volumes of Dumas loaned to her by Mr Grosvenor. In Paris she parted from her father and was escorted on the train to Bucharest by the Lascelles's eldest son Billy, with whom she had already conducted a mild and intermittent flirtation. The journey, described in long and colourful letters to friends and family, was a triumphant passage through the baroque palaces and fun-loving cities of central Europe in that interval of relative peace between the Franco-Prussian War and the later aberrations of the German empire.

From Vienna she reported that they had taken Billy's younger brother Gerald aboard the train at Munich and were enjoying themselves immensely. They arrived in Bucharest in time for

Christmas. She wrote to her sister Elsa: 'What an amusing morning you must be having – I wonder what you have got for Christmas presents? I came down to breakfast this morning with my arms full of all the presents from Sloane Street which were opened in the dining room ... The Roumanian language is so like the French that one can understand all the words written up on the shops. This evening Auntie Mary is going to have a Christmas dinner party with a real English plum pudding ... '

Two days later she was writing to her stepmother: 'Today is the great day – the first ball day. I am looking forward to seeing all those people very much ... ' In the next few weeks she came to close quarters with several men and women who were to influence her future; with Valentine Ignatius Chirol, her 'beloved Domnul' of later years, who became the Foreign Editor of The Times and the power behind a good many political thrones, though he was sick for much of the time that Gertrude was in Bucharest; Charles Hardinge, who as Lord Hardinge of Penshurst was to become Viceroy of India at a critical juncture of her life; the two Lascelles boys and their sister Florence; and of course with members of other diplomatic missions and the nobility of Rumania. She began to display the expert interest in architecture that was to enliven her journeys wherever she went: 'It is almost the only old piece of building in Bucharest, and to judge by the carving on the capitals on the pillars and over the low doorway I should think it could not be earlier than the fifteenth century,' she wrote, with reference to a church she found. And she maintained her interest in home affairs, especially the eternal Irish problem, while she travelled. 'Cousin of My Heart,' she wrote to Horace Marshall who was about to take his finals at Oxford. 'Your letter amused me immensely and made me feel that I must be at Leeds talking to you – or watching you grappling with the amazing coils of Theocritus. But no ... I must be thinking about dressing for the ball to which we are going ... You, I know, share with me that condition of general amusement with all the world we have yet seen and you will not therefore be surprised to hear that I am having a particularly good time and that I am enjoying myself extremely.' A few days later she wrote in less frivolous vein apropos the discovery that a famous letter published in The Times in 1887 and purporting to come from the pen of Parnell had been forged by the Irish journalist Pigott, who was ruined by the discovery and subsequently shot himself in

Spain: 'That old scoundrel Pigott!—peace be to his ashes! What apes the Times people have been. Fancy building a Palace of Justice with Pigott for a foundation stone ... I never could see myself that Mr Parnell's private character had much bearing on the Union.'

Her audacious approach to the male-dominated world in which she moved found another expression in her retort to a foreign statesman who was discussing weighty matters of European politics with Sir Frank Lascelles. To the dismay of her hostess she told him: 'Il me semble, Monsieur, que vous n'avez pas saisi l'esprit du peuple allemand.' Her stepmother, commenting many years later, observed: 'There is no doubt that ... it was a mistake for Gertrude to proffer her opinions, much less her criticisms, to her superiors in age and experience.'

She did not neglect the social side of her visit. 'I can't attempt to tell you whom I danced with for it was impossible to remember them all ... ' At a concert she shared a box with Uncle Frank and the two boys opposite that of Rumania's poet Queen Elizabeth, who was better known by her literary name of Carmen Sylva. And the highlight of the stay was a charity ball at which the Queen went over to Mary Lascelles and Gertrude and had a long talk with them. She finally presented Gertrude with ten francs and sent her to buy tombola tickets. 'I drew nothing but blanks. But wasn't it sweet of her?'

She spent nearly four months altogether in Bucharest before leaving for Constantinople. Even at the last moment the leisured party put off its departure. On April 20th she wrote to her father: 'We have put off our going to Constantinople till Saturday, for the weather has become deliciously warm again and we are all going down to Sinaia tomorrow. Last night Mr Chirol, Uncle Frank, Billy and I went to see one of the great midnight services ... ' There followed one of those descriptive essays that were to flow more frequently from Gertrude's pen as the years went by.

The whole sight of the church crowded with people carrying lighted tapers, the splendidly dressed priests, the smell of incense and the curious ceremonies was rather interesting but it gave me a disagreeable impression I think. It was so extraordinarily undevout; the people stopped in the middle of a sign of the cross to gossip with their neighbours and the very priests when they swung incense exchanged humorous remarks with the congregation.

By the first week of May they were at the gateway to the East, surrounded by the Byzantine and Islamic splendours of Constantinople. Gertrude's first impression was muted. 'The people are so fearfully sophisticated, they address you in very bad English, and in order to gain your confidence assure you that they recognise you perfectly and remember having seen you often in Glasgow or Liverpool or some other place you have never been to.' The view soon brightened. She and Billy took a caïque and rowed up the Golden Horn nearly to the Sweet Waters. 'It was perfectly delicious with a low sun glittering on the water, bringing back the colour to the faded Turkish flags of the men of war ... '

They dined with the Embassy secretaries. 'I sat between Mr Lowther, who is not nice but is rather funny, and Mr Findlay who is good but dull.' The paradox was not lost on Gertrude. Her relationships with men were ill-fated from the beginning and there can be no dissent from the words of an earlier biographer who had the advantage of womanly insight: 'Men interested Gertrude more than women, and on the whole I think she got on with them better; but she had too strong a streak of masculinity in her own make-up, and she was too prone to intellectual argument, so that in spite of her essential womanliness, her in many ways delightful femininity, her very warm heart and her craving for affection and desire to be liked, she was not perhaps the sort of woman men want to marry. In fact I rather fancy she frightened off even those she cared for most.'

In June 1889 she was back in London. Many years later her sister Elsa re-read her youthful letters and wrote: 'I feel ... that they close the last chapter of absolute happiness in Gertrude's life.'

She had passed through the Bosporus and had seen from a distance the ornate splendours of the palace and seraglio whence the Sultan Caliphs had ruled for some five centuries, secretively and often fearfully, over the Arabian peninsula, Syria, Mesopotamia and much of eastern Europe and north Africa, and held spiritual sway over the faithful of Islam. She had approached the high ingate to the Sultan's palace, the *bab al aly*, which the

French satirically dubbed *la porte sublime*, and she was fascinated by the thought of what lay beyond in the Asiatic dominions of Turkey. For the moment, however, she had to draw back from the tantalising mysteries of the East and return to London with Billy Lascelles. There was a good deal of tut-tutting from her stepmother about their open and unchaperoned association. 'Billy and I sat in the garden and had a long talk ... he wanted to take me with him to Paddington and send me back in a hansom, don't be afraid, I didn't go – what would have happened if I had, it was ten o'clock?' She stayed on at Sloane Street for a week or two, visiting her friend Mary Talbot who was then working with the Whitechapel Mission, attending French literature classes at Caroline Grosvenor's home and spending much of her time with the Russells of Audley Square and the Dover Street fraternity, before making her way to Redcar where she rejoined her younger sisters and Hugo.

The children of Hugh's second marriage by now ranged from eight to eleven years in age and Hugo, the eldest, was away at boarding school. Gertrude took their education in hand whenever they were together at Red Barns, though she had some difficulty with Molly. On one occasion she asked her younger sister if she could tell her the religion of the inhabitants of Rome. Molly looked round the room for inspiration and in the end answered desperately – 'Quakers'. Her stepmother – whose delight in her family, in which she included Gertrude as one of her own, was unceasing – devoted herself mainly to Hugo's musical development. Perhaps she saw in him an outlet for her own frustrated talent for she noted every stage of his precocious progress. At ten months, she recorded, he could sing Rubinstein's Melody in F; at fourteen months he was giving voice to 'Men of Harlech', 'Rule, Britannia!' and 'John Peel'; at sixteen months to 'God Save the Queen' and at twenty months to 'London Bridge' and 'Sur le Pont d'Avignon'. At six the young prodigy was taken to London to hear Rubinstein play and after the recital he was introduced to the great man who lifted him up, kissed him and said, 'Mind you are never a musician.' 'A stupid thing to say,' remarked Florence.

In fact, the sensitive Hugo was to go on to Eton where much of his musical talent was thwarted by masters who told him that he must drive away the tunes which came constantly into his mind by 'thinking of something else' and he went on to Oxford and was eventually ordained, though on the way he formed a lasting friendship with the most learned of all English men of music, Donald Francis Tovey.

The word most frequently used by Florence to describe her own happiness in the family life of which she had become the centre was 'radiant'. Hugh was away for much of the time and often appeared at Red Barns only on Sundays. 'He was big brother, comrade and teacher in one,' according to his wife, and when he was with his family he entered into their childhood high jinks with enthusiasm, though he preferred to sit with Gertrude and talk philosophy, religion and politics. The children created a world of their own in the garden at Redcar: a derelict outhouse which they called their 'Wigwam'; and the family adults and servants were regularly invited to tea with its occupants, which included a pet raven known as Jumbo. Carefully worded invitations to parents, Gertrude, Maurice, grandparents and Bobby the bootboy were always replied to with ceremony. 'I shall have much pleasure in accepting your kind invitation to tea on Saturday 23rd,' responded Bobby to one such request for his company, while grandma Olliffe addressed her reply to 'Monsieur et Mesdames de Viguevamme'; 'Lady Olliffe will do herself the honour of taking tea with her young friends at 5 o'clock this evening.'

The children called the garden 'Paradise'. Their young lives in that secure devoted world came close to the description of their choosing. Only poor Hugo suffered the ordinary torments of life at this period. Just before Gertrude returned to Redcar in the summer of 1889 Florence had a letter from him which said, 'Dearest Mammy, It really isn't such a terrible thing to have an Eton jacket all the week, is it? The boys say that I am a swell, but it's better to be that than a guy ... ', and a few days later, 'I have quite got over my homesickness now, but when I think of Beethoven's Sonata in A flat it makes me feel rather unhappy and inclined to cry.'

Gertrude's time with the children during the summer holiday was restricted by a scheme which her stepmother had conceived soon after the birth of her last child, Molly. 'I had no more children,' she wrote, 'those three were all-sufficing to me, and brought me, as they have done ever since, unalloyed happiness.' She began to return to writing plays and to embark on a project of sociological research which if not unique in its day was certainly remarkable. She assembled a group of ladies in and around the Cleveland area where the family's Clarence ironworks was situated, with the object of visiting a thousand homes of working people and assessing the problems and deprivations of their lives. Gertrude appears to have been appointed treasurer of the group for in October 1889 she sent a note to Florence from Red Barns to tell her: 'The ladies of Clarence were friendly, and oh, unexpected joy! their accounts came right ... ' Over a period of several years these visits gave rise to a highly informative and useful document on the steel industry of the north-east of England and the needs and expectations of those who worked in that industry.

Florence charted the growth of the industry from its tentative beginnings at the turn of the eighteenth century when her husband's grandfather Thomas Bell, already the owner of a successful alkali plant at Jarrow, went into partnership with the barrister and classical scholar James Losh and a mutual friend George Wilson to form the ironfounding company of Losh, Wilson and Bell at Walker-on-Tyne in 1807. Later came the establishment of the first of the Cleveland factories by Henry Bolckow, a Newcastle corn merchant who came originally from Mecklenburg in Germany, and a knowledgeable Welshman John Vaughan, and the subsequent arrival of the Bells led by Sir Lowthian, the 'high priest' of chemical metallurgy, in 1854. She traced the Quaker influence on the development of the town of Middlesbrough which grew up around the ironworks; the effects of the railroads and shipping routes on the initial prosperity and eventual decline of the industry; the growth of its population from thirty-five souls in 1811 to nearly a hundred thousand at the end of the century; the discovery of the rich ores of Eston in the Cleveland Hills which brought ironworkers flooding in from Staffordshire, Scotland and South Wales to work the puddling furnaces of Middlesbrough in the 1850s until the town supplied one third of the country's pig-iron and Britain's output exceeded that of the rest of the world. 'In less than a century,' she wrote at the end of her report, which she completed in 1907, 'the proprietorial presence of the iron industry had come and gone. Meanwhile, Bell and others had made great fortunes, Teesside had become a vital part of the might of England and British iron had fed the growth of railways, bridges and communications throughout the world.'

The Bells had become rich indeed, though many less responsible manufacturing families had spent the fortunes made in those halcyon years as quickly as they made them and had gone into oblivion. Sir Lowthian Bell owned Washington Hall (he gave it away as an orphanage in 1891), Rounton Grange and Arncliffe Hall in Yorkshire, as well as a London home. There was also Red Barns, while Lowthian's brother John had a magnificent home called Rushpool Hall at Saltburn, with a heated indoor swimming pool and his yacht moored nearby, and a comparable house in Algiers known as Mustapha Rais, which Lizzie Bell inherited on his death. Lowthian's family all enjoyed a standard of living of that order, as did the Bolckows, Dormans and other iron-making dynasties. The masters of the district were not above competition in such matters as the size of their respective establishments, the splendour of their carriages or the number of their mistresses.

When Florence had completed her programme of enquiry, over a period of nearly thirty years, she called it *At the Works* and dedicated it to Charles Booth, the author of *Life and Labour of the People of London*, in recognition of his 'wise and sympathetic counsel'. One passage in particular defines her own attitude to life:

> We move through a world filled with labels, and we are most of us content to accept the mere name on the label for that which it represents ... Commerce, Prosperity, Industry, the Iron Trade, War, Peace – what do these all mean? I confess that as I try to grasp them I can represent them to myself, always and ever, in terms only of human beings: they all mean the lives, the daily actions, of thousands of our fellow creatures.

The vapid social life of the *salons* and dining tables of London still beckoned Gertrude during the three years between her first European tour and her next journey abroad. By 1890 she had become friendly with another family which was to play an important part in her future life, the Mallets. Louis du Pan Mallet, whom she met at the Russells' Audley Square home along with his father and namesake Sir Louis Mallet, had just joined the Foreign Office. He was later to become précis-writer to Lord Lansdowne, private secretary to Sir Edward Grey and Permanent Under-Secretary, and ambassador at Constantinople. Gertrude wrote to her stepmother on February 15th, 1890 from Audley Square, reporting on the latest society prank in which the Mallets were playing a crucial part, the 'Pessimist Society' and its associated magazine the *Mausoleum*, to which she was asked to contribute. She went on, 'It's so nice being here!' Dinner guests included the Blennerhassets, Lord Carlisle, 'some Strachey people' and 'some stray men'. She sat next to Leo Maxse, the editor of the *National Review*, with her cousin Flora Russell on the other side of him. 'We talked and laughed merrily the whole dinner through. We played a delightful game, which consists in reciting in order of demerit all the people you dislike – the person who keeps it up the longest wins. The great point is to pick somebody whom you know the other players like – we all agreed on Lady Carlisle.' After dinner she talked to Lady Blennerhasset. 'She told me the best thing she had done was to burn a complete book which was quite ready for the press – after reading one of her published works I can readily believe it. I alluded to Madame de Staël – she seemed surprised that I had seen it; I daresay it would be rather a shock.' Examples of Gertrude's self-confidence and the catholic nature of her interests when she was just twenty-one abound in this long and rambling letter. She was joined after dinner by another Russell boy, 'a brother of Lord Ampthill's, who ... knew Maurice at Eton ... we talked about games and schools and I liked him'. Then came Auntie Maisie and Lord Carlisle: 'We discussed football and the church! He was very surprised to find what a lot of ecclesiastical gossip I knew, and I that he should know about football.' She ended the letter: 'I have been reading Mr Morley's *Walpole* which Sir Louis Mallet says is *supreme* – it is most brilliant and interesting.'

When she first came down from Oxford Gertrude had taken to needlework, not so much to mend her clothes since she constantly bought new gowns (dresses were worn by the lower classes at that time), as to occupy her hands when she sat and talked. By now she exhibited another of the traits that seemed to carry her from extreme decorum to the verge of Victorian social censure; she started to smoke cigarettes, a habit that remained with her for the rest of her life, though such was her *savoir faire*, it seems to have caused little comment among her friends or, in later years, her political superiors.

The year 1890 marked her introduction to Ibsen's plays. 'Mother and I went to see The Doll's House,' she told her father. 'We were very much struck by it. It is extremely good in some places and extremely bad in others, ludicrously and crushingly bad. But above all it is original, one has seen nothing the least like it before and I feel about plays that it is such a comfort to get out of the stereotyped type of plot – the husband and the wife and the other young lady and all the other people who crowd the English stage. The mere fact that the Doll's House was new made it rather impossible to form a just criticism ... one felt that the basis for comparison was swept away.'

It was, however, her first encounters with Henry James at the Audley Square table that caused her to send the most detailed reports of life in London to her stepmother. Florence and James had been friendly since her childhood days in Paris.

> Dinner at the Arthur Russells' was most amusing. I sat by Bernard Holland who is a very funny person and charming to talk to ... Flora was on the other side of him, Claud of me and beyond Claud Lady Colville. She was rather bored poor lady, for she could not talk to Lord Arthur who took her in and she could not very well talk to us because we were too far off ... after I talked to Mr Holland for a long time ... then came heaps of people, Leo Maxse, the Grenfells, two Oxford young men who I know and like, the Maurice McMillans to whom I talked, they asked after you – so did Henry James who was in great form ... Henry James said 'M-did Mrs Bell enjoy herself in London, and is she glad to be at home – but perhaps the two clauses of my question are not quite hum – ah – consistent'.

A few days later, she wrote of another meeting at the Russells' place: ' ... presently Henry James appeared and delivered himself on the subject of David [Mrs Ward's The History of David Grieve]. Oh it was so good – he is the critic – so moderate, so just; and so contemptuous! Every sentence hit the nail right on the head, and every nail ran down into the coffin of Mrs Ward's reputation as a novelist. He thinks the Paris part the worst: "the poor lady" he said with a little shrug of the shoulders "and David – a shadow, a character indefinitely postponed, he arrives nowhere." H. J. thinks Robert [Robert Elsmere by the same author] a much better book than David. He said to Mrs W. that he thought the book lacked the purpose of the last. "Purpose," said she, "why this one has two purposes." Isn't that comic! "Two purposes said he, are as bad as ten or twenty." ' She concluded: 'Dearest, dear mother, it is so flat and horrid without you. I hope you find your husband a consolation to you, you see I haven't one to console me, that's why I miss you so much. Mother dearest, three score years and ten is very long, isn't it?' It was not the only time that Gertrude was to cry out for that consolation.

4

Persian Pictures

Are we the same people I wonder when all our surroundings, associations, acquaintances are changed? Here that which is me, which womanlike is an empty jar that the passer by fills at pleasure, is filled with such wine as in England I had never heard of ...

She went to Persia in the spring of 1892, travelling with her cousin Florence Lascelles (whose father was by then ambassador in Tehran). They went by the long rail route through Germany and Austria to Constantinople and on to Tiflis, Baku and the Caspian Sea, Gertrude reading Strabo 'who mentions nearly all the little towns which exist today'. She wrote some of the most descriptive letters of this holiday to Horace Marshall. After the above lines which captured her first questioning feelings she wrote: 'How big the world is, how big and how wonderful. It comes to me as ridiculously presumptuous that I should dare to carry my little personality half across it and boldly attempt to measure with it things for which it has no table of measurements that can possibly apply. So under protest I write to you of Persia: I am not me, that is my only excuse. I am merely pouring out for you some of what I have received during the last two months.' And so she pours out her impressions, vivid pictures which seem, even at a distance of almost a century, still to shimmer in the cool streams of Tehran, Kashan and Isfahan. Men with flowing robes of green, white and brown, women who lifted their veils as she went past to reveal lustrous eyes, luxurious vegetation and the nothingness of stony desert – 'Oh the desert around Tehran! miles and miles of it with nothing, *nothing* growing; ringed in with bleak bare mountains snow crowned and furrowed with the deep courses of torrents. I never knew what desert was till I came here ... ' The hospitality of people to whom she was a stranger, the enchanted prince whose home and garden belonged to his guests, beggars who 'wear their rags with better grace than I my most becoming habit' and the commonest women whose veils 'are far better put on than mine'. The never-ceasing compliments, the unstinted hospitality – 'Ah, we have no hospitality in the west and no manners.' And then – 'Say, is it not rather refreshing to the spirit to lie in a hammock strung between the plane trees of a Persian garden and read the poems of Hafiz ... '

She arrived in Persia with a smattering of the language, learnt in the course of six months' tuition at home along with Latin, which she found harder than Farsi, stumbling as best she could over the 'horrid catching briars of prepositions and conjunctive moods'. She found an amiable old teacher in Tehran who knew too much Persian for her and not enough French (and no English) and so they carried on long philosophic discussions, he expressing the viewpoint of 'an oriental Gibbon' in Persian, she delivering her sermons in French, and neither being greatly the wiser in the end.

She had not been long in Persia before she met one of the Legation secretaries, Henry Cadogan. She and Florence Lascelles, it was said, imparted an unaccustomed gaiety to the diplomatic missions, British and foreign, almost as soon as they arrived. Within a very few days Gertrude was describing the *real* treasure of her journey: ' ... it certainly is unexpected and undeserved to have come all the way to Tehran and to find someone so delightful at the end – he rides with us, he arranges plans for us – he shows us lovely things from the bazaars – he is always there when we want him and never when we don't. He appears to have read everything that ought to be read in French, German and English.'

Gertrude also made an impression on the German chargé d'affaires, Dr Friedrich Rosen, an able linguist who did much to help her Persian studies so that before she left she could read and write the language well and speak it tolerably. Cadogan, ten years older than Gertrude, was an all-round sportsman, good it was said at bezique and billiards as well as tennis, and agreeably intelligent. Rosen often invited them to his home together and they would ride into the surrounding country as a threesome or with uncle Frank and Florence. 'We would ride all over Shimran at the foot of the Alburz mountains, and visit every gorge formed by a stream of clear water running down from the snows ... We often had tea or a moonlight picnic in beautiful gardens, whose gates were hospitably opened to European visitors.' Rosen remembered Cadogan as 'an unusual type of Englishman', devoted to books, music and conversation. When visiting the German minister's house on one occasion he issued instructions at the gate that no other visitor should be admitted while he was within as he would be listening to Frau Rosen's music or reading poetry to his hosts. Rosen recalled the moment when the Englishman and Gertrude came together in a manner which transcended their hitherto uncomplicated companionship. They were at a picnic and while the other guests talked Gertrude and Henry Cadogan wandered off together and he saw him lift her up on to a gate where they sat oblivious of the rest of the company, reading verses of Hafiz to each other. At that moment he thought he divined a deeper involvement.

Coincidence is hardly to be avoided in a social circle as wide and contiguous as that in which Gertrude moved. Almost everyone she knew was in a position of some power or influence. Almost every branch of her family contained a noted politician, diplomat or scholar. Everywhere she went she met somebody who could smooth her path or afford her a useful introduction. It was no surprise to her, therefore, to discover that Dr Rosen's wife was the daughter of Monsieur Roche who was a lifelong friend of her stepmother's. Needless to say, Gertrude's mother and father also knew the Cadogans and young Henry was, in any case, an old friend of Mrs Norman Grosvenor, so that it would not be difficult to find out about him. The romance flourished and the elated couple rode across the Kavir desert and along watercourses of the Lar to the whitewashed tower where the Zoroastrians flung their dead for the vultures to devour; they visited the racecourse, and sat in the long grass 'looking at the lights changing on the snow mountains' and reading Catullus. There was a party to celebrate the Queen's birthday on May 24th. 'We had tents, provisions and a band in the garden but oh! the people are so dull.' At dinner Gertrude was seated next to a Persian who had been at Balliol for four years and an old bearded man with whom she spoke in 'ollendorfian' Persian. 'Mr Cadogan and I agreed that it would be perfectly delightful if all the horrid colleagues had not been there.'

She had reported her every move to her parents in the usual

flow of affectionate correspondence, and her father was worried. He decided that it would be a good thing if he and Florence went out to Tehran to take Gertrude home with them. On June 20th, 1892 she wrote artfully to her father: 'I think you must let me know as soon as you get this letter what you intend to do. I have two or three plans in my head ... but first I think Mother ought seriously to consider whether it would be wise for her to come. Of course when we came everything was perfectly easy; Mr Churchill [Harry Churchill, first secretary of the Legation] was with us who knows the country thoroughly, trains of servants were sent down and we had every comfort. But the simple particular can't travel like that ... it is impossible not to be in a draught because the doors don't shut; I can't help thinking that the journey would knock Mother up and after much thought I really don't advise her to come ... ' She went on to suggest that he, her father, might come out the following March and that meanwhile she should winter in Tehran. It is unlikely that Hugh failed to see the stratagem, but Gertrude was saved from the threatened parental visit by the dissolution of Parliament in London and the decision of Lord Salisbury to appeal to the country. Hugh, a lifelong Liberal as was his father before him, felt unable to support Gladstone on the Irish question and so decided to stand for election, unsuccessfully as it proved, as a Unionist candidate.

And so Gertrude was able to enjoy four more months in the company of Henry Cadogan. Eventually a stay which she would gladly have extended into eternity was cut short by a sudden outbreak of cholera. One of the worst-affected areas was around Dehsashoub where the Rosens lived, and Frau Rosen caught the disease, though she eventually recovered from it. There was panic among the servants, and in the fearful atmosphere that prevailed tempers became frayed; Gertrude even quarrelled with her beloved Henry. 'Mr Cadogan and I had a serious difference of opinion and I sent him away goodnightless!' But she saw that the sun might 'go down on her wrath and rise – on nothing', and she quickly repaired the breach. Persians and Europeans were dying all around them, 'the long lines of new mounds in the graveyard gave one a sudden shiver'. Curiously, or perhaps predictably, the most urgent concern of most of the British colony was that the servants might desert them. Gertrude's special concern at the time however was the long-awaited reply to a letter she had written to her parents telling them that she had become engaged and asking permission to marry Mr Cadogan. 'Today or tomorrow I shall get the much wished for letters from you and Papa,' she wrote. The letter did eventually arrive but it did not contain the reply she hoped for. For all its sympathy and understanding, it made clear their disapproval of her intended marriage to 'an impecunious diplomat', and they doubted from what they had heard of Mr Cadogan whether he would make Gertrude happy. They had heard, it seems, that he had gambling debts and was of an arrogant disposition. They asked Gertrude to return home, indeed insisted that she should, so that she could think about the matter away from the glamour and romance of Persia.

On a Sunday in mid-September she wrote to her stepmother: 'I can't tell you how I long for these days to be over ... Yesterday afternoon we sat in the Movara garden and discussed it in all its bearings ... We talked much of you; I had given him several of your letters to read for I wanted him so much to know you ... "Perhaps when you go home she will write once to me," he said, which sounded so pathetic and made my own unhappiness seem so endlessly selfish, for I have you for help and consolation when I go home and he has nobody ... He was devoted to his own mother who died a few years ago ... The thing I can bear least is that you or Papa should ever think anything of him which is not noble and gentle and good. That is all of him that I have ever known ... I can't call for more of your sympathy than you will give, can I? Oh Mother, Mother.'

She had written despairingly to friends and relatives asking them to intercede with her father and seeking their advice. In July she had written an anguished letter to Valentine Chirol, asking him what she should do. She returned home by way of Constantinople and the first part of the journey was made by boat across the Caspian Sea. 'So we steamed away across the Caspian, and the sleepy little place vanished behind the mists that hung over its lagoons and enveloped its guardian mountains – faded and faded from our eyes till the Shah's palace was no longer visible; faded and faded from our minds, and sank back into the mist of vague memories and fugitive sensations.' She arrived in London late in October. Florence was waiting for her and soon they were joined by a sympathetic but unmoved Hugh. Gertrude's sister Elsa was to write in later years: 'But alas! beyond love and sympathy he could not give her what she wanted.'

Nine months after Gertrude's departure Henry Cadogan went to the Lar river in winter and fell into its icy water. He died from pneumonia within two days.

For the next four years she travelled extensively in Europe and when she was in England spent as much time as she could with her family at Redcar. The wounds of her first love healed slowly and she did not reproach her parents. Indeed she sought solace in them: 'Dearest, dearest, I did not think we could ever be closer to one another than we were, but I understand what love is, and so what yours is to me. What it is to be back and have my Mother again! I don't really want anybody but her, except you –.' Thus she wrote to her father soon after her return.

Between her travels she began to write an account of her journeys in Persia, and to translate the verse of Hafiz. The series of short essays on the land in which she had travelled and revelled and finally fallen in love was, in a way, an experiment in writing. She did it chiefly for her own amusement but friends persuaded her to show it to a publisher, Richard Bentley, who was keen and so she allowed it to be sold, though anonymously. Her first book, *Safar Nameh: Persian Pictures*, a book of travel, did not win universal acclaim for her literary skill when it appeared in 1894. But it had enormous charm. 'Charm but not actual achievement,' wrote Janet Hogarth.

Three years later in 1897 she was to publish her first and only verse, a translation from the *Divan* of Hafiz. The work was prefaced by a masterly critical essay which included a life of the Persian poet comparing him to his contemporary, Dante. She drew on Goethe, Villon and other poets of the West for her comparative assessment, showing the breadth of her reading and the depth of her critical vision. The work was an eloquent statement of the varied and complex attributes of Gertrude's brilliant mind, of her astonishing sense of word-play, her intellectual vitality, and not least of her temerity, for she had started to learn Persian a mere two years before she began to translate the work of the finest writer in the language. Her assurance would have been envied by many a recognised expert on Persian literature, as indeed would the achievement. The distinguished Koranic scholar A. J. Arberry has said of her translations: 'Though some twenty hands have put Hafiz into English, her rendering remains the best!' He was speaking in 1947. Perhaps one verse from *Poems from the Divan of Hafiz* reveals the truth of something that another famous English figure of the East, Sir Ronald Storrs, was to say of her in years to come: that she was compounded almost equally of head and heart.

> Light of mine eyes and harvest of my heart,
> And mine at least in changeless memory!
> Ah! when he found it easy to depart,
> He left the harder pilgrimage to me!
> Oh Camel-driver, though the cordage start,
> For God's sake help me lift my fallen load,
> And pity be my comrade on the road!

5
Family Matters

By the dawn of 1893 Gertrude's natural ebullience had come to the fore and the only apparent evidence of her recent torment was her growing irritation with the attentive Billy Lascelles. He suffered amiably the backlash of her ill-fated romance. 'How odd it is,' she wrote, 'to realise that those fires are ashes now.' It was the first real indication that her feelings for Billy had ever amounted to more than cousinly affection. ' ... no vestige of a spark, thank goodness! no excitement, no regret ... we can never be any nearer, never, never.' But she had not forgotten or grown distant from the scented gardens of Persia.

She spent much of the winter in London and the summer in visiting. During August she was in Canterbury: 'We spent a madly amusing five days ... we danced every night, saw a good deal of cricket ... you discuss byes and wides and Kemp at the wicket and Hearne's batting ... a restless sort of summer.'

Back in London she was able to re-establish links with school and Oxford: with Edith Langridge now doing good works among London's poor for the Lady Margaret Hall settlement; Maggie Benson, youngest of Archbishop Benson's daughters, an outstanding classical scholar who was soon to join the Sisterhood of the Epiphany, eventually to become its mother superior in India; the dark-eyed Mary Talbot about to embark on a supremely happy and tragically brief marriage; and Janet Hogarth, her lifelong friend who married her own Oxford tutor W. L. Courtney, 'the tall figure that must always turn down New College Lane', critic and editor of the *Fortnightly Review*.

At Redcar, where she continued with her Farsi and Latin studies and embarked on Arabic, she enjoyed the companionship of her sisters and her young brother who had just won a scholar-

ship to Eton. She had hardly seen Hugo in two years. In July 1891
he had written from boarding school: 'My dearest Gertrude, I
wish you *many many* happy returns of your birthday, and I hope
you will like my present ... There was a cricket match here on
Saturday against Sunningdale ... Aren't you sorry that Eton
were beaten at Lords?' Hugo was not much of a sportsman,
preferring the excitement of music to that of the rugger field and
cricket pitch, but to mitigate the inevitable bullying of public
school and to impress Gertrude, who was keen on practically
all sports and had an appreciative eye for the skills of her white-
flannelled countrymen, he pretended an interest. From Eton he
wrote to sister Elsa ' ... will you ask Gertrude if she would mind
giving me some instruction in general history and literature in
the holidays. I intend to do a lot of sap then.' And to Gertrude
herself: 'Next week we have to do a copy of Latin verses on
Verona i.e. a description of the City, mention of Catullus who
was born there, and the story of Romeo and Juliet. Could you
give me some help in the first of these?'

In April 1893 she was off on her travels again, this time with
her father. They set out for Algiers to visit uncle John Bell's
widow Lizzie and her daughters, travelling through France by
train to the Mediterranean and returning by way of Switzerland
and Weimar in Germany where her brother Maurice was staying
to improve his German.

From Nîmes she wrote: 'Took a carriage and drove past the
Arena and to the garden where lies the Temple of Nymphs. The
frogs croaked and the little owls screamed in the trees, and the
warm scented night with all its sounds was so like those other
nights in a far away garden where the owls scream. I cried and
cried in the Temple of the Nymphs, and filled the Roman baths
with tears which no one saw in the dusk.' Persia came fitfully to
her thoughts as it would time and again on her restless voyage,
pressing on by train and boat as if, even in the summer of youth,
she must wander if only to escape. From Avignon she wrote
to grandmother Laura Olliffe in London: 'The Pont du Gard
sends you a little piece of Thyme to remind you of your visit
there. What a place it is! Papa and I had a delicious day there ... '
On Thursday April 20th they went to Arles. Next day they were
in Marseilles, and the next they crossed to Algiers.

The stay at Mustapha Rais with aunt Lizzie does not seem to
have been an unqualified success. She told her stepmother:

'Everything seems to run into a mad luxuriance – even the architecture, which is all twisted columns and twisted arches, and twisted elaboration and designs, and everywhere tiny marble courts with fountains in them, roped over with banks of roses. But it's very beautiful to see. I could wish man were not so vile! Aunt L. is the very most wearisome woman the Almighty ever invented.' She sat with her cousins Lilian and Clara after dinner, looking down over the town and beyond to the lights of the harbour, 'with the sweet smell of roses everywhere and the garden full of nightingales ... '

The journey home was described in a flurry of letters to her stepmother, capturing in short graphic passages the people, the sights and sounds and incidents. Her alarm at the thought of having to tip the servants. Chillon: ' ... the whole place full of memories of those wonderful people at the beginning of the century. Shelley's name is cut on one of the pillars – more interesting than fifty holy prisoners!' The funicular train ride to Glion where she had cakes for breakfast and went into the meadows: 'They were lovely those meadows ... full – full of flowers. Whole hillsides were white as if snow had fallen on them – white with the big single narcissus. I never saw anything so beautiful.' There was the meeting in Switzerland with old uncle Tom Bell, Grandfather Lowthian's only surviving brother, 'a gentle old thing with blue eyes like Grandpapa's. He collects butterflies'. And a vivid account of her attempt to mend Lord Granville's tricycle in Potsdam from which she was rescued by the footmen of the British Embassy. Her stay with Maurice at Weimar produced the comment: 'He is an odd creature, Maurice, full of perception.' She arrived back in England to find that her stepmother was the secretive cause of one of the sensations of the London theatre in late Victorian times. Florence's closest friend and the most frequent of all the visitors to her London and Redcar homes was the actress Elizabeth Robins whose current stage attachment was to the Independent Theatre founded by J. T. Grein in London's Strand. She had often tried to persuade Florence to write a play for the company but without success until she produced a Swedish short story of Strindbergian starkness. Florence was so moved by the plot that she straight away sat down and wrote the play, transferring the characters and situations to the industrial north of England. Miss Robins rushed to London with the work and read it to Grein. 'I shall never forget the impression it made upon me,' wrote the theatre's director. 'The first act, with its glorious sunshine, its idyllic picture of a woman's love and a woman's admiration for the physical beauty of her husband, charmed me ... I could barely grant her time to pause ... and the deeper grew the gloom of the action the more did it thrill me ... when it was over ... I was speechless and overcome ... We shall do that play; we will produce it as soon as we can. It is a beautiful tragedy.'

Florence laid down the condition before handing over the play that her name should not be associated with it and that her authorship should never be divulged. It was William Archer who had induced Elizabeth Robins to find an author for the story, which was called *Befriad* in Swedish. At first Archer doubted whether the subject could be presented on the stage at that time: the brutal death of the husband in a factory accident, the effect of the sight of his mangled body on his pregnant wife, her belief that her unborn child would manifest his physical beauty and the inevitable dénouement – a deformed child, a distracted mother's murder of the infant, the penalty, the agony of the death cell. 'The thing would be utterly, unspeakably brutal and hideous – That made the temptation quite irresistible,' wrote Archer. Whenever he spoke of the author it was of 'him'.

The play, *Alan's Wife*, had its first performance on Tuesday May 2nd, 1893, following a season of *Hedda Gabler*. Its effect on public and critics alike was sensational. As the curtain came down on the final act the audience rose in mixed joy and fury, applauding wildly or shaking their fists as they saw fit. There were loud cries of 'Author! Author!' and Grein was eventually forced to go on to the stage to admit that he did not know the identity of the writer, but that if he did he would 'shake him by the hand', a remark that was greeted with a chorus of hear-hears! and a loud cry from the auditorium 'Shake him by the throat!' Bernard Shaw was impressed by the work and whenever Archer pestered him for a new play during the next few years, he would reply, 'Put on Mrs Hugh Bell's play'; it seems that he at any rate knew the identity of the author. One side of a divided critical reaction was typified by A. B. Walkley's article in *The Speaker* of May 6th, 1893:

It is a philosophical commonplace that nature is, in some aspects, unjust, immoral, malignant, ferocious, 'red in tooth

and claw'. Life presents us occasionally with cases of unspeak-
able calamity for which there can be no compensation; wrongs
that can never be righted; hopeless, heartless, odious things
which put the glib commonplaces of the pulpit and the copy-
book to rout, and leave poor, mocked mankind shaking their
fists in impotent rage at the sky ... a case without consolation
or redress. It is the case which has been represented at the
Independent Theatre by the anonymous author of *Alan's Wife*,
and presented with no attenuation, but rather persistent
aggravation of its horrible circumstances ...

Gertrude returned at the height of the storm and she, like her
stepmother and the rest of the family, kept a resolute silence about
Alan's Wife. There is something very revealing about the episode.
The parents Gertrude so admired, whose precepts she so readily
embraced, exhibited in an unusual degree the classical Victorian
dilemma of trying to uphold outmoded social proprieties in an
age addicted to reason and rationality. Gertrude sensed the inconsistency just after Oxford. She wrote to her stepmother from
London in July 1889: 'We drove in a hansom to the exhibition
and Captain —— brought me home, I hope that doesn't shock
you; I discussed religious beliefs all the way there and very meta-
physical conceptions of truth all the way back ... I love talking
to people when they really will talk sensibly and about things
which one wants to discuss. I am rather inclined to think however
that it is a dangerous amusement, for one's so ready to make
oneself believe that the things one says and the theories one
makes are really guiding principles of one's life whereas as a
matter of fact they are not at all.'

The Bells, civic and industrial leaders and local benefactors
through three generations, looked upon a changing world from
a position of free thought and social insulation. As Florence
shied away from the stage that was her real *métier*, so Hugh looked
at industry with academic detachment. He spent a fortune building
offices and local monuments which became showpieces of the
Gothic revival. He travelled up and down the country addressing
his meticulously marshalled arguments to meetings of the
Liberal Party, businessmen's gatherings and 'free' trades unions,
in a piping, professorial voice. He often went to local engagements in his first motor car, a 'baby' Austin, and he wore a top
hat on important occasions, especially during his period of office

as Lord Lieutenant of the North Riding of Yorkshire. He made a ready impression on his audiences. In later years he was usually chauffeur-driven in a Daimler car. He was one of the most sought-after speakers among the industrialists of his time, and it has been said of him that he was a gifted actor. When off duty he was usually to be found shooting, dressed in the tweeds of the country squire, or riding to hounds. He was well read and remarkably energetic. But he was not greatly interested in the gritty matters of production methods and techniques of which his father had been a pioneer. He was a man given to the general rather than the particular. There are clues to the adult Gertrude in the time and climate of her growth to maturity.

6
Round the World

The years from 1894 to 1897 were quiet by Gertrude's standards. She travelled between Redcar and London and at either end bicycled between engagements. She also spent a lot of time in Switzerland where she tried her hand at mountain climbing and soon became addicted to it; and she returned to the antiquities of Italy.

Her diary provides the main clues to her movements at this time though a few letters survive to help us trace her journeys and impressions. There was a journey through France to Switzerland and Italy in 1894 with Mary Talbot, Gertrude sleeping little for she dreamt of printer's proofs: 'a nightmare of proofs woke me'; her *Safar Nameh* was nearing publication. 'There was a hard frost on the ground, and winter takes all the colour out of Switzerland, but after Lucerne we got into beautiful hilly country, lakes and snow peaks.' Then Milan and Santa Maria delle Grazie where she saw Leonardo's *Last Supper*, 'very old and battered, peeling from the walls of the desolate old room ... The peaceful figure of the Christ, with sorrow lying heavy on the eyelids, stands out with wonderful saintliness between the two agitated groups of apostles pressing hither and thither, wondering, questioning, plotting, protesting.' Bologna: 'Oh, Bologna is a heavenly place – all the streets are arcaded, and you walk through long vaulted aisles, and see down vistas of columned courtyards and long, arched streets, pink and yellow with stucco and rich with carving.' Florence, where the sun shone on Giotto's tower and on the figures of the Baptistry gates, and she watched a 'stormy gorgeous sunset ... and the long Arno valley growing darker and darker all except its gleaming river', and saw

Michelangelo's *David* and Botticelli's *Primavera* in the Accademia: 'There is a Virgin enthroned with saints which seemed to me almost too *maniéré* – and the dear Botticelli can be *maniéré!*' To the Uffizi where she discovered Botticelli's *Birth of Venus*, 'he is indescribably lovely when he's pagan.' And all the while taking lessons, studying her grammar, Persian, Arabic, Italian, German. 'Spent the morning reading and writing. After lunch came Professor Falarsi who galloped us through the *Inferno* in a thrilling manner – and in two hours!' And then the sudden, emphatic assertion, even in her personal diary, letting it be known that it is no ordinary eye that glimpses the wonders of the world: 'Fra Angelico is the one person who ever succeeded in giving bodily form to the spiritual – witness the Transfiguration.'

In the summer of 1894 she was back at Redcar helping Hugo, Elsa and Molly with their school work and cycling to the Bell ironworks at Port Clarence for tea with the womenfolk of the steelworkers, and reading whenever there was a spare moment. Later, in London, she sat in the park with Billy Lascelles and helped him with his racing accounts. 'We walked and I was comforted,' she recorded. She went back to Switzerland, this time with her family, where they met up with the Rosens and memories of Persia flooded back. She read the letters between Jonathan Swift and Vanessa and observed: 'I wonder if any man, beginning with the man to whom these letters were first addressed, has ever understood how much they meant, and if any woman has failed to understand. Swift did not care for her – that's how a man writes who does not care. And how it maims and hurts the woman!' She thought of Henry Cadogan: ' ... and today a year ago the shadow fell very near me. I thought of him much last night, and of all he had been to me and still is.'

There was another family holiday in Switzerland in 1895, and through that year she worked on the *Divan* of Hafiz, completing the task early in 1896. Heinemann the publisher took an immediate liking to it when she showed it him: 'He is an interesting little man is Heinemann.' Her 'pundit' (Denison Ross, head of the London School of Oriental Studies) called on her frequently when she was in London. He congratulated her on her proficiency at Arabic. 'I think his other pupils must be awful duffers. It is quite extraordinarily interesting to read the Koran with him – and it is such a magnificent book! He has given me some *Arabian Nights* for next time, and I have given him some Hafiz poems to

read, so we shall see what we shall see. He is extremely keen about
the Hafiz book.'

The early part of 1896 was spent in London, much of it with
the Stanleys and Grosvenors. She attended a party at the home of
Lord and Lady Portsmouth where she met Viscount Haldane
and his daughter Elizabeth, 'whom I have long wished to know'.
She and Elizabeth dined with the Stracheys, St Loe Strachey
having just reviewed her *Persian Pictures*. Her sisters were now
living in London with her and attending her old college. 'Moll
looked charming last night,' she wrote. She continued to work
hard during the daytime. 'I studied my grammar this morning and
went to the London Library where I looked through volumes and
volumes of Asiatic Societies.' A day or two later: 'I stayed in and
read some most illuminating articles on Sufyism.'

By springtime wanderlust had returned and she arranged to
visit Italy with the Grosvenors and Mrs Green, accompanied part
of the time by her father. She was back in London at the end of
April. 'I went to the British Museum on my bicycle this morning.
It adds a great joy to my studies and I feel all the brisker for it.
The children have had a tennis court marked in the square. I am
just going out to see them play. They are looking blooming and
are such angels! However we will try not to be too foolish about
our family.' Her stepmother was at Redcar at this time with the
'dear friend of all of us', Elizabeth Robins. 'Give my love to
Lisa,' wrote Gertrude. 'I wish I could come and have a long talk
with her to-night over the fire.' Her Arabic was coming on well:
'I shall soon be able to read the Arabian Nights for fun.' There
were more indications of her appetite for work and of her social
insularity in her letters and diary. ' ... I went up to the Museum
this morning and read a Persian life of Hafiz ... I think I got the
meaning of it with the help of a Persian dictionary, but a Latin
translation is not so clear to me as it might be ... I didn't go to
Lady Pollock's on Tuesday, because I had promised to go to a
party at Audley Square and I couldn't combine the two unchaperoned ... I am going down to Caroline (in Kent) for
Whitsuntide. I want to bicycle down if I can get an escort, it's
only 17 miles ... ' It seems she did not find an escort for she went
by train and took her bicycle with her to the wooded suburb of
Beckenham and she wrote home to Florence: 'It is so perfectly
delicious here. I arrived all right and bicycled up from the station
in time for tea. Afterwards we went on a long expedition all

round and about, the common is too heavenly, a mass of broom and hawthorn.' Then she said, 'We have spent an extremely lazy morning basking in the sun and talking and idling about. I expect it's rather cockney outside ... '

By summer, social activity had reached a climax: Ascot with the Lascelles and other relatives and friends – Uncle Frank was now ambassador at Berlin and was able to slip over to London at intervals – and Lord's for the annual confrontation of Eton and Harrow, and an endless procession of parties and dinners. In June she writes: 'We have had a most delightful day. We started about 10.30, Gerald, Florence, Uncle Frank and I, got to Ascot half an hour before the first race, which we saw from the top of the Royal Enclosure stand ... My gown was a dream and was much admired. I am going this evening with Aunty Mary and Florence and the Johnsons to sit out of doors in the Imperial Institute and listen to the band – rather nice as it is very hot ... What a dear Lord Granville is ... ' She reassured her stepmother, parenthetically, 'I didn't bet, I need not say.' In July: 'Hugo came up in great form and we started off for Lord's together, but on the way discovered that we had lost the blue tassel on his umbrella, which saddened us dreadfully! So we tried in many shops to get one, and failed alas! However, we were comforted at Lord's when we saw that many Eton boys had no tassel.' They ate greengages for lunch and made wishes as the fruit was the first of the year, and Gertrude asked Hugo what he had wished: ' "Why I wished Eton might win – what in the world is there to wish for besides?" He was such a darling!'

At the beginning of 1896 Mary Talbot left her work among the poor of London's Bethnal Green, which she combined with her duties at Lady Margaret Hall, in order to marry the Reverend Winfrid Burrows. Mary was thirty-four at this time, six years older than Gertrude, and by the end of the year she was expecting twins. Gertrude made frequent journeys to the vicarage in Leeds where her friend now lived. Towards the end of the year she met Janet Hogarth at tea in London and seizing her arm she said, 'It's all right, Janet; I've seen Mary and she's radiant.' Gertrude remarked to her stepmother that Mary had said to her that whatever might happen she had no regrets, for her happiness had been so great that it was worth any sacrifice. She died soon after the birth of twin girls.

By mid-January 1897 Gertrude was in Berlin. On the 22nd she wrote to her sister Elsa: 'I made my bow to the Kaiser Paar on Wednesday. It was a very fine show. We drove to the Schloss in the glass coach and were saluted by the guard when we arrived. We felt very swell ... We all hastily arranged one another's trains and marched in procession while the band played the march out of Lohengrin. The Emperor and Empress were standing on a dais at the end of the room as we walked through a sort of passage made by rows and rows of pages dressed in pink. The "Allerhöchst" looked extremely well in a red uniform – I couldn't look at the Empress much as I was so busy avoiding Aunt Mary's train. She introduced me and then stood aside while I made two curtseys. Then I wondered what the dickens I should do next, but Aunt Mary made a little sign to go out behind her, so I *enjambed* her train and fled!'

All over Berlin there was *Kunst und Kultur* to mark the sixtieth year of sovereignty of Wilhelm II's grandmother Victoria: plays, music, banquets; the British in Berlin were, for the moment, favoured guests. Gertrude and cousin Florence spent hours on end at concerts and plays and the opera, followed usually by dancing late into the night. 'Do you know they are giving John Gabriel tonight!' The same morning the two young women went to a concert. 'They played a quartet of Mendelssohn's quite deliciously and a great Beethoven quartet, do you know it, Op. 132 – it needed a lot of knowing I thought and far more intelligence than I could give it.'

They were lent a sledge and went for a snow-ride into the Grünwald – 'it is really a magnificent forest ... it looked too lovely under the snow. All the pine trees were covered with a thin white frost ... too delicious.' And another concert: 'We heard a thing of Haydn's and a thing of Brahms ... There were not many people, mostly students from the Hochschule, and oh how those men played! I never enjoyed music more.'

Then came an invitation from the Emperor to share the royal box at a performance of *Henry IV*. Gertrude went with her cousin Florence, chaperoned by Countess Keller, a lady-in-waiting at the Court. 'The play was very well done. The Falstaff excellent and the whole thing beautifully staged,' Gertrude wrote. In the interval after the second act, the two young women were sent for and they were conducted to the Kaiser Paar. 'We made deep curtseys and kissed the Empress's hand, and then we all sat down, Florence next to the Emperor and I next to the Empress ... The Emperor talked nearly all the time; he tells us that no plays of Shakespeare were ever acted in London and that we must have heard tell that it was only the Germans who had really studied or really understood Shakespeare. One couldn't contradict an Emperor, so we said we had always been told so ... ' It was a moment of unusual reticence on Gertrude's part.

There were the inescapable Court balls and gargantuan meals, and Gertrude cycled round the Embassy in the rain to keep herself in trim. They had dinner before their departure with Cecil Spring-Rice of the Foreign Office, later to become her cousin Florence's husband, and with Lord Granville. As they departed from their last meeting with their royal hosts, the Emperor and Uncle Frank sat and examined a sheaf of telegrams that had been handed to the former. The girls pretended not to listen, but they heard references to Crete ... Bulgaria ... Serbia ... mobilisation, and so forth. The Empress kept looking at Wilhelm anxiously — 'she is terribly perturbed about it all and no wonder for he is persuaded that we are all on the brink of war ... '

Yet another cloud came to darken a life of such material comfort and ease. In April, soon after Gertrude's return from Germany, Lady Mary Lascelles died after a brief illness. Her aunt had seemed in good health when they were together and the news came as a great shock.

At the end of 1897 came the first of two round-the-world voyages Gertrude was to make in that well-worn and often tedious tradition of the rich in Victorian times. But journeys were seldom tiresome or without incident for her. This time she enjoyed the company of her brother Maurice, of whom she had seen little in recent years, chiefly because he was content to spend most of his time in the North working among the steelmen. He was said to be a young man of great charm and unpretentiousness who moved easily among the workers at the Bell factories and who knew literally hundreds of them and their families personally. They travelled on the Royal Mail Steamship *City of Rio de Janeiro*. On December 29th she wrote to her father: 'We are safely aboard with all our belongings and we have magnificent state rooms to ourselves ... so you see it's quite perfect ... We are both much excited ... and amused. It's awfully interesting watching the people who come aboard. Some look rather nice I think, but

for the most part they don't look as nice as we do!' Maurice had
bought a book called *Manners for Women* with the help of which,
according to Gertrude, he hoped to be able to give her some
useful advice. Apparently its most illuminating item was the
revelation that Englishwomen of the right sort could use a needle
as skilfully as they could ride a bicycle – thus 'encouraging
Maurice to hope that his buttons may be sewn on during the
journey'.

To her sister Elsa she wrote one of those long and affectionate
letters which interspersed her voluminous correspondence with
her parents: 'You can't think what a joy it was to hear about all
your doings ... I am glad Moll went to the ball ... Now I am
going to tell you about San Francisco. I must tell you that San
Francisco is not finished; the streets are the oddest jumble, first a
tall building 25 storeys high, then a wooden lean-to, then another
great elaborate place, and so on. Moreover the roads except for
the tramlines are either a sea of mud or a wilderness of inlaid
cobblestones. Directly you get outside the town you find yourself
in great tracts of sand overgrown with green shrub ... To the
right of you is the bay, a constant delight to look upon, studded
with islands, filled with ships, its exquisite shores retreating
further and further away from the Golden Gates until it looks
almost like the sea itself except for the vaguest lines of land in the
far distance ... '

In March they were in Tokyo. A lengthy and effusive letter
from Yokohama to her stepmother depicts the Japanese capital:
'Dearest Mother, Where, where shall I begin! If I were to tell you
all the delicious things we have seen and done during the last
three days, I should write a letter as long as from here to Redcar ... '
She describes a journey by rickshaw: 'You get into a little peram-
bulator, a blue man in a mushroom hat picks up the shafts and
trots off with you ... His name was written on his hat in English
and his address (I imagine) in large white Japanese letters on his
blue cotton back.' There are minute descriptions of Yokohama
and Tokyo, shops, prices, people, scenes. It was winter when they
were there and people sat 'bundled in their wadded clothes over
a pan of charcoal', and Gertrude had in a few days picked up
enough Japanese to converse with them quaintly. 'Say I: "It is
cold," then seeing that he is mopping his brow with a cotton
handkerchief, I remarked, "Isn't it hot?" He took off his ... hat
and tucked it under the seat saying, "It's very hot, honourable

E

young lady esquire" ... The conversation ended, as all conversations do end in Japan, with peals of laughter.' The piquant observations fall one on another in the pages of her letters: theatres decked with flowers and coloured streamers, a Shinto version of the baptismal ceremony, her first glimpse of Fuji, the sacred mountain seen through a cluster of trees, a Buddhist temple ... 'gateway after gateway of carved and lacquered wood, court after court cloistered with lacquered pillars, planted with pines and here and there an exquisite plum or almond ... ' It was a joyous, blissful world which Gertrude inhabited at the end of the nineteenth century. Then came the long journey home, described as minutely as the outward trip: fellow guests at the Captain's table, a dance on board, golf on deck and a piquet tournament, onward to Hong Kong and across the oceans and seas to England. And then, hardly stopping to collect herself, more journeys to Bayreuth, Switzerland and the Dauphiné.

Surely by now Gertrude had begun to question the point of all this roaming? Was this life of endless, restless travel what she really wanted, or was she perhaps merely escaping, or searching for a husband or a challenge for her keen intelligence? Or was wandering an adjunct to her passion for languages; preparation, perhaps, for tasks of which she was as yet barely aware?

7

Jerusalem

She set out for the Middle East again in November 1899 at the invitation of the Rosens who by now represented the Kaiser in Jerusalem. She stopped on the way at Smyrna, the busiest trading town of Asia Minor then, making the last part of the voyage in a Russian vessel, the s.s. *Rossia*, which carried about four hundred Christian pilgrims. She wrote to her stepmother: 'The pilgrims are camped out all over the deck. They bring their own bedding and their own food and their passage from Odessa costs them 12 roubles. They undergo incredible hardships: one woman walked from Tobolsk, she started in March.'

She did not stay at the German consulate but at the Hotel Jerusalem, presumably because the Rosens lacked the space to accommodate her, but she had most of her meals with them. Almost her first action on arrival was to hire a horse and an Arabic teacher, Khalil Dughan. 'My horse is much admired,' she wrote to Florence. 'My teacher, also, is a success.' She was, nevertheless, having a surprisingly difficult time with her Arabic — surprising in view of her earlier protestations and the ease with which she had learnt Persian. She told Elsa, 'I must go to bed quickly so as to be up early and prepare my lesson before my Arab comes (I may say in passing that I don't think I shall ever take to Arabic, but I go on struggling with it in the hope of mortifying Providence by my persistence! I now stammer a few words to my housemaid — him of the fez — and he is much delighted ... '

She spent most of her time in Jerusalem touring with Dr Rosen's sister-in-law, Charlotte Roche, armed with a large Kiepert map of Palestine, keeping her family informed of her progress with a procession of vividly descriptive and sometimes

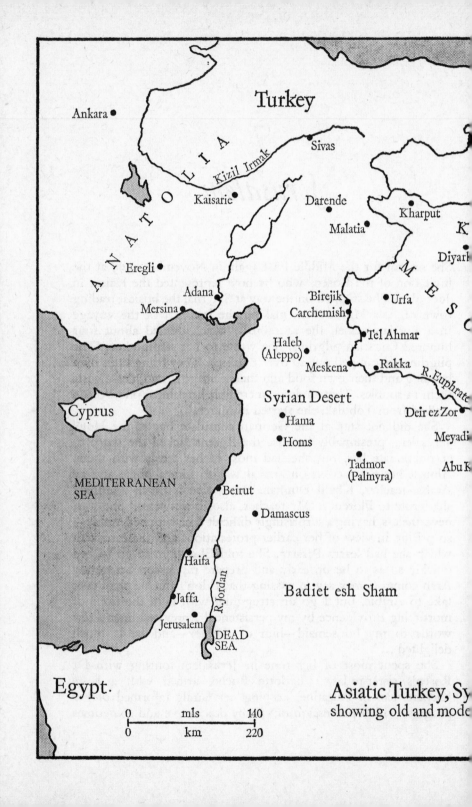

Asiatic Turkey, Sy
showing old and mode

Russia

Baku

zerum

Julfa

R. Araks

CASPIAN
SEA

Kizil Uzun

L.VAN

Tabriz

L.URMI

D I S T A N

Nineveh

at

R. Tigris

Jesire

Mosul

Erbil

Sulaimaniya

Kirkuk

Persia

A M I A

na

Tekrit

Kermanshah

Haditha

Hit

Falluja

Baghdad

Kasr
Temail

Ctesiphon

Museyib

Babylon

Dizful

Karbala

Hilla

Kut

Ukhaidir

Shuster

Najaf

Diwaniya

Amara

Nasiriyah

l Mesopotamia

Basra

e names

PERSIAN
GULF

Kuwait

cryptic observations. To Elsa: 'Charlotte and I went down to the Church of the Holy Sepulchre and I left her sketching while I explored it *gründlich* by the light of a taper which I bought from a priest. He intended me, I fancy, to use the taper for other purposes but I found it necessary as the church contains shrine within shrine and many of them very dark. It is most curious, half a dozen churches in one, of the most various dates. It is, you may fairly say, a summary of the whole bible ... all the sacred places huddled together under one roof, most convenient for the pilgrims. The people there are the most interesting part – from all countries and praying with every degree of fervour, with a couple of Turkish soldiers on guard to keep them from belabour-ing opposite sects!'

She called on the English consul Mr John Dickson and his wife but otherwise spent most of the time with the Rosens and her Arabic teacher. Her days were carefully mapped out. Study in the morning after being awakened by her befezzed housemaid, who prepared her bath and looked after her with motherly concern; then lunch with the Rosens, riding until five in the afternoon, more work until seven, and then dinner with the Rosens. 'I aim at being back by 10 to get another hour's work but this doesn't always happen, especially now when Nina [Rosen] is very busy preparing an Xmas tree and we spend our evenings tying up presents and gilding walnuts, Dr R. reading to us ... ' She started to make headway with her Arabic under Khalil, 'I learnt more about pronunciation this morning than I have ever known'. Her private lessons in Persian and Arabic, which she had begun three years before at home in England and continued under Denison Ross, are unlikely to have given her a native gift of pronunciation. Her new teacher gave her some fascinating lessons. One of them began: 'The Arabs are the oldest race on earth; they date from the Flood.' Her conversations with her 'housemaid' were perhaps more instructive, as a letter home suggests:

> Comes my housemaid.
> 'The hot water is ready for the Presence,' says he. 'Enter and light the candle,' say I. 'On my head,' he has replied – That means it's dressing time.

Christmas came and went in persistent rain and the century turned its last leaf to the welcome accompaniment of sunshine. *Heil dir, Sonne!* she exclaimed to the Rosens. But her effervescent letters did not always conceal the shadows of distant events. In January she received news of the death of one of her best-loved and most devoted aunts, Ada, who had looked after her following her mother's death when she was three years old, and who had married an officer of the Yorkshire Regiment, Lt-Colonel Arthur Fitzpatrick Godman. They lived near the Bells at Smeaton Manor in Northallerton, and Gertrude had seen her in the agony of a long-drawn-out illness. The Boer War, the first real test of Britain's imperial power and the capabilities of its generals since the Crimea, was not going well; and Maurice was about to leave for South Africa in command of the Volunteer Service Company of the Yorkshire Regiment. Her letters show a constant concern. Early in February 1900 came the announcement of General Buller's retreat, just as Maurice's company set off, but news of the relief of Ladysmith came as her brother was on the high seas and so, for a while, Gertrude and the family were able to concentrate on less worrying matters. Elsa and Molly, her half-sisters, were now grown young women, enlivening a social circle of which Gertrude had already become a familiar member. It has been said of them that they were archetypal ladies of 'good family', impressive in appearance, utterly correct in behaviour and with upright postures which even in Victorian England, where all ladies of breeding sat and walked with a plumb-line erectness, were remarkable. They seem to have had less of Gertrude's earnestness about them. Both were said by many people who met them (and who were able to recall them in the latter half of the twentiety century) to have been brilliant and delightful conversationalists; an impression borne out by Virginia Woolf who, as Miss Stephens, wrote to Emma Vaughan, her 'beloved Todelkrancz', in June 1900: 'Since I wrote ... we have been to Cambridge for the May week and I have danced at my first Ball. It was the Trinity ball, and the largest of all ... Florence and Boo were there, and Alice Pollock and the Hugh Bells (If you know them – MAP calls them "the most brilliant girl conversationalists in London" – and Thoby was much attracted by them and them by him) ... ' Three years earlier the girls had started a magazine called the *Monthly Cousin* which was produced partly on a typewriter and partly by hand and to which all members of the family and their friends were expected to contribute. Gertrude sent her sisters some picturesque eastern essays for editorial consideration.

She asked her stepmother to send her a telegram as soon as she had news of Maurice's arrival in South Africa and to ensure that her latest article for the *Monthly Cousin* was not offered for publication elsewhere since 'The style of it was only suited to that journal.' By late February 1900, when rain had returned to prevent long excursions, she was able to announce that she could read from the *Arabian Nights*, 'just for fun'. 'Do you know these wet afternoons I have been reading the story of Aladdin to myself for pleasure, without a dictionary! It is not very difficult, I must confess, still it's ordinary good Arabic, not for beginners, I must confess, still it's too charming for words ... I really have learnt a good deal since I came for I couldn't read just for fun to save my life.' She had found a Syrian girl companion by now whose elocution was even more to her liking than Khalil's.

Thus armed with an elementary understanding of the tongue and guided by Dr and Nina Rosen, she prepared to make her first journeys into the Syrian desert. She had sent home for a wide grey felt sun hat, 'not double, but it must be a regular Terai shape and broad brimmed'. Even before that piece of headgear arrived she cut an uncommon figure in Jerusalem where most days she was seen riding side-saddle to places of interest, examining the shrines of Christianity, Islam and Judah with great interest and increasing knowledge. If she was expecting to have to climb or to forage in the desert she might wear trousers, an almost unheard of sartorial departure for a woman; but she would still ride side-saddle. In the conflicting order of social priorities to which she and her family clung, ladies did not ride astride a horse. She would often ride over from the German to the British consulate while she was in Jerusalem to take tea with Mrs Dickson or to visit her husband at his vineyard, to which, surprisingly, was attached a soap factory. She partnered Mrs Dickson at whist parties among the English community. Sometimes she would go alone to places of interest, on other occasions she would be joined by the Rosens on a picnic ride to some historical site or a high spot from which they could gaze down at the Mediterranean or the Dead Sea – 'It's true I could bicycle to Jericho with my feet up'. The tomboy, if less prominent than a few years before, was still an attractive part of her.

She explored a new path to Bethlehem with the Rosens: 'It was lovely, a beautiful valley full of Olives, but the road shocking, as all the roads are.' On another ride with the Rosens they were attacked by dogs, the German Consul just saving himself from being thrown over a precipice by jumping from his horse with celerity. She learnt to read Genesis in Hebrew with Dr Rosen's help: 'It's extraordinarily near Arabic, much nearer than any two European languages I can think of.' And ever the worried enquiry about Maurice, the keen interest in the activities of her sisters as they traversed France, Italy and Switzerland and the *salons* of London in her recently implanted footsteps, and of brother Hugo now at Oxford.

On March 2nd she wrote to her father: 'The R's and I have been planning expeditions. We mean to go for ten days into Moab about the 18th. It will be lovely. We shall take tents, Dr R, Nina and I. Our great travel is not till the end of April, but I shall go to Hebron sometime early in April. Goodbye!'

She set out on her first desert journey on Monday March 19th, 1900, at the age of thirty-two. The road was thick with tourists, all accompanied by their donkey caravans, servants and badawin guides. There were no extraordinary dangers in these Syrian *vilayets* of the Ottoman empire, though it was common enough for American and European tourists to go home with hair-raising tales of narrow escapes from wild tribesmen in these stony and often flower-carpeted fringe deserts; and of course the badawin guides exaggerated the dangers out of sheer venality. Despite romantic stories which surrounded the journeys of Lady Hester Stanhope and Gertrude herself, to say nothing of later visitors whose powers of literary invention were to touch the hearts and minds of generations of Englishmen, the so-called Bible lands were not the stuff of great voyages of exploration.

Gertrude took things very much in her stride. In fact, she went without the Rosens on this first excursion, arranging to join them for a second journey in early April. She was accompanied by a cook named Hanna, 'that H is such as you have never heard,' she told her father, and a Christian guide named Tarif. In four hours she reached Jericho, famished, and went straight to the Jordan hotel for a meal. She had hoped to camp in the Jordanian desert that night but the tents were so far behind on the baggage mules that she was compelled to return to the hotel to sleep. They left early next morning with an extra *agheyl* – a Turkish guide – to see them along the Jordan valley to Madeba. Tamarisks blossomed in 'full white flower' and the willows were in 'the newest of leaf'. Of the Jordan plain she wrote: 'It was the most unforgettable sight — sheets and sheets of varied and exquisite colour — purple, white, yellow and the brightest blue — and fields of scarlet ranunculus.' As they passed across the scented plain they were joined by a cheerful party from Bethlehem, a fat man on a donkey and a small thin man who walked beside him, the portly one dressed in white with a yellow *kaffiyah* ('the thing they wear round their heads bound by ropes,' she explained for the benefit of her father) and a fair beard. He turned out to be another Christian 'Praise be to God!' and so they journeyed together across a carpet of flowers, the men stopping every now and again to pick Gertrude a bloom or to let off their breech-loader guns at pigeons which invariably flew off untroubled. 'May their house be destroyed,' exclaimed the Christian every time he missed. They left the floral plain behind and went towards Tell Kufrein where they saw the first black tents of the desert. All around barley was in ear and one of the Adwan Badu — 'Arabs *par excellence*' — played a reed pipe. 'It was much more Arcadian than Arcadia,' she wrote. They crossed Wadi Hisban 'which is Hesbon of the fish-pools in the Song of Songs', and went on to Ayun Musa, 'a collection of beautiful springs with an Arab camp pitched above them', where the women were unveiled and wore long blue cotton gowns. They bought *laban*, sour goat's milk, from them and went on to an encampment of the Bilka Arabs, where they pitched their own tents. It was raining and a strong wind was blowing when they left next morning, and Gertrude composed a letter to her family:

> At 7 it began to rain but I nevertheless started off for the top of Siagheh, which is Pisgah, sending the others straight to Madeba. I could see from it two of the places from which Balaam is supposed to have attempted the cursing of Israel and behind me lay the third, Nebo-Naba in Arabic. The Moses legend is a very touching one. I stood on the top of Pisgah and looked out over the wonderful Jordan valley and the blue sea and the barren hills, veiled and beautified by a cloud and thought it was one of the most pathetic stories that have ever been told.

She met an American photographer in a waterproof coat, took coffee and a cigarette and waited at a Latin monastery for her next official guide, who turned out to be a big, handsome and cheerful Circassian. They took the Roman road, hewn out of the solid rock of the gorge, which led through more flowers to their next stopping place. The Turks were nervous of English influence in Syria at this time and Gertrude had decided to pretend German nationality in order to extract the utmost co-operation from them. On Saturday March 24th, after nearly a week of gentle travelling, she wrote to her father: 'Grüsse aus Kerak! do you know where to find it on the map? ... I am going on to Petra ... I would telegraph to ask your permission, but there's no telegraph nearer than Jericho!' The Turkish governor or Mudir gave her another Circassian soldier to help her on her way, though he was reluctant to let her travel in a region inhabited by the Bani Sakhr and other tribesmen who paid little regard to Ottoman regulations. From Kerak they could look down the steep valley below them across the Dead Sea to the hills of Judea. They went on along the Roman road to Wadi Musa, six hours distant, stopping to purchase a lamb and some milk from the badawin and soon after seven in the evening they entered the defile which led to Petra, the Bab as Sik, no more than eight feet wide in places and half-a-mile long. 'We went on in ecstasies until suddenly between the narrow opening of the rocks, we saw the most beautiful sight I have ever seen. Imagine a temple cut out of the solid rock, the charming façade supported on great Corinthian columns standing clear, soaring upwards to the very top of the cliff in the most exquisite proportions and carved with a group of figures as fresh as when the chisel left them – all this in the rose red rock, with the sun just touching it and making it look almost transparent.'

They camped under a row of tombs, with pillars and cornices, topped by a great funeral urn, 'extremely rococo, just like the kind of thing you see in a Venetian Church above a 17th century Doge leaning on his elbow ... ' Next day she went to the top of Mount Hor: 'No daughter of yours could be content to sit quietly at the bottom of a mountain when there was one handy!' She and her guide climbed to the summit where they found Aaron's tomb. 'I have never seen anything like these gorges; the cliffs rise to a thousand feet on either side, broken into the most incredible shapes and *coloured*.' They returned the way they had come, meeting a party of *slubba*, desert tinkers, who were travelling on the pilgrim way from Mecca to Damascus. These happy people, despised by the Arab tribesmen, were always willing to help the wayfarer as that great Arabian traveller Charles Doughty had discovered on his weary way, and they danced around Gertrude's tent, content that they had been near the Prophet and had seen the holy city. One of her muleteers was a Druse. 'If all his sect are like him, they must be a charming race. He is a great big hand-some creature, gentle, quiet and extremely abstemious.' She decided that she would like to go to the Hauran desert and to take Muhammad the Druse with her. She arrived back with the Rosens on Saturday April 8th, sunburnt, 'a rich red brown, not at all becoming', and began immediately to arrange for the next journey, to the Hauran, with her hosts and her muleteers. She wrote to Elsa, discussing her sister's views on Italy and sending an illustrated article on Petra, written *en route*, for the *Monthly Cousin*. Gertrude was now an accomplished photographer and she began to send home some of the thousands of pictures of the East which were to supplement the written accounts of her travels. And a word for her other sister whom she persistently regarded as the most frivolous member of her family: 'Tell the ditty Moll ... that I've got a present for her. It's a complete Bethlehem costume, with the high hat and veil and everything. She can wear it to the next fancy dress ball if she likes.'

Before setting off for Jabal Druse, the mountainous home of that sect which stands somewhere between Islam and Christianity and which neither cares for greatly, she went to the Russian consulate and watched from its balcony the ceremony of the Orthodox at the Church of the Holy Sepulchre. She was intoxicated. 'I never felt so excited in my life,' she wrote. 'Suddenly the sound of the crowd rose in a deafening roar and I saw a man running from the sepulchre with a blazing torch held high over his head. The crowd parted before him ... Then followed a most extraordinary scene. On either side of the sepulchre people fought like wild beasts to get to the fires, for there were two issuing from the two windows of the sepulchre, one for the Greeks and one for the Armenians. In an instant the fire leapt to the very roof; it was as though one flame had breathed over the whole mass of men and women ... there was nothing but a blaze of light from floor to dome, and the people were washing their faces in the fire. How they are not burnt to death is a real miracle ... Well, I can scarcely tell you about it sensibly, for as I write about it, I am overcome by the horrible thrill of it.'

By the last week of April she was ready to leave for her first journey into genuinely difficult and hazardous territory. 'Oh,

Father dearest, don't I have a fine time! I'm only overcome by the sense of how much better it is than I deserve!' She and the Rosens kept together for the first week as they made their way north-east from Jerusalem, crossing the Jordan near Salt and making their way across country towards Damascus. By the end of April they had made leisurely progress to Deraa and when the following morning Gertrude looked through the flap of her tent she could see Mount Hermon, snow-capped and gleaming, in front of her. On the eastern horizon she could just make out the Druse mountains. They breakfasted in front of the Rosen tent as usual, and then parted for the time being, she going east with her caravan and they striking out westward to Lebanon. She rode for three hours with Muhammad and Yakoub her muleteers and Hanna the cook, though she usually went on ahead while they coped with the baggage animals; and she began to familiarise herself with the tribal *diras*, or pasture lands of the country, a knowledge that she was to put to vital use in years ahead. 'The maps mark this as Anizah country,' she would note, 'but they appear to have withdrawn their black tents further eastward, probably because of the encroaching Turkish government.'

Before they left Jerusalem, Dr Rosen had insisted that if Gertrude was going into the desert on horseback she must learn to use a 'gentleman's saddle'. It meant a break with one of the fixed customs of life but she was eventually persuaded and already she felt the benefit after years of side-saddle riding. The chief comfort of her journey, she said, was her *masculine* saddle. 'Never, never again will I travel on anything else; I haven't known real ease in riding till now.' She was disconcerted, how- ever, to find that wayfarers now thought she was a man approach- ing and addressed her as '*Effendi*' until they saw her skirt. 'You mustn't think that I haven't got a most elegant and decent divided skirt,' she assured her father. In this volcanic region most of the houses were built of black basalt rock — 'When the Romans built a great colony here in the first century, about, they built entirely with stone' — for there were no trees for wooden building. She made her way to Jizeh and then on to Bosrah, black and imposing, 'a mass of triumphal arches with the castle dominating the whole'. She was surrounded by past magnificence and present squalor, as she put it. Here came the inevitable moment of bargaining with the Turks. The Mamur, the Sultan's land agent in the province, was a Beiruti who spoke Arabic but his colleague was a Turk and had to speak to Gertrude in very inadequate French. She was able to convey to them, however, her urgent desire to see the Mudir, the governor of Bosrah. They took coffee and engaged in the customary polite exchanges and she told him that she wished to look upon Salkhad in the heart of the Druse country.

'*Salkhad!*' said the Mudir. 'There is nothing there at all, and the road is very dangerous. It cannot happen.' 'It must happen,' said Gertrude uncompromisingly. 'The Mutasarif fears for the safety of your Presence.' 'I wish to look upon the ruins.' After two days of fruitless exchanges she decided to make a dash for it. She was taken to see the military commander, the Rais al Askar, who was being shaved while Gertrude sipped coffee, and put her case to him and he promised to let her know his decision. He did not come to her by nightfall. Next morning she had gone. 'I've slipped through their fingers, and as yet I can hardly believe my good fortune.' Gertrude decided that she had better avoid Salkhad as the Turks were sure to pursue her there. Instead she made for a place called Areh where, according to her information, a powerful Druse shaikh lived. They made a long journey through the night, bitterly cold in contrast to the hot day, by a well-made Roman road. At last they saw a man in a cornfield with the white turban and black kaffiyah of the Druse and Gertrude practised the formal address she had learnt, 'Peace be upon you! oh, son of my uncle!' He put them on the road to Little Heart, the highest point of the Jabal Druse, on the way to which they found the little village of Miyemir. Druse women in their blue and red robes and white veils drew water from the pump, and by them stood a 'most beautiful boy of 19 or 20'. His name was Saif al Din and at first he dismissed the pleas of Gertrude and her party to guide them to Areh, but after a while he touched his heart and his forehead in token of obedience and set off with them. They sang on the way and Gertrude 'laughed with joy' as they passed through meadows and cornfields and vineyards.

'Are you German?' she was asked as soon as she met the villagers of Areh, and when they learnt that she was English she was invited to the house of one Hammad, who piled up cushions for her to recline on and with many words of gratitude to Allah put a stool at her feet and water by her side to wash her hands, and plied her with endless cups of coffee. It was a hospitable beginning to a propitious stay. She was taken to see Yahya Beg, the paramount shaikh of the Druses by the attentive Hammad, their little fingers entwined as he led her to the great man of his people. 'I would defy anyone not to treat Yahya Beg with respect,' she observed. He was a big man of fine stature and manner, who summoned the Englishwoman to sit with the others squatting on his carpet and eating from a central platter, and soon he was asking her about her travels, and her family. As she told her tale he would say, *Daghty, daghty*, 'it is true, true'. By the time she was ready to leave after five days at the heart of Jabal Druse, the people called her *Okhty*, 'sister'. She drank tea with them and gave them passages from the Bible to toy with – they were especially pleased with 'Love Thy Neighbour' – and finally set off for Damascus on Wednesday May 9th. She rejoined Charlotte Roche there two days later. She had asked her parents' permission to go on to Palmyra for a fortnight accompanied by three Turkish *agheyls* and on her return to join Charlotte again for a final journey over the Baalbek Hills to Beirut, and thence by boat to Haifa and on to Jerusalem.

> As we drew near Palmyra, the hills were covered with the strangest buildings, great stone towers ... some more ruined and some less ... They are the famous Palmyrene tower tombs ... I wonder if the wide world presents a more singular landscape.
>
> Except Petra, Palmyra is the loveliest thing that I have seen in this country, but Petra is hard to beat.

She returned home in June. Before she left she wrote to her father: 'But you know ... I shall be back here before long! One doesn't keep away from the East when one has got into it this far.'

8
Courage and Determination

Before she and Maurice left on their round-the-world voyage at the end of the Queen's Diamond Jubilee year, the family had spent a brief holiday in the Hautes Alpes. They stayed at La Grave under the shadow of the Meije, a mountain which challenged the most experienced of Alpine climbers. Gertrude wandered off one night and slept at the refuge, striding back the next morning with her first serious mountaineering ambition fixed firmly in her mind. She had to wait until the summer of 1899 before she could undertake the mission however.

Meanwhile she contented herself with a stay at Redcar with her sisters and Hugo; a brief sojourn in London spent mainly with the Russells of Audley Square; a visit to northern Italy on her own; a few weeks in Bayreuth with Hugo, the Lascelles and Chirol; and a journey to Greece with her father and her uncle Thomas Marshall, a classical scholar who had published a translation of Aristotle's works. In Athens she met for the first time her friend Janet's archaeologist brother, Dr David Hogarth, who showed them some recent finds — pots of 4,000 B.C. from Melos. 'Doesn't it make one's brain reel!' They had travelled to Athens by way of Corfu, a cheerful threesome despite the disparity of their ages. She found her uncle Tom a 'most amenable and agreeable' companion as they made their way along the coastline of Greece by horse-drawn carriage and eventually by train on the last stage to Athens. They stopped at several sites of ancient Greece on the way, she and Marshall spending a 'delicious' time amid the ruins of a Doric temple. But Gertrude wondered how her uncle managed when he travelled alone. 'He is absolutely ignorant and incapable about ways and means, added to which he has the untravelled Englishman's incapacity for making himself understood in any language except his own.' However, they got around together quite happily and went on conducted tours with Dr Hogarth and the illustrious Professor Doerpfeld, head of the German school of archaeology in Athens. 'He is a most agreeable person, extremely good looking and he consents with alacrity to our request that we be allowed to attend his lectures.'

On her way back she visited the Vatican and saw the Sistine Chapel, wondering where else in the world one could spend such a morning, and then they went on to Arcadia. 'Arcadia, I regret to say, is not the Arcady of the poets. The mountains are bare and rocky ... ', but she took a knowledgeable delight in the flora of the region, the blue stylosa iris 'which we forced last winter', anemones of scarlet, white, purple and blue and great colonies of cyclamen.

Perhaps the most enjoyable experience of the year was the journey to Bayreuth in the company of Hugo, now a grown young man whom she found 'one of the most delightful people in the world', though she argued with him constantly, except on matters of music in which subject he was vastly her superior. Donald Tovey joined them and gave a performance of part of *Die Meistersinger* after tea, on a very bad piano. At supper after a performance of *Parsifal* they were joined by Hans Richter, along with Frau and Siegfried Wagner. 'It had been a splendid performance, Richter conducted and the whole thing swung along magnificently. Frau Wagner and he came in to supper arm in arm and they had a tremendous reception.' Only Sir Frank Lascelles, carrying on his official duties bravely following the loss of his wife, failed to enjoy the excitement of musical debate and fine performance as much as he might have done in the past. For Hugo and Gertrude it was 'thrilling to see the home and be in the atmosphere of it all'.

For Gertrude, however, those enjoyable summer months were no more than an interlude in her preparation for the assault on the Meije. She arrived at the first camp on the afternoon of Friday August 25th, 1899 where she was joined by her French, German and English companions at the Refuge de l'Alpe after a two-hour walk from the base. After an early supper she went to bed and set off at 4.30 the next morning, arriving at the top of the *clot* at 8.10 in the evening. 'The Meije looked dreadfully forbidding in the dusk,' she wrote. She slept on straw that night

with a cloak for a pillow, packed as 'tight as herrings' between an
Englishman, two Germans and the guide Rodier. They went to
bed at 8 and at midnight they went down to the river and bathed.
'It was a perfectly clear night, clear stars and the moon not yet
over the hills.' They made their way to the first climb at 1 a.m.,
finding their way by lantern, arriving at the glacier at 1.30 when
they all harnessed their ropes, in Gertrude's case for the first
time. The first three hours of the climb was up 'very nice' rock. 'I
had been in high feather for it was so easy, but ere long my hopes
were dashed.' There followed a difficult and tiring two and a half
hours and at some points she had to be lifted up by her rope like a
parcel. 'The first half-hour I gave myself up for lost. It didn't
seem possible that I could get up all that wall without ever
making a slip. You see I had practically never been on a rock before. However, I didn't let on ... ' Soon she found it quite natural
to be hanging on by her eyelids over an abyss. ' ... We passed
over the Pas du Chat, the difficulty of which is much exaggerated ... ' They were at the foot of the Pyramide Duhamel and
they went on until they sighted the Glacier Carré where they
rested at 7.45 in the morning. At 8.45 they were at the top of
their first ascent between the Pic du Glacier Carré and the Grand
Pic de la Meije. They left at 9 a.m. and reached the summit at
10.10 encountering only one really difficult stretch at the Cheval
Rouge, an almost perpendicular and flat red stone. 'We stayed
on the summit until 11. It was gorgeous ... I went to sleep for
half-an-hour.'

The way down was more testing than the ascent. At one stage
she clung to a rock, suspended in mid-air for ten minutes with
La Grave beneath her. They took three hours to complete their
passage down to the Pic Central, spending a final hour negotiating
ice and rock until finally they came to the Glacier Tabuchet, at
which camp Gertrude had left her clothes. She changed from
her climbing trousers back into a skirt for her reappearance at
her hotel at 6.30 on the Sunday evening.

'I'm really not tired but my shoulders and neck and arms feel
rather sore and stiff and my knees are awfully bruised,' she told
her father. 'Dearest Papa!' she concluded, 'I shan't have nearly
enough money! I suppose I may draw large cheques? ... Oh, I'm
going to become a member of the German and Austrian Alpine
Club!' Her letter had begun on a less lighthearted note. Florence
had sent her a batch of correspondence relating to the family

dispute with the Bodleys which was now reaching a very acrimonious pitch. 'I have just been reading the Bodley correspondence,' she wrote after awakening from the long sleep which followed the previous day's climb ' ... it seems as if the moment has perhaps come to take action against them. Evelyn's last letter looks like the beginning of more bothers which it would be best to forestall. But it will be tiresome for you I am afraid, for there seems such a lot for them to say to which people who know neither you nor them will be inclined to listen. It can't, however, in the end be anything but satisfactory to you, and it would be a great comfort if they could be silenced forever ... Grandpapa, I observe, goes off on a side issue and considers only what concerns himself. I suppose it's natural but it's not agreeable.'

She returned home to Redcar in the middle of September to a domestic atmosphere heavy with dispute.

From July to September 1900 she was in the Swiss Alps. From Chamonix she describes the build-up of an Alpine expedition, 'meeting one's guides, talking over the great ascents that looked so easy on the map,' and laying out her clean new mountain clothes. Her father had been unwell while she was at home, and she promised him in her letter that she would go with him to Italy for a short holiday when she returned. Meanwhile, she told him, 'Mont Blanc mocked from across the lake', and she went off with that sense of exhilaration which always took hold of her when she was faced with the physical challenge of a great mountain or desert. 'It's a delightful place inhabited by English and American climbers, the people are most close and understanding of one's wants.' She wrote to Florence with that note of humility which mountains can induce in the proudest of people: 'I learnt a great deal from the Dauphiné last year, but oh dear! one's self-satisfaction is a good deal lessened when one is with people who really can climb.'

She was driven by foul weather from Montanvert, her base for further climbing, but she tackled the Mer de Glace before leaving for home. She and her guide climbed up the great effluent glaciers of the sea of ice: 'They are a continuous mass of the most wildly broken ice ... and great masses are constantly breaking away and crashing down.' She traversed the Grepon and Dru, and returned to England in a reasonably contented frame of mind. Now, in her thirties and as widely travelled as anyone of her age could

reasonably expect to be, she seemed to feel less need for circum-
spection in her letters home, though she maintained the somewhat
farcical habit of asking her father's permission to move on from
place to place, even in those lawless parts of the East to which
she was attracted and of which Hugh Bell knew little or nothing.
She announced that she would be dining with a young man, a
fellow climber, on the way home and that they would be joined
by another mountaineer whom she had 'picked up' casually in
Paris.

The rest of the year 1900 was spent mostly at Redcar in the
company of Hugo, her parents and sisters then being in London.
She had brought some cedars with her from Lebanon – 'Shall
we try to make them grow at Rounton? It would be rather fun to
have a real Cedar of Lebanon – only I believe they don't grow
more than about 20 feet high in 100 years, so we at least will not
be able to bask much under their shadow.' She supervised the
planting of one on the lawn at Rounton and gave others to
members of the family. She spent Christmas with Hugo, and her
young brother seems to have been put through a severe programme of physical training. Hunting figured largely in her
scheme. 'I looked after him to the best of my ability,' she told her
parents, 'which is a difficult thing to do in the middle of a run.'
He fell off his horse at one stage and appears to have lost a few
teeth for a little later she reports that at the beginning of the
month there was another hunt in which 'Hugo fell off ... but lost
no more teeth'. According to Gertrude he 'bore himself like a
man'.

In the absence of Florence, Gertrude stepped into the breach
at Middlesbrough and arranged teas, lectures and Christmas
festivities for the families of the workpeople at the Bell factories.
On Christmas Eve she wrote to her stepmother: 'Hugo and I are
very happy. He's delightful to be near, and we feel extremely
peaceful and comfy.' She wrote almost daily letters to her brother
Maurice in South Africa, and she kept in constant touch with
Chirol who had just succeeded Sir Donald Mackenzie Wallace as
director of the Foreign Department of The Times after twenty-
eight years in the Foreign Office, in which period he had served
in several parts of the world.

The death of Queen Victoria in 1901 left almost everyone of
whatever degree of prosperity with a feeling of personal loss and
profound uncertainty. Even Gertrude, who was seldom thrown

off balance for long by those events over which she had no control, was undecided what to do. In January she was at Redcar looking after her father who was still recuperating from his long-drawn-out rheumatic illness of the previous year. Her stepmother persuaded her to pay a flying visit to London in early February, however, for the Queen's funeral and she described the procession in a letter to Chirol:

> We had seats in Piccadilly, just opposite Dover Street, and we got there soon after eight. By nine all the entrances into Piccadilly were blocked, and lots of people never got to their seat at all ... About ten Lord Roberts appeared and rode up and down past us, much cheered. Soon after eleven the troops began moving past—the Colonials very gallant, the new Irish Guards with their green cockades. Leveson-Gower was among the blue-jackets; and among the Field Artillery I was charmed to see Laurence Godman [her cousin], looking delightful with his bearskin crushed down on to his lovely little face ... Then we saw the cream-coloured ponies coming down the great silent street, and it was almost impossible to believe that Queen Victoria was not alive behind them, the living centre of it, as she had been before ... Then the crowd of Kings, and Kings to be, King Edward very dignified, the Emperor a little behind him, very white and evidently much moved ...

The rest of that year until late summer was spent at Redcar and, occasionally, at Rounton where grandfather Lowthian, now old and ailing, was still in residence. So quickly had the youthful years passed that she now regarded her own father, as children will, as a lovably eccentric old man, though he was only fifty-seven. In August she wrote to her stepmother who was then in London: 'Father came in at four and announced that he wanted to bicycle ... Dear old thing.' A few days later she departed for Switzerland again.

On Wednesday August 21st she met up with her guides Ulrich and Heinrich Fuhrer in the Bernese Oberland, and she was obviously in a happy frame of mind for she had rare words of praise for a woman acquaintance, Lily Grant Duff, who was staying at the same hotel. 'Lily looked very pretty in her big hat and mountain clothes,' she told her father.

Among the mountains and the climbers, her pleasure was

unconfined. In August she told Florence, 'I am established for a day or two in this enchanting spot (Rosenlaui in the Oberland), having been driven out of the higher mountains by a heavy snowfall on Monday, which renders the big things impossible ... Here there is a fascinating little rock range, which can be done in almost any weather.' Before tackling those fascinating little rocks she met an English family and they spent a lively afternoon playing cricket to the amusement of their European companions, with fir-tree branches for stumps, and large butterfly nets handy to fish out the balls when they went into the river. Early in September she wrote to her father from the same area:

I am now going to give you a history of my adventures. Friday: we set out before dawn, the mists lying low everywhere ... We cast round and finally decided on a place where the rock wall was extremely smooth, but worn by a number of tiny water channels. These gave one a sort of handhold and foothold. Just after we started it began to snow a little. The first 100 feet were very difficult and took us three-quarters of an hour. The rock was excessively smooth and in one place there was a wall some 6 ft high where Ulrich had to stand on Heinrich's shoulder. Above this 100 feet it went comparatively easily and in an hour we found ourselves in a delightful cave, so deep that it sheltered us from the rain and sleet ... Here we breakfasted ... The next bit was easy ... but presently we found ourselves on the wrong side of a smooth arête which gave us no hold at all. We came down a bit, found a possible traverse and got over with some difficulty ... We know that neither the N. nor the S. side of the Gemse Sattel, as we have called it, has been done. Indeed the S. side *may* be impossible, but I don't think it is ... the experts may be mistaken.

Two days later, after being held up by snowfalls they tackled another peak, the Klein Engelhorn. 'It looked most encouraging, the lower third was composed of quite smooth perpendicular rocks.' They completed a difficult traverse to take them above smooth and precipitous rocks and 'here we were on an awfully steep place under the overhanging place'. First Ulrich tried to climb up the overhang by standing on Heinrich's shoulders. Then Gertrude clambered up on to Heinrich and Ulrich on to Gertrude. 'It wasn't high enough! I lifted myself still a little higher—always with Ulrich on me, mind!—and he began to raise himself by his hands.' As Ulrich's foot left her shoulder Gertrude put out her hand and straightened her arm to make a ledge for him. He called out, 'I don't feel at all safe—if you move we are killed.' Grtrudee assured him that she could stand there for a week. The guide got himself up into 'a fine safe place'; then it was Gertrude's turn. The three of them were roped together and she was able to make the ledge on which Ulrich was perched with the help of the other two, but Heinrich, left to last with no shoulders to stand on, could not get up 'with fifty ropes'. Then, in her account of this dangerous ascent, Gertrude delivers a characteristic aside: 'The fact was, I think, that he lost his nerve.' She was speaking of one of the most distinguished and courageous of Swiss guides, who like his cousin of the same name was a legend in the Alps. Ulrich and Gertrude went on to the summit of the Klein Engelhorn, rescuing Heinrich on the way down. When she retold the story to her stepmother, Gertrude remarked that Ulrich had admitted to her that if, when he had asked her if she felt safe she had replied that she did not, he would have fallen and they would all have gone over the edge. Gertrude told him after the event, 'I thought I was falling when I spoke.'

'What do you think?' she asked her father at the end of her report, 'Seven new peaks—one of them first-class and four very good. One new saddle also new and first-class. That's not bad going is it?'

By mid-September she was back in England, none the worse for a wet and hazardous expedition. She called on the Stanleys, Chirol, Lisa Robins, the Pollocks, Humphry Wards and other friends, and spent Christmas 1901 at Red Barns.

The year 1902 began and ended with sea journeys which, had she not made such descriptive use of them, would seem nothing more than ostentatious extensions of a life marked by unquestioned privilege and unlimited parental indulgence. In January she, her father and Hugo left Liverpool on a voyage to North Africa, Sicily, Malta and Italy, and on the first day out, the 14th, she wrote to her stepmother: 'We sat next the Captain at lunch. Mr Moss next Hugo and a Mr and Mrs W. and their daughter and two B's (father and daughter) opposite. Mr W. has a Lancashire accent you could cut with a knife, is a vulgar beast, but interesting and not unpleasant. Mr B. is sanctimonious, and I like him not. Miss M. pleasant and inoffensive.' She seldom erred on the side of charity in describing her companions. Hugo and Gertrude played bridge, read Sicilian history and argued amicably through cold blustery winds, and their father wrote an article about Trades Unions which he read to them from time to time. Gertrude thought it was 'excellent'. She caught a cold on the early part of the journey and was sick going through the Bay of Biscay; but neither malady confined her. She arranged to have the upper deck marked out for golf practice and went on with her Italian as the ship proceeded towards the Mediterranean. She continued to work at her Arabic, and less systematically at Latin, the syntax of which, along with Arabic pronunciation, presented the only serious obstacles to her formidable powers of learning. They went ashore at Algiers and Gertrude was 'much entertained at talking Arabic'. She found the 'better classes' quite easy to understand. She felt the pull of the East again: 'I find it catching at my heart again as nothing else can, or ever will I believe, thing or person.' On January 23rd they entered Malta harbour, and so began a week of photographing and drawing ruins of that ancient island, interrogating and describing its people, and hectic socialising. Dinner with the captains of H.M. ships in the harbour: 'I sat between Captains Leveson and Farquhar, and was very much amused.' Lunch with the C.-in-C., Admiral Sir John Fisher on the flagship *Renown*, 'rather an outsider, but an amusing person. His mother was a Cingalese, and he and his daughter have a most distinct touch of the Oriental'. To the opera for *Cavalleria*, 'of which we could only endure half', and the Council Chamber 'hung with Gobelins given by Louis XIV'. By the end of the month they had journeyed to Sicily. 'After lunch we drove out ... to the Latomia dei Cappuccini, that tragic place which is now a fruit garden, full of oranges, lemons, flowering almonds, pomegranates, and olives ... Here the Athenians sighed their lives away, out of sight and earshot of the blue waters they had ruled and lost. So on to San Giovanni where we saw boring catacombs, and the place where St Paul is supposed to have preached.'

Almost every page of her letters of this period was filled with the freshness and enchantment of discovery in a Latin land dotted with the remains of ancient Greece. At Taormina: 'Hugo and I got up at six and went to the theatre to see the sun rise. Unfortunately it was sirocco, and a very stormy sunrise, with

1 Gertrude, aged eight, and her father painted by Sir Edward Poynter, R.A., in 1876

2 Portrait of Gertrude's mother, Maria (Mary), in 1867

3 Gertrude's stepmother, Florence, from a photograph taken at the time of her marriage to Hugh Bell

4 Florence Bell reading in the 'Common Room' at Red Barns, 1905

5 The Bell family with their cousins the Walter Johnsons in 1883.
Gertrude is in the centre of the back row

6 Rounton Grange, Northallerton, designed by Philip Webb, showing
part of the gardens laid out by Gertrude

7 Washington New Hall in 1858 from a drawing bearing the initials of the architect, A. B. Higham

Etna mostly hidden. But for all that it was a revelation of beauty ... and then the theatre, the perfect theatre, framing sea and town and mountains through its broken arches, and itself the most exquisite warm colours of brick and stone.' And again: 'One's eyes, one's whole mind are brimmed full of beauty in that place — the eternal Greek beauty set in an Italian landscape.' At Santa Flavia they were joined by a youthful Winston Churchill, six years younger than Gertrude and as yet better known for his part in the Omdurman battle and the Boer War, and his book *The River War*, than for his politics. 'He appeared at 9.30,' she wrote to her stepmother on Sunday February 9th, 'and took us sight-seeing.' They went back to Mr Churchill's villa, leaving a card at the home of friends on the way and calling at the residence of a priest of the Chapel Royal, where they saw a collection of ancient Sicilian coins. As the journey progressed, Gertrude's father became weary with the discomfort of travelling on small steamers and cramped trains, and the rheumatism which was increasingly troublesome during the rest of his life became extremely painful, though a local chemist supplied a liniment which Gertrude rubbed into his limbs to good effect. They returned to their starting point, Taormina, which they eventually left 'with a terrible tearing of the heartstrings' for Naples via Paestum or Pesto as it is now called, with its 'fine and noble columns, just right in height and diminution', and the Temple of Neptune.

The family party split up after a tour of Neapolitan sights, Hugo and their father returning to England and Gertrude going on alone to Asia Minor. On Saturday March 15th she wrote to Florence from Malcajik: 'Dearest Mother, I am delighted to get your satisfactory telegram about Maurice [her brother was just home from the Boer War with a shoulder wound to show for his service] ... I was welcomed here on last Wednesday with the greatest warmth. On Thursday ... I went off early and spent the day at Ephesus ... We travelled with a comic party, American Catholic Bishop, a dear old thing, two American priests and a young Englishman — what he was doing in that quarter I can't think. They are going to Syria so I shall probably meet them again.' She was accompanied for much of the time on her travels along the west coast of Asiatic Turkey by the Van Heemstras and Van Lenneps, wealthy and academically distinguished families of Dutch origin. She spent several weeks with them, sampling the 'delicious' climate and country, and joining archaeological digs at a Byzantine tumulus and at the ancient Ionian site of Colophon where the shrine of the Claros Apollo was unearthed. She went on to Smyrna (modern Izmir): 'You should see me shopping in Smyrna, quite like a native only I ought to have more flashing eyes.' She called at Pergamos to survey its temples and palaces, at Magnesia and Sardis, picking up a copy of Herodotus in French with the aid of which she was able to follow the routes of earlier travellers in the region. At Sardis she remarked: 'I was delighted that I had Herodotus so fresh in my mind ... It's a madly interesting place ... Some day I shall come and travel here with tents but then I will speak Turkish, which will not be difficult ... '

In the third week of March she was cruising along the coast of Cyprus aboard the s.s. *Cleopatra*, a large vessel with only three first-class passengers, two men and Gertrude. One of her fellow passengers was the young Englishman she had met at Ephesus with the American bishop, Mr Paton, who turned out to be a student of Dante, 'an agreeable enough travelling companion'. The ship's doctor, a fiery Czech, proved the butt of Gertrude's dislike this time. He was 'consumed with a hatred of all things German ... rather like Sidney Churchill [the brother of Harry Churchill at the British Ministry in Tehran] – a man with a grievance against the world in general for being as it is. The Captain was a 'charming little Italian' and they all spoke his language at meals. 'I began with French but there were so few things they could say in French that I found it better to be comparatively dumb myself in Italian.' By now Gertrude had learnt to print her own photographs and spent many hours on her long journeys in improvised darkrooms. There was a short stop at Rhodes, time enough to examine the fortifications of the crusading Knights. She arrived at Haifa at the end of March and found temporary accommodation at Mount Carmel, before moving down into the town to engage in more linguistic exercises.

She found two shaikhs who agreed to act as instructors at Mount Carmel. 'I love my two shaikhs. It's perfectly delightful getting hold of Persian again, the delicious language! But as for Arabic I am soaked and sodden in it and how anyone can wish to have anything to do with a tongue so difficult when they might be living at ease, I can't imagine. I never stop talking it in this hotel and I think I get a little worse daily ... The birds fly into my room and nest on the chandelier!' There were two kindly old Americans staying at the same hotel, professors of divinity, and Gertrude could not resist the temptation of putting them together with her Persian instructor Mirza Abdullah, who promptly asked one of the Americans what he considered were the proofs of Christ's being God. 'The American answered in the most charming manner,' writes Gertrude, but Mirza Abdullah was not satisfied. 'He speaks as a lover, but I want the answer of the learned,' said the Persian. The two men debated for an hour and at the end Abdullah was unable to understand why the professor accepted one prophet and rejected another. 'I am bound to say I quite sympathised with him,' remarked Gertrude. This was cosmopolitan Syria, swarming with sightseers and students of divinity and horse traders of all nationalities, some of whom Gertrude had already met in the course of her travels. She rode every afternoon, read for between five and seven hours a day, had Persian and Arabic lessons, entertained parties of European and Oriental notables to tea and still found time to write the most explanatory and descriptive letters home. Having read the back copies of *The Times* which were sent to her by her father each day wherever she happened to be, she wrote to her stepmother: 'Read old Timeses all the evening. Though I haven't alluded much to politics, I am really thrilled by the Liberal split. I wonder if Lord Rosebery will be strong enough to re-form the party?' Her politics seem to have been undergoing some re-appraisal at this time. In her letters to Valentine Chirol, which were almost as copious as those to her parents, she entered into long discussions about the rise in the power of organised labour and the increasing influence of the trades unions, and seems on the whole to have taken a favourable view of those developments.

In another letter home from Haifa she remarked: 'I have called on all the missionaries! Heaven preserve us, what a collection of scarecrows!' On another occasion: 'Two clerics to dinner, one a Syrian, and the other the vicar of an East End parish.' Again: 'Dearest Mother, I now take my meals with a black. He's a fellow lodger in this hotel. He's a very pleasant black, and since he talks Arabic to me his colour leaves me quite indifferent.'

She rode the length of Mount Carmel to the Druse villages at the south-east, and there she received news of her old friends among the Druses of the Hauran. She rode over to Acre and along the Nazareth road where she was joined by a guide called

Solomon, mounted on a donkey, who took her to see the site of
Elijah's sacrifice. She returned to England in May 1902.

Before she could accompany Hugo on a long-awaited sea trip she
had to return to the Engelhorn range to complete some of the
climbs that had been frustrated earlier by bad weather. She spent
the month of June at home in Redcar and London and in July she
was back in the Oberland.

At about this time she wrote an undated letter to 'Ever my dear
Domnul' to sympathise with him at the threatened takeover of
The Times newspaper by a rival publishing group, and to compliment him on his talents; and she added an interesting footnote
to the effect that Ibn Rashid, the Amir of the Central Arabian
province of Jabal Shammar, was 'on the warpath' and that she
could not be sure that this would be 'a good year to visit him'.
This is the first reference in her letters to any ambition she may
have entertained to explore inner Arabia. Mountaineering was her
priority at the moment, however, and she left home with no more
demands on her family than a request to her sister Molly to obtain
for her two gold pins for her necktie and thick black garters.

She was met by Ulrich and Heinrich Fuhrer and was surprised
to find another woman climber there, Fräulein Kuntze, who was
somewhat put out to discover that Ulrich, with whom she had
been climbing, was contracted to act as guide to Gertrude. The
Englishwoman was uncommonly generous in her references to
the German girl; 'very good indeed she is,' she told Florence.
Gertrude had become a celebrated figure in the Bernese Oberland.
She was stopped by a guard on the train and asked if she was *the*
Miss Bell who had climbed the Engelhorn the year before. 'This
is fame,' she wrote with amusement and pride. The first few
days consisted of gentle climbing and reconnoitring 'a charming
little rock or two'. Then on July 13th they attempted what they
called 'the first of the impossibles', the Wellhorn arête. They
literally ran up the first part of the mountain, the Vorder Wellhorn.
Then they roped and started to work around a smooth and nasty-
looking overhang which took them four hours of 'very fine arête
climbing'. They arrived at a long knife-edge exposing a precipice
with a drop of some 2,000 feet beneath them. They reached the
summit after several hours of dangerous climbing in freezing
cold, and returned safely to base. 'If the weather holds we shall
go on to Grimsel,' she said, 'for the second impossible is now in

our minds.' On the last day of July she and the guides set out to conquer the Finsteraarhorn by its then unclimbed north-east face.

Gertrude wrote a detailed account of the attempt to her father in early August. They made good progress early on and by soon after midday – they had started out at 5 a.m. – were on to the arête, and after a few more hours of heavy rock and ice work they were within sight of the summit. Suddenly the weather broke and heavy snow impeded their progress. Then came thunder and lightning, their axes attracting the lightning. They could not go on, in either direction. They bivouacked for the night in a crevice which protected them from falling stones and avalanches. They remained roped together. By next day the ridge had grown narrower with the snowfall and its sides steeper. The summit was about a thousand feet above them and even in those incredibly dangerous conditions they decided, more at Gertrude's instigation than at the wish of the guides, to go on. A thick mist came up to add to their difficulties. 'Once we got to the top we could get down the other side in any weather,' said Gertrude. As it was they could not attempt the journey down the north-east buttress. They crept along the knife-edge of a col, but it proved too difficult for even the brilliant Ulrich. The awful alternative of the descent down the arête was better than trying to go on. They had been fifty-three hours on the rope and had had little sleep. Gertrude and one of the guides tumbled down on to a ledge and though they had a fixed rope to hold on to it was a frightening experience. By six in the evening they were attempting to climb down a chimney, the one that had already caused them trouble in the ascent. They were standing on an upright at the top of a tower when there was a blue flash. Gertrude's ice-axe jumped in her hand and she thought she felt it getting hot through her woollen glove. 'It's not nice to carry a private lightning conductor in your hand in the thick of a thunderstorm,' she said. They survived that danger, but they were forced to stop again because Heinrich had fallen into soft snow on the mist and rain-swept glacier. She and Heinrich slept in sacks, Ulrich insisting that Gertrude should lie on his while putting her feet into her own. They awoke at 4 a.m. A few hours later they reached safety.

Gertrude had failed to conquer the Finsteraarhorn, but her fame among mountaineers was now such that she was offered a place in the next Himalayan expedition planned by Dr C. F. de Filippi. Five years after the event, a letter from the guide Ulrich

Fuhrer was published in the *Alpine Journal* in which he recalled the climb and said: 'The honour belongs to Miss Bell. Had she not been full of courage and determination we must have perished.' Another distinguished mountaineer, Colonel E. L. Strutt, who became editor of the *Alpine Journal*, wrote in 1926: 'Her strength, incredible in that slim frame, her endurance, above all her courage, were so great that even to this day her guide and companion Ulrich Fuhrer—and there could be no more competent judge—speaks with an admiration of her that amounts to veneration. He told the writer some years ago, that of all the amateurs, men or women, that he had travelled with, he had seen but very few to surpass her in technical skill and none to equal her in coolness, bravery and judgement.'

When Gertrude wrote to her father to describe an event that was to become legendary among Alpine climbers, she began by describing the flora of the region. 'I was delighted by the exquisiteness of the flowers ... Isn't it odd how the whole flora changes from one valley to another.' Not all of her climbing expeditions were recorded in her own letters or in mountaineering publications, but one Alpine authority listed her new routes or first ascents in the Engelhorner as best he knew them: In August 1901, Similistock, King's Peak, Gerard's Peak; September 1901, Vorderspitze, Gertrude's Peak (named after her), Ulrich's Peak, Mittelspitze, Klein Engelhorn, Gemsenspitze, Urbachthaler Engelhorn; July 1902, Klein Similistock. That authority, W. A. Coolidge, stated that one well-known climber had told him that his most vivid recollection of Mont Blanc was the effort required to follow Miss Bell. And he added, 'They tell me she was the best of all lady mountaineers.' When she returned from the Finsteraarhorn, she and her guides had frostbite of the hands and feet. It was to all intents the end of her climbing career.

9
Durbar

The rigid Victorian society in which Gertrude grew to maturity
threw into sharp relief the aims and activities of those women who
were intelligent and intrepid enough to seek recognition in a
world designed by men; a world in which the place of women
was clearly defined. She was not alone in her determination to
break through the barriers of nineteenth-century convention, but
she did not have to try as hard as many of her sex. Her family was,
by the standards of the age, enlightened, and it had the means to
provide her with opportunities which in any age would seem
generous. Gertrude did not regard her own liberated existence
as anything more than a natural expression of her own ability and
enterprise. She was no early feminist; indeed she distrusted and
disliked her own sex, seldom missing an opportunity to comment
on their ineptness or their unfitness to engage in those activities
which were better left to men. If she found an equal footing on
mountains and in deserts, or in academic life, it was not because
she demanded any special 'rights' or fought any battles of emanci-
pation, but because in her own view she merited the freedoms
that were accorded her. She both acknowledged and breached the
conventions of her age. She distrusted the notion of equality but
it would have been a brave man who denied her the right to an
equal place in his midst. By the time she was thirty, she was
remarkably well travelled, yet she persistently asked her father's
permission to proceed from one place to another, even in later
years. She travelled alone or with male companions in deserts and
on mountains, but she never went out in London without a
chaperone. She would rationalise opposite positions with conviction. Politically she was emphatic, and sometimes equivocal.
When she wrote to Chirol at the time of Maurice's departure to

South Africa, she observed: 'There are good sides to the melan-
choly picture, such as the spirit of the nation, and its instant
response to calls upon it. It never seems to have lost heart for one
moment, and not to waste its time in useless recrimination, but
to turn all its mind to the important business of pushing the
matter through. And the Colonial loyalty has been splendid. But
oh! how I hope we shall take all this to heart, and never again be
found embarking on a war with neither soldiers, nor guns – nor
ministers! I feel that all the *kudos* goes to the Boers; their resistance
has been a piece of almost unparalleled courage, bother them!'

In the Jubilee year of 1897 she had written to her parents from
Potsdam; 'Did you drink the Queen's health ...? Such a subject
for congratulation.' When she had recovered from the initial
shock of the death of the old Queen she wrote to her stepmother:
'Aren't you glad that our new King is Edward VII? I'm delighted.
I have been riding this afternoon.' Now Lord Curzon was pre-
paring his durbar to announce to the princes and people of the
sub-continent of India the accession of Edward VII, King
Emperor. It was a rare opportunity to savour the glory of
Empire and Gertrude and her brother Hugo set off for the great
event, the first stage of her second world cruise, at the end of
November 1902. Just before they left Redcar, the Reverend
Michael Furse, a don at Trinity College during Hugo's time at
Oxford (later the Bishop of Pretoria and of St Albans), visited the
family at Red Barns. Years later he recalled a conversation with
Hugo and his 'charming sister' Gertrude. They were taking an
evening walk when Gertrude turned on Furse and said, 'I suppose
you don't approve of this plan of Hugo going round the world
with me?' 'Why shouldn't I?' replied Furse. 'Well, you may be
pretty sure he won't come back a Christian.' The visitor asked
her why that should be. 'Oh, because I've got a much better
brain than Hugo, and a year in my company will be bound to
upset his faith,' said Gertrude. 'Oh will it? Don't be too sure
about that,' said Furse.

Several members of the Russell family, Lord Dartrey and other
friends accompanied them on the journey to India, most of which
was spent in theological dispute between brother and sister. Here
was the blue-stocking at her most persistent. They had hardly
reached the Thames Estuary before Gertrude began to put Hugo
to the sword. Fortunately both kept diaries during the voyage so
that we have a two-sided account of the debate that occupied

them as they went round the world. On Thursday November 27th aboard the s.s. *China* off Marseilles, Hugo noted: 'Gertrude is an excellent person for a travelling companion, for besides the fact that she has been in the East before and takes a great interest in things Oriental, she also (which is of great interest to me) holds strong atheistic and materialistic views, the effect of which will be, as Michael Furse says, to put me on my mettle. She holds them sometimes aggressively: I think that aggression on her part will probably be met by aggression on mine and that we shall thereupon be rude and quarrel!' Hugo had begged his sister before leaving to refrain from quarrelling and she had assured him that nothing was further from her mind. She opened the debate, however, with a jocular story to do with the Archbishop of Canterbury, Dr Temple. When he was Bishop of London, said Gertrude, he drove from Fulham in a cab, but his fare did not satisfy the cabman who told the bishop, 'If St Paul were here he would give me one and sixpence,' to which Temple replied, 'If St Paul were here he would be at Lambeth, and that is only a shilling fare.' Hugo appreciated the joke. As the good-humoured exchange proceeded, he even admitted to some shortcomings in Genesis, especially with regard to Methuselah's reputed age. But his sister was not prepared to let the discussion rest there. She wanted to know if Christians still held to the theory of verbal inspiration. Hugo replied:

'It has been impossible during the nineteenth century to hold that all scripture was verbally inspired.'

'Then what do you mean when you say inspiration?'

'I would confine inspiration to the things which concern human nature exclusively, not the external world of which men's views must be modified by the progress of science. Spiritual insight into human nature can, it seems to me, be given by revelation and not disproved.'

'Then what about Muhammad?'

'I should say he was certainly inspired—although being a man he was liable to err and misinterpret, and the revelation to him may only have been partial.'

'On that supposition surely it was very deceitful of God to give one revelation at one time and 600 years later to give another which would lead men astray. And the fact that Christians take upon themselves to preach to Muhammadans

G

must be derived from a fresh revelation, posterior to the time of Muhammad, since the Muhammadan revelation was posterior to the Christian.'

'The Christian revelation was itself one which could not be supplanted. It was expressly for all times – besides which it seems to me to be in accord with what is best in human nature.'

'Then you are accommodating it to fit in with your views on human nature ... '

So the discussion proceeded as the s.s. *China* ploughed eastward, Gertrude and her brother hardly pausing for breath. Even the letters home which would normally have occupied several pages each day were few and far between. But there was no animosity as yet, 'Hugo is the most delightful of travelling companions,' she told Florence early in December. 'We spend a lot of time making plans with maps in front of us. We are chiefly exercised as to how many of the Pacific Islands we shall visit.'

They arrived in Bombay on December 12th. 'You can't think how charming and amusing and agreeable the Russells have been,' she wrote to Florence, adding: 'Our servant met us at the quay; he seems a most agreeable party and he's going to teach us Hindustani.' Within a few days she was telling her stepmother: 'We have become almost unrecognisably Indian, wear pith helmets – and oh! my Hindustani is remarkably fluent ... We are addressed as *Your Highness*.' They were in Bombay within a year of the great plague epidemic in that city but life seems to have returned to normal, though it is unlikely that Gertrude would have been put out had the disease been rampant. The Governor, Lord Northcote, she found 'charming, delightful to talk to, and she is even more charming'. While her companions sat in the English club or in their hotels writing letters home and taking cool drinks, Gertrude rushed around the city observing and describing its buildings and people. Two excited elderly Parsees grabbed her as they passed and told her that 'the ceremony had begun' and before she could protest she was in a courtyard witnessing a marriage ceremony.

Gertrude and Hugo went on to Agra and Jaipur and arrived in Delhi at the end of December, where they were guests of the Viceroy in his visitors' camp. 'Dearest Mother, Where shall I begin in this tale of our wonderful days?' They had completed

the last part of the journey partly by train and partly by horse,
Gertrude's costume consisting of a sun helmet, a cotton gown
and a fur coat, a combination which she found suited to the
variations of the Indian climate. At Agra they saw the palaces of
Akbar and his successors and rode out to see remains of the old
Moghul empire. Gertrude was once more in that world of
antiquity which she knew almost instinctively:

> Outside we found a solemn Muhammadan waiting for us who
> said, 'I am guide – my name Chisti. I am very holy man.' With
> which he marched us off to the great mosque ... One of the
> most magnificent gates in the world leads into the mosque,
> colossal, standing on top of a long flight of steps coming up
> from the town inlaid with bold designs in white marble,
> topped by a long scroll of inscription, the famous verse from
> the Koran: Jesus said, 'This world is a bridge, make us
> abiding' – It is almost too significant a motto for the deserted
> palaces of the capital of a dead empire.

The Russells, Arthur Godman her first cousin, Valentine Chirol
(who had arranged to meet her in Delhi before she left London),
and many other familiar faces were awaiting her at Delhi. After a
visit to the polo ground she remarked that they had met 'all the
world'. But she was about to witness a world whose splendours
she had scarcely imagined. 'Pack six kings dressed in green,
yellow and gold, and a state treasury of pearls and emeralds, into
one landau, harness six horses to it, with postillions clothed in
every colour of the rainbow, put four mounted lancers in front
and four behind, and you have just the beginning of the vaguest
idea of what a Raja looks like when he goes out driving. And you
meet twenty of them in half an hour.' Gertrude was in Delhi at
the high summer of empire.

The excitement built up day by day to the climax of the great
event itself in the first days of January 1903. Nobody was better
than Gertrude at conveying the enchantment and, if need be, the
impiety of a great occasion:

> The function began with the entrance of the Delhi siege
> veterans – this was the greatest moment of all, a body of old
> men, white and native, and every soul in that great arena rose
> and cheered. At the end came some twenty or thirty Gurkhas,
> little old men in bottle green, some bent double with years,

some lame and stumbling with Mutiny wounds. And last of all came an old blind man in a white turban, leaning on a stick. As he passed us, he turned his blind eyes towards the shouting and raised a trembling hand to salute the unseen thousands of the race to which he had stood true. After that the Viceroys and Kings went by almost without a thrill ...

And then the great procession itself, Lord Curzon representing the King, amid all the panoply of Imperial India.

First soldiers; then the Viceroy's bodyguard, native cavalry; then Pertab Singh at the head of the Cadet Corps, all sons of Rajas; then the Viceroy and Lady Curzon, followed by the Connaughts, all on elephants; and then a troop of some hundred Rajas on elephants, a glittering mass of gold and jewels. The Rajas were roped in pearls and emeralds from the neck to the waist, with cords of pearls strung over their shoulders, and tassels of pearls hanging from their turbans; their dresses were shot gold cloth, or gold embroidered velvet. The elephants had tassels of jewels hanging from their ears ... It was the most gorgeous show that can possibly be imagined.

Lord Curzon had said before the show that if there was a single case of cholera in Delhi he would remove the entire event to Agra. He need not have worried. It went off without a hitch, or at any rate with none that the Viceroy himself was aware of. Gertrude observed the arrival of Lord Kitchener; everyone stood up and cheered him and the band played 'See the Conquering Hero'. And she noticed that the troops refused to cheer Curzon, whose aides-de-camp moved up men of the Yorkshire Regiment and other British soldiers to step into the breach, but they remained silent. 'It's very curious collecting opinions about Lord Curzon,' she told her stepmother. 'I am gradually coming to the conclusion that he is something of a great man, but there is no doubt that he is extremely unpopular ... Even Arthur [Russell] who is by no means anti-Indian says, "Since Lord Curzon's time the natives have learnt to push you off the pavement" ... [quoting an officer at the Durbar]: "You get sharp words and bad manners from him, but you find that the thing that needs doing gets done, without months of official letters, and yards of red tape" ... Then again, all the Frontier people are fire and flame for him; Mr Cox out in Muscat, Mr Hughes Buller in Kashmir ... '

There were countless parties, lunches, dinners and meetings with royalty and politicians, at which Gertrude was usually accompanied by Domnul and the Russells. She was introduced to the Aga Khan by Lord Carlisle. There was talk of the insoluble problems of India, of its outrageous wealth and poverty; and continuing theological dispute with Hugo. As they journeyed across country to Udaipur and Jaipur, Chitor and Alwar, and back to Delhi, Gertrude demanded of her pacific young brother an explanation of the mystical. 'Gertrude could not see why one revelation should be more valid than another, since both were supposed to come from God,' wrote Hugo as Gertrude harped back to an earlier debate. 'Then she interrogated me about the Old Testament.'

'How about Hezekiah and Moses?' I couldn't say that the shadow went backwards ... 'Then how about the burning bush?' This I couldn't explain ... Then to New Testament miracles. 'Do the orthodox (by which she meant me!) accept them? or are they not thought necessary to the Christian faith?' I said they are not necessary, except the Resurrection, which is absolutely ...

Before dinner one evening they were visited by an Indian hospital assistant of some education who overheard them in discussion and sought to join in. He was brought up to worship Rana and Krishna, but as a student had adopted the faith of Arya Samaj, with its belief in one indivisible God. Hugo asked him politely if this sect, rebelling against the orthodoxy of popular Hinduism, was likely to spread, and if so whether it would touch the lower classes. The visitor said that it was spreading among educated men, but that the lower classes were never likely to adopt it, adding as an afterthought that if they did the educated men would be unable to find servants. Gertrude took no part in the conversation. When the Indian had departed she said to Hugo, 'None of your blasted equality for him.'

From Alwar to Lahore ... 'We left a Hindu city to find a Muhammadan; we left marble temples, and find tiled mosques; and we have exchanged a slender and naked Hindu population for the stalwart men of the north, Sikhs and Pathans, long-coated, with beards dyed with henna ... speaking a tongue bristling with Persian words.' They found Willie Peel and Lord Killanin on the way, and went on to the North-West Frontier with the Russells.

Gilbert Russell relayed a story he had been told of that dangerous and lawless region. A British regiment was being harassed by an Afridi sniper who made them the targets of his rifle practice every night, and eventually they asked a member of the Khyber rifles to investigate and see if he could rid them of the nuisance. The native soldier returned shortly after, bearing a human head, and he was complimented on his promptness in dealing with the matter. 'Oh yes,' he said, 'I know all about his ways. He was my father.'

They looked into the forbidden land of Afghanistan and saw the Kabuli caravan emerge from the gorge. 'The wild, desolate valley was full of camels, and men, and ponies, tramping, tramping up to Kabul, and down to Peshwar. It was a wonderful thing to stand at the gates of Central Asia, and see the merchant trains passing up and down on a road older than all history.' As they took a last look at that infamous pass she wrote: 'Think of conqueror after conqueror standing there and looking down on the richest land of Asia! Aryans and Greeks, Mongols and Pathans – they have all looked down that valley, and smelt the hot breath of India, and the plunder to come, Alexander, and Timur, and Muhammad of Ghazni, and Barbar – who comes next over the Pass?' Before leaving the Frontier she washed her hair for the first time since Bombay. 'Pfui!'

By the end of January they reached Calcutta and then went on to Darjeeling and the Himalayas, balm to Gertrude's poetic soul. 'At 4.30 Hugo came into my room and said, "Get up, get up! the moon's shining on all the snows!" and I jumped out of bed and into a fur coat.' In her excitement Gertrude ate a hurriedly prepared egg with sugar instead of salt, and they rushed off on their horses, Nepalese guides panting behind, Kinchinjunga before them.

That was a ride! We dashed on to the Tiger Hill, which is about 900 feet high. As we got to the top I saw the first sunbeam strike the very highest point of Kinchinjunga – Nunc Dimittis there can be no such sight in the world – Away to the west, and 120 miles from us, Everest put his white head over the folded lines of mountains.

She vowed that she would return to climb Kinchinjunga, that 'white dream suspended between earth and heaven'.

The rest of the journey was a saga of tourism intermingled with dispute which became more affected and inconclusive as time went on. Burma, Hong Kong, China, Japan; new places and places she had seen before; new experiences and old. Elephant rides, boat trips along the Irrawaddy, diplomatic receptions and bizarre conversations, colourful natives and eccentric Englishmen —it was a keenly observed journey but hardly enjoyable, especially for Hugo who, by the time they had reached America on the way home, was heartily fed up with his sister and elected to separate from her and make his own way across the United States. On the way from Calcutta to Burma there had been a characteristic exchange. They talked of English and French novels and differences of national temperament which the two literatures exemplified. Hugo thought the English character was so made as to lean less towards its vices. Gertrude said that the worst of English vices was a lack of discrimination. Hugo responded that he could not see how discrimination was a moral virtue, or the want of it a vice. 'Of course, it is one of your vices not to be able to see that,' said Gertrude. They went on to talk of democracy and John Stuart Mill. 'The greatest good of the greatest number' was a pointless idea, insisted Gertrude. The important thing was the happiness of the 'agent'. Sentiment, she said, was the most dangerous of frailties. 'It makes the world stagnate more than anything else.'

In Canada Gertrude went off to climb the Rocky Mountains. When she and Hugo met up again they found themselves arguing about reason and emotion. She did not, she told him, approve of his tendency to appeal to the emotions rather than the mind. She would rather people stayed wicked than that they should be reformed by appeals to the emotions. Hugo asked her why she climbed the Rocky Mountains. Was that not simply for the pleasure she would get? And what sort of pleasure was that? Was it not simply and solely an emotion? Gertrude had replied that it was emotion controlled by reason. She went on to Boston to meet Lisa Robins while Hugo stayed in Chicago. 'The air was electric,' Gertrude wrote in her diary. Brother and sister returned to England on July 26th, 1903.

10

Inheritance

Hitherto Gertrude's travels had been little more than sightseeing tours, the gratification of the wish of a wealthy and greatly indulged young woman to see the world and to soak up impressions and knowledge as she went. She was thirty-two years of age at the turn of the century. She was, like her stepmother, fluent in English, French and German, and in addition she could speak and write Arabic and Persian, was passably proficient at Turkish and could hold a tolerable conversation in most parts of India, and in China and Japan. If she was an historian by formal learning, she was by inclination and acquired knowledge a wide-ranging scholar with an almost intuitive understanding of ancient architecture and archaeology. She had proved herself a woman of immense courage in her mountaineering exploits, and a writer of real ability. She could have rested on her laurels at this stage of her life in the assurance that she had seen as much of the world as any human being could reasonably wish to see, and achieved a great deal more than most; that she had come to know almost everyone who mattered in government service and was related to a good many of them, and had received a warm welcome at the courts of emperors and the hearths of ordinary mortals. She could, like several of her well-known contemporaries in London society, have slipped comfortably into one of those cosy and exclusive London 'sets'. But she was too active by nature to become part of any fixed group. A dinner-table conversation was as much as she could endure of those discussions which always began with 'I think' and 'In my opinion', and she would usually go away to lampoon her fellow guests in letters to the family. She delighted in the company of the Stanleys and Russells, the Maxses and Cecils, and the theatrical friends of her stepmother and Elizabeth Robins, but her incursions into these passive debating circles were almost always attenuated by a desire to rush off to her mountains, or see friends in the country, to walk, cycle or ride by horse across the dales and moors of her northern homeland; to read and study. Bertrand Russell recalled Gertrude telling him at this time that she would not wish to live in a university town because its inhabitants 'knew nothing of the great world without'.

She had by her own exacting light achieved little to date. Now she sought some tangible objective beyond the ordinary limits of travel and writing. She despised the idea of writing books or articles for the Press in order to see her name in print. When she was prevailed on to produce a book or an article she preferred anonymity and only agreed to use her name under insistent editorial pressure. Her mind turned more and more to the largely unexplored deserts of central Arabia, and to the work in archaeology that had been going on with much-publicised vigour for some thirty years on the peripheries of those deserts, in Syria and Mesopotamia.

Before she left on her world cruise with Hugo, negotiations were in progress regarding the family businesses, the outcome of which was to have an important bearing on the Bell family's future. In 1901 Gertrude's grandfather decided to amalgamate the Bell companies with other concerns in an effort to provide the financial, managerial and—above all—the technical resources necessary to their survival. He was now eighty-five and in failing health. The strikes and lockouts of the 1880s in the north-east of England had come as a warning that drastic changes were necessary. Even more importantly, Britain's lead in the manufacture of iron and steel had been eroded to the point where she was already a poor fourth behind the United States of America, Germany and Japan. Like his own father Thomas, Sir Lowthian Bell had been a life-long advocate of technical education, but by the turn of the century he was the only technologist of any real merit among the ironmasters of the north, and perhaps of the whole country. His domestic competitors were mostly entrepreneurs. As an historian of the industry has written: 'He was an outstanding scientist and he had a fine head for that business to which he directed his scientific talent ... But to these he added other gifts. He was a first-rate statistician and one of the com-

paratively few industrialists of the age to see the importance of
relating business to economic trends which he analysed so
shrewdly ... ' Bell lost the battle for technical education, while
the Krupps of Germany and their like in America, Asia and
Europe won it. Britain was to pay a high price for its folly, and
Lowthian Bell was one of the few men who understood just how
great it would be. In his own family, where no grandchild,
nephew or niece had been denied the very best education that
money could buy, not one followed in his footsteps. Maurice,
popular with the workpeople and a good manager, took over
many of the family responsibilities at the Works, but he was no
technician. In Lowthian's younger days Washington Hall, where
Gertrude's father grew up, was alive with scientific and philosophical debate of the highest order. The ironmaster of
Washington counted among his close friends and acquaintances
Charles Darwin and Thomas Huxley, Robert Stephenson, Baron
Armstrong the armament king, William Morris, Burne-Jones, and
some of the distinguished Quakers of the region of whom his
wife and father-in-law were notable representatives. His own
education in Scotland, Germany, Denmark and France, in the
course of which he distinguished himself as a chemist and
physicist, had made him an international figure by the time he
reached his early twenties. His published works, *Chemical
Phenomena of Iron Smelting* and *Principles of the Manufacture of Iron
and Steel*, were standard textbooks for many years. It can only be
regarded as a peculiarly English fact that this extraordinary man,
acknowledged even by the Krupps of Germany as the leading
technical authority of his age, was listed in most directories of
the time under the heading 'Merchant'; to the end of his days,
even within his own family, he was spoken of as a 'trader'.

Thus Gertrude's grandfather very sensibly decided in 1901 to
unite his companies with those of a competitor, Dorman Long.
That company, a relative latecomer to the area, had been exceptionally successful under the technical management of Sir
Arthur Dorman, a Kentish farmer who went north in 1875, and
the financier Albert de Lande Long. They purchased a majority
of the ordinary shares of Bell Brothers, and Sir Lowthian Bell
became chairman of the new organisation. Already Lowthian
had sold off the chemical companies which he founded in con-
junction with his father-in-law, Hugh Lee Pattinson, to the
Brunner Mond Company. The firm's rail interests had been

amalgamated with the North East Railway which in turn became part of the London and North Eastern Railway. It was a condition of the new arrangement that Hugh Bell became a director of all the companies concerned. As a result, the Bells became exceedingly rich in terms of liquid cash overnight. Part of the money was invested in new family estates. Part was distributed to grandchildren, nephews and nieces, all of whom received £5,000. The residue went to Gertrude's father. An incidental consequence of the arrangement was that Hugh, in becoming a director of the London and North Eastern Railway, found himself at board meetings sitting alongside Sir Edward Grey, soon to become Britain's Foreign Secretary.

Three years later, five days before Christmas in 1904, Sir Lowthian died at his London home at the age of eighty-eight. His passing went virtually unnoticed. In November of that year Gertrude had visited him at Belgrave Terrace, and wrote to her stepmother: 'I called on Grandpapa ... He was very doddery I thought, poor old dear.' It was the last surviving comment on him, apart from an obituary in *The Times*. When he died Gertrude was in Paris on her way once more to the Middle East. Her father had inherited the baronetcy and the residue of his estate, three-quarters of a million pounds. The new Lady Bell, in the collected letters of Gertrude which she published years later, mentioned that 1904 was the year in which her daughter Molly married Charles Trevelyan, thus establishing another link with a family of many talents, but she does not refer to the death of Sir Lowthian.

11
Asia Minor

Early in 1901, before she set out for the Delhi Durbar with Hugo, Gertrude had engaged the services of a maid, Marie Delaere, at an annual remuneration of £22 plus washing ('I think you always give washing?'). She had also found an opportunity to join forces again with Janet Courtney, and she enjoyed a 'wild afternoon' walking through the slums of East London with Hugo: 'It really is most extraordinary to see the edges of London.' After her return from the world voyage she divided most of her time between Redcar and London, much of it in the company of her young cousin Sylvia Stanley, the daughter of Lyulph and aunt Maisie, and her brother Edward. In 1903 Edward Stanley joined the British Civil Commission in Nigeria, and so another spate of correspondence ensued between Gertrude and one of her many friends and relatives in government service. She wrote to him soon after his arrival in Nigeria:

> Yes, Marcus Aurelius is a good counsellor, if one can follow his advice. I mostly find myself rebelling against it, with an uncanny sense of being too hopelessly involved in the mortal coil to profit by it. What is the use of bending all one's energies to the uncongenial thing? One is likely to do little enough anyway, but if half one's time is taken up persuading oneself one likes it or at least conquering distaste there is very little left to achieve success with.

Even in her most personal letters, Gertrude usually wagged an admonitory finger. She reported most of her activities to Edward Stanley during 1903; being at home she had little cause to write to her parents and one of the few substantial gaps in their lifelong correspondence occurs at this time. 'Last night I went to a ball at your house,' she tells her cousin, 'a very exceptional thing for me to do and enjoyed myself so much that having gone for a moment, I stayed for three hours. A most pleasant party ... I had an amusing dinner the other day sitting between Lord Peel and the Aga Khan. Do you know who he is? He is a direct descendant of the Prophet, supreme head of half the Shia world, an English subject, enormously rich (his sect allows him £180,000 a year) and a pretender to the throne of Persia ... He explained to Gilbert Russell, whom he knows very well, that he was so rich that £2,000 was to him as 6d is to other people. "Then", said Gilbert, "could you change me a shilling?" '

She had been taken ill during a stay at Redcar and the doctor diagnosed anaemia, but she was not subdued for long. In November 1904 she left for Paris with Sylvia Stanley and there met Salomon Reinach the director of the Museum at St Germain, and the French explorer Dussaud. 'I had a most enchanting evening with Reinach. I got there at 7.30 and left at 11.30 and we talked without ceasing all the time ... This morning I went to the Bibliothèque Nationale. Reinach gave me a letter to one of the directors and I was received with open arms ... I looked at two wonderful Greek MSS – illuminated – from 12 to 3.30! and I am going back there to-morrow to see ivories and more precious MSS ... It is perfectly delightful.' On November 10th: 'To-day I went to the Louvre in the morning then at 12 with Reinach to St Germain ... Now I'm going to dine with him and spend the evening in his library. He wishes me to review a new book of Strzygowski's for the Revue Archéologique – I think I might as well try my prentice hand ... '

Reinach's commission was to have a profound effect on the course of her life from then on. In early January 1905 she was sailing towards Beirut aboard the s.s. Ortona, wishing that Hugo was with her for she began to reflect nostalgically on his kind and considerate manner, despite the brushes of their long voyage. But Hugo was now preparing to take holy orders. His sister's sustained attack on his faith had not shaken his belief, and not even an offer from The Times to become its music critic had changed his mind about the ministry. From Beirut she reported on January 18th that she was 'deep in the gossip of the East', and she went on to Haifa in that state of intoxication which always overcame her as soon as she set foot on the soil of the Middle East. She arrived at Haifa on February 1st and from there rode into Jerusalem where her first caller was the British Consul, Mr John Dickson. He told her that an Englishman named Mark Sykes and his wife were nearby, and she quickly went in pursuit of them. 'They received me with open arms, kept me to dinner and we spent the merriest of evenings. They are perfectly charming. I've got a dog, an extremely nice dog of the country. He sleeps in my tent, and he is perfectly charming. He is yellow. His name is Kurt, which is Turkish for Wolf.' Gertrude's light-hearted account of the meeting with the Sykeses was not by any means complete. The young Englishman who at that time traversed the same paths as she in Syria and the Levant was a near neighbour of the Bells in Yorkshire, son of a baronet and one of the county's richest landowners. But they had little in common besides wealth and proximity of birthplace. Eccentric, mercurial and opinionated, Sykes was to wander confidently through the corridors of power in the years ahead, always to turn on his heels at the last moment. Staunch Catholic, Tory-democrat by self-applied political label, brilliant and vituperative in his writings and speeches, and contemptuous of desert Arabs and all subject peoples, he soon turned on the woman whom he saw as a competitor on his eastern travels. He described her as a 'Bitch' and 'an infernal liar'. Their dinner in Jerusalem, it seems, became an exercise in showmanship, each trying to outdo the other in Oriental learning, knowledge of routes and the prices of animals and guides, with Mrs Sykes, Edith, trying stoutly but ineffectually to keep the peace. Soon after their meeting Edith returned to England and Sykes wrote to her apropos Gertrude's suspected desire to go ahead of him and thus pre-empt his Syrian journey: 'Confound the silly chattering windbag of conceited, gushing, flat-chested, man-woman, globe-trotting, rump-wagging, blethering ass!' The unseemly exchange reached a climax when Gertrude was alleged to have told the Wali of Damascus that Sykes's brother-in-law was the Prime Minister of Egypt, thus ensuring that he, Sykes, was denied permission to go on into the desert. In fact, the brother-in-law, Sir Eldon 'Jack' Gorst, had been adviser to the Khedive on financial matters before becoming the Resident in Cairo in succession to Cromer. When Sykes did eventually obtain permission to move on, with the help of the British Consul, he found that Gertrude had taken his proposed route. He described her as 'the terror of the desert' and said she left every place she visited in 'uproar'. In fact either party to this abrasive encounter was capable of causing a good deal of uproar, both among their eastern hosts and their fellow countrymen. For the moment they avoided each other, he returning to Constantinople as the impetuous honorary attaché at the British embassy, she continuing her travels. For the next two months she wandered happily on horseback among the Syrian Arabs and the Druses, through Palestine and the Levant, from Haifa to Rameleh and Tneib, meeting up with the Bani Sakhr tribesmen by whom she was greeted with the remark which followed her for the rest of her life, and long after her death: *Mashallah! Bint Aarab*, 'As God has willed, a daughter of the Arabs', though she rendered it rather freely as 'daughter of the desert'. She crossed the Jordan and the Mecca railway, joining a raiding party, or *ghazu*, and parleying with the Druses whom she told, to their apparent sadness, that Lord Salisbury was dead, and to whom she explained the complexities of fiscal policy in the world so that they became convinced Free Traders. And on to Damascus, where she arrived at four in the afternoon to find men of all kinds gathered in prayer, 'from the learned Doctor of Damascus down to the raggedest camel driver', and she was constrained to say 'Islam is the greatest republic in the world, there is neither class nor race inside the creed'. She took off her shoes and followed them as they responded to the chanting of the *imam*.

> 'Allah!' he cried, and the Faithful fell with a single movement upon their faces and remained for a full minute in silent adoration, till the high chant of the *imam* began again: 'The Creator of this World and the next, of the Heavens and the Earth, He who leads the righteous in the true path, and the evil to destruction. Allah!' And as the name of God echoed through the great colonnades, where it had sounded for nearly 2,000 years in different tongues, the listeners prostrated themselves again, and for a moment all the church was silence ...

So from the Great Mosque on to the coffee houses and to the Governor's residence. 'This has been a visit to Damascus that I shall not easily forget. I begin to see dimly what the civilization of a great Eastern city means.' She went on to Baalbek, Homs, across the foothills to the plain of Hama and Apamea, overlooking the Orontes Valley, a square mile of temples built by Seleucus Nicator, now in ruins. 'Now think how Greece and the East were fused by Alexander's conquests. A Greek king, with his capital on the Euphrates, builds a city on the Orontes and calls it after his Persian wife, and what manner of people walked down its colonnades, keeping in touch with Athens and with Babylon?' Now she made her way to Aleppo, where she picked up her guide Fattuh, an Armenian Catholic who was to become her constant companion, and beyond to Konia, the Ottoman vilayet which embraced Cilicia and Cappadocia. 'What a country this is!' she wrote to Florence Lascelles, 'I fear I shall spend the rest of my life travelling in it.' She crossed the Cilician plain by horse, with only a very small caravan since her muleteer and baggage animals, hired at Alexandretta, had disappeared *en route*, arriving at Adana on April 23rd, where she was joined by Mr George Lloyd, another of those itinerant Englishmen of the East who were at that time gravitating to the same archaeological focal points like moths circling a light. Since reading and reviewing Strzygowski's *Kleinasien: ein Neuland der Kunstgeschichte*, Gertrude had been fascinated by the ruined Seljuk mosques and the Byzantine churches of Anatolia, and she saw in this little-known region an outlet for her passionate interest in architectural history. She could not have chosen a better site for exploration since Sir William Ramsay, the great ecclesiastical historian and epigraphist, was there at the same time. She described Konia for her father's benefit; the burial place of Jelal ed-Din Rumi, Persian founder of the order of Dervishes; conspiratorial chatter with Pashas exiled by the Turkish Sultan over lunch with the Loytveds, representatives of the German Empire; the Kara Dagh, a great isolated mountain rising out of the plain, and at its feet Maden Sheher and Binbirkilisse (Barata), the place of the Thousand and One Churches, the number reflecting a fanciful Turkish habit which found its way to the West of giving any unknown number the figure 1001.

'If you had read (and who knows? Perhaps you have!) the very latest German archaeology books you would be wild with excitement at seeing where I am,' she told her father. As for the tomb of the Jelal ed Din Rumi, the air was full of the music of his verse. 'Ah listen to the reed as it tells its tale: Listen, ah, listen, to the plaint of the reed. They reft me from the rushes of my home, my voice is sad with longing, sad and low,' Gertrude translated as she went along.

Ramsay, the quiet Scot whom David Hogarth and many other young archaeologists of the time sought to work with (he sent

Hogarth off to learn epigraphy in Greece before allowing him to
return to the master), had been in the region in 1882 with Sir
Charles Wilson and had written in the *Athenaeum* drawing
attention to the need for an architectural and historical investigation of its derelict churches. The letter had attracted Gertrude's
attention and she unblushingly wrote to the famous author of
innumerable works on the Church and the Roman Empire,
suggesting that they should carry out such an investigation
together. Now they met for the first time. On May 16th she
wrote: 'The consul and his wife met me at the station and dined
with me at the hotel and I found there ... Professor Ramsay, who
knows more about this country than any other man, and we fell
into each other's arms and made great friends.'

Gertrude had already examined the territory and many of the
churches – she counted twenty-eight in all – and as soon as she
met the Professor she asked him to accompany her to one of
them where there was a barely decipherable inscription she
wanted him to look at and copy, which she believed to contain
a date for the building. She was right. The chronology of the
churches, said Ramsay, centred on the inscribed stone she had
discovered. There was little time to go further into the matter
then. They arranged to meet again at the site in about a year's
time.

Gertrude returned home to her family which had now moved
into her grandfather's home at Rounton. She promptly took
charge of the garden and with the help of the Bells' Scots gardener
turned it into one of the horticultural show-places of the north of
England, between times noting in a diary some intimate discussions on political, military and imperial matters with 'Springy',
Sir Cecil Spring-Rice, her newly acquired brother-in-law G. M.
Trevelyan, Dr Rosen, Sir Alfred Lyall, Valentine Chirol, Sir
Frank Swettenham, Professor Ramsay and a host of other
visitors. She also began another account of her travels in the East
which she called *The Desert and the Sown*.

In the autumn she went to Paris to continue her work on
ancient manuscripts with Reinach, and returned to England for a
few weeks, during which time she attended a house party at the
home of Lord Roberts. 'It's very amusing being in military circles.
The party is the Roberts family, Sir Ian Hamilton, and a few other
soldiers ... It's interesting seeing Lord "Bobs". He is, of course,
quite a dull little man ... Sir Ian tells thrilling tales.'

She set off again in December 1906 to join Ramsay in Anatolia.
She was accompanied as far as Cairo by her father, who was sick
for much of the time, and Hugo who joined them on his way back
from Australia. She spent a 'most successful' afternoon with Lady
Anne Blunt who was dressed in badawin costume among her
horses, chatting in her garden, with wolves and foxes for companions, about her errant husband Wilfrid Scawen; and she
dined with the Cromers:

> Lady C., Lady Valda (Machell) and I were the only women so
> I sat on the other side of Lord C. and had a quite enchanting
> talk with him. He is the nicest person in the world, without
> doubt. He was very eager to know if there was anything I
> wanted and when I said I wanted to have a good talk with a
> learned shaikh, he was much concerned about it, saying to
> Mr Machell, across the table, 'Look here, Machell, you must
> find us a good shaikh. Just think who is the best.' So they are
> thinking.

Her father's ill-health, though he was recuperating by the end of
January, made it necessary for her to return to England with
him. They arrived home in early February 1907 and Gertrude
departed for the East again a month later, again travelling via
Cairo and the hospitable Cromers and meeting *en route* Lady
Ottoline Morrell, 'preposterously clothed' and Salomon Reinach's
brother Theodore, 'stupendously learned'. She moved on through
Smyrna and Miletus, discovering the Greece of Asia, 'the Greece
that Grote didn't know'. She wrote: 'The seas and hills are full
of legend and the valleys are scattered over with the ruins of the
great rich Greek cities. Here is a page of history that one sees with
the eye and that enters into the mind as no book can relate it.' Her
thoughts turned abruptly homeward at this stage, however, as the
result of a telegram from her sister Elsa telling her that she was
about to marry her naval officer fiancé, Herbert Richmond. 'It is
unsatisfactory for the family rather, still I wish I were with you
all the same,' Gertrude wrote to her stepmother, somewhat
mysteriously. She reconciled herself to missing a wedding which,
she said, she viewed 'with mixed feelings', because she could not
leave Sir William Ramsay in the lurch. On Saturday May 11th,
1907 she noted: 'Ramsay arrives in three days and I've got a
hundred thousand things to do so I'll write no more now,'

though she did find time to write to Elsa and to note regretfully: 'I can scarcely bear the idea of not being at her wedding.' The Ramsays arrived on Friday May 24th, when Gertrude was in the middle of digging. They appeared in donkey carts and Lady Ramsay got out and began to make a pot of tea in the open while the learned Sir William started to discuss the problems presented by the Church on which Gertrude was working as though he had been there all along. The work which they performed in uncovering and deciphering old and worn legends, in uncovering brick and stonework, in establishing an elaborate chronology, is told in the book they wrote together at Rounton Grange and published in 1909. It provides a considered account of the project, unlike the letters which were often scribbled on the spot or before a well-earned sleep. *A Thousand and One Churches* also provides an early insight into a skill which was later to earn Gertrude a reputation that was unique in government service of being able to take the driest, most mundane contemporary or historical subjects and invest them with the force and colour of her easy, compelling writing style.

There was, however, one other lesson in eastern thought which impressed itself on her before she left for home with her rubbings and measurements, and her full if barely legible notebooks. She found herself in a garden with her servant Fattuh, and what she describes as 'the following preposterous conversation' took place:

GB – loq: Oh! Fattuh, to whom does this poplar garden belong?
F – To a priest, my lady.
GB – Does he mind our camping it it?
F – He didn't say anything.
GB – Did you ask him?
F – No, my lady.
GB – We must give him some backshish.
F – At your Excellency's command.
A pause
F – My lady ...
GB – Yes?
F – That priest is dead.
GB – !!! Then I don't think we need bother about the backshish.
F – No, my lady.

'Speech,' she observed, 'does not serve the same purposes east and west.'

Ramsay wrote the first and fourth parts of the book and Gertrude the second and third parts, and they dedicated it to Professor Josef Strzygowski whose book was 'our constant companion during many weeks in Maden Sheher'. Remarkably, it was Gertrude who, sitting in her study at Rounton on her return to England and working alongside the man who was acknowledged to be the foremost authority on such matters, wrote the most detailed architectural notes, taking each church as she went and dissecting it, technically and historically. Maden Sheher, she noted, is really made up of two parts, Binbirkilisse and Deghile, the cities of the valley and the hill, sixty miles south-east of Konia itself in ancient Iconium. An island of volcanic mountain, oval in shape, rises out of the Lycaonian plain; the Kara Dagh or Black Mountain. Its highest peak is called Mahaletch, which Ramsay and Gertrude thought was a corruption of the Christian St Michael, for it was crowned at a height of 7,000 feet by a great church with a monastery attached to it. From there they gained a magnificent view across the plain to the snow-clad Taurus ridge. At the northern base of the Black Mountain lay Maden Sheher, a stretch of fertile land, cultivated in part, and Binbirkilisse, the place of the churches they had come to record. It was fortunate that they arrived when they did, for two years later when Ramsay returned to the site some of the structures had collapsed beyond recognition – settlements, forts, monasteries and churches finally succumbing to the erosion of time and the insistence of subsiding land.

Gertrude had already written an account of her preliminary researches in a letter to *Revue Archéologique* of January 1905, where she went into the geometry of the cruciform structure. 'The structural scheme of the cross-in-square must have been early understood. Millet has pointed out that in the great vaulted buildings of Rome, such as the baths of Caracalla and the basilica at Maxentius, it is only necessary to substitute the dome on pendentives for the intersecting barrel vault in order to arrive at the cross-in-square ... '

In the opening chapter of *A Thousand and One Churches* Ramsay wrote: 'A defenceless city like this must have fallen easy prey to the Arab invaders, who began to overrun Asia Minor soon after

A.D. 660. In the terrible centuries which followed, when every
year one or more raids swept over Anatolia, such a city was
necessarily deserted ... '

Gertrude was assured in her detail and emphatic in her conclusions: 'No. 1 is the largest church in the Kara Dagh ... It is a
true basilica, the nave being raised above the aisles and lightened
by round-headed windows pierced in the upper walls, five on
either side.' And then: 'In Mahaletch we have an admirable
example of Anatolian custom. The Christians must have re-
sanctified a mountain, immemorially honoured, by crowning it
with a mausoleum chapel and a church. So at Ivriz the sacred
valley was consecrated by chapels, so on the Lake of Egerdir the
pagan shrine on the north-eastern shore was taken over and is
still used by the Christians. The custom of the country enforced
itself on all new-comers, and when in their turn the Turkish
invaders found a Christian chapel on the hill-tops, they too
adopted the site as a place of pilgrimage and sanctified it with the
grave of a holy man ... For in Anatolia, custom is stronger than
the strongest. Conquerors come and go, but the final victor is the
land itself.'

Her chapter on Ecclesiastical Architecture opens like a rondo
after a comparatively solemn middle movement, and becomes in
the end a testament to a new-found faith:

> One of the most remarkable experiences of travel is that which
> assails him who passes from the seaboard of Asia Minor and
> gains the central plateau. He leaves behind him a smiling
> country full of the sound of waters, with fertile valleys, hills
> clad in secular forests, coasts that the Greek made his own,
> settling them with cities, crowning them with temples,
> charging the very atmosphere with the restless activity of his
> temper ... If this is the first it is also the final impression ...
> Race, culture, art, religion, pick them up at any point you
> please down the long course of history, and you shall find
> them to be essentially Asiatic.

Her journey in 1907 was beset with difficulties, but nothing quite
compared with the problems of archaeological research at Maden
Sheher. Sir William Ramsay was, in her word, a 'chaotic' traveller.
His mind was so full of ecclesiastical history that he seldom knew
where he was and if left to his own devices would forget where
his camp or his hotel was; on occasion he even lost his clothes.

Lady Ramsay took it on herself to minister to his practical needs, but Gertrude had to look after him in matters of work and to keep a constant eye on his notes, drawings and rubbings, which he was always liable to leave under a heap of rubble. In addition she commanded a workforce of thirty-one Turks who were detailed to clean out parts of the churches she and Sir William wished to investigate. All day long the air was thick with '*Effendim! Effendim!* come and look at this', or '*Effendim*, this is good', only to find that their discoveries were usually of the most insignificant kind. Still, she was devoted to her Ottoman workforce, writing to her 'Beloved Hugo' in July: 'They are perfectly charming ... we are all on the most friendly terms.' The biggest blow came in July after a month of excavation when her ever-present Armenian companion Fattuh became seriously ill. When he was with Gertrude in Konia two years before he had suffered the inevitable consequence of trying to keep up with her in the near delirium which always accompanied a new discovery or a memorable sight. She had rushed madly into a church and Fattuh, trying dutifully to share her enthusiasm, rushed after her and gave his head a terrible blow on a low doorway. Ever since he had suffered from acute pains in the head and on this visit he collapsed. 'I fear there must be something wrong. I cannot of course leave him in this state to go back to Aleppo,' she told Lady Bell in mid-July. She thereupon telegraphed the British Ambassador in Constantinople and the Grand Vizier, telling them that she wished to take Fattuh with her to the capital to receive specialist attention, making mental reservation of the fact that there was a German doctor at Smyrna who would be able to tend the patient in emergency. Fattuh would not receive much of a welcome among Turks with a long and vicious record of persecuting the Armenian race.

She nearly gave up at one stage. She wrote confidentially to Chirol expressing doubts about the country, the people and her own ability. 'This is not my country – I must break the news gently to the good Ramsay. I have not the training for it ... No I shall go back to Arabia, to the desert, where I can do things and see things that Ramsay and his learned like could scarcely do and see ... ' But the depression did not last, and she was soon digging and note-taking again. She also mentioned to Chirol the helpfulness of the young vice-consul at Konia, Captain Doughty-Wylie, who had shown some interest in her and her work, 'a charming young soldier with a quite pleasant little wife'.

At the end of July she was in Constantinople once more, writing first to her father. 'Beloved father. I arrived last night – with Fattuh! The tale of bringing him here amounts to an epic ... I shall have to be a few days here ... I can't leave Fattuh all alone here till I am satisfied that he is out of the wood.' The ambassador Sir Nicholas O'Conor placed the embassy yacht *Imogen* at her disposal and her next letter was written to her stepmother while cruising in the Bosporus. In it she said she was having a fine time and had met Ferid Pasha, the Grand Vizier. 'He is a very great man, and I strongly suspect that he will play a large part in Turkey, very possibly mould Turkish history at some time or another. Moreover he was kinder to me than words can say ... ' As she wrote those words the exiled Young Turks were gathered in secret enclaves in Macedonia, Paris and Switzerland; within a year the Sultan Abdul Hamid II and his ministers were to become the victims of a palace revolution and the Turkish Empire was to find a new master, Mehemet V. Gertrude added: 'Fattuh is rapidly recovering, and I very much hope that he'll be out of hospital by the time I leave.'

By early August she was on her way back to Britain. 'I expect I shall be back in London about the 7th or 8th and I should be most grateful if Marie [her maid] could be sent up to meet me there. I shall have to stay a day or two to get some clothes.' Among the first visitors when she got back to Sloane Street was Sir Edward Grey, Foreign Secretary in the Campbell-Bannerman administration and shortly to join Asquith in the new Liberal government. There would probably have been a post in the government for Gertrude's father but his political ambitions seemed condemned to failure despite his being offered good constituencies.

Gertrude wrote to Chirol following Grey's visit, discussing the possibility of an election and its likely outcome. She noted the rising power of Labour and thought it no bad thing.

12
Mesopotamia

Everything now was bent towards archaeology and the East. She no longer thought in terms of 'going abroad' so much as of visiting her home and friends between carefully planned journeys which focused and absorbed all the resources of her mind and body. Nevertheless such interludes in her travels gave her immense pleasure. She always looked forward to seeing her family, especially now that both her sisters were married and Molly had children of her own. 'I don't think I ever saw anything more adorable than Moll's children,' she wrote while visiting Charles and Molly Trevelyan at their home at Cambo in Northumberland. She also maintained her links with friends and more distant relatives who constituted a not inconsiderable portion of *Who's Who*. She entertained a great deal while she was at Rounton during the relatively quiet years of 1907 and 1908. The procession of visitors included writers, artists, diplomats, explorers and politicians, several of whom were to become closely involved with her own journeys and political activities in the East. Her visitors in the later months of 1907 included the Lascelles and the Russells, George Lloyd, Percy Loraine, Sir Edwin and Lady Egerton, G. W. Prothero, Sir Ernest Shackleton and the young Captain Frank Balfour of whom she was to see much in the years ahead. In October of that year she began a course of instruction in the techniques of travel and exploration at the Royal Geographical Society in London, concentrating on survey methods and map projection under Mr Reeves of the Map Room.

The only notable event of 1908 was a holiday spent among the hills and mountains of north Walesalong with Chirol, Frank Balfour and others. By this time Gertrude was a brilliant conversationalist and raconteur, her extensive travels and her wide reading in several languages combining to give her storytelling, whether at the dinner table or an impromptu gathering, an air of confidence. No less an authority than Lisa Robins declared that Gertrude recited poetry better than anyone she had ever heard. During the leisurely weeks of their Welsh holiday Gertrude and her companions called on Admiral Sir William Goodenough at his country home and that distinguished traveller recalled how she sat on a bench in his garden with Valentine Chirol and 'told stories, some serious, some amusing, some almost frivolous, while a group of children sat spellbound listening to the strange but absolutely true things that they heard'.

She spent Christmas 1908 with the family at Rounton and immediately after the holiday sailed for Alexandria aboard the s.s. *Equator*, her objective the Roman and Byzantine fortresses and churches along the banks of the Euphrates in Mesopotamia. She arrived at Beirut in February 1909 where she was joined by Fattuh, now recovered from his head injury, and they made their way to Aleppo and the river which runs from the Anatolian heights to the ancient sites of Babylon and Sumeria until it joins its twin, the Tigris, and becomes the Shatt-al-Arab. This was to be Gertrude's most important exploratory journey. As her small caravan made its way between Rakka and Ana along the east bank of the Euphrates on the route from Tel Ahmar to Hit, she was in territory much of which was unknown to the West. As always she camped in style, the attentive Fattuh making sure that her table was well laid with the fine linen and cutlery and platters which she always took on her desert voyages. After her evening meal she would work on her notebooks and maps, recording the measurements of height and latitude she had obtained during the day. She made copies and rubbings of Hittite inscriptions which David Hogarth had sighted on a brief excursion the year before and had asked her to record, and she was able to make a useful contribution to maps of the region in the course of her first and only journey of actual geographical discovery. But her chief interest was not so much in the Hittite and other ruins that she encountered on the first part of her route as in 'the father of castles' about which she had heard repeated stories, lying on the west bank of the river some 120 miles south-west of Baghdad at Ukhaidir. The French traveller Massignon had described its unique palace briefly and other Europeans had visited the site but there was no detailed record of it. Here was an opportunity to use her undoubted gifts as an archaeological and historical scholar. She crossed the Euphrates into the dangerous tribal territory of the Duleim and eventually reached the palace of Ukhaidir in late March. She was greeted by a massive structure the dating of which has always been in some doubt, though the later parts were certainly built by one of the Abbasid princes, probably in the second half of the eighth century A.D. Gertrude was able to stay for only four days during which time she sketched as much as she could, showing the central gateways, complex fortifications, mosques, audience chambers and living quarters. She had to enlist the services of her Arab companions and Turkish military guides, or *agheyls*, in measuring the features of the palace, and she ran into inevitable difficulties. 'When my soldiers come measuring ... nothing will induce them to leave their rifles in their tents. They are quite intolerably inconvenient; the measuring tape is forever catching round the barrel or getting caught in the stock, but I can't persuade them to lay the damnable things down for an instant.'

She returned to the palace in 1911, eventually producing a book of painstaking scholarship which was published by the Clarendon Press in 1914. In the meantime, she published an account of the vaulting of the palace in the *Journal of Hellenic Studies*. When she came back just over eighteen months later, the German archaeologists of the Deutsche-Orient Gesellschaft had found their way from Babylon to Ukhaidir. They generously allowed her to use their architectural drawings and they freely compared notes, and although their book on the subject came out two years before hers there was no animosity between them; in fact, their respective works complemented each other. She wrote in her preface:

> With this I must take my leave of a field of study which formed for four years my principal occupation, as well as my chief delight. A subject so enchanting and so suggestive as the Palace of Ukhaidir is not likely to present itself more than once in a lifetime, and as I bring this page to a close I call to mind the amazement with which I first gazed upon its formidable walls; the romance of my first sojourn within its precincts; the pleasure, undiminished by familiarity, of my return; and the regret with which I sent back across the sun drenched plain a last greeting to its distant presence.

And so she went across the Euphrates in search of forts and monasteries, drawing her incomparable word-pictures as she went, and then north-east to Kurdish territory. Of the nun at Khark she wrote: ' ... young and personable, and she found the religious life very much to her taste. Her sacred calling gave her the right to come and go as she pleased, to mix in male society, and even to put forth her opinion in male councils. Moreover it provided her with an excuse for claiming audience of me on the evening of my arrival. "I have come to see my sister," I heard her announce. "Does she speak Arabic?" And before Fattuh could answer, she had presented herself at the tent door. The object of her visit was to ask me for a revolver.' At the same place Gertrude's saddlebags containing her precious notebooks, photographs and cameras were stolen, and she sent the local Kurdish chief off into the desert to look for them. When he could not find them she summoned the Turkish *kaimakam*, the governor of nearby Midyat, to complain to him. The saddlebags were found with all their contents except her money, which was later refunded by the Ottoman authority. To her dismay, her adventures in the wild country of the Kurds reached the British Press. 'One might think that in the Tur Abdin one was safe from horrible newspaper notoriety.'

There was also a study of Ali Beg the chief of the Yezdis, the so-called 'devil-worshippers', who still plied their ancient caravan route through Asia Minor: 'He is a man of middle age with a commanding figure and a long beard, light brown in colour, that curls almost to the waist. He was dressed from head to foot in white, and as we sat together in the divan, I thought that I had seldom drunk coffee in more remarkable company. I told him that I knew his people in the Jabal Simun and that they had spoken to me of him as the ruler of all. "The ruler of us all," he replied gravely, "is God".'

At Samarra on the Tigris she met the distinguished German archaeologists Buddensieg and Wetzel. 'The pleasure at being out of the heat and dust of a camp ... and into a cool clean house, is scarcely less great than that of having intelligent, learned people to talk to,' she wrote. She made notes of the finds there and copied many inscriptions in her notebook, which the Germans signed to signify their approval of her work.

In August 1909 she was at home in Yorkshire drawing the castle of Ukhaidir, 'it is coming out beautifully. I can scarcely bear to leave it for a moment,' and contributing a chapter on the Armenian monasteries she had studied on her way to Diyarbakir

to a book which Strzygowski was writing. There was a brief
diversion at this time caused by the highly publicised activities of
the suffragette movement. Gertrude would, of course, have been
a welcome addition to the ranks of those who sought women's
suffrage, but she was totally opposed to the movement. She
neither sympathised with its aims nor approved of the methods
employed by her sex in attracting notice to their cause. In 1908
she had joined the movement against the extension of the franchise
to women, along with the Countess of Jersey, Mrs Humphry
Ward and others, and was a founder member of the Anti-suffrage
League, later absorbed into the 'heterosexual' League formed by
Lords Curzon and Cromer. Free Trade remained her political
cornerstone, and though she more and more flirted with a Fabian
brand of socialism, she was, like her father, given at heart to a
Spencerian notion of progress through competition and the
pursuit of excellence.

As Gertrude travelled in and around that fertile crescent which
sweeps from the Nile to the confluence of the Tigris and Euphrates,
she became ever more familiar with a group of fellow countrymen
who shared with her the means to travel at leisure and who were
drawn, much as she, by archaeological discovery and the infinite
mysteries of deserts and forbidden cities. Increasingly she found
herself enmeshed in the politics of the region, in that futile
attempt by westerners to move among tribal peoples and to
examine and categorise them with the aid of their own predilections
and their own divergent philosophies. They fascinated each other
almost as much as they were collectively fascinated by their Arab
hosts, all scribbling descriptive diary notes and letters home, so
that we are presented with a many-sided picture of the British
brigade in Arabia in the early 1900s. Gertrude was in many ways
the central figure, the least committed politically, the most widely
travelled and, though it was not a factor that entered into her
calculations, the lone woman. Most of the others were in government service and, like their German counterparts throughout
these peripheral lands of the Ottoman Empire, they combined
the roles of travel and archaeology with that of 'intelligence' or,
in plain language, spying.

Perhaps the foremost among them was David George Hogarth,
now almost as well known to Gertrude as his sister Janet, a small
man with a goatee beard who wandered in Macedonia and the

Levant after escaping from the clutches of Sir William Ramsay, and who succeeded Sir Arthur Evans as Keeper of the Ashmolean at Oxford. He was six years Gertrude's senior and wrote learned books about Arabia, its inhabitants and its explorers without ever going beyond its fringes, for he was no explorer. He was a prodigious scholar, a walking encyclopaedia in matters Greek, Arabic and archaeological, though he did not speak Arabic and was more attracted by writing than by digging in his devotion to the latter pursuit. He looked forward to spending 'quite a respectable portion of eternity in talking to Herodotus'.

Then there was Mark Sykes, the bane of Gertrude's eastern paradise, a peripatetic gatherer of alarmingly biased information. He admired the Turks and approved their method of rule, *divide et impera*, and he spoke of the Arabs of his own day with a contempt that has seldom been equalled. He had travelled among these people from boyhood with his father, and he wrote of his visit to a tent of the Wuld Ali tribesmen: 'Now at the moment I stepped into a tent ... I was immediately impressed by the fact that there never could be, and never would be, any fellow-feeling between them and me.' Of the Shammar badawin he wrote: 'A rapacious, greedy, ill-mannered set of brutes ... These animals are, unluckily, pure badawin, and have not been tinctured with either Turkish or Kurdish blood, which always has a softening and civilising effect on these desert tramps.' He was hardly more complimentary about the town Arabs. Sir Mark Sykes was to become the principal adviser to the British government on its war-time relations with the Arabs in just a few years. Meanwhile he wandered among these tribal people, writing passionately of the achievements of the Caliphates, ever praising the Turks and denigrating his hosts.

There was Captain Hubert Young, bristling with military zeal and anxious to meet everyone who mattered, British, German and Arab; George Lloyd, cool and precise; Auberon (Aubrey) Herbert, bohemian and myopic, who made the journey across Sinai in 1907, a feat at that time considered remarkable; and at Carchemish in the north-east corner of Syria, T. E. Lawrence, 'Ned' or 'the little fellow' as they called him, a bright classical scholar and aspiring Arabist, working for Hogarth alongside Leonard Woolley amid the ruins, and keeping his eye on the Germans who were also digging there, on behalf of Military Intelligence.

Gertrude returned to Mesopotamia in January 1911 after spending a few months at home completing her current literary tasks and making a brief journey through Italy and Germany. By now she had completed another book, a record of her 1909 trip which she called *Amurath to Amurath* and which the publisher hoped would rival the success achieved by *The Desert and the Sown* in the three years since its publication. She travelled by way of Beirut and Damascus (where she was delayed by snow) and through the Syrian desert to the Euphrates, ' ... too heavenly to be back in all this again, Roman forts and Arab tents and the wide desert', marching sometimes thirteen or more hours a day, and often getting nowhere. However, she found a short-cut to Ukhaidir which took a day or two off her expected travelling time.

On March 4th she wrote: 'We left Ukhaidir this morning. I wonder if I shall ever see it again and whether I shall ever again come upon any building as interesting or work at anything with a keener pleasure.' From there her caravan set off for Najaf, sister city of Karbala on the Euphrates, the two sacred centres of the Shia sect of Islam which stems from Ali the cousin of the Prophet and the husband of Muhammad's daughter Fatima. As they marched through threatening weather they found the corpses of sheep and donkeys that had been trapped by the snowfall of January, which had covered not only Damascus but much of the Syrian desert. When the desert-dwellers first saw it, she was told, they thought it was flour. The region through which they now travelled was occupied by the Bani Hassan tribe and the plain was aglow with their camp fires. Gertrude's party stopped briefly at the ruin of Khan Atshan, 'a splendid ruin of I should think the 9th century, about the time of Samarra', which provided her with useful information in her attempt to date the palace at Ukhaidir. They reached Najaf on Tuesday March 7th, 'a walled town standing on the edge of a cliff of the dry sea and surrounded on the other side by a flat plain. Above the walls rises the golden dome of Ali's tomb which is the place of pilgrimage of all the Shia world'. She was taken sightseeing by the chief of police, but there was little to interest her since she was not allowed into the mosque nor even to pass close to it, and so she went on to Babylon.

I rode off with a guide, and lunched on top of the Tower of

Babel. You know what it was? It was an immense Babylonian temple dedicated to the seven spheres of heaven and the sun god. There remains now an enormous mound of sun-dried brick, with the ruins of a temple to the North of it and on top a great tower of burnt brick, most of which has fallen down. But that which remains stands up, like a finger pointing heaven-wards, over the Babylonian plain ...

She went on to Hillah, where her rifle was confiscated by an officious policeman, and then to Baghdad, where she was met by the British Resident, Lt-Colonel J. G. Lorimer. 'Mr Lorimer says that he has never met anyone who is in the confidence of the natives in the way I am,' she wrote, 'and Mr Lorimer, I should wish you to understand, is an exceptionally able man!'

Lorimer was, in fact, the last in a line of British representatives in Baghdad who left behind them an illustrious record and a heritage without compare in the imperial history of their country. Europeans had, of course, gone to Baghdad through the centuries to trade and to savour the atmosphere of a past enveloped in the mists of time and dimly portrayed in the literature of Greece and Rome. There was the Englishman John Eldred who went there in the reign of Elizabeth I, and a German contemporary, the physician Leonhart Rauwolff, who was there in 1575; the rabbis Benjamin of Tudela and Pethahiah of Ratisbon, who wrote accounts of the place in Latin; and the Pope's Vicar-General at Babylon in the eighteenth century, l'Abbé de Beauchamp; the Frenchman Tavernier; and perhaps the best informed of all the early travellers, the Italian nobleman Pietro della Valle, the first to write intelligently of Babylon and the mounds at Hillah and Birs Nimrod. But it was to the British Residency, established in 1783 by the East India Company, that there came a procession of men of unrivalled gifts and industry. In 1808, by which time the Residency had assumed consular status, came Claudius James Rich whose prodigious oriental attainments were regarded by his superiors as the least of his merits. It was through his scholarship and enterprise that serious archaeological research was started among the ruins of Assyria and Babylon. It was through his charm and personality that Britain's place was established in this important outpost of the Ottoman Empire. He entered Baghdad in style, with a sepoy guard, his wife Mary carried on a *palankeen* or mule-borne litter with a retinue of Armenian servants.

They left in 1821, to the cheers of the populace, and he went on to
Persia, to see Persepolis and the tomb of Cyrus where he contracted cholera while tending the victims of the disease and died,
leaving a fine collection of cylinder seals and clay tablets with
inscriptions in the wedge-shaped, or cuneiform, script for others
to decipher. He also left to others his formula for dealing with the
Turk: 'Nothing but the most decisive conduct will do; any other
will increase the insolence of his disposition,' he wrote. Then came
Colonel Taylor, who was in Baghdad with the remarkable
missionary Anthony Groves at the outbreak of the plague
epidemic of 1831. A hundred thousand people from a population
of a hundred and fifty thousand died, but Groves and Taylor
lived through it. Taylor was so good a scholar that Arab divines
were said to seek his advice on the translation and interpretation
of ancient manuscripts in their possession. He was the first to
investigate the pre-Babylonian sites of Sumer in the south. In
1843 came Henry Creswicke Rawlinson, who by almost incredible
feats of physical bravery and mental application found the key
to the cuneiform language by comparing the Old Persian,
Elamite and Babylonian inscriptions dedicated to Darius, King of
Kings, on the massive rock of Behistan, and who sat in his 'tree'
house on the Tigris, a home-made wheel splashing water over it
to keep him cool while he worked through the hot Mesopotamian
summers, translating the first legends of mankind written on
tablets of clay. He occupied the Residency with wild animals
that became his pets, including a leopard, a lion cub and a
mongoose, and it was said of him that he was so popular among
the people that even his pets commanded respectful attention,
and that when he appeared even the Shia and Sunni zealots
stopped fighting. After him came Henry Layard, supreme among
the archaeologists of the region, who in the wake of Rawlinson's
achievements uncovered the treasures of Nineveh, the royal
library with its incomparable store of records, the palace of
Sennacherib at Kuyunjik. There were others, of course, not least
the French Consul at Mosul, Paul Émile Botta, who was the first
among the serious excavators of Mesopotamia, but the work of
the Britishers who came as soldiers and achieved near miracles of
scholarship and discovery is unparalleled in the annals of the
British Empire. Gertrude, as she trod the paths made by these
men, was more aware than most people of her day of the heritage
her predecessors had left behind, and the book in which she told

her story, *Amurath to Amurath*, was a sensitive account of that awareness.

J. G. Lorimer, her host in Baghdad, was a steward of the Residency in the mould of Rich, Rawlinson and Taylor. He was engaged in the compilation of a *Gazetteer of the Persian Gulf* which became the most reliable and authentic guide ever put together of Britain's long involvement in the area, of the histories of the Arab princes and shaikhs from the coast to central Arabia who had ruled under Turkish suzerainty for more than four centuries. What Gertrude did not know at that time was that Lorimer was engaged in a long-drawn-out dispute with his own government arising out of the rivalry between the Foreign Office, which since Palmerston's time had dedicated its support to the crumbling Ottoman Empire, and powerful factions within the Indian administration that supported the aspirations of Arab rulers. It was a battle in which, in years to come, Gertrude was to find herself playing an important part.

For the moment she was content to enjoy the hospitality of the Resident, and to take a ride up-river on the official launch with Sir William Willcocks, 'a twentieth-century Don Quixote, erratic, illusive, maddening and entirely lovable', with whom she discussed the possible irrigation of the desert regions and the proposed extension of the German railway from Baghdad to Basra. They moved on towards the Persian frontier along the Diala river and then westward again along the Himrin range, stopping at the fortress of Kasr Shirin, 'one of the most beautiful places I have ever seen', crossing and re-crossing the Zab river, on the way to Mosul. On the road at Kalat Shergat she met the German archaeologists who now, since the funds once provided for British archaeologists by the British Museum and the *Daily Telegraph* had dried up, had become the dominant force in Assyriology. She was warmly welcomed by them and she spent three days in the company of their leader, the distinguished Dr Walther Andrae. 'His knowledge of Mesopotamian problems is so great and his views so brilliant and comprehensive.' Fattuh became ill again on their journey north through the tribal *dira* of the Shammar, but a native doctor was called who bled him copiously and, it seems, to good effect. They were now on the well-trodden desert road from Mosul to Mardin, Urfa and Carchemish, where she hoped to meet Hogarth. In early March, as Gertrude's caravan was on its way to Baghdad, Hogarth's

I

assistant Lawrence had written to his brother: 'We are expecting Miss G. Bell (whose book 'Between the Desert and the Sown', you might like).' On May 18th Gertrude wrote to her stepmother: 'The Kaimakam came over ... and told me that Mr Hogarth had left but that Mr Thompson was still at Carchemish. Accordingly I went there — it was only 5 hours' ride — and found Mr Thompson and a young man called Lawrence (he is going to make a traveller) who had for some time been expecting that I would appear. They showed me their diggings and their finds and I spent a pleasant day with them. 'Three days later Lawrence wrote to David Hogarth: ' ... Gerty has gone back to her tents to sleep. She has been a success: and a brave one. She called him (Thompson) prehistoric! (apropos of your digging methods) till she saw their result ... ' In a letter to his mother on May 23rd, however, Lawrence inferred one of those head-on disputes to which Gertrude's unequivocal manner was always liable to give rise: ' ... we showed her all our finds, and she told us all hers. We parted with mutual expressions of esteem: but she told Thompson his ideas of digging were prehistoric; and so we had to squash her with a display of erudition.'

Gertrude called on Fattuh's wife, Zekiyyah, on the way through Aleppo and had coffee with her, and then took her servant to see an American doctor in Beirut. 'I can't say how sorry I am, always, to say goodbye to this delightful country where I have to leave so many friends.'

13
Encounter

Not Amurath an Amurath succeeds,
But Harry, Harry!
Henry IV, Part 2

Gertrude's latest book detailing her studies and wanderings in
the Turkish dominions of Asia Minor was published in 1911. She
addressed a dedicatory letter to Lord Cromer, indicating the pace
and perception of her travels with a skilful blend of ardour and
understanding. 'Liberty—what is liberty? I think the question
that ran so perplexingly through the black tents would have
received no better a solution in the royal pavilions which had
once spread their glories over the plain. Idly though it fell from
the lips of the Badawin, it foretold change ... I saw the latest
Amurath succeed to Amurath and rejoiced with all those who
love justice and freedom to hear him proclaimed. For Abdul
Hamid, helpless as he may have been in the hands of the weavers
of intrigue, was the symbol of retrogression ... ' She was not to
find the new Sultan any more trustworthy than the last as a
custodian of liberty as time went by, but for the moment Mehemet
V embraced the eager hopes of the Young Turks and Gertrude
thought him worthy of a fair trial. Perhaps because, as Hogarth
put it, the new book contained 'maturer science and less careless
rapture' than her *Desert and the Sown*, the public reaction to it was
little more than polite. *Amurath to Amurath* was well reviewed in
some quarters and barely noticed in others. The autumn months
of 1911 and much of the next year were spent mostly at home.
There was plenty to do, however, and much to catch up with. 'I
was back in time for the Coronation and enjoyed it immensely,'
she told Chirol, 'especially the actual ceremony (I had a very good

seat in the Abbey), which was the most splendid thing I ever
beheld, and the naval review.' Her cousin Florence Lascelles had
married 'Springy', Sir Cecil Arthur Spring-Rice, a Foreign Office
Under-secretary. Elsa as well as Molly now had a family, Valentine
Chirol had retired from *The Times* with a knighthood and had
gone to the Far East to establish a base in Delhi as a freelance
contributor to the paper. Maurice, whose collar bone had caused
him a good deal of trouble since he returned from the Boer War,
had gone off to Germany for a cure. Hugo was finally ordained
in 1908 and he was now about to join Bishop Furse in Pretoria,
after four years as the curate of Guiseley Parish in Leeds where he
worked hard for an annual stipend of ten pounds under the
incumbent, the Reverend J. F. Howson. And her childhood
companion Horace Marshall, now a successful lawyer, was
anxious to spend some time with her, as were Janet Courtney and
Lisa Robins among her devoted and widely scattered friends.
The garden at Rounton and her book about the palace of Ukhaidir
also took up a lot of time. Her letters to Chirol provide the clues
to her activities and intentions at this time. By November 1912
she was caught up again in the women's suffrage controversy.
'My dearest Domnul ... Life was nearly wrecked for a month by
arranging an anti-suffragist meeting in Middlesbrough on the
largest scale. It was interesting but it took an appalling amount
of time.' She was also involved in the world-wide fund for the
relief of Constantinople following the great fire in the city and the
subsequent outbreak of cholera early in the year. 'My preoccupation now is Asiatic Turkey,' she told Domnul in the same letter.
'What will happen now that Ottoman prestige has vanished into
thin air? It's a curious problem, and I should not be surprised if
we were to see, in the course of the next ten years, the break-up
of the empire in Asia ... '

But there was a more intense preoccupation in her life at this
time, the 'charming young soldier' Major Charles Hotham
Montagu Doughty-Wylie of the Royal Welch Fusiliers, known to
his friends as Richard or Dick. He had found himself drawn to
the effervescent intelligent woman who called on him to collect
her mail and present her compliments soon after her arrival at
Konia. She too looked forward to his frequent visits to Maden
Sheher where he watched the ardent team at work. He was a
strong, sensitive man, the nephew of Charles Doughty, the
greatest of all the outsiders who went to Arabia and wrote about

it. He was not an intellectual in any accepted sense but he was well aware of what was going on in the world at large and knew of the fame that now attached to Gertrude, for *The Desert and the Sown* had already been acclaimed in the Press and Professor Hogarth had declared it to be not unworthy of a place alongside Doughty's *Arabia Deserta*: indeed, he pronounced it 'among the dozen best books of Eastern travel'. In any case her fame as a traveller in the East went before her by now, among the natives and the British communities of the Turkish coastal regions. His distinction was of a different kind. He was by common consent one of the bravest and most fearless of soldiers, and his presence in the diplomatic world at that time was brought about by the need for respite after a series of wounds which had won him medals and acclaim in almost every battle in which Britain was engaged from the time he joined the army in 1889 until the East African campaign of 1903. He had fought at Hazara, Chitral, Crete, and in the Nile Expedition, winning medals and clasps as he went. In the Boer War he received severe injuries and was awarded the Queen's medal and three clasps. At Tientsin during the Chinese rebellion he raised a corps of mounted infantry and was again wounded. There were few more dashing or renowned men in the British army. He was the same age as Gertrude, born on July 23rd in 1868, nine days after her. And in 1904, a year before Gertrude's first visit to the plains of Anatolia, he had married Lilian, the daughter of Mr John Wylie of Westcliffe Hall, Hampshire, and widow of Lt Henry Adams-Wylie of the Indian Medical Service. Doughty-Wylie was a hero figure, Gertrude a rich and brilliant woman with connections at the highest levels of government. The Doughtys of Theberton Hall, Leiston in Suffolk, ranked high enough in a world where acceptability was the first hurdle in any acquaintanceship. There was no more to the matter in 1907.

Then in the following year while Gertrude was between journeys, Doughty-Wylie as he had become (Lilian Wylie, who was always known as Judith, had insisted on her own surname being attached to those of both her husbands) found himself in the news. It was the year in which the mass-slaughter of the Armenians began once again in the Ottoman dominions, as an ugly accompaniment of the Young Turks' rebellion. Mobs roamed the area of his consulship murdering Christians with a fanaticism bred of years of festering hatred and recrimination.

Railway tracks and even the roads of the main towns were littered with corpses of innocent victims. Doughty-Wylie put on his military uniform, gathered up a small group of Turkish troops, and rode through the centre of the storm in the towns of Mersin and Adana in pursuit of the rebels. At this first attempt to quell the angry mobs a bullet smashed his right arm. But a few days later he was out on patrol again when the killing resumed. His action, according to Press reports, had saved hundreds and perhaps thousands of lives. He was awarded the C.M.G. and the Turkish Order of Mejidieh for his bravery. Messages of thanks and congratulations came to him from all over the world, including the governments whose nationals had been saved by his action. He immediately set to work to organise relief for 22,000 refugees, while his wife organised three makeshift hospitals for the treatment of the seriously maimed and sick. It may be assumed that one of the letters of praise that followed the Adana Massacre as it came to be called was from Gertrude, for she kept a Press cutting describing his actions. They may have been in correspondence before, but if they were no letters have survived. In 1909, when an uneasy peace had been restored to the area covered by the Konia vice-consulate, he returned to the post which he had occupied for a year before going to Asiatic Turkey, that of consul in Addis Ababa. There are suggestions in later letters that he and Gertrude were writing to each other fairly regularly at this stage, she describing her journeys to Ukhaidir and Babylon and her return to the Anatolian plain, he presumably discussing his consular activities. Their friendship was warm, perhaps feeding on mutual admiration and Gertrude's skill as a letter writer, but no more. Then in 1912, the year in which Gertrude remained so contentedly tied to England, he arrived in London to take up an appointment as Director-in-Chief of the Red Cross relief organisation founded in Constantinople during the recent Balkan War, as a result of which Turkish power in Europe was virtually ended. They may have met in the late spring in London, when she was staying at Sloane Street, 'grappling with the problem of clothes', lecturing at the behest of Herbert Richmond's brother Ernest, who was director of antiquities in Jerusalem, and visiting a music hall with her Stanley cousins. It was a light-hearted period. She spent Christmas with the family at Rounton and a few days later, on January 2nd, 1913, she wrote to Domnul telling him that she had given up a plan to accompany the Italian writer and

traveller Cavaliere Filippo de Filippi on a scientific expedition to
Karakoram. 'The nearer I came to it, the more I could not bear
it. I can't face being away from home for fourteen months. My
life now in England is so delightful that I will not take such a
long time out of it.' It was something of a change of face for
Gertrude who had never before cast more than a brief backward
glance as she went off to the far corners of the earth. Miss
Elizabeth Burgoyne in her *Gertrude Bell: from her Personal Papers*
wrote: 'The intensity of Gertrude's nature, combined with so
much vitality and charm, made it inevitable that men should be
drawn to her, and she to them; and about this time her whole
being was dominated by her friendship with a man who was
already married. The fire, quelled for many years, blazed afresh,
and she was deeply in love; but, all too soon, an equally fierce
sense of honour forced her to turn away from the possibility of
happiness. She had for some time contemplated an expedition
to Hail; now, towards the end of 1913, it became a means of
escape, and passages in her letters to Sir Valentine Chirol show
her mental turmoil and her pain.' In June she was elected to
Fellowship of the Royal Geographical Society on the proposal
of Leonard Darwin. But Hail was not much in her thoughts
at this time. Doughty-Wylie came to London again and she went
to Sloane Street to be close at hand. She entertained thoughts
only for England and the soldier from Constantinople. In July
she invited him to Rounton, a daring thing to do since he was in
England without his wife, not a woman to take lightly what
would have been regarded as a social indiscretion in those days.
The visit seems to have survived any such hazard. On August
13th he wrote:

My dear Gertrude, I am so very glad you took me to Rounton.
I so much enjoyed it, the people, the place, the garden, the
woods, everything. They are a vital setting to my friend,
however many other frames she fits in. And I am so glad you
told me things, and found you could talk to me. It's that I
like – just openness and freedom to say and do exactly what
one wants to do. In your mind I think there was a feeling,
natural at first openings of doors, that it wasn't properly
appreciated. But it was – I love openness – I've always ever
since those early Turkey days wanted to be a friend of yours –
Now I feel as if we had come closer, were really intimate

friends – I've gained so much and I want to hold it. The loneliness – why we are all born alone die alone really live
alone – and it hurts at times – Is this nonsense or preach-
ments? I don't care – I must write something, something to
show you how very proud I am to be your friend. Something
to have meaning, even if it cannot be set down, affection, my
dear, and gratitude and admiration and confidence, and an
urgent desire to see you as much as possible ... All the good
luck in the world, Yours ever, R.

On August 16th he wrote to her from his club, telling her that he
had accepted a post with the International Boundary Commission
in Albania. Then on August 20th, when he returned to London
from a visit to his Suffolk home: ' ... your letters waiting for me
... wonderful letters my dear, which delight me. Bless you. But
there can be no words to answer you with. Well – let's talk about
other things – do you know this?

> Men say they know many things
> But lo, they have taken wings
> The Arts and the sciences
> And a thousand appliances –
> The wind that blows
> Is all that anybody knows.

He went on: 'My wife is in Wales. She'll come up when I wire to
her and go with me – till we see the hows and whys and wheres ...
I have turned into my old bachelor quarters in Half Moon Street,
no 29. Write to me there ... while I am alone, let's be alone. Ah
yes, my dear, it's true enough what I said about solitude, on
every hill, in every forest, I have invoked and welcomed her ...
And you, too, know the goddess well, for no one but a worshipper
could have written what you did about the hush of dawn in the
garden.' Then there was a strange recall of Rounton, a reference
to a lone woman that was to have a strange, almost macabre
significance in the future. ' ... Did I say all this to you before? Or
dream I did? By the way, talking of dreams – Rounton ghosts
visited me the next night also. Is there any history of them ...?
some shadowy figure of a woman, who really quite bothered me,
so that I turned on the light. It wasn't your ghost, or anything
like you; but something hostile and alarming ... ' For the first
time he signed a letter by his familiar name, Dick.

He reverted to his curious vision in another letter: ' ... and she of the second night was a long, shadowy woman thing that swept and swept across my bed like a hawk, stooping and said nothing, and I didn't know who the devil she was, but she meant attack, and I wanted the light ... '

It is a pity that in attempting to reconstruct the story of their relationship we have to rely chiefly on his side of the story, not Gertrude's, whose life is otherwise almost over-documented. But Doughty-Wylie was a married man and her letters could hardly be paraded or easily kept, though he claimed overtness with his wife at this time. On August 22nd he writes: 'My dear. This shall go to speak with you at Naworth – to give you my love and a kiss as if I were a child or you were ... Yes for a little time we are alone but it's only a little time. Judith knowing you well and having always before seen your letters would find it very odd to be suddenly debarred them and on voyages our lives are at close quarters ... '

There is no doubt that Gertrude was deeply and passionately involved and she may perhaps have been urging him to some decisive break at this time. Her letters, had they not been destroyed, would almost certainly have painted a picture of a woman who was desperate in her devotion and driven by an overwhelming desire to bring this of all her relationships to a successful conclusion. She was, after all, in her forty-sixth year. Yet, even in the intimacy which shows through his letters, there was still a note of formality in the affair. On August 26th, in the absence of the expected daily letter, he wrote: 'A blank day, my dear. I am tempted to wonder – did I say too much? Or was it that you thought the time had passed? Or were you too occupied? Away with all such things. In the chains we live in – or I live in – it is wise and right to wear them easily.'

Next day, the time of his departure for Albania drawing close, he discusses their mode of address when he was abroad: 'Of course call me Dick in letters and I shall call you Gertrude – there is nothing in that – many people do – my wife doesn't see my letters as a rule, but as she often writes to you herself we have always passed them across – but oh how I shall miss them! ... We look over the edge of a dream – a thing lovely and to be desired ... There is another thing that has to be done – tonight I shall destroy your letters – I hate it – but it is right – one might die or something, and they are not for any soul but me ... '

There was a strangely oblique reference to sexual intimacy which seems to have hovered in their correspondence without ever finding explicit expression: 'Last night, a poor girl stopped me – the same old story – and I gave her money and sent her home ... So many are really like me, or what I used to be, and I'm sorry for them ... These desires of the body that are right and natural, that are so often nothing more than any common hunger – they can be the vehicle of fire of the mind, and as that only are they great; and as that only are they to be satisfied ... '

And an abrupt warning in another letter, which otherwise conveyed the passion of past weeks: 'My dear, if I can't write to you, I shall always think of you telling me things in your room at Rounton, showing me something of your mind and something of mine ... The subtle book eludes, but our hands met on the cover. And you'll go on being the wise and splendid woman that you are, not afraid of any amazement and finding work and life and the fullness of it always to your hand. And I shall always be your friend.'

The Doughty-Wylie letters were kept under lock and key for the lifetime of his widow, who lived until 1960, and access to them was carefully guarded by Gertrude's family. One of the first outsiders to see them after her death, Mr Seton Dearden, asked: 'Was this all this emotional, sex-starved woman, reaching her climacteric, wanted? Was this all that love, coming late in life, could offer her? And why this constant variance in tone in his letters from talk of physical love, to mere friendship?' It is a question to which, even in the light of ensuing correspondence, there is no clear answer. There was time for one more letter before Doughty-Wylie left England.

Judith has not turned up, she is coming by the night train. I am swallowed up in friends from every side that seem to grow in this Club – from Abyssinia, China, the Sudan, Iceland, Cairo, and my own regiment. I have to dine – and play – there's no escape. But I snatch a minute to greet you ...

It was the last letter from London. The next letters were from his ship as it sailed through the Mediterranean and between the Greek islands. They became down-to-earth, descriptive of places, only occasionally showing the fervour of a few weeks ago. And now that he had gone she began to prepare urgently for the desert journey, the next best thing to being in England with Dick Doughty-Wylie.

'Monastir is a nice place,' he wrote, 'cool and eastern – I feel almost as if we were back in Konia ... except that there is no hope of GB walking in covered with energy and discovery and pleasantness ... '

On September 29th he was writing from Monastir while coping with the affairs of Albanians and Serbs and the Balkan Boundary Commission: 'It was so very nice of you my dear friend ... I take this enormous bit of paper to expose to you my enormous affection ... ' In October she sent him some books and proofs of articles she had written, and he responded: 'I do like your writing – you very clever and charming person – and you in your desert ... ' At the end of the month he was wishing her *bon voyage*. 'I don't know if this will reach you before you push off – if it does, my dear, it is to wish you all the luck and success, all safety and reasonable comfort (both of those last your fiery soul is apt to despise) ... Have a good journey – find castles – keep well – and remain my friend. Ps. As to *proces verbaux*, the great thing is to put in my colleagues and leave out myself.'

She did not leave until mid-September as it happened. On the 9th he wrote again, 'two long, delightful letters ... And you'll be gone – and before you come again, I wonder where we shall be – I suppose Africa. Thesiger wants to come home – and I know the run of things. *Ma salaami*. Dick.'

The flame had not gone out. It still flickered as she set off for Hail in central Arabia.

14
Hail

In the winter of 1909 Lt-Colonel Percy Cox, the Indian Government's Resident in the Persian Gulf, was on leave in England and a mutual friend, Richmond Ritchie, arranged for Gertrude to meet him so that she could discuss with him her long-entertained plan to journey into central Arabia. She wanted to start at one of the Gulf states, presumably Kuwait or Ujair on the Al Hasa coast, and make her way through the territory of Najd to Hail in Jabal Shammar at its northern extremity. Cox declared that tribal conditions in that area were too unstable to allow of such a journey and so she reconciled herself to taking the northern route from Damascus. It was a sensible decision from many points of view. Not even Charles Doughty had been able to face the rigours of southern Najd and the dangers posed by its wild and fanatical tribesmen. The greatest of all Arabian explorers, Charles Huber, turned back on his tracks only to be murdered by his own guides. The Austrian Baron Nolde was driven to suicide by the attempt. Things had improved since early 1902 when Ibn Saud or, to give him his full name, Abdul Aziz bin Abdurrahman al Saud had returned to Riyadh from his enforced exile in Kuwait and set out to restore the kingdom of his forefathers, the Wahhabi empire, which once embraced almost the entire peninsula of Arabia. But his territory was closed to the outside world. Two men had visited Riyadh from the outside in the intervening years, the Dane Raunkiaer and the Englishman Gerald Leachman, but they had been taken under escort to the Saudi capital and were lucky to escape with their lives. More importantly, Britain was engaged in delicate negotiations with Turkey in 1913 with the object of strengthening Ottoman authority in its Asian dominions, especially in central Arabia, and Ibn Saud was

angrily resisting the attempt to make him the *kainakam* of the
Sultan in lands over which he ruled as the strongest and most
widely respected prince of the desert. Captain W. H. I. Shakespear,
the Political Agent in Kuwait and Ibn Saud's bosom friend, had
been deputed to negotiate on Britain's behalf with the ruler of
Najd and he had fought a long and angry battle with his own
government on the Arab chief's behalf. Now, Whitehall had
reluctantly agreed that Shakespear should be allowed to make a
journey of exploration across the peninsula from Kuwait to
Aqaba, calling at Riyadh on the way in order to placate the angry
and defiant Ibn Saud. It would have been the height of folly for
anyone else to have attempted such a journey at that time.

Thus Gertrude and Captain Shakespear set out for central
Arabia at almost exactly the same time, she heading for the
capital of Jabal Shammar, home of the Rashid, the usurping
family which Ibn Saud had thrown out of Riyadh twelve years
before.

If she left England with a heavy heart in 1913, Gertrude's
resilient nature came partly to her rescue. Within a month of
Doughty-Wylie's departure, and within two weeks of setting off
for the East herself, she wrote to her father:

> Last night I went to a delightful party at the Glenconners' and
> just before I arrived (as usual) 4 suffragettes set on Asquith and
> seized hold of him. Whereupon Alec Laurence in fury seized
> two of them and twisted their arms until they shrieked. Then
> one of them bit him in the hand till he bled. And when he
> told me the tale he was steeped in his own gore. I had a great
> triumph on Monday. I got Edwin Montagu to lunch to meet
> Major O'Connor and the latter talked for 1¼ hours of all the
> frontier questions – admirably E.M. sat and listened for 1½
> hours and then summed up the whole question with complete
> comprehension. I was enchanted. He is not only able E.M.,
> he is the real thing – he's a statesman ...

She travelled to Alexandria aboard the s.s. *Lotus*, arriving in
Damascus on November 25th, 1913. Her first call was on
Muhammad al Bessam, the son of Doughty's generous host in
Anaiza, who knew of good riding camels that were going
cheaply in Damascus. She found him an indispensable support
whenever she arrived in the Syrian city and she relied on him

heavily for advice and guidance. He told her that it was 'perfectly easy' to get to Najd that year, and she told her stepmother: 'I will let you know anyhow from Madeba – look for it on the map east of the north end of the Dead Sea.' She intended to take the routes due south from the Damascus oasis previously followed by Leachman and another traveller Musil, thus avoiding the Hijaz railway. A last-minute hitch made her change that plan, however. Fattuh became ill again and the idea of a long desert journey without her trusted servant was out of the question. She therefore took a route which curved round the Druse mountains through the lava tracts north-east of the Dead Sea and thence to the railway. Fattuh was to rest up and make his way by rail, some three weeks after her departure, to the village of Ziza where she would meet him. While these elaborate plans were being laid she kept up a lively, untroubled correspondence with her parents while unburdening her heart to Doughty-Wylie in Albania and her soul to Chirol in Delhi.

Towards the end of November she received a number of letters that can have done little to lessen her desire to see the former again. 'How are you my dear ... feeling the desert and the journey and the adventure on you – but well I hope and stronger ... And so you start – God go with you – and the luck of the world ... I am nervous about you somehow, lest things should go wrong. And I tell myself I am a fool – why should they go wrong? Yes – I'm very fond of you – I think, I have thought for a long time, that you are delightful and wise and strong, and such as my soul loveth. And in thought, on a swifter camel, into the desert I go with you ... I shall go on writing, but for tonight goodbye, my dear, keep well, be happy ... and don't forget me and our talks at Rounton ... ' That was dated November 21st. Two days later he wrote: 'Tomorrow probably you'll be in Damascus, and then begins the real adventure ... I can follow you by memory fairly well. A little south of Maan and from there to Hail is surely a colossal trek. For your palaces your road your Baghdad your Persia your O'Conor and your Fars ... I do not feel so nervous – but Hail from Maan – Inshallah! ... Yes you are a rolling stone – so are all people worth having – if not in body then in mind – for after all it is the mind that really matters ... '
And then, congratulating her on her latest book, *The Palace and Mosque at Ukhaidir* which had just been published, he went on in the way of those who live out their passions and desires in the

mind: 'It's late and I'm all alone, and thinking of those things, of philosophy and love and life – and an evening at Rounton – and what it all meant. I told you then I was a man of the earth, earthy ... You are in the desert, I am in the mountains, and in these places much could be said under the clouds. Does it mean that the fence was folly, and that we might have been man and woman as God made us and been happy ... But I myself answer to myself that it is a lie. If I had been your man to you, in the bodies we live in, would it change us, surely not. We could not be together long, and there's the afterwards sometimes to be afraid of ... Do you ever think like this? ... And still it is a great and splendid thing, the birthright of everyone, for woman as for man, only so many of them don't understand the simplicity of it. And I have always maintained that this curious, powerful sex attraction is a thing right and natural and to be gratified, and if it is not gratified, what then; are we any worse? I don't know ... '

It does not need any great perception to read between those lines, or to imagine the kind of letters that Gertrude was addressing to Albania; the kind of questions she was asking. Yet she went about the mundane tasks of organising her journey from Damascus with every appearance of single-minded concentration. On November 28th she wired her father for £400: 'This is not a gift for which I am asking. I wish to borrow the money from the National Bank.' Bessam had found her a guide and two personal servants one of whom, Muhammad Murawi, had travelled four years earlier with Douglas Carruthers, the man who was to draw up her maps when she returned to London. The wealthy and powerful Bessam had told her that she would need plenty of money with which to buy gifts for the princes of Hail. She purchased twenty camels, hired cameleers and a *rafiq* or guide, Hamad of the Ghiyadh tribe, and set off on December 16th. It seems that she was in touch with T. E. Lawrence, still digging and spying on the Germans at Carchemish, for he wrote to his brother on December 10th 'Miss Bell passed straight through from Beirut to Damascus ... and will not visit us till Spring.' Before leaving England she had written to Chirol: 'I want to cut all links with the world ... The road and the dawn, the sun, the wind and the rain, the camp fire under the stars, and sleep, and the road again ... '

Her first camp was at Adhra on the edge of the Damascus oasis near Dumeir. She was on the road she would normally have

taken to Mesopotamia and the prying eyes of Turkish officials
were probably averted for that reason. On December 21st she told
Lady Bell: 'We have reached our first goal and a very curious
place it is, but I will begin at the beginning. It was horribly cold
last night ... it was impossible to keep warm in bed ... I am not
cut out for Arctic exploration ... The men's big tent was frozen
hard and they had to light fires under it to unfreeze the canvas ... '
She climbed to the top of the volcano to take bearings and
insisted on her rafiq going with her. 'Oh! Hamad,' she said as they
breasted the slope, 'who can have lived in this strange place?'
She received the kind of reply familiar to those who travel with
the Badu, 'By God we would learn from you. But, indeed, oh
lady, there is no guide to truth but God.' They were held up next
day by what Gertrude described as a 'preposterous and provoking
episode'. They were attacked by Druse horsemen, one of whom
covered them with his rifle while another drew sword and
demanded of Muhammad his camel and saddlebag. Her men
were stripped of their revolvers, cartridge belts and cloaks, and
her camel was struck by a swordsman. They were rescued in the
nick of time by some Druse shaikhs who recognised her servants,
and their possessions were restored to them. Ahead of them lay
some stony hills, and cold rain came to hinder their progress.
However, they crossed the wadis of Muqati and Umqad and on
Christmas Day she found herself, as if by way of a heavenly gift,
among the ancient ruins of a fortress which had in its time seen
Roman occupation. She was able to spend the day taking measurements and copying inscriptions from the Greek, Safaitic and
Kufic. Three days later they were in sight of the southern end of
Jabal Druse and in the territory of the Ruwalla tribe, one of the
greatest desert groupings in all Arabia. But she did not meet
them; instead she ran into the Bani Sakhr tribe and was entertained by their shaikh, Ibn Mit'ab, who had two years before
betrayed the great chief of the Ruwalla, Ibn Shaalan, to his pro-
Turkish foes, the Shammar. By the end of the month she was in
the volcanic country between Jabal Druse and Wadi Sirhan
where she found a Roman fort and springs, and stopped to copy
an inscription of Diocletian, emperor of the eastern provinces of
the Empire in the third century A.D., at Qasr al-Azraq.

'What sort of Xmas Day have you been spending?' she asked
her family. 'I have thought of you all unwrapping presents in the
Common Room and playing with the children.' She was now

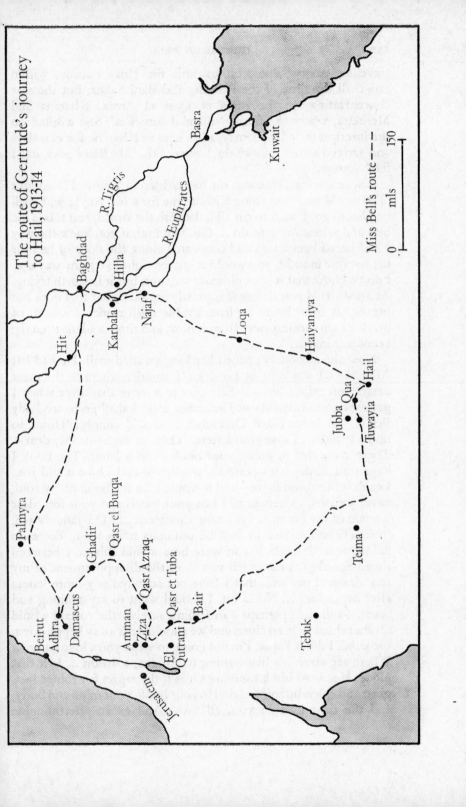

The route of Gertrude's journey
to Hail, 1913-14

Miss Bell's route ----

0   150
mls

Basra

Kuwait

R. Tigris

R. Euphrates

Baghdad

Hilla

Hit

Karbala

Najaf

Loqa

Haiyaniya

Hail

Qua

Jubba

Tuwayia

Palmyra

Beirut

Adhra

Damascus

Ghadir

Qasr el Burqa

Amman

Ziza

Qasr Azraq

El

Qutrani

Qasr et Tuba

Bair

Tebuk

Teima

Jerusalem

travelling almost due west towards the Hijaz railway, within
range all the time of the Ruwalla and Bani Sakhr, but she was
concentrating on the ruins of Qasr al Amra, Kharana and
Meshetta, where she found 'splendid surprises'. She worked on
the inscriptions of the Umayyad palaces at Kharana for two days
and arrived at the railway on January 6th. 'My letter goes and I
fetch letters.'

Before leaving Damascus she had written to 'Beloved Domnul':
'The world must get along without me for a bit. Anyhow, I shall
be glad to go. I want to cut all links with the world, and this is the
best and wisest thing to do ... Oh, Domnul, if you knew the way
I had paced backwards and forewards along the floor of hell for
the last few months, you would think me right to try any way out.
I don't know that it is an ultimate way out, but it is worth trying.
As I have told you before it is mostly my fault, but that does not
prevent it from being an irretrievable misfortune – for both of
us. But I am turning away from it now, and time deadens even the
keenest things ... '

Now she anxiously opened her long-awaited mail. He had left
Albania and was now in London. 'I wonder where in the great
desert you might be? – I shall miss you more than ever when I
get back to London about December 20th. I shall go to see Lady
Bell ... ' A letter dated December 23rd said simply: 'Home to
find 2 letters ... I love your letters.' Then on the 28th: 'My dear –
There came this morning your book – and a letter. The book I
have read all day – it's perfectly wonderful and I love it and you.
I can't write about it yet – and it would take the book of my soul,
never written, to answer it. I kiss your hands and your feet, dear
woman of my heart. Let it be for a moment ... ' On January 5th,
from Theberton Hall in Suffolk, ominous reference to domestic
differences: 'Tonight if you were here would this be a between
time? Should I want to tell you ... of the disappointment of my
relations and my wife that I have not acquired any more letters
after my name? ... Not a bit. I should want to say nothing and
listen, – and then perhaps – ah I think surely – the curtain would
lift that shuts us in so close, and we should drift away happy down
the wind. I don't know. I'm not going to write you a love letter ...
Where are you? It's like writing to an idea, a dream ... Is it that
gloom that is so black tonight? Or is it the regret for things lost,
great and splendid things I find in your book, your mind and body,
and the dear love of you, all lost.' And as an afterthought:

'Would you like me to write you a love letter — to say in some feeble whisper what the mind outside is shouting — to say, my dear, how glad and gratified and humble I am when I think of you ... '

But the last letter had not reached her yet. It was to follow her across the desert, and in the meantime she started to keep a secret journal, as well as her little pocket diary. On January 11th, as she waited and argued with the Turks who had followed Fattuh to Ziza and had been ordered to take her to Amman, she wrote:

> I have cut the thread. I can hear no more from you, or from anyone ... We turn towards Najd, inshallah, renounced by all the powers that be, and the only thread which is not cut runs through this little book, which is the diary of my way kept for you.

She pulled every possible string to obtain permission to move on, but the Turks were obdurate and even the new ambassador in Constantinople, her friend Sir Louis Mallet, warned her that H.M. Government would disclaim responsibility for her if she went on. In the end she decided to slip away without her documents, though three jemaders deserted her for fear of reprisal. She found fresh camelmen and with Fattuh now attending to her welfare as best he could, they set off south-eastwards to Tuba. Somewhere along the line, perhaps about now, she wrote again to Chirol:

> I have known loneliness in solitude now, for the first time, and in the long days of camel riding and the long evenings of winter camping, my thoughts have gone wandering far from the camp fire into places which I wish were not so full of acute sensation. Sometimes I have gone to bed with a heart so heavy that I thought I could not carry it through the next day. Then comes the dawn, soft and beneficent, stealing over the wide plain and down the long slopes of the little hollows, and in the end it steals into my dark heart also ... that's the best I can make of it, taught at least some wisdom by solitude, taught submission, and how to bear pain without crying out.

Her journey from now on was over a well-worn route. The Italian Carlo Guarmani, the Austrian Baron Nolde, Wilfrid and Lady Anne Blunt, Doughty, Carruthers, Leachman, and many others had traversed the path through Wadi Sirhan, east of the region later called Transjordan, to the Great Nafud, the land of orange-red sand dunes. In fact, Gertrude took a safer route than most, for she avoided the wells to the east and west of her path where trouble was always likely to accompany the raiding parties when they went in search of water; she relied instead on the *khabari*, or ponds formed by rain in the desert. The lessons she had taken in surveying techniques and map projection at the Royal Geographical Society were to prove useful on the journey. She was armed with a 3-inch theodolite, and she took accurate sightings for latitude as she went. But too much has been made of Gertrude's journey to Hail as a notable feat of exploration. She was not in any serious sense of the word an explorer. 'That's the trouble with wandering,' she once wrote, 'it has no end.' For her there was a succinct truth in the remark, precisely because she did not seek a conclusive goal. Her interests were those of the scholar, the historian and archaeologist; her approach to travel was philosophical, though it was accompanied by courage and endurance of the highest order. She did not seek to discover new places or to map unknown or unexplored areas, and the efforts of some writers to portray her as 'The Daughter of the Desert', as a kind of schoolgirl's 'Lawrence of Arabia', do justice neither to her nor to her real achievements. Even David Hogarth, who was no traveller himself, tended to look with awe on her journeys and to equate them with those of other voyagers who were bent on discovery in the unmapped territories of central Arabia. The geographical features of her route were clearly marked on the maps of London, Constantinople and Simla. A woman was largely protected by her sex in the desert. Unless she carried valuable articles to tempt the natural cupidity of the badawin she was unlikely to attract much more than an amused and uncomprehending interest. The desert Arab's sense of self-importance forbids a serious concern for the activities of a woman, whatever her nationality or the novelty of her appearance. Indeed, many remarkable tales of women's exploits in the East have gone more or less unnoticed. When Sir Leonard Woolley returned to England from his excavations at Ur of the Chaldees, for example, he met a little old lady named Miss Tanner who exhibited a surprising knowledge of the region in which he had been digging. When he asked her how she had acquired her knowledge she replied that she had wandered through Iraq and southern Iran in the early 1880s accompanied only by a Christian dragoman and had camped for three nights on the top of the ziggurat which he, Woolley, had excavated.

If Gertrude was not engaged in a unique or unprecedented journey, she nevertheless put all her considerable resources of endurance and initiative to the test. There were plenty of hazards along the way. She took the path which leads west of Jauf, the desert township which was the traditional home of the Shaalan family, hereditary amirs of the great Anaiza tribal confederations and paramount shaikhs of the Ruwalla, though the place had until recently been occupied by Ibn Rashid's men. The road took her through the territory of the chief of the Howeitat tribe, Shaikh Auda, by whom she was well received. She called at his *harim* and was made to feel at home by the belligerent but likeable ruffian who waged incessant war on Turks and fellow Arabs and kept a careful count of his victims. She also found a starveling family of Shammar on the way and allowed them to join her caravan. A shaikh of the Wuld Suleiman barred her way at one point until she surrendered a revolver and pair of Zeiss binoculars, a small price to pay for safe passage in Wadi Sirhan; the Howeitat men with her prevented any further extortion. The rest of the route ran parallel with the much-used caravan road to Hail. Only cold weather hindered their journey seriously. In mid-February there was frost on the sand. As they neared Hail a messenger came from the Amir Ibn Rashid to say that he was with a raiding party and would not be able to welcome her to his capital, but that his shaikhs would receive her. In sight of the first mountain of Jabal Shammar, Jabal Irnan, Fattuh came to her and said that a camel had sat down and could not be made to stir. 'Muhammad, Fellah and I went back with some food for her, thinking she might be weary of walking in the deep sand and that with feeding and coaxing we could get her on, but when we reached her we found her rolling in the sand in the death agony. Muhammad said, "She is gone. Shall we sacrifice her?" I said, "It were best." He drew his knife and said, "In the name of God. God is most powerful." With that he cut her throat ... I am deeply attached to all my camels and grieve over the death.'

On February 24th she wrote: 'We are camped within sight of Hail and I might have ridden in to-day, but I thought it better to announce my coming and therefore I sent on Muhammad and Ali and have camped in the plain a couple of hours or so from the town ... I hope the Hail people will be polite. The Amir is away raiding and an uncle of his is left in charge.' Hogarth was to write of her visit to the Rashid: 'No European, other than a Turkish officer, was known to have been seen in Hail for over twenty years, and no European woman for more than thirty. The all-powerful Amir Muhammad ibn Rashid, who protected more than one western visitor, had died half a generation ago; and since his death murder after murder had thinned the princely house. Its power had been waning for some time in comparison with that of the Amirate of Southern Najd; and one result of the growing preponderance of the Ibn Sauds in central Arabia was likely to be the accentuation of Wahhabism, heretofore lukewarm. Miss Bell might well be doubtful how she would be received.'

In fact, Hail was a veritable metropolis of trade and was in regular communication with the outside world. The Turks visited the place in considerable numbers and Shakespear, travelling in the opposite direction, met numerous people in the desert who had passed Europeans on their way to the capital of the Rashids. Lady Anne Blunt, the only other woman to penetrate to central Arabia up to that time, had left a colourful description of the place. And of course two of the finest writers in the entire world of travel literature, Palgrave and Doughty, had given accounts of it generations before. But Gertrude's powers of description were in no way diminished by the knowledge of famous precedents:

And now I must relate to you the strange tale of my visit ... When we had been on the road for about an hour we met Ali on his camel, all smiles. They had seen Ibrahim, the uncle in charge. He was most polite and ha! ha! there were three slaves of his household come out to receive me ... So we came up to the walls of Hail in state ... At the doorway of the first house stood Muhammad al Murawi ... I walked up a long sloping passage ... to an open court and so into a great room with a roof borne on columns and divans and carpets round the walls. It was the Roshan, the reception room. Here I sat and one of the slaves with me. These slaves, you must understand, are often very important personages. Their masters treat them like brothers and give them their full confidence. Also when one of the Rashids removes the reigning prince and takes his place (which frequently happens) he is careful to murder his slaves also, lest they should avenge the slain ... Thereupon there appeared ... two women. One was an old widow, Lu-lu-ah, who is caretaker here, as you might say. The other was a Circassian, who was sent to Muhammad al Rashid by the Sultan as a gift. Her name is Turkiyyeh. Under her dark purple cloak — all the women are closely veiled here — she was dressed in brilliant red and purple cotton robes and she wore ropes of bright pearls round her neck. And she is worth her weight in gold as I have come to know. She is a chatterbox of the first order and I passed an exceedingly amusing hour in her company ... After lunch Ibrahim paid me a state visit, slaves walking before him and slaves behind. He is an intelligent and (for an Arab) well educated man. He was clothed in Indian silks and carried a gold mounted sword ... As he went he whispered to old Muhammad al Murawi that as the Amir was away and as there was some talk in the town about my coming, a stranger and so on, he was bound to be careful and so on — in short, I was not to leave the house without permission ...

After her reception in the great Roshan or Khawa she remained in honourable captivity for several days, confined to her room in the guest house, though visited from time to time by Fatima, the young Amir's devious grandmother, and other notables. Eventually Ibrahim invited her to visit him at the fortress of the amirs and so she found herself back in the Roshan. She was conducted by slaves and found Ibrahim and a large company sitting on carpets. They all stood as she arrived. She sat on the right of the Amir's uncle while slaves poured tea and coffee. Finally censers were brought in and swung three times before each guest, a signal that the reception had ended. Gertrude had already sent gifts of silk to all the chief inhabitants of the royal household, and revolvers and Zeiss glasses to the Amir and Ibrahim and their slaves. She tipped the doorkeepers generously as she went. Life was expensive in Hail and she was running short of money. In Damascus she had paid Ibn Rashid's agent £200 so that she could draw the money by letter of credit in Hail. When she asked for the money it was decided that the requisite document was made out to the credit of the Amir's treasurer who was out riding with him and could not be paid until he returned. What she did not know at that time was that the young and irresponsible head of this homicidal family, who had been in the custody of the Sharif of Mecca until his recent return to occupy the throne, was

in the process of murdering his uncle, the Regent Zamil ibn
Subhan, with Turkish connivance. Zamil was a level-headed man
and a good ruler who had been in communication with Ibn Saud
in the hope of restoring peaceful relations between the two great
seats of power in central Arabia. Saud ibn Rashid the twenty-
year-old Amir, and another Saud, a nephew of the Regent, were
together with the raiding party near a place called Abu Ghar when
a slave was instructed to shoot the Regent in the back. As Zamil
was murdered his brothers and slaves tried to ride away but they
were shot down too. And while the murder was taking place the
Amir and his accomplice rode past without even turning to look.
That all happened in early April. It was perhaps a good thing that
Gertrude did not wait for the Amir's return. She appealed to his
uncle but Ibrahim insisted that no money could be paid until Ibn
Rashid returned. She told him that if that were the case she must
go and would be grateful for the services of a rafiq.

She wrote: 'That morning I must tell you he had returned the
gifts I had sent to him and to his brother Zamil, who is away with
the Amir. Whether he did not think they were sufficient or what
was the reason I do not know.' She took the gifts with her to her
audience and asked Ibrahim to take them back, which he did.
They can have been of little use to his brother.

Next day I sent a messenger out for my camels – they proved
to be two days away – and again I sat still amusing myself as
best I might and the best was not good. I had no idea what was
in their dark minds concerning me. I sat imprisoned and my
men brought me in rumours from the town ... The general
opinion was that the whole business was the work of Fatima,
but why, or how it would end, God alone knew. If they did not
intend to let me go I was in their hands. It was all like a story
in the Arabian Nights, but I did not find it particularly enjoyable to be one of the dramatis personae. Turkiyyeh came again
and spent the day with me and next day there appeared the
chief eunuch Sayid – none more powerful than he. He came to
tell me that I could not leave without permission from the
Amir.

Gertrude appealed, protested and drank tea endlessly. She was
allowed to wander in the garden with the male Rashids, 'all that
have not been murdered by successive usurping amirs', and in
the end decided to deliver an ultimatum. 'I wish to leave tomorrow,'

8 Portrait of Gertrude, 1921

9 Lt-Col. C. H. M. ('Dick') Doughty-
Wylie, V.C.

10 Colonnaded street in Palmyra, 1900

11 Church at Binbirkilisse, 1907

12 View of ruins at Ukhaidir, 1911

Opposite:

13 Gertrude outside her tent at Babylon, 1909

14 German archaeologist, Dr Buddensieg, with an Arab assistant, 1909

15 Gertrude taking measurements at Ukhaidir, 1909

16 By the Euphrates, near the excavations at Babylon

17 German archaeologists at work, Babylon, 1909

18 The German excavations at Babylon, 1909

she told them, and asked again for a rafiq. But the eunuch told her that nothing could be done. 'I went to the men's tent (after prayer) and spoke my mind ... without any Oriental paraphrases and, having done so, I rose abruptly and left them sitting – a thing which is only done by great shaikhs, you understand.' That evening Sayid the eunuch returned with £200 and told her she could go. With great dignity she replied that she had no intention of leaving that night but wished to see the town in daylight next day, after which she would go on her way. She was shown the sights next day with great ceremony, and took tea with Turkiyyeh and Fatima.

Her subsequent description shows that she had absorbed much in her confined stay:

The narrow strip of palm gardens ... between the twin ridges of Jabal Sumra widens out as it issues from the gorge, and in the verdure lies the town of Hail. To the south west a few walled palm groves, planted in the shining mirage of the plain, rise fantastically green against the black crags. To the south the plain has its way. It is as though you looked over the level floor of the world ... Hail as it stands today is of comparatively recent date but it preserves a traditional architecture which goes back, I make no doubt, to very early times. Arab princes before the Prophet must have received the poets of the Age of Ignorance in just such palaces as those in which the Shaikhs of Jabal Shammar hold their audiences. The battlemented ring of mud wall encircles Hail, the line broken at regular intervals by ruined towers, battlemented also, machicolated, narrowing upwards like wingless windmills ... Dominating the city, the great round towers of the Qasr, the Amir's palace, crown the massive defences which guard the secrets and the domestic tragedies of the Rashid. You pass under the bastion formed by the summer palace of the Amir Muhammed ... and so through the Medina Gate under the watchful eye of its slave gate-keepers ... Though it is a town, like any other, of streets and houses, Hail retains something of the wilderness. There is no clatter of civic life. Silent ways are paved with desert dust ... the creak of wheels is not heard. The noiseless slow footfall of the camel is all the traffic here ... Since 1893 no European had set eyes on Hail ... Three times in the last eight years the grown men of the Rashid have fallen to the sword of one of their own stock, their bodies scarcely cold, thrust hastily into the deep wells of the Qasr, their women given no interval to mourn husband and child before they were portioned out among the usurpers ...

When I returned again to Damascus the man of Najd came to me and said: 'Have you news of that which has passed in Hail since you left? Of Ibrahim?' Ibrahim was him who received me in the Shammar city. 'No, God save you,' said I. 'But what has befallen Ibrahim ...?' He looked at me in silence and drew his fingers across his throat.

The life of the town is untouched by this blood strife. What the Shaikhs do may be reprehensible but they are the Shaikhs ... Under their leadership the Shammar tribes have lorded it over northern Arabia ... my gatekeeper was Chesb, booty of war, but he seemed to have identified himself with the interests of his new masters. He was not behind the men of Hail in piety ... His chant woke me every morning before sunrise. 'Allahu akbar, Allahu akbar – God is great, God is great. There is no God but God. And Mohammed is the prophet of God. God is great. God is great.' Low and soft, borne on the scented breeze of the desert, the mighty invocation, which is the Alpha and Omega of Islam, sounds through my memory when I think of Hail.

'I go to Baghdad,' she wrote with relief on leaving the city of Al Rashid. The road was infested with lawless tribesmen who were up in arms against the Turks, and there were some nasty moments, but within a fortnight she and her companions had made their way along the ancient road of the Persian pilgrims, and she was in sight of Najaf and familiar landmarks.

More letters awaited her in Baghdad. Doughty-Wylie had written to his famous uncle to tell him of Gertrude's journey and to pass on her good wishes. 'I wrote to my uncle and he thanks you and wishes you a safe journey. It's troubled me before but it is now worse ... And the desert has you – you and your splendid courage, my queen of the desert – and my heart is with you ... If I was young and free, and a very perfect knight, it would be more fitting to take and kiss you. But I am old and tired and full of a hundred faults ... '

The syntax became positively wild. ' ... you are right, – not that way for you and me – because we are slaves, not because it is not the right, the natural way – when the passions of the body flame and melt into the passions of the spirit – in those dream ecstacies so rarely found by any human creature, those, as you say, whom God hath really joined – In some divine moment we might reach it – the ecstacy. We never shall. But there is left so much. As you say my dear, wise Queen – all that there is we will take.'

'It's the last letter. There is so much to say ... Tell yourself the thousand things that you would hear and I tell. If I can content you let me do it. If you want me let me be there, the little things, the big things, say them all ... But now you are at Hail. Now we'll go back to that court of your heart ... '

But it was not the last letter. As the weeks went by he wrote every day or two and the letters piled up along her route.

'I cannot tell you how much it moves me to hear you say – No, not that – to see it written by you, that you might have married me, have borne my children, have been my life as well as my heart ... '

Again: 'You give me a new world, Gertrude. I have often loved women as a man like me does love them, well and badly, little and much, as the blood took me, or the time or the invitation, or simply for the adventure – to see what happened. But that is all behind me.'

'And you shall walk in my garden, even ghostwise and imperfect in this life – and I will walk in yours, ghostwise also, and still more imperfectly.'

January 15th: 'Already it seems a long time since I wrote ... This morning they wrote to me to go to Abyssinia, and I am going about the end of the month ... Where are you now? By the Belka castles, working like ten men, tired and hungry and sleepy ... Like that I love to think of you: sometimes, too, (but it's beastly of me) I love to think of you lonely, and wanting me ... '

In the last week of January Doughty-Wylie called at Sloane Street where he met Gertrude's father. Then he went to the Foreign Office to an interview with Sir Edward Grey. He was due to leave London for Addis Ababa in a few days. 'Yet go I must ... There's anarchy out there, complete and beastly. Thesiger has gone away to East Africa. I go to Kartoum and Cairo to see K [Kitchener] and Wingate. Perhaps I can hear in Cairo. Your father will let me know, dear old man ... '

'A line, my dear. I have some minutes and every minute I miss you.'

'I love you – does it do any good out there in the desert? Is it less vast, less lonely, like the far edge of life? someday perhaps, in a whisper, in a kiss, I will tell you ... '

'It's magnificent; love like this is life itself ... This shall go to Lorimer in Baghdad. Oh, where are you, where are you? And I too go away in a few days.'

'Well, I go. Africa draws me; I know I shall have things to try for, to climb over, to get round, to win; more probably to lose. But of them I scarcely think: it is only that I love you, Gertrude, and shall not see you ... '

'But, I have a thing to ask – wire to me – *British Minister, Addis Ababa* – your safe arrival. *Safe Baghdad.* How immensely happy I shall be to see it. *Ma salaami.* Dick.'

15
War

The journey to Hail ended in a mood of despondency. In March she wrote from Baghdad: 'The end of an adventure always leaves one with a feeling of disillusion—don't you know it? I try to school myself beforehand by reminding myself of how I have looked forward at other times to the end, and when it came have found it—just nothing. Dust and ashes in one's hand ... This adventure hasn't been successful either. I haven't done what I meant to do. But I have got over that now ... '

She set out for Damascus and wrote to her parents in early May to tell them that she expected to be in Constantinople on the 8th, and in London about a fortnight later. She was welcomed to the Turkish capital by Sir Louis Mallet who had been sent there by Sir Edward Grey in a last-minute effort to rescue from the fire that charred chestnut of Liberal foreign policy, the consolidation of Turkey's Asiatic empire. 'Sir Louis is perfectly delightful. He is tremendously full of his job and we have talked for hours,' she wrote.

Sir Louis reported to the Foreign Secretary on May 20th, giving his chief—to whom he had acted as private secretary and assistant under-secretary of state for the past eight years—an account of Gertrude's journey and of her impression of the ruling family of Hail:

Domestic intrigue in the Rashid family has been and is increasing. During the past five or six years two convulsions occurred at Hail and on each occasion the ruling Amir and as many of the male members of the family as could be seized, had been put to the sword. Since her departure, Miss Bell states, the Amir's chief adviser whom she did not see, and his representative in Hail who received her (both cousins of the Amir's mother), have been murdered ... Miss Bell has kindly promised to furnish you with a detailed account of her travels, the results of which will be of great interest and value, as no European has visited Hail for more than fifteen years ... As she was desirous of meeting Talaat Bey and I thought that there would be no harm in his Excellency hearing some first hand information respecting the present situation as regards Ibn Rashid and Ibn Saud's prospects and influence, I invited him to meet her at dinner. His Excellency was more impressed with Miss Bell's knowledge than she with his. He told her that he proposed to appoint Ibn Saud Vali of Nejd giving him practical independence but placing a small Turkish garrison in Ojair and El Katif and that the frontier between Ibn Rashid and Ibn Saud would be demarcated. Miss Bell told Talaat Bey that she thought that this latter proposal was quite impracticable, which indeed it seemed to be.

When she finally reached London Gertrude was in a tormented state of mind. The emotional tie with Doughty-Wylie, far from diminishing as the result of her Arabian journey, had intensified. In April, before leaving Baghdad she had told Chirol: 'I expect I shall be in Damascus by the end of the month, and the middle of May will probably see me in C'ple – if Sir Louis is there. If not, I should perhaps come back via Athens. I don't mind much either way, indeed I am profoundly indifferent. But I don't care to be in London much, and if there is no reason for hurrying, I shall not hurry ... You will find me a savage, for I have seen and heard strange things, and they colour the mind. You must try to civilise me a little, beloved Domnul. I think I am not altered for you, and I know that you will bear with me. But whether I can bear with England ... I come back ... with a mind permanently altered. I have gained much and I will never forget it. This letter is only for you – don't hand it on to anyone, or tell anyone that the me they knew will not come back in the me that returns. Perhaps they will not find out.'

The England she eventually returned to was changed perhaps as much as she. In that sultry summer political tempers were frayed on all sides and ominous threats of war, civil and international, threw dark shadows over the country. The Irish troubles were at another peak in their long history of bigotry and vehemence; the suffragettes still pursued their cause with much shouting and biting and chaining to railings; the German Emperor rattled his sabre. A few months earlier London had welcomed the chief minister-elect of Turkey, Hakki Pasha, in the vain hope that if war should break out between the British Empire and the German and Austro-Hungarian Empires, the fourth great imperial force would at least remain neutral in return for British favours. Domestic life had changed too. Her sisters were preoccupied with their growing families. Her parents had just returned from a visit to the United States, and her letters to them had piled up at Rounton. They had left Southampton on March 7th in company with Bertrand Russell, who had been invited to deliver the Lowell lectures in Boston and to act as temporary professor of philosophy at Harvard. The voyage was not without its lighter moments according to Russell:

> I sailed in the *Mauretania* on March 7th. Sir Hugh Bell was on the ship. His wife spent the whole voyage looking for him, or finding him with a pretty girl. Whenever I met him after the sinking of the *Lusitania*, I found him asserting that it was on the *Lusitania* he had sailed.

No sooner had Russell parted from the senior members of the Bell family than he found himself in a train compartment listening to two fellow passengers discussing Gertrude's brother-in-law, George Trevelyan. Although they moved in much the same circles and met frequently, Gertrude and Bertrand Russell were too alike in sharpness of mind and assurance of opinion for their mutual comfort. They gave each other a wide berth intellectually, seldom referring to each other in their letters.

After her parents' return Gertrude stayed with Florence in London, busy with the captioning of her hundreds of photographs of central Arabia and her maps. Little interest was shown in her achievement by a nation preoccupied with more pressing affairs.

On June 7th the *Times* correspondent in Cairo reported that Captain Shakespear had passed through at the end of his trans-Arabian crossing and had called on Lord Kitchener, the Resident, and Sir Reginald Wingate the army Sirdar and Governor of the Sudan, a singularly unfruitful visit according to Shakespear. A leading article in the newspaper conjectured as to the explorer's route, and remarked on Gertrude's trek. She responded with a letter published on the 13th of the month:

> Sir, I heard recently in Damascus that Captain Shakespear's intention was to travel north from al-Riyadh, leaving Hail to the west and touching the wells of Laina visited by Captain Leachman in 1912; thence to Jauf and to the head of the Gulf of Aqaba. It is, however, useless to speculate as to his route, as we shall shortly have a description of it from himself, and all who are interested in the exploration of Arabia may rest assured that one so well qualified as he will give us information of singular value. Since you make allusion to my more modest journey, will you permit me to describe the course I took? ...

She went on to give an account of her journey from Damascus to Hail and the return along the pilgrim route to Najaf and Baghdad. She ended with a brief reference to the current conflict in central Arabia.

> My belief is that Ibn Saud is now the chief figure in central Arabia, although the Ottoman Government was still pursuing its traditional policy of subsidising and supplying arms to the Rashids. Captain Shakespear will be able to give us more certain information as to the relative positions of the protagonists.

The Times railed at Britain's spineless and confused approach to eastern problems at this juncture and in a leading article on June 29th it made a pertinent attack on the Asquith Government's attempt, shared by its Liberal predecessors, to take power away from the Government of India and place it in the hands of a Foreign Office preoccupied with European and domestic affairs and incapable of taking a genuinely 'imperial' view. Under the heading 'Council of India Bill', it observed:

> One of the deplorable results of the intense preoccupation of the country in the Ulster problem is that many often gravely important issues, both Imperial and foreign, are receiving insufficient attention ... The attempts to undermine the Council began as soon as the Liberal Party entered office. From the moment when Lord Morley became Secretary of State for India, he set himself up to belittle and to contract the functions

which his Council was intended to exercise ... He sometimes
went to lengths which were almost unconstitutional.

The newspaper had put its finger on the difficulty which faced
successive Viceroys and their Residents in eastern territories.
Since the Government of India started to shed its authority – a
process which may be said to have begun even before the Council
of India, in the wake of Palmerston's policy of thwarting Russian
and French ambitions by bolstering the Ottoman domains – it had
also shed its resolution. By the first decade of the twentieth
century the Viceroy and his Foreign Secretary were merely
cyphers of the Foreign Office in London, unable to act independ-
ently or directly in any of the territories over which they tradition-
ally held sway. What was worse, they were often unable – or
unwilling – to support their own men in the field, men whose
knowledge of the political and historical backgrounds of the
territories they administered or advised was usually immense. It
was in that atmosphere of conflict between two of the principal
departments of State in the British administration, the Foreign
and India Offices, that Gertrude began to become involved in
the politics of the Middle East. And it was in the shadow of
Grey's determination to maintain the tottering empire of the
Turks that an angry and frustrated Captain Shakespear arrived
in London in June 1914. Less than twelve months before the
Foreign Secretary had stated Britain's position in the clearest
terms. 'The only policy to which we can become a party is one
directed to avoid the collapse and partition of Asiatic Turkey,'
he told the India Office. Sir Louis Mallet minuted his observation
while recording his chief's remarks – 'for another policy would
once again bring into question the possession of Constantinople,
and probably result in a European war'. When those notes were
made, Grey and Mallet knew perfectly well that war with Germany
was inevitable and that Turkey would assuredly join the Kaiser,
though on the resignation of Britain's ambassador at Constantinople, Sir Gerard Lowther, in 1913, Mallet himself rushed to the
Turkish capital in a last-minute attempt to foster the neutrality
of the Ottoman power. Meanwhile Sir T. W. Holderness, the
Permanent Under-Secretary at the India Office, told Mallet: 'I
gather privately that FO are much frightened of Sir Percy Cox
and Captain Shakespear, whom they suspect of all sorts of
designs ... the point is not what Sir Percy Cox or Captain

L

Shakespear say and think, but what Lord Crewe says and thinks, and that his Lordship is uncommitted.'

Although Gertrude and Shakespear were naturally keen to meet, for they shared a common knowledge of the tribal dispositions and conflicts of Arabia which was unique among their contemporaries, there is no evidence that they did so. They certainly corresponded, however, and they both spent a lot of time at the Royal Geographical Society where the director, Dr Scott Keltie, pressed them into giving accounts of their journeys while they worked in the map room and sorted through their unique photographic records of central Arabia. But they were too busy in other directions to prepare detailed and illustrated lectures. Shakespear was fighting a daily battle with the India and Foreign Offices, writing long reports which stressed the urgent need for a treaty with the rising star among the desert princes, Ibn Saud, and being told that such an agreement was neither desirable nor possible. He also spent a good deal of time at his parents' home in Brighton, while Gertrude travelled between Sloane Street and Rounton. She also devoted herself once more to the activities of the suffragettes, joining Janet Courtney, Millicent Garrett Fawcett and others, to warn that 'militant victory is empty if it demonstrates the effectiveness of lawless violence'. And Doughty-Wylie still occupied her mind. Nevertheless, the two travellers found time to play a protracted game of hide-and-seek with Dr Keltie.

On June 13th, Keltie had written to Gertrude:

Dear Miss Lothian Bell, I am very much interested to see your letter in to-day's 'Times'. I did not know you were back ... May we look forward to your giving us a paper at the beginning of next session at one of our meetings ... with maps and slides?

A week or so later she wrote to acknowledge the Society's decision to award her its gold medal and the attendant monetary prize: 'Dear Dr Keltie, The Geographical Society is doing me far too much honour and I feel profoundly that my travels have not deserved the recognition which they are about to make to me. But since they are determined about it I must express my very grateful thanks. Yes, of course I will come to the meeting on Aug 26th. I think I should probably like to have the money in the form of an instrument, but will you let me have a day or two to consider the matter?'

August 4th from Rounton: 'Dear Dr Keltie, I am not coming to London this week. My brother's Territorials are mobilizing and I do not wish to leave home while he is here. The next few days will enable us to ... form clearer decisions, but it looks as if maps of Arabia must give place to more pressing matters.'

September 8th, still at Rounton: 'Dear Dr Keltie, I do not think there is any reason why I should not give the lecture in November ... Do you know what has become of Captain Shakespear? ... Ps. Please note that my second name has a *w* in it!'

September 9th, from Dr Keltie: 'I know the tendency here to mis-spel [*sic*] your second name and I am always correcting it ... It would be a good thing if you could come to London on 21st to start the map. The sooner the better as our draughtsmen have been busy ever since the war began, and are still busy in doing work for the War Office ... I expect Captain Shakespear has gone off somewhere: he was eager to go. He was not allowed to go into active service although he was not required to return to his post. But I know he volunteered for service of any kind he could under-take under the circumstances. I wrote to him a day or two ago but have not heard from him yet.' On September 22nd the director wrote to tell her that Hilaire Belloc had been persuaded to give a 'war lecture' in place of her long-postponed paper. 'If it is con-venient we should take your paper on 7th December.'

By December Gertrude had followed Shakespear into whatever service she could profitably render her country. Neither delivered their promised papers, though many years later in a much-changed world others did it for them.

Gertrude wrote to Keltie again on November 6th: 'I am going next week to help Lady Onslow to run her hospital. I have asked some of my friends at the Red X to join me in the first suitable job abroad that falls vacant ... and I have written to friends of mine in Paris asking whether I could be of use to them in any way ... Arabia can wait, can't it?'

On November 19th she wrote from Lady Onslow's Clandon Park Hospital at Guildford: 'I'm busy all day long here and I expect before the end of the month to go to France. I am so sorry. I must ask you to forgive me.'

By the end of November she was in Boulogne where she worked in Lord Robert Cecil's office for tracing the missing and wounded, together with Flora and Diana Russell. Her father had asked her if she would like a motor car sent over. 'Ian Malcolm has brought a motor car over with him so for the moment that's all we want,' she replied. 'But I can't be certain that we may not want one later, for this whole thing is in the course of organisation ... and I wish you could hold your hand till I see what happens ... Will you ask General Bethune to send us out as complete a list as he can of the Territorial Battalions – something corresponding to the Army List for regulars ... ' Gertrude was seldom far from high-up sources of assistance when the occasion demanded. She told Doughty-Wylie: 'I had a hideous interview with the passport people at the Red Cross ... age 46, height 5 ft 5½ ... no profession ... mouth normal ... face, well ... I looked at the orderly: "Round," she said ... '

She worked in Boulogne for three months, throwing herself into the tasks of organisation necessary to keep track of the missing and wounded in the terrible conditions of war in Europe in the late days of 1914 and the ensuing year. 'In time I think we ought to have one of the best run offices in France. We are already scheming to get into closer touch with the front which is our weak point. Lord Robert asked the Adj. General to let us have a representative and he refuses categorically ... We have the most pitiful letters and we see the most pitiful people ... '

By January 1st, 1915 she was writing to her stepmother: 'A happy New Year. What else can I wish you? Diana and I caught ourselves wondering last night whether the next 31st Dec. would find us still sitting at our desks here ... ' In fact, Gertrude was back home in March reorganising the London office for the missing and wounded, which was in a chaotic state. She was joined there by her cousin Sylvia Stanley. But already more congenial work was beginning to materialise. In September 1914, just after the outbreak of war, the Director of Military Operations had been in touch with her for a report on her views on Syria which had been requested by Wyndham Deedes of Intelligence in Cairo. On September 9th, the D.M.O. sent a copy of her confidential report to Sir Edward Grey:

Syria, especially Southern Syria, where Egyptian prosperity is better known, is exceedingly pro-English. I was told last winter by a very clever German named Loytved and an old friend of mine now at Haifa, that it would be impossible to exaggerate the genuine desire of Syria to come under our jurisdiction. And I believe it. Last Autumn an additional impulse was given to this sentiment by the dislike of growing French influence. This dislike is universal. Germany does not count for much either way in Syria. On the Baghdad side we weigh much more heavily in the scale than Germany because of the importance of Indian relations – trade chiefly – the presence of a large body of German engineers in Baghdad, for railway building, will be of no advantage to Germany, for they are not popular. On the whole I should say that 'Iraq' would not willingly see Turkey at war with us and would not take an active part in it. But out there, the Turks would probably turn ... to Arab chiefs who have received our protection. Such action would be extremely unpopular with the Arab Unionists who look on Sayid Talib of Basra, Kuwait, and Ibn Saud, as powerful protagonists. Sayid Talib is a rogue, he has had no help from us, but our people (merchants) have maintained excellent terms with him ...

It was the first official report in Gertrude's hand, a hand that was to become famous in Government circles for its easy style, its familiarity with eastern problems, and its provocative and erudite commentary; and it showed that even while travelling unofficially in Syria and Mesopotamia (or Iraq as she more correctly called it), she kept her ear carefully to the ground.

Meanwhile, the Royal Geographical Society had heard that she was back. 'I heard yesterday that you were back in London and naturally take the first opportunity of writing to ask you whether there is now a chance that you will be able to deliver your promised paper,' wrote the director on April 12th. 'I am in London but I might just as well not be, as far as you or anyone else, outside the Wounded and Missing Office, is concerned. I am in this office from 9 am till 7.30 pm, seven days a week and I see no likelihood of the hours being shortened,' she replied. While she was working with the Red Cross in France, Captain Shakespear had been dispatched by the Government to central Arabia to attempt to gain the support of Ibn Saud in the event of Turkey's entry into the war. On January 5th, 1915 he wrote to her from Majma'a in central Arabia:

Dear Miss Bell, I am in camp here with Bin Saud, and having the luxury of being halted for a few days am banging off some letters. I can't remember when I last wrote but think it must have been before I went down to Aldershot ... just as that got going nice and smoothly the India Office wired for me and fired me out here 'to get into personal touch' with Bin Saud. It was a weary long voyage out ... I had got as far as Karachi when war with Turkey was announced ... Here I find immense relief that we have turned the Turks out of Basra and not a trace of any fanaticism or of feeling against the British. Bin Saud is as pleased as possible. He is making preparations for a big raid on Ibn Rashid with a view to wiping him out practically and I shouldn't be surprised if I reached Hail in the course of next month or two as BS's political adviser!! I expect you are having a pretty busy time with a hospital or something ... I am afraid Dr Keltie will be rather annoyed with me — no lecture and no paper for the Journal ... If you aren't too busy and can spare a line about your doings and how the lecture went at the RGS you can help my loneliness out here ... I trust you had a better Christmas and New Year than I ... a 22 mile march and New Year's Day my second bath in 20 days ...

Within three weeks of writing that letter, Shakespear was dead, killed in the battle that was to have wiped out the pro-Turkish desert force of Ibn Rashid. With his death the British abandoned Ibn Saud altogether. Shakespear's maps and some of the most detailed and valuable notes ever compiled on the Arabian terrain were included along with Gertrude's observations on the War Office and Royal Geographical Society maps. In June she was approached by the Director of Naval Intelligence. Britain's policy in Arabia was about to take a dramatic turn and Gertrude's expertise was needed in that theatre of war.

16
The Arab Bureau

When the call came it was as though everything that had gone before was but preparation for this moment. Politics were food and drink to Gertrude's alert mind. The Middle East was her spiritual home. Though she was anxious to help her country in any way that was open to her, service in some part of the Arab world was inevitably her first wish. Her travels and her friendships in government converged on that territory which, however imprecisely, was called Arabia. Her connections with men of power at home and in the Middle East pointed inexorably in that direction. Sir Edward Grey, Sir Louis Mallet now back at the F.O. as Permanent Under-Secretary, Lord Hardinge of Penshurst, Viceroy and Governor General of India, Edwin Montagu and Sir Arthur Hirtzel at the India Office, Winston Churchill and after him Balfour at the Admiralty – all were long-standing friends or acquaintances, some of them familiar since girlhood. Ambassadors and consuls strung across the world from the Far East to America were known to her personally. Politicians and diplomats on both sides of the fence in the war now raging in Europe and the Middle East had been her willing hosts over the years. Her relatives the Trevelyans, Russells and Lascelles occupied positions of authority in Whitehall and the legations of H.M. Government overseas. Harold Nicolson, with whom she had become acquainted at the Constantinople embassy, was now an under-secretary at the Foreign Office. Her brother-in-law Rear-Admiral Sir Herbert Richmond was deputy Director of Naval Operations. As the year progressed and the toll of casualties mounted on the European fronts, some of the Britishers she had met in the deserts and towns of the Levant and Syria, Mesopotamia and Egypt, were busy with

schemes which had a particular need of her experience and knowledge. Even the emotional turmoil which still raged in her
through the last months of 1914 and the early part of 1915
pointed with almost sinister insistence towards the East.

In February 1915, when she was working for the Red Cross in
France, a telegram was dispatched from Intelligence Cairo to the
War Office in London. It read: 'Major Doughty-Wylie, former
Consul at Adana, arrived from Abyssinia. I suggest I might keep
him here for employment. Do you concur? He is en route for
England. I have not yet mentioned this to him. Maxwell, C-in-C.'
It was the period of the Turks' abortive attempt to cross the Suez
Canal, of the reinforcement of enemy forces outside Ismailia and
on the Tigris in Mesopotamia. German intelligence agents were
swarming through Syria. The propaganda of the Young Turks
and the Committee of Union and Progress, and of the Germans,
was proving effective in Jerusalem, Damascus, Baghdad, Basra
and other centres of the Pan-Islamic movement. The systematic
murder and abduction of the Armenians had begun again, for the
third time in half a century. On February 14th Britain's ambassador
at Petrograd wired that according to Russian intelligence a strong
Turkish force was on its way to Baghdad. On February 20th Lord
Kitchener told General Maxwell that a naval force was on its way
to bombard the Dardanelles and later the same day Maxwell was
told that he should warn a force of 30,000, made up of Australian
and New Zealand contingents, 'to prepare for service'. Major
Dick Doughty-Wylie was thought an ideal intelligence officer for
the campaign being planned; a campaign which, according to
Kitchener's telegram to Maxwell, would demand 'specially competent officers' who would have to be capable of 'acting inde-
pendently' until the main force under Birdwood joined them.
However, he was allowed to proceed to London on leave and
Gertrude rushed from France to meet him.

A month before she had written from her office in Boulogne:

Dearest, dearest, I give this year of mine to you, and all the
years that shall come after it, this meagre gift — the year and me
and all my thought and love ... You fill my cup, this shallow
cup that has grown so deep to hold your love and mine.
Dearest, when you tell me you love me and want me still, my
heart sings — and then weeps with longing to be with you. I

have filled all the hollow places of the world with my desire for you; it floods out to creep up the high mountains where you live.

Then there was silence, and depression. 'Fear is a horrible thing, don't let me live under the shadow of it.' Then the meeting in London. Whatever happened or was said on that occasion it was certainly coloured by the knowledge that he must depart again in a few days to join Sir Ian Hamilton's staff as the Gallipoli force assembled. It is some weeks later, when he has left for the Mediterranean, that we pick up the threads of correspondence. His letters were censored and necessarily brief. On February 26th she wrote to him:

I can't sleep – I can't sleep. It's one in the morning of Sunday. I've tried to sleep, every night it becomes less and less possible. You, and you, and you are between me and any rest; but out of your arms there is no rest. Life, you called me, and fire. I flame and am consumed. Dick, it's not possible to live like this. When it's all over you must take your own. You must venture – is it I who must breathe courage into you, my soldier? Before all the world, claim me and hold me for ever and ever. That's the only way it can be done. No: I don't permit an ultimatum; whatever you wish I shall do. But it will come to the same in the end. Do you think I can hide the blaze of that fire across half the world? or share you with any other?

And so the passion spilled on to the page, pleading, exhorting, imploring. 'The day shall be made light for you, and the night a glory,' and finally, 'If it's faith you think of, this is faithlessness – keep faith with love – Now listen – I won't write to you like this any more. Take this letter and lay it somewhere near your heart that the truth of it may bore its way into you through the long months of war. I've finished. If you love me, take me this way – if you only desire me for an hour, then have that hour, and I will have it and meet the bill ... and if you die, wait for me – I'm not afraid of that other crossing; I will come to you.'

And so, in the end, in her forty-seventh year and in the desperation of a longing she had not known in such intensity before, she turned, for the first and last time in her life, to the supernatural. His replies were guarded. His own wife had seen him off to the war tearfully, and had written that if anything happened to him she would kill herself. He wrote to her and to Gertrude as he made his way towards the Middle East. To the latter: 'As for your delightful letters, I have had, as you know, one batch – the [one] which contained the ultimatum – my dear, I have read it – God knows – but of that I cannot write.' And later: 'As to the things you say of some future in far off places, they are dreams, dream woman – we must walk along the road – such heavenly madness is for gods and poets – not for us, except in lovely dreams.'

On April 20th, another letter:

> My dear, Tonight I pack up all your letters and leave them addressed to you ... Tomorrow, if the weather moderates, I am embarking on a collier, the 'wreck ship', or wooden horse of Troy – which we are going to run on the beach and disembark by an ingenious arrangement ... If I can get ashore, I can help a good deal in the difficult job of landing enough troops to storm the trenches on the beach – and to see the most dashing military exploit that has been performed for a very long time ...

The next day, as he was due to embark, there was a brief, affectionate note with a suspicion of presentiment: 'So many memories my dear queen, of you and your splendid love and your kisses and your courage and the wonderful letters you wrote me, from your heart to mine – the letters, some of which I have packed up, like drops of blood.' Now the passion was as much his as hers, and promises made in the heat of the moment looked only too likely to be fulfilled:

> My dear, don't (this is what weighs me down) don't do what you talked of – it's horrible to me to think of it – that's why I told you about my wife [her threatened suicide] – how much more for you – don't do anything so unworthy of so free and brave a spirit. One must walk along the road to the end of it. When I asked for this ship, my joy in it was half strangled by that thing you said, I can't even name it or talk about it. As we go steaming in under the port guns in our rotten old collier, shall I still think of it ... Don't do it. Time is nothing, we join up again, but to hurry the pace is unworthy of us all.

And finally the answer to the question which must spring irresistibly to mind:

Was it perhaps some subtle spirit of foreknowledge that kept us apart in London? As I go now I am sorry and glad, but on the whole glad – the risk to you was too great – the risk to your body, and to your peace of mind and pride of soul ... I must stop. Now, as I write, I know also that you will do nothing to yourself. Peace be upon you; for you have still the garden and the trees to walk under, where there is nothing but peace and understanding ... *Ave valeque*.

The rest is history. The story of the carnage of Gallipoli, the harvest of Churchill's insistence and Kitchener's vacillation, has been told time and again. And no story of gallantry among all the gallant acts of those days in April 1915 outshines that of Lt-Colonel 'Dick' Doughty-Wylie, as he led his Australian troops from the wreck-ship *River Clyde*, jumping on to the backs of dead men as they landed, to make the final assault on the old Turkish fort at Hill 141 under heavy artillery fire. He was shot through the head at the moment of victory as the Turks ran away and his men stood and cheered him. His last request was said to have been that someone tell the authorities of the bravery of the Royal Navy Commander Unwin and the boy Drewry. In the late afternoon of April 29th his body lay stretched out on the beach. They buried him where he was and Lt-Colonel Williams said the Lord's Prayer over his grave and bade him farewell.

He had won the highest commendation of the Ottoman Empire for his initiative and bravery during the Armenian massacres. His own countrymen awarded him the Victoria Cross posthumously. It is said that Gertrude was at dinner with friends when she heard the news and that she concealed her anguish. But in the days and weeks that followed she was numbed and inconsolable, though she found comfort in the calm and affectionate attendance of her sister Elsa, whose good sense, reinforced perhaps by Gertrude's own fundamental atheism which precluded any serious hope of reunion in an afterlife, prevented the suicide that she threatened before and after Doughty-Wylie's death.

There was a strange aftermath to the story of heroism which marked the death of one of the bravest of British soldiers and which so affected the lives of two remarkable women. His wife Lilian, or Judith, a member of the Union des Dames Françaises, and a nurse at St Valéry-sur-Somme at the time that Gertrude was in France, wrote in her diary: 'The shock was terrible. I don't quite know what I did for the first sixty seconds. Something seemed to tear at the region of my heart. All my life was so much of his life, all his life mine. I suppose I shall have to pick up the pieces ... just a lonely widow ... '

On November 17th a woman is said to have landed at Gallipoli and laid a wreath on his grave. Though hostilities were still in progress the Turks 'fired neither bullet nor shell' during the ceremony, according to the report of two British naval officers who said they witnessed the event. Gertrude boarded a troopship on that very day, bound for Cairo. Doughty-Wylie's ghostly dream seems to have pursued him beyond the grave.

Field-Marshal Lord Kitchener, when he was British Resident in Cairo before the outbreak of war, had engaged in secret talks with Abdullah the son of Husain the Sharif of Mecca, the exact details of which were never disclosed, though it is known that Abdullah sounded out the Resident on Britain's attitude should the Arabs rebel against their Turkish overlords. Kitchener, the leonine, imperious bachelor on whom an ill-prepared British Empire looked as saviour and guide in the war, had been a law unto himself in Cairo. Succeeding Sir Eldon Gorst but inheriting Cromer's mantle he was virtually the ruler of that country whose importance to the Powers lay not in itself but in the Suez Canal which divided it from Sinai and the Arabian peninsula and provided access from the Mediterranean to the Red Sea. Great though his power in Egypt was, Kitchener regarded it as a second-best prize for his valiant work in the Boer War and other notable campaigns of the British army. He had expected to be made Viceroy of India after Curzon with whom he fought an unceasing and vitriolic battle during his time as Commander-in-Chief of the Indian army; it is said that he even built himself a private residence in Simla to await his return. But he was offered Cairo and he made do with it. From his vantage point at the north of the Arabian peninsula he set out to devise an 'Islamic' policy of his own in total disregard of all the schemes of the Indian Government connected with Arab lands, and he gathered round him a group of admiring assistants of whom the chief were 'Fitz', Colonel Oswald Fitzgerald his devoted Secretary, and Ronald Storrs his Oriental Secretary. When war was imminent in the summer of 1914 Kitchener was home on leave. As soon as a declaration of hostilities seemed inevitable he decided to hurry back to Cairo but was intercepted at Dover where a telephone message from the Prime Minister was delivered asking him to return to London. His appointment as War Minister followed. Sir Henry McMahon the Foreign Secretary to the Government of India, who was also in England at the time, was appointed to Cairo as Resident in his stead. Kitchener was not pleased by his detention in London and it is said that he spent some time at the Foreign Office discussing Egyptian affairs, before being called to a private meeting at 10 Downing Street on August 5th to be told that he was summoned to join the Government. Before he left for Dover a few days earlier he had let it be known that he still wanted to be Viceroy of India. In 1910, when Hardinge's predecessor Lord Minto was seriously ill, the King was said to be 'violently in favour of sending Kitchener back'. Lord Morley, the Secretary of State, refused the King's wish as Kitchener 'had become hopelessly idle'. But the old soldier's popularity with the British public was such that his claims could not be denied in war. In the first month of his vitally important job as War Minister he meddled constantly in Arabian and Egyptian matters, and it was a telegram of his on September 24th, 1914 to the Residency in Cairo which began a chain of events that was to cause interminable rivalries among the allied powers, realignment of loyalties among the Arabs, and the making and breaking of promises on a heroic scale. His message referred to an intelligence report of September 6th regarding the attitude of Husain the Sharif of Mecca, and went on: 'Tell Storrs to send secret and carefully chosen messenger from me to Sharif Abdullah to ascertain whether should present armed German influence at Constantinople coerce Caliph against his will, and Sublime Porte to acts of aggression and war against Great Britain, he and his father and Arabs of Hijaz would be with us or against us.'

The reply came more than a month later, on October 31st. It said that the messenger had returned from Mecca and that Abdullah's response was 'guarded, but friendly and favourable', and that he desired a closer understanding with Britain. Lord Kitchener was reminded that the message only repeated proposals made to His Majesty's Agency on January 8th, when he had met Abdullah in Cairo. There was also reference to a private conversation with the messenger, Muhammad Farouki, in the course of which he is alleged to have said, 'Stretch out to us a helping hand and we will never aid these oppressors'. On the day that

Abdullah's message was received, Kitchener sent another telegram:

> Lord Kitchener's salaam to the Sharif Abdullah. Germany has bought the Turkish Government with gold, notwithstanding that England, France and Russia guaranteed the integrity of the Ottoman Empire if it remained neutral in this war. The Turkish Government have against the wish of the Sultan through German pressure committed acts of war by invading the frontiers of Egypt ... If the Arab nation assist England in this war that has been forced on us by Turkey, England will guarantee that no internal intervention takes place in Arabia and will give the Arabs every assistance against external foreign aggression. It may be that an Arab of the true race will assume the Caliphate at Mecca or Medina and so good may come by the help of God out of all the evil which is now occurring.

Kitchener's message was delivered five days before Turkey came into the war. It made the first reference in an official document to the 'Arab Nation', an idea foreign to every Arab except perhaps the ambitious Sharif of Mecca; it implied a promise of the Caliphate which had nothing whatever to do with Britain; and it marked the beginning of negotiations which were to go on for eighteen months until the Sharif of Mecca believed himself to be, and called himself, the 'King of the Arab Lands', and until he and his sons had been promised virtually the entire peninsula.

In 1936, Gertrude's most distinguished successor among women travellers in Arabia, Freya Stark, wrote to Venetia Buddicom: 'A publisher asks if I will write a life of Gertrude Bell. I don't know what to say. I don't know if I want to write anything; on the other hand I should like to get all that Eastern Arab history clear in my own mind. I am not very fascinated by her as a woman ... ' Her desire to clarify her view of eastern Arabian politics would have met with formidable difficulties at that time, when none of the official documents were available. Even since those documents – or most of them – have become available, many a noted historian has tried to find his way through that labyrinth of opinions, myths and legends, and outright lies, and has had to admit in the end that he has been dealing not so much with fact as with romance. At least we now have access to some of the bricks from which that cosmic castle of Britain's Arab policy was constructed. We know that if Kitchener was its architect, Sir Mark Sykes, that 'bundle of prejudices', the *enfant terrible* of Gertrude's far-off and carefree journeys in Syria and the Levant, was its mason. They had, incidentally, repaired their relationship following meetings in Constantinople and England at the time of the Balkan War of 1912.

In November 1915 Gertrude wrote to her father: 'Captain Hall [Director of Naval Intelligence] sent for me this morning and told me that Cairo had cabled that they would like me to come out. Further moves depend on them, but at least, he says, I shall be on the spot and ready to go. I'm taking all my kit; he quite agrees that it is as well to be prepared. You will be up, won't you, before I go? I know mother is coming on Tuesday. They pay my travelling expenses and give me my billeting allowance. I think I'm justified in accepting that, don't you?' A few days later, she was on the P & O ship *Arabia* off Marseilles. 'Dearest Father, I spent some hours ... hanging about the quay – hours not very much cushioned by making the acquaintance of the Bishop of Jerusalem and his wife ... The ship is crowded – innumerable women and babies. If I had babies I don't think I would take them travelling about at this juncture.'

The events of the past year had not left her without scars, but here was a new and absorbing task to occupy her and she grabbed at it. Her concern now was for Maurice, who had been in France with his Territorial unit almost since the start of hostilities. On November 30th she arrived in Cairo where she was met by Hogarth and Captain Lawrence and taken to the Grand Continental Hotel where they were all three billeted. On the day of her arrival she wrote: 'Dearest Mother, I telegraphed you this morning after my arrival and asked you to send out by Lady B. another gown and shirt. It looks as if I might be kept here some time ... I have not yet been to see the McMahons but I must leave a card on them today. For the moment I am helping Mr Hogarth to fill in the intelligence files with information as to the tribes and shaikhs. It's great fun and delightful to be working with him. Our chief is Colonel Clayton whom I like very much. This week Mark Sykes passed through and I have seen a good deal of him ... We reached Port Said after dark on Thursday night. Captain Hall, the brother of our Captain Hall (he is head of the Railway here) made every possible arrangement for my

comfort and Captain Woolley, ex-digger at Carchemish and head
of the Intelligence Department at Port Said came on board to
meet me. Next morning I came up here. Mr Hogarth and Mr
Lawrence (you don't know him, he was also at Carchemish,
exceedingly intelligent) met me and brought me to this hotel ...
Mr Hogarth, Mr Lawrence and I all dined together; at our table
sit two Engineers, Col. Wright (brother of Hagberg) and very
nice and Major Pearson. Occasionally we have Mr Graves into
dinner—he was *Times* Correspondent in Constantinople in
former days. I knew him there. Now you have my circle ... ' One
of her first encounters in Cairo was with Lady Anne Blunt, her
famous predecessor at Hail, at her stables outside the city. She
also ran into her cousin Liz Lascelles. Hogarth was due to return
to London in a week's time, 'which will leave a terrible gap'. On
December 7th she wrote to her father, 'I was so glad to have M's
[Maurice's] letter bless him! ... He is back by now in France ...
one looks on and half despairs of an end to it. But perhaps, after
all, the end will someday come with a rush and take us all by
surprise ... Mr Hogarth will come and see you when you are in
London and give you news of me ... '

While Gertrude was working at her assessment of the Arab
tribes her friends in Cairo were in almost hourly communication
with London. On December 13th Lt-Colonel Gilbert Clayton,
the director of Civil and Military Intelligence in Cairo, wrote to
Sykes: ' ... I hope you have been able to do some useful work in
forwarding the various projects which we are agreed upon as
advisable ... I have already started the nucleus of a Near East
Office, but so far I am confining myself to making it deal with
political suspects of all kinds, and pan-Islamic propaganda ...
Hennessy and Philip Graves are working at this at present, and I
am only waiting to hear from you, and to get another man or
two, to expand it ... ' Sykes replied in characteristic vein:

My dear Clayton. I am delighted to do anything to get the
closest co-ordination between all our intelligence. I am entirely
at your service in this matter ... I propose, if you concur, that
Hogarth shall come out again in January, as soon as he has got
his notes in order for printing. The WO and ourselves [Foreign
Office] are pooling our Intelligence ... By yesterday's telegram
from C-in-C East Indies, Admiral Peirse, I see he has appointed
Lt-Cdr Mansell to work on staff of GOC Egypt. I am writing

to Admiral Peirse again to suggest that Mansell shall work
with you. He is a very able fellow ... I shall feel happy if he is
working in your office, because I am not going to send you a
rotter ... I had a delightful letter from Miss Bell. She is
evidently perfectly happy in Cairo.

With that letter Sykes enclosed a draft of the proposed functions
of an 'Arabian Bureau'. They were: first, to harmonise British
political activity in the north-east of the Arabian peninsula, and
to keep the Foreign and India Offices, the Admiralty, War Office
and Government of India simultaneously informed of the general
tendency of German and Turkish policies. Second, to co-ordinate
propaganda in favour of Great Britain among non-Indian
Muslims, 'without clashing with the susceptibilities of Indian
Muslims and the Entente powers.' The head of the Bureau was to
be Sir Mark Sykes and his deputy, Lt-Col. Parker. An officer was
to be appointed to tour the Persian Gulf and visit prisoners of
war in India, and to transmit any information gleaned through
the Chief Political Officer in Mesopotamia, Sir Percy Cox. On
December 28th Sykes again telegraphed to Clayton: 'In my view
and Fitzgerald's FO should run Bureau at least nominally ... The
WO, FO and IO are slow and the Admiralty has barged in and
seized me and the Bureau ... The Admiralty want to annex the
Bureau as part of their network and keep me in an office in
London ... The merit of the Admiralty is that it alone achieves
anything, has large funds and does things.' At the same time
Sykes wrote: 'Basra: when we have settled into our stride try
and gently get a giver and receiver.' Native agents were to be
recruited in Karak, Mecca, Madina, Damascus and the Hauran
desert. The Bureau men in Cairo had already formed themselves
into an organisation with its own office and telegraphic address –
appropriately enough they chose the code name 'Intrusive' – and
were in the process of establishing their own espionage network
separately from that of new G.O.C.-in-Chief, General Sir
Archibald Murray, who so far knew little of these proceedings,
though he was suspicious and by no means happy with what was
going on around him.

On January 1st, 1916 the Foreign Office cabled Clayton, still
officially the military intelligence chief under Murray: 'Do you
consider any existing organisation would be hampered by
Bureau?' Clayton replied, through the Resident McMahon, that

M

the organisation must be in Egypt and 'under the control of His Excellency the High Commissioner, but endowed with a considerable measure of independence'. On January 6th, the Prime Minister asked for an Interdepartmental Committee to sit urgently to consider the formation of an 'Islamic Bureau', and it met under the chairmanship of the Director of Military Intelligence, Brigadier-General G. M. W. Macdonogh. It was agreed at that meeting that Sykes's original objectives were satisfactory and that the organisation should be called the 'Arab Bureau'. On the 20th of the month, Lord Kitchener's secretary Colonel Fitzgerald wrote to Clayton: 'Many thanks for your letter of 28 December, and all its news, which was interesting to both Lord K and myself ... India has been very suspicious but Herschell [Hirtzel], who was the IO representative of the Inter-Departmental Committee, is sympathetic, and will put it to India in such a way that I do not think we shall have any trouble from them in the future.' While all this was going on Sykes was engaged with M. Georges Picot of France in negotiating an agreement which divided Ottoman Asia into mandates and spheres of influence.

Chirol was in India as the correspondent of *The Times*, and on January 16th Gertrude wrote to her father: 'I rather hope that I may hear this week from Domnul in reply to a cable I sent him saying I might come out to India at the end of the month. My chief here is warmly in favour of the idea.' On January 24th: 'I can't write through censors and I must therefore send you a private word by bag enclosed to the Hogarths to tell you what I am doing – it is of course only for Mother and Maurice ... When I got Lord H's message through Domnul I suggested that it might be a good plan if I, a quite unimportant and unofficial person, were to take advantage of the Viceroy's invitation and go out to see what could be done by putting this side of the case before them ... ' The next day to her mother: 'The news about Maurice filled me with such immense relief ... The knowledge that he is safely at home makes me feel indifferent as to going to India which did seem a fearfully long way from home ... Anyhow I think I ought to go and that's an end. I have practically finished the Tribal book I have been doing as far as it can be finished here, but I look forward to getting a lot of fresh material in India ... '
She had summarised her work in Cairo and the drift of events in the East in a letter to Lord Robert Cecil, a month before. On December 20th she had written:

Dear Lord Robert, It is very nice to be able to write to you by
bag for otherwise I could talk of nothing but the weather and
my health, both of which are too good to call for any comment.
They have set me to work here on Arabia, tribes and geography.
There is nothing else to be done at this moment; we are
marking time, not very successfully, I fear, in Mesopotamia,
and waiting for the Turkish attack on the Canal. News from
Syria is lamentably scanty and when it comes not of a very
valuable kind. It looks as if they are going to tackle the
Mesopotamian expedition before they come here, and as far
as Egypt is concerned that is most fortunate, for until the last
three weeks no preparations had been made to meet them, and
the troops in this country were mostly details or raw and quite
incoherent masses of Australians. It is almost incredible that we
should have taken such a risk – quite incredible let us hope to
the enemy. The negotiations with the Sharif have, however,
been very skilfully conducted, and as long as we can keep him
in play there is no fear of a big religious movement. He is the
only person who can raise a *jehad*. The Turks, preaching at the
instigation of the Germans, are as little likely to carry conviction this year as they were last ... Meanwhile we are
hampered both by the French and by India as you know. The
Sharif has not shown himself unreasonable. We could probably
come to terms, but never on the basis of relinquishing the
whole of Syria – and the demands put forward recently by
Picot extended French Syria from the Mediterranean to the
Tigris. It would be wise to give the French a very long rope;
when they come to consider the administration of such a
Syria as that it is not improbable that they would find it a bigger
business then they were prepared to undertake. But the weaving
of long ropes takes time and it is time which is lacking. A
serious Arab movement, if it were once to be set on foot,
would turn them out of N. Africa just as easily as it would turn
us out of Egypt ... The weakness of the argument is that the
Arabs can't govern themselves – no one is more convinced of
that than I – and when they come to us for help and counsel
(as they will) the French will not regard it favourably. However, perhaps we need not look so far ahead ... As for the
India difficulty, the retreat in Mesopotamia may help to bring
the Indian Government into line. Mesopotamia is far less
complicated a question than Syria; it is decades behind Syria

in culture, and the Arab unionist movement has scarcely begun there. We shall not be able to annex either of the two provinces, Bastar or the Iraq, but no one will object to our administration there if it is not graduated through an Indian bureaucracy. Colonisation would have to be very carefully and delicately handled. I could write a great deal on that subject but I won't! ...

Gertrude's grasp of the political issues was amply shown in that letter, written only a month after joining the rudimentary Arab Bureau in Cairo. Equally, the contradictions which were to dog Britain and her allies in the peninsula for generations to come are not hard to detect. Lands were being apportioned which had never belonged to either Britain or France, and which did not exist in the Arab mind, for no Arab was a Syrian or Mesopotamian – he had never heard such names, being Damascene, or Beiruti or Aleppi perhaps, or a Shammari or Ruwelli, but never a 'national' in the Western sense. Britain, in any case, had yet to conquer the vilayets of the Ottoman Empire to which she and France attached convenient but meaningless labels. Gertrude departed as Hogarth returned to the scene, an honorary Lt-Commander in the Royal Navy, to take effective charge of the Bureau under Clayton's overall direction. Storrs remained in the background, fastidious in habit and choice of friends, conversing on art and classical music in Arabic and German and translating Husain's wordy communications into English. Lawrence, contemptuous of the military, was made a temporary captain in the army; and he was soon to be fitted up with Arab dress of pure silk, with gold-threaded *agal* and gilded sword, at the insistence of Faisal, son of the Sharif, at a cost, it is said, of £20,000. The desert was thick with messengers carrying demands for money and territory from the Sharif, and the Foreign Secretary asked McMahon to check the translation of a document on one occasion. Does he 'demand or request'? he asked. Graves, Newcombe, Dawnay, George Lloyd and others gathered around, and McMahon carried on his negotiations with the Sharif. During 1915, Hogarth had started to produce at frequent but irregular intervals a secret intelligence document called the *Arabian Report* which was issued by the Admiralty to carefully selected individuals in Government service. In February 1916, it became the *Arab Bulletin* and Gertrude made the first of a long and brilliant series of contributions to its pages.

Thus began the so-called Arab Awakening, which men in the mainstream of the war were to label 'a side show' and then, with redoubled scepticism, 'a side show of a side show'. Gertrude had picked up the stirrings of revolt years before and now she, Hogarth, Lawrence and the others set out to make them articulate. The word 'Liberty' had gone forth, as she had noted in her preface *Amurath to Amurath*, from printing presses made available by missionaries in Baghdad, Basra and Damascus:

> The sense of change, uneasy and bewildered, hung over the whole Ottoman Empire; it was rarely unalloyed with anxiety; there was, it must be admitted, little to encourage unqualified confidence in the immediate future. But one thing was certain; the moving Finger had inscribed a fresh title upon the page.

On December 7th the Cabinet had decided to order the final withdrawal from the Dardanelles. On January 1st she had written to Lady Bell: 'My dearest Mother, I wonder, if I could choose, whether I would not have the past year again, for the wonder it held, and bear the sorrow again. And dearest, not least of all the wonder would be your kindness and love, yours and Father's, bless him a thousand times. I can't write it off yet, but I ask myself what I should have done without it and find no answer. I don't speak of these things now; it's best to keep silence. But you know that they are always in my mind.' A few days later: 'Yes, the retreat from Gallipoli was wonderful. It doesn't bear thinking about. But it was no good staying ... the folly and muddle of it all, and the vain courage.'

She was given three hours in which to pack for India and left aboard the troopship *Euripides* on January 28th, 1916. She arrived in Karachi on February 7th.

17
Oriental Secretary

Gertrude arrived in India at the nadir of the allies' fortunes in the war. The appalling casualty lists from the Western and Russian fronts and the tactical stalemate of the European campaigns gave the public of the allied powers no hint of relief from their sacrifices. Now the Dardanelles were closed and only the long Arctic route to Russia remained open. The great hero of the British public Lord Kitchener was in disgrace, having been told that the new Chief of the General Staff Sir William Robertson would henceforth have direct access to the Cabinet and War Committee and that he, Kitchener, would have no further say in strategic matters. Sir Henry McMahon carried on his negotiations with the wily Sharif of Mecca in an effort to raise an Arab rebellion in return for the stewardship of practically all Arabia and a sum of £225,000 a month from Britain. In Mesopotamia, the capture of Basra, the advance through marsh and swamp to Nasiriyah on the Euphrates and Amara on the Tigris, and the capture of Kut-al-Amara, the little township in a bend of the Tigris about 300 miles from Basra, had provided the only comfort for Press and public of the Allied Powers in 1915. The commander of the assault on Kut, General Sir Charles V. F. Townshend, issued a statement on September 28th, 1915 which said: 'The battle of Kut-al-Amara may be said to be one of the most important in the history of the British army in India.' There had, he said, been 'nothing of its magnitude either in the Afghan War or the Mutiny', for it was fought against troops 'equally well armed and of equal numbers to ourselves'. His remarks were reported gleefully and gratefully, and the high command began to entertain a grander strategy in Mesopotamia. The Turks were in retreat. Baghdad, showpiece of the second Arab Empire, a name which rang a bell everywhere in the world, was the prize to which they turned their attention. Townshend was a keen student of military history and he came to Mesopotamia in the footsteps of one of his heroes, Belisarius who delivered Rome from the Barbarians, and Ctesiphon from the Persians in A.D. 541. 'It was evident to me that Sir John Nixon [Commander-in-Chief of Indian Expeditionary Force 'D' in succession to General Sir Arthur Barrett] intended to make a dash for Baghdad with my present inadequate force,' wrote Townshend. Intelligence at Cairo and London reported meanwhile that Enver Pasha had reinforced the Turkish army with units of the famous Constantinople Fire Brigade force and that a new commander had arrived at Baghdad, Nureddin Pasha. And so in November the army pushed on to Ctesiphon, virtually to the gates of Baghdad. The Indian army could afford 9,000 troops for the exercise. The German High Command estimated that 90,000 would have been needed to ensure success. Some 8,500 British and Indian soldiers, with bayonets fixed, drove a superior enemy force before them and captured the ancient fortress. 'The Indian battalions were composed in great part of raw recruits. I am not surprised that the press at home called them the *Invincibles*', wrote their commander in his diary. 'I am perfectly convinced that no body of men ever had harder fighting, be it in the Peninsular Wars, the Crimea or even ... France or Gallipoli.' Those men, the Dorsets, the Mahrattas and Punjabis, had fought for a year in the swamps and marshes of southern Mesopotamia, often at temperatures of 113 degrees in the shade. Horses had died by the hundred from sheer physical exhaustion. Now came the counter-attack. Another 4,500 men died on the long retreat back to Kut-al-Amara where Townshend thought he would find shelter. Instead, a brave, weary army found itself trapped. By the time Gertrude arrived in India, the General and his men at Kut had begun to face the longest, the most courageous and the most humiliating siege in the history of the British army.

'We reached Karachi on 6th [February 1916] and I'm cabling to Domnul to let him know,' she told her father. She was asked to talk to the officers of the Rifle Corps on Mesopotamia, and to the troops 'about anything'. 'Poor dears, I shall love to do anything to amuse them.' She went to see the new Delhi, revived as the capital city of the Raj in India after George V's Durbar of 1912, touring the city with the Viceroy and the architect Lutyens. She also saw a good deal of Domnul; '... there was Domnul on the platform and a Vice-Regal motor waiting outside. You may imagine my joy!' But most of her stay in India was taken up with an attempt to allay Lord Hardinge's misgivings about the activities of the Arab Bureau. He had already been told that the Bureau intended to set up a branch office in Basra. Indeed, three officers of the body were already making plans to go there on one of the most extraordinary missions of the war – Admiral Rosslyn Wemyss, now in command of the Red Sea Fleet and an enthusiastic supporter of the schemes of the Bureau, Aubrey Herbert and T. E. Lawrence. A hard-pressed Sir Percy Cox had already had a visit from Storrs's Circassian friend and the chief rival of Enver Pasha for the leadership of the Young Turks, Aziz al Masri; having failed in his battle with Enver, al Masri came over to the Allies' side and lived in the shade of the Residency at Cairo, but he was not well received in Basra. The Viceroy had from the beginning insisted that he wanted no part of the Arab Bureau's plans, that he did not approve of its personnel, and that anything it did or attempted to do was almost certain to cause trouble among the millions of Muslim subjects in the sub-continent. India had a special difficulty in this connection. Its Muslim population was almost entirely of the orthodox Sunni persuasion which was upheld, even if it was not dignified, by the Sultan in his position as Caliph of Islam. Unlike the Shia of Persia and, in the main, of Mesopotamia, the Sunnis of India had no quarrel with their Caliph and were not keen to fight against the Turkish army. Their reluctance was of a very human nature. They knew that if they went away to fight against the Turks their village priests would condemn their action so that when they came home they would be unable to find a place in the community, shunned by their elders and prospective wives. Yet, in the end, they fought and distinguished themselves on the battlefields of France and Mesopotamia. Lord Hardinge had warned, however, that if anyone was foolish enough, for example, to bombard the coastal regions of the Holy Hijaz, he might well have a revolution on his hands. That was the essence of his message to Gertrude. If he was presented with a *fait accompli*, however, what about Gertrude herself taking on the job of Arab Bureau representative in Basra? He could trust her, or at any rate his successor designate Lord Chelmsford could, for he was to retire in two months' time. Gertrude was not keen on the idea initially. She had looked forward

to returning to Cairo, to that intellectual elite of the Grand
Continental Hotel which she found so congenial. She does not
seem to have needed too much persuasion, however.

Two letters of the time exemplify the argument that was going
on between Cairo, London and India. On November 3rd, 1915
Aubrey Herbert, back in London from his visit to Basra, wrote
to Clayton in Cairo: 'My dear Colonel, I got back here four days
ago ... I have seen Eric Drummond, Nicolson and George
Clarke ... Also Gabriel and Fitz. Lord Lansdowne has told me to
see him. Tomorrow I hope to see Grey ... FO have got pretty
cold feet ... They trust Egypt with the running of the Arabian
Question. They realise that Arabia ought to fall under Egypt and
not under the India Office ... One of the difficulties lies with the
Government of India, as you know ...' Herbert ended his note
with a colourful observation: 'There is one thing I ought to tell
you about the FO. They have been pretty hard taskmasters in the
past and unjust to their servants ... Now, however, after this
muddle, they are ready to give a much freer hand in many parts.'

On November 28th, 1915 Lord Hardinge had written to
Wingate, following a note he had received on the 'second mission'
of Arab Bureau officers to the Sharif on November 1st:

> My dear General. The principal objection which I have to the
> memorandum is contained in the translation of a note on the
> boundaries, where the limits of the proposed Arab state are on
> the east to be the Persian frontier to the Gulf of Basra, and
> thence to the Indian Ocean. This means the surrender of all the
> advantages for which India has been fighting in Mesopotamia
> during the past year and the creation of an Arab state lying
> aside our interests in the Persian Gulf, which would mean
> commercial ruin for many of our undertakings, and probably
> chaos in those provinces. Moreover, what appears not to have
> been realised is that two thirds of the population in Baghdad
> and Basra are Shias, and the Shia holy places of Karbala and
> Nejef are in the province of Baghdad and have no connection
> whatever with Mecca or the Sharif thereof.

After dealing with the religious aspects of the matter, Lord
Hardinge, in one of the most revealing and sensible letters in this
long-drawn-out dispute, went on to say that Wingate and his
colleagues could try to help the Sharif if they wanted to, but that
India should not be asked to make sacrifices for Arabs who 'have

been fighting against us the whole time and have no claim whatever upon us. I cannot tell you how strongly I feel upon this point.'
Then:

> ... these expeditions, to East Africa, Mesopotamia, Dardan-
> elles, Salonika, and elsewhere ... are all blunders. The war will
> not be won in any of these outlying spots, but in Flanders, and
> it is there that we should have concentrated all our strength in
> order to give the Germans a smashing blow at the earliest
> possible date ... All these diversions mean weakness in the main
> theatre, and it seems to me we have been outwitted by Germany
> and are literally playing her game ... Hardinge of Penshurst.

The Viceroy's view was shared at this stage by the Prime Minister,
the C.I.G.S., and a majority of the Cabinet. While Gertrude was
staying at Vice-Regal Lodge, Hardinge sent a secret telegram to
London: 'We agree scheme as detailed in papers received. We
understand Political Officers will not be called on to act at dicta-
tion of Bureau and that we shall receive copies of important
papers issued and received in this connection. I propose to
depute Mr A. B. Fforde, Indian Civil Service, to represent Indian
Government.' Gertrude seems to have carried out her mission with
some skill, since two months before the Viceroy had told the
Secretary of State, Austen Chamberlain, that he was entirely
opposed to selecting a liaison officer in India or Mesopotamia.
He would be dangerous 'unless under close control'. In the meantime, Gertrude had agreed to go to Basra, if not to stay, at least
to keep a temporary eye on the Bureau. 'I've just come in from
another dinner at Vice-Regal Lodge. At the beginning of dinner
the V. sent me a scribbled card to say that it was all settled about
my going ... It is interesting, deeply interesting, but oh, it's an
anxious job. I wish, I wish, I knew more – and was more. And
I am overwhelmed at meeting with so much kindness and
confidence.' It was agreed that Mr A. Brownlow Fforde should
be paid as though he were a first-grade magistrate and revenue
collector in India, and his appointment was confirmed by Sykes.
He arrived at the Grand Continental, Cairo, in March where nobody wished to have anything to do with him or to provide him
with useful work. He spent the entire war from then on in a
running fight with the India Office over his pay – 'I hope you will
defeat the financial purist who wishes to reduce my pay by one
third,' he told the Permanent Under-Secretary on 20th March –

and in wandering around the suqs and bars of Cairo where he accidentally uncovered one of the boldest German espionage missions of the war.

Gertrude left India for Basra on March 1st, 1916. Before departing she wrote a note to Captain Hall at the Admiralty, anticipating her arrival: 'Before I came to Basra I remember your putting your finger on the Baghdad corner of the map and saying that the ultimate success of the war depended on what we did there. You are one of the people who realised how serious are the questions we have to face ... I have had a most useful fortnight here ... I have got on terms of understanding with the Indian FO, and the ID [Intelligence Department]. It is essential that India and Egypt should keep in the closest touch since they are dealing with two sides of the same problem ... '

On March 3rd she wrote to her father: 'We are within half an hour of Basra. I've come on a transport ... steaming up the river all the morning through a familiar landscape of palm grove and Arab huts, with apricot trees blooming ... I wish I knew how Maurice is and were certain that he is not going back to France yet.' She stayed for the first two weeks with Sir Percy and Lady Cox, and was soon engaged in a hectic round of activity. 'I'm still with the Coxes, but I only dine, sleep and breakfast here – for I go to lunch next door to GHQ ... I went to the Intelligence Department this morning, saw Colonel Beach who is at the head of it, and Captain Campbell Thompson whom I had known when he was an archaeologist ... I'm now looking for a servant. It's delicious weather ... muddy, stagnant creeks and crowds of Arabs – but I like it! ... I dined last night with some American missionaries called Van Ess. I also saw Mr Dobbs. He is now a Political Officer here ... the Head of the Revenue Office and so has been brought into very close knowledge of all the Turkish system ... I am still with the good Coxes. Sir Percy is most charming, well read and interesting and a really considerable politician ... I walked with ... a nice and intelligent young man called Bullard who was for a long time at the Embassy at C'ple. We walked right out of the palm groves into the desert the first time I had seen it for two years ... The hasty recall of General Aylmer is sufficient comment of recent events here. Heaven send someone more competent to command, otherwise I see no chance of advance until the Russians clear the way for us – not a satisfactory thought.'

In April she wrote to her stepmother: 'I'm thankful to hear that Maurice won't be fit to go on active service for another month ... I notice now that there is an attempt on the part of the Government to shuffle the blame for the reverses here entirely on the shoulder of the Generals in Mesopotamia, whereas everyone knows that they were ordered to advance from home beyond all gainsaying. If only we can make a success of Kut ... We are still in the middle of our battle which has been interrupted by rain and wind and floods. It's more an aquatic achievement than a military one out here, and rain immobilises everyone. You can't move for mud. How Kut holds out still I can barely guess.'

On April 11th, Sir Arthur Hirtzel, director of the Political and Secret Department of the India Office, minuted a message to the Viceroy:

> I do not like the idea of another Bureau in Mesopotamia, but it is perhaps best to leave GOC to make his own arrangements, on the clear understanding that he is to work in subordinate co-ordination with, and not on equal terms with, the Bureau in Cairo.

On April 26th the Viceroy cabled back:

> Please explain precise purport of your words ... I confess I do not understand exact status of Mesopotamian branch of Bureau. Cox is I understand working in perfect harmony with Hogarth. Major Blaker has been appointed special liaison officer by GOC Force 'D', but there are apparently other officers e.g. Lawrence, who have been sent to Mesopotamia with special instructions of which we are unaware. I should be glad to have information of names of all such officers sent and the nature of their instructions ... To obviate confusion, suggest that Blaker and all other officers with special political instructions should be considered under Cox ...

The stranded soldiers at Kut had been under siege now for five months. The German General Von der Goltz had just taken charge of the enemy force and he squeezed the British troops with native thoroughness. Since December, when General Townshend at the head of the retreating army watched his men file past him, hunger had gradually added its grim effect to the exhaustion from which the men suffered on arrival. 'As I watched the exhausted troops dragging themselves by me — for it could hardly be called marching — past the line of block-houses into Kut, I thought of what Jomini had said of retreats: *Courage and firmness in adversity is more honourable than enthusiasm in success*,' wrote their commander.

Now, after months of waiting for relief which never came, all their food was gone. Every animal in the force had been slaughtered to feed the dying soldiers and civilians locked in the town, despite Townshend's assertion early in the siege that there was food enough for the town's population — five to six thousand householders — and the army, for three months. As they faced rain and cold and daily shelling by the enemy, the troops were forced to go out into the fields to search for berries and some chose poisonous fruit to hasten their deaths. The villagers too turned to the berries for survival and the trees were soon practically bare. In December Townshend had tried to turn the villagers from their homes but Cox interceded on their behalf and in the end only 700 or so tribesmen and strangers were sent out to find their way through the Turkish lines. Many of the soldiers, determined that the children should not die unnecessarily, gave them the last of the berries. But the fears of Lord Hardinge began to be realised. The Indian troops who had fought so bravely though they had no quarrel with the enemy they were sent to fight, starving and hardly able to walk, began to desert to the Turkish lines. Others shot off their trigger fingers to avoid combat. Those who were caught were brought back and shot on Townshend's order as an example to the others. Yet at another stage of the siege an officer on watch saw General Von der Goltz inspecting his troops and shot at him from his roof-top vantage point. 'I was angry,' wrote Townshend, 'for he is one of the finest military strategists in Europe.' Aylmer had taken six weeks in preparing to relieve the beleaguered army. In March he had suffered many casualties, and Townshend told his men that the attempt to relieve them had failed. The Turkish commander Khalil Pasha asked them to surrender as they had no further chance of rescue. As they were decimated by hunger and disease the men heard by field radio a Reuter report of a debate in the House of Lords, initiated by Lord Beresford, as to whether their commander had been consulted before the disastrous advance on Ctesiphon.

In mid-April Townshend was conducting the last rites of his command, writing to the Government of India an official note that his Hindu troops had eaten horseflesh only after receiving permission from the Pandits and their Maharaja and that 'therefore no stone should be cast at them'. There was a last-minute attempt to run the blockade of the river but it failed. By April 23rd they were ready to concede defeat.

It was at this point that Captain T. E. Lawrence and Aubrey Herbert appeared on the scene. Accustomed to carry bags of gold along the road from Cairo to the Hijaz in order to further the Arab rebellion, they came to Kut, on whose authority was never clear, to bribe the Turkish Commander and Von der Goltz into letting the prisoners go. Cox was horrified when he heard of the scheme and refused to be connected with it in any way. The fact that he did not turf Lawrence and Herbert out of the country when he heard about their plan can only argue that they had the backing of Whitehall.

The sum offered was £1 million. The enemy commanders replied that they were 'gentlemen' and could not be bribed. They were then offered £2 million, the balance to be paid at a later date. The answer was the same. On April 25th Townshend asked the permission of the Government to seek surrender terms. Admiral Wemyss as the senior officer present was consulted by radio and replied: 'With your prestige you are likely to get the best terms.' Khalil Pasha met Townshend aboard a Turkish patrol boat and demanded unconditional surrender. The British General asked for parole of his force. On the instructions of Enver Pasha this was refused. At the last Townshend was offered his own liberty if he did not destroy his arms and equipment, but he refused. On April 29th, before the radio was destroyed, a message was received from the naval force that had tried to relieve them: 'We, the officers and men of the Royal Navy, who have been associated with the Tigris Corps and have, many of us, so often worked with you and your gallant troops, desire to express our heartfelt regret at our inability to join hands with you and your comrades in Kut.' Townshend and his men spent the rest of the war in Turkey, where they were honourably confined.

On May 28th the new Viceroy, Lord Chelmsford, told London: 'You are I think aware that Captain Lawrence was recently deputed here temporarily from Egypt in connection with certain projects of which the Arab Bureau was one ... In view of modified aspect in which this institution is presented to us by Lawrence, I propose that Miss Gertrude Bell and not Major Blaker should act as corresponding officer for Mesopotamia. To this end I contemplate ... giving her definite official status by Force Routine Order and placing her services at Cox's disposal granting her a fixed allowance a month for them ... She is herself quite prepared prima facie to fall in with the arrangement.'

Next day Hirtzel entered a minute in the India Office records: 'Whole position of Arab Bureau and everything connected with it unsatisfactory. But Clayton being asked to come to London as soon as possible ... Miss Bell's knowledge is of course enormous.' The anger of the generals in Mesopotamia at the Bureau's foolish and provocative antics was at boiling point, and General Lake, latest of the army commanders there, telegraphed: 'I find it difficult to accept position implied without full discussion ... The experiment made in attempting to handle affairs in Iraq through Cairo without previously consulting us can hardly be regarded as fortunate ... During past few weeks the experience gained by one or two officers in Cairo who have paid visits here has I hope resulted in a considerable removal of wrong impressions.'

'Seem to be getting into a tangle,' wrote Hirtzel. Almost the same words were to be used by the Secretary of State Austen Chamberlain before he resigned his Cabinet post in the backlash of the Mesopotamian disasters and the Arab Revolt.

No sooner had Cox and the Generals got rid of Lawrence and Herbert than Lloyd appeared on the scene. At the moment of the Kut débâcle, he was in Basra making his own plans for the Bureau office there. He wrote to Wingate, now playing an increasingly important part in Bureau affairs, on May 27th:

My dear General,
I have delayed in writing to you until I had some time in which to size things up a little here, as owing to having missed Lawrence on my arrival here I had to begin rather in the dark. As regards the general situation here things are for the time at a standstill ... the Government of India seem to have been doubly cursed with a Commander in Chief with too little grip and a Finance Member called Mayer with too much ... The Turks have now retired on one bank of the river, probably because they have succeeded in giving us the knock they desired ...

Then to the Arab Bureau:

Cox has talked to me a good deal about this, and when I arrived I found him still not fully alive to the main objects of the thing ...

Shortly after my arrival he received a rather testy telegram
from India referring to L's visit and expressing some bewilder-
ment as to the status of the bureau ... He hinted that I should
become the bureau's correspondent here but I said at once
that I was not a good enough Arabic scholar ... He agreed to
this and I suggested that Gertrude Bell, who appears to be
determined to stay out here, should be the correspondent with
Blaker the nominal correspondent providing the necessary male
and military attributes ... Gertrude Bell seems to be the perfect
person for the job ... Sir Percy Cox agreed but said that the
correspondent ... if he had access to his information and
worked from his office would have to come under his control
to a certain extent. That is just the difficulty ... These fears all
seem to date from Mark's visit [Mark Sykes] who seems to
have been amazingly tactless, and not only to have rather
blustered everyone but also to have decried openly everything
Indian in a manner which was bound to cause some resent-
ment ... I think G.B. may be relied upon not to create difficulties. I have written to Deedes who will tell you of how my own
plans are shaping ...

On May 27th also, Gertrude wrote to her mother to tell her of the
excitement caused in Basra by news of the Russian advance into
Persia, and the fall of Erzerum. 'We have had in Basra 3 of the
Cossack officers who rode over the hills to Al Gharbi. They had
the time of their lives here.'

At Nasiriyah she stayed with Major Hamilton, the Political
Agent from Kuwait and heir to the barony of Belhaven and
Stenton. But she spent most of her time at the Euphrates town
with Captain G. F. Eadie 'who knows more about the tribes than
any man in Mesopotamia'. They worked every day from breakfast
to tea, riding together before they started work, often in the company of General Brooking. She wrote to Chirol: 'You don't know
how difficult my job is here; but I continue to be very glad to be
here. As for all the part that doesn't concern me, it is still out-
rageously bad. Insufficient ice, insufficient mosquito nets, insufficient rations at the front, a colossal, far-reaching insufficiency
and incompetence. Since the Crimea I don't think there has been
such a campaign.' She went on to Suq al Shuyakh, where she met
another 'charming' young Political Officer, C. J. Edmonds, 'as
clever as can be'.

She was now the official correspondent of the Bureau and the only woman who was formally part of the Expeditionary Force in Mesopotamia. She was shortly to become, in addition, Sir Percy Cox's Oriental Secretary, responsible for dealing with local notables and filtering them through to her chief. She undoubtedly found solace in her new work, a barrier against any too vivid a memory of recent events. But that apart, she was by nature a prodigious worker, and the dual task which confronted her was tailor made. Nobody was more capable of taking the bare bones of a contemporary happening and giving them historical flesh. She began to make the first of her major contributions to Hogarth's *Arab Bulletin*, now a regular fortnightly document, to assemble intelligence information from briefings with the army authorities and interviews with tribal shaikhs, to translate the Arabic correspondence of the office, and—as was to become her increasing habit—to take on tasks which some of her colleagues considered to be the proper preserve of the chief of the civil administration. One of the first jobs she undertook was to write to Ibn Rashid with a plea that he should preserve his neutrality. Her letter, written in May, according to a subsequent note to her parents, had little effect on that irresponsible and recalcitrant young man, which would not have surprised her or Cox if they had turned to the files in their own office in which Captain Shakespear and the former Resident Lorimer had warned that no good would ever come of trying to accommodate Ibn Rashid and to set him up as a counter to the ambitions of the rising star of the desert, Ibn Saud. 'We didn't succeed in roping in Ibn Rashid. Everything that could be done was done; he was forgiven seventy times seven, but he wouldn't listen to our piping ... He's ignorant and foolish beyond belief ... But it's not the immediate war problems here I think of most; it's the problems after the war, and I don't know what sort of hand we shall be able to take in solving them.' It is remarkable how much highly confidential information she was able to pass to her parents and to Chirol in those days of censorship; but the censor's pencil never held much fear for Gertrude, any more than did the conventions of Government service which at the very least frown on open criticism of superiors. The ever-present tragedy of the civil power in these early days of the Mesopotamian campaign was the deaths of Lt-Colonel Lorimer and Captain Shakespear in 1914 and 1915 respectively. Lorimer had been moved from Baghdad (where by virtue of the rising

N

authority of the Foreign Office in those regions he reported
through Constantinople to Sir Edward Grey) to Bushire, while
Cox went to Simla to take over Sir Henry McMahon's job as
Foreign Secretary there. Lorimer was killed in his office by a self-
inflicted shot through the head sustained, remarkably for so experienced a soldier, while cleaning his gun. As for the intrepid
Captain Shakespear, he had taken one look at the High Command
in Basra as he passed through on his way to meet Ibn Saud, and
decided that if he had to serve under them he would be court-
martialled within a week. Already he was a legendary figure
among the young officers and 'Politicals' who came to the area at
the beginning of the war. Without Lorimer or him, however,
there was nobody who was capable of dealing with Ibn Saud or
of coping effectively with the tribal leaders in and around lower
Mesopotamia. Captain Leachman, who had been appointed to
succeed Shakespear and who was now one of the political officers
on the spot, was the bravest of men, but irresponsible. He was
regarded as the most insubordinate of officers, and he attracted
the worst elements of the Arab community whom he cursed
roundly in his colourful dog-Arabic.

Thus Gertrude had to start virtually from scratch in her
assessments of the Arabs who could make or mar the work of the
administration. Not the least of the problems confronting it was
that of accommodating the ruler of Najd, whose influence with
the tribes was immense, without upsetting the vain and ambitious
Sharif of Mecca. At this stage Gertrude had not met the formidable Abdul Aziz bin Abdurrahman al Saud, but she had heard a
great deal about him and in response to repeated requests from
Hogarth she sent him for publication in March, soon after her
arrival, a sketch based on notes supplied by Dr Harrison of the
American Mission in Kuwait and Bahrain, who had been to
Riyadh to treat the Amir for a minor ailment at the end of 1915.
It was a naïve account. 'He possesses great personal charm, with
a ready and attractive smile. He is a great kingly-looking man
like an Assyrian picture. He says, seemingly with pride, that he
has been married 65 times; each wife lasts about three days; he
divorces each one, giving them to his shaikhs or to his ordinary
followers. In civil matters he shows unusual kindness and
patience; his internal policy is good and strong. His external
policy consists in flirting with the Sharif of Mecca, and in punish-
ing Ibn Rashid whenever he can. He is capable of doing so unless

Ibn Rashid gets in alien support ... When war broke out Ibn Saud sat on the fence. Captain Shakespear brought him back to our side but when Captain Shakespear was killed in a skirmish, Ibn Saud behaved badly and created the impression that he was unreliable... To his people he is quite a hero ...' There was reference to the influence of Shaikh Mubarak of Kuwait (who died in 1915) on the warrior of Najd, and a remarkably misleading statement to the effect that Ibn Saud had concluded a treaty with the Turks behind Mubarak's back. In compiling his account of these events in the *Bulletin* for March, Hogarth wrote:

> It is in the last degree undesirable that we should be drawn into Central Arabian politics. It should not be forgotten that of the two, the Sharif and Ibn Saud, Ibn Saud is 1) the less powerful potentate and 2) far less able to influence the present general Eastern situation in our favour. It is worth considering whether a similar treaty (to that signed by Cox and Ibn Saud in 1915) could be made with Ibn Rashid, the rival Amir of Jabal Shammar.

Some fundamental misconceptions of British policy in Arabia were demonstrated in that paragraph.

In the summer of 1916, just as Gertrude had organised her office at G.H.Q. to her satisfaction and had begun to settle in to her work and a new social existence, she was struck down by jaundice. She was back in circulation within two months, however. Among the closest of her early friendships was that with the Reverend John and Mrs Van Ess of the American Mission of the Dutch Reformed Church. Mrs Van Ess, in her account of the ripening friendship, wrote: 'Her first task was to organise all the available information about the tribes, and to compile a Gazetteer [bringing up to date Lorimer's earlier study of the Persian Gulf area]. John was very knowledgeable about tribal Iraqis from his extensive tours of the marshes and desert during his first term, and she constantly consulted him. Her erect figure, and her eager animated face crowned with grey hair, became familiar in our home, and her delightful human qualities, her sparkle and intelligence and zest for life, made her a most welcome companion.' Often when Mrs Van Ess came into her living room she found Gertrude and her husband sprawled on the floor, with maps and charts spread out around them and would compliment them on their goodness in praying together. John Van Ess was probably the best Arabist in the English community, with the possible exception of Mrs D. L. R. Lorimer, wife of the late Resident's brother. Mrs Lorimer became the first editor of the *Basra Times* when it was instituted by the British. Van Ess had compiled an Arabic grammar which Gertrude had read and she sent him one of the ditties such as she composed for the *Monthly Cousin* and the *Christmas Surprise*, compiled at Rounton each year for the amusement of family and friends:

> V is for Van Ess, he once wrote a book
> Perhaps you have seen it, or a copy you took,
> He deserves a gold medal, without any doubt,
> Not for what he put in but for what he left out.

Van Ess promptly composed a reply:

> G is for Gertrude, of the Arabs she's Queen,
> And that's why they call her Om el Mumineen,
> If she gets to Heaven (I'm sure I'll be there!)
> She'll ask even Allah 'What's your tribe, and where?'

Om el Mumineen. Mother of the Faithful. Gertrude acquired many designations among the Arabs, but the one by which she became best known was a peculiarly Iraqi form of address, *Al Khatun*. It is a word little used in other Arab territories and was translated by British officials as 'The Lady', but it really means 'a lady of the court' and has religious undertones. She was also called *Es-Sitt*, another Arab word for 'Lady'. Mrs Van Ess records one of Gertrude's earliest confrontations with a tribal leader. She was received none too cordially, Arabs at that time being unaccustomed to women inhabiting any sphere save the harem, but she put her case with the usual vigour. The Shaikh listened and when she had finished said to his followers:

> My brothers, you have heard what this woman has to say to us. She is only a woman, but y'Allah, she is a mighty and a valiant one. Now, we know that God has made all women inferior to men. If the women of the Angleez are like her, the men must be like lions in strength and valour. We had better make peace with them.

After Lawrence's visit to the front line in the spring he and Gertrude spent some time together in Basra and in May she took him to see the Van Esses. Even then he had the delicate, effete manner which made him such an oddity among the gregarious Arabs of the desert, physically repelled as he was even by the shaking of hands. 'He was an unimpressive young man at this time, and had very little influence on the Arabs of Iraq,' Mrs Van Ess wrote in her diary.

Two other acquaintances of this period were to help Gertrude over the dark days of her first year in the country, when the British army was trying to reorganise and to stabilise its position after the disaster of Kut. H. St John Philby, a young Political Officer just arrived in Basra to reinforce the civil side, proved welcome company with his keen and controversial mind, and both the Van Esses and Gertrude took to him immediately, though their friendship was to receive some hard tests as time went on. But Major Reader Bullard was perhaps her favourite among the Political Officers of the period. Gertrude found him a stimulating conversationalist and an agreeable companion on her early morning riding and swimming expeditions. As she approached her fifties she kept remarkably fit and must have looked some years younger than her actual age. In June 1916 a young officer stationed at Nasiriyah, John (later Sir John) Jardine wrote to his brother Lionel, himself a Political Officer in the post-war period: 'This evening we had a thrill. A Miss Gertrude Lothian [sic] Bell (41) came to tea with the C.O. She is to do Intelligence work here as she has travelled among the Arabs. A woman fairly knocked us over after 6 months. As she walked through the camp, the guard turned out by mistake and wept tears on their bayonets. I see a fool of a bishop has been preaching about sex hatred. He wouldn't find much of it in IEF "D". She wore a green hat and scarf, white blouse and fawn tussore skirt ... '

In the hot summer months she worked with fiendish energy compiling intelligence reports and information summaries, and contributing some brilliant articles to the *Arab Bulletin* which became popular reading-matter in high places. Among the dozens of intelligence reports she filed in her first few months there was an eye-witness account of the continuing atrocities against the Armenians, obtained from a captured Turkish soldier:

The battalion left Aleppo on 3 February and reached Ras-ul-Ain in twelve hours ... Some 12,000 Armenians were concentrated under the guardianship of some hundreds of Kurds, drawn not from the local tribes, but from the urban riff-raff of Mosul, Bitlis, and Diarbekir. These Kurds were called gendarmes, but were in reality mere butchers; bands of them were publicly ordered to take parties of Armenians, of both sexes, to various destinations, but had secret instructions to destroy the males, children and old women ... One of these gendarmes confessed to killing 100 Armenian men himself ... [they] were dying of typhus and dysentery, and the roads were littered with the decomposing bodies. The empty desert cisterns and caves were also filled with the corpses ... The Turkish officers of the battalion were horrified by the sights they saw, and the regimental chaplain (a Moslem divine) on coming across a number of bodies, dismounted his horse and publicly prayed that the Divine punishment of these crimes should be averted from Moslems, and by way of expiation, himself worked at digging three graves ... No man can ever think of a woman's body except as a matter of horror, instead of attraction, after Ras-ul-Ain ...

And while Gertrude worked at her routine tasks, her friends in Cairo were bringing the Arab Revolt to fruition. Even the army command, which had all along poured cold water on the schemes of the Bureau which most of them looked on as little more than a mischievous prank, now began to see at least one advantage in these costly antics. The rebellion of a few tribesmen in a part of the Ottoman Empire which was of no military or civil interest to Britain, since it already controlled the Red Sea, might not be of great significance in itself, but the propaganda value was obvious. It is difficult to say exactly when the Revolt started. On June 7th, Ronald Storrs interviewed the Sharif's youngest son Zaid near Jidda. He was told then that Zaid's brothers Faisal and Ali had attacked Madina on June 4th with the intention of cutting the Hijaz rail link. At that meeting Storrs was told that the Sharif himself would shortly attack the Turkish garrison in Mecca, while Abdullah would take Taif and a nephew would occupy Jidda. The Sharif's proclamation of the rebellion was dated June 5th and that is usually taken as the actual date.

In the name of God, the most merciful, the compassionate. O, Our Lord, judge between us and between our people in truth. Thou art the best of Judges ... To all our brother Moslems. It is well known that the first people who recognised the

Turkish Government amongst the Moslem Rulers and Emirs
were the Emirs of Mecca ...

There followed the announcement of the rising and the final
appeal to God 'who is our sufficient defender'. Thus began a
saga which was to infuriate the G.O.C.-in-Chief Egypt and the
Viceroy of India, help to discredit the British Government, cause
a rift among the allies, absorb millions of pounds of public money,
cause dissension among the most famous and reliable fighting
forces in British India, and find its way into the history books by
virtue of the English public's insatiable need for heroes as the
private war of an Englishman called 'Aurens', better known to
the Arabs as 'Abu Khayyal' or 'Father of the Shadow'.

It is not easy in retrospect to comprehend the activities of the
Arab Bureau opposed, as they were, by the Prime Minister, the
Secretary of State for India, the Viceroy, the Chief of the Imperial
General Staff and, not least, the G.O.C.-in-Chief Egypt. Yet
junior officers in the Bureau's service were able to wander freely
around the Middle East with inexhaustible supplies of money, in
defiance of generals and in open contempt of official policies and
campaign strategies, at a time when the allied cause and the lives
of millions of men hung in the balance. The only possible explanation is to be found in Kitchener's early support. So strange a
creature as the Bureau, nominally owned by the Foreign Office,
funded by the War Office and effectively controlled by the
Admiralty, could not have survived without the most powerful
of patrons. It was one of the supreme ironies of history that on
the very day that the Arabs raised their banners in revolt, Field
Marshal Lord Kitchener was drowned when the cruiser *Hampshire*
sank in the icy waters of the North Sea.

On July 6th there was a meeting of the War Committee, called at
the request of the Chief of the Imperial General Staff, General
Sir William Robertson, to discuss the Arab Revolt. Sykes was
asked to address the Committee. He said that the Government
should adopt a consistent pro-Arab policy in the Middle East and
that in execution of that policy Sir Percy Cox should be appointed
High Commissioner of Eastern Arabia, Hadramaut and Aden,
and should be directly responsible to the Foreign Office instead of
the Indian Government 'as at present'. Cox would have charge of
all negotiations with the Arab tribes 'from Aden to Mesopotamia

inclusive'. Sykes, with Gertrude virtually at the helm in Mesopotamia, felt safe in his dealings with that territory, and by the same token he was becoming worried about the direction of Bureau policies in Egypt. He damned McMahon with faint praise. 'With regard to Egypt, I am strongly of opinion that Sir H. McMahon requires help in the way of instructions. There has been a steady effort to carry on the administration as though very little was afoot, with the result that people have gone in for junketing, entertainment, and have drifted into a tendency to let things slide ... Native and civil British opinion was that Sir Henry McMahon was only a temporary holder of the position, and that Lord Kitchener was coming back ... I now come to the Gulf and Mesopotamia and the political work of Sir Percy Cox. This is the most difficult thing I have to say ... that the Government of India is incapable of handling the Arab question ... Lastly, it is useless to ignore the jealousy which subsists between Simla and Cairo. This is an old-lasting feud, but real nevertheless ... I cannot speak too highly of Sir Percy Cox's work ... but he will never be free so long as it depends upon Simla. The only way to unity and co-ordination ... is to place the political affairs of Mesopotamia, Aden and Muscat directly under the Foreign Office, London and appoint Sir Percy Cox High Commissioner with equal rank to Sir Henry McMahon ...'

The unimaginative and loyal McMahon was about to take the rap for negotiations which had, by common consent, entangled the Government in a web of intrigue and promises from which it would have great difficulty in extricating itself; negotiations in which he, McMahon, had been the unsuspecting intrument of wild and dishonourable men. While McMahon's negotiations had been in progress, Sykes had been formulating the secret Sykes–Picot agreement designating British, French and Italian spheres of control and influence in the Ottoman dominions, which was to cut across some of the promises made to Husain. And Husain for his part was already calling himself *Malik al Bilad al Aarab*, King of the Arab Lands, to the consternation of the French who suspected that he included metropolitan Syria in 'Arab Lands'. Britain insisted that he should style himself 'King of the Hijaz' but he held to the end that he had been promised not only the Caliphate of Islam but the kingship of a territory which embraced most of the peninsula and included part of what became French-mandated Syria and British-mandated Palestine. Meanwhile, his

son Faisal took up the cudgels in company with the men of the
Bureau, and set out on a path that was to make him Gertrude's
protégé in Iraq, as post-war Mesopotamia came to be named.
Mark Sykes produced a regular summary of the Arab Bureau's
intelligence reports for the benefit of Britain's military and civil
leaders. It was invariably hotheaded and usually studied in its
insolence. On one occasion he remarked: 'In it (Arabian Report
No. XV) Sir Henry McMahon tells Lord Grey that the Sirdar has
told him (Sir Henry McMahon) that he (the Sirdar) proposed to
tell Colonel Wilson to tell the Sharif certain things, but that he
(Sir Henry McMahon) has made certain alterations in the text
which the Sirdar desires Colonel Wilson to convey to the Sharif,
and that the Sirdar concurs in the amendments ... It is very lucky
for us that for the moment nothing is happening in Arabia that
requires either thought or decision ...' By September, the India
Office was so fed up with his sarcastic intervention that it decided
no longer to send copies of the *Arab Bulletin* to the Viceroy unless
they contained essential information, and it put a total ban on
Sykes's summaries – 'They are exasperating even in a temperate
climate,' wrote Hirtzel. There was a final and appropriately
bizarre drama attached to the Sharif's revolt. The Viceroy Lord
Chelmsford read about the event in the Press and, indirectly, in
communications from the India Office, but he wondered if he
might see a copy of the proclamation. Nothing arrived for a
month and he complained to London. It was eventually discovered
that someone in the Foreign Office had confused 'Simla' with
'Sirdar' and his copy had been lying on Wingate's desk.

As the 'illicit adventure' unravelled itself in the Hijaz, Gertrude
was recovering from jaundice, and helping Sir Percy to prepare
for a durbar in Kuwait at which Ibn Saud was to be the guest of
honour and to be made a Knight Commander of the Most
Honourable Order of the Indian Empire. Meanwhile, she went up
to Nasiriyah again, chiefly to inspect the ziggurat of Ur which
she was busily protecting from 'the ravages of Generals and railway engineers'. In a description of the journey she wrote: 'From
its summit you can see another immense mound, and then the
desert, and the desert, and the desert. Loftus dug at Ur a long time
ago, but no doubt there is much yet to be explored. The brick
wall is, if I remember, Parthian, though the site goes back to the
beginning of historic time.' On November 25th she wrote: 'Sir

Percy has been holding a fine durbar of Arab chiefs at Kuwait and Ibn Saud is to pay us a visit here ... The whole business is a tall feather in Sir Percy's cap.'

Britain was becoming increasingly concerned about Ibn Saud. Brigadier-General Macdonogh, the Director of Military Intelligence, had observed in connection with the Sykes–Picot agreement and the other activities of the Bureau: 'I must confess that it seems to me that we are in the position of the hunters who divided up the skin of the bear before they had killed it.' Ibn Saud took much the same view of what was going on. He told Cox that he was not concerned who held the Caliphate when he was asked somewhat nervously if he approved of Husain taking on the distinction. But he was concerned at the Sharif's self-made title 'King of the Arabs' and at the increasingly bombastic attitude of the man he regarded as no more than an upstart appointee of the Turks who enjoyed practically no tribal support. There was also a suspicion that Ibn Saud was merely biding his time with Ibn Rashid and that he would strike when circumstances were favourable to him rather than to Britain. Thus, having spurned him for five years past and rejected his plea for an alliance, Britain was now entertaining him royally. The Prince of Najd arrived in Basra at the end of the month and on December 1st Gertrude wrote: 'We had an extraordinarily interesting day with Ibn Saud who is one of the most striking personalities I have encountered. He is splendid to look at, well over 6 ft. 3, with an immense amount of dignity and self-possession. We took him in trains and motors, showed him aeroplanes, high explosives, anti-aircraft guns, hospitals, base depots – everything. He was full of wonder but never agape. He asked innumerable questions and made intelligent comments. He's a big man ... ' If Gertrude was impressed, the guest was flabbergasted. He could hardly believe the evidence of his senses when he arrived in Basra to find that he was being greeted by a woman. Ibn Saud, even by 1916, had met few women outside the harem. They had no place in public life as far as he was concerned, and of course none in his kingdom would have been permitted to show herself in public without the *burqa* or face mask. Yet here he was being greeted and shown around by a woman whose manner was totally uninhibited and who insisted on talking to him as an equal. Philby was to write some years later: ' ... he certainly did not like her, while the fact that she was accorded precedence, not only over himself but also over all the British civil and military chiefs, did not seem to him to be in keeping with the dignity of man. And many a Najdi audience has been tickled to uproarious merriment by his mimicking of her shrill voice and feminine patter: "Abdul Aziz! Abdul Aziz! look at this, and what do you think of that?" and so forth.'

One positive result of the meeting between Ibn Saud and Cox was the temporary suspension of one of the Amir's most rigorous desert campaigns. Ever since the battle of Jarab in 1915 at which Shakespear was killed, Abdul Aziz had been determined to destroy the Ajman tribe whose desertion caused that death and let Ibn Rashid's army off the hook. He pursued them to Kuwait where to his intense anger they were given refuge by the Shaikh after a battle in which Ibn Saud himself was wounded and his favourite brother, Saad, was killed. It was a major feat of diplomacy on Cox's part to persuade him to give up that pursuit, however temporarily.

Gertrude's description of the visit to Basra appeared in the *Arab Bulletin* of January 12th, 1917. It was a generous and accurate portrayal of the great Arab leader, whose qualities had perhaps suggested to her that rather than toying with the Rashid family and the princes of Mecca, both Britain and the Turks would have done well to take him seriously from the beginning. It was one of Gertrude's best-known contributions to the *Bulletin* and was subsequently reproduced in the *Arab War*. It recounted the exile of the Sauds in Kuwait following the ascent of Muhammad ibn Rashid, 'Doughty's grudging host' in Najd. It told of the young Abdul Aziz 'eating the bread of adversity' while he waited under the protection of Shaikh Mubarak; of his return to Riyadh on the first day of 1902 and the fight to recover the lands of his forefathers; of the battle of Jarab and the death of Captain Shakespear, and it describes the ceremony at Kuwait on November 20th, 1916. 'On that memorable occasion three powerful Arab chiefs, the Shaikh of Muhammerah, who though a Persian subject is of Arab stock, the Shaikh of Kuwait and Ibn Saud, Hakim of Najd, stood side by side in amity and concord and proclaimed their adherence to the British cause.' A brief reference to Ibn Saud's speech, 'as spontaneous as it was unexpected', and then a characteristic descriptive passage:

Ibn Saud is now barely forty, though he looks some years older. He is a man of splendid physique, standing well over six feet, and carrying himself with the air of one accustomed to command. Though he is more massively built than the typical nomad shaikh, he has the characteristics of the well-bred Arab, the strongly-marked aquiline profile, full-flesh nostrils, prominent lips and a long narrow chin accentuated by a pointed beard. His hands are fine, with slender fingers ... and in spite of his great height and breadth of shoulder he conveys the impression common enough in the desert, of an indefinable lassitude ... the secular weariness of an ancient and self-contained people, which has made heavy drafts on its vital forces and borrowed little from beyond its own forbidding frontiers. His deliberate movements, his slow sweet smile and the contemplative glance of his heavy lidded eyes ... Nevertheless report credits him with powers of physical endurance rare even in hard-bitten Arabia. Among men bred in the camel saddle he is said to have few rivals as a tireless rider. As a leader of irregular forces he is of proved daring, and he combines with his qualities as a soldier that grasp of statecraft which is yet more highly prized by the tribesmen ... Politician, ruler and raider, Ibn Saud illustrates a historic type. Such men as he are the exception in any community, but they are thrown up persistently by the Arab race ...

Whitehall was impressed by the article, as by almost everything else that came with the familiar initials GLB attached to it. The Secretary of State for India told Cox: 'We are publishing Miss Bell's article, omitting reference to Shakespear's friendship and earlier relations with Bin Saud'. It was clear the way the wind was blowing. Britain was committed to its Sharifite policy. Austen Chamberlain also declared that it was unwise to refer in future, in published material, to our hitherto 'secret' treaty with Ibn Saud. He referred to a virtually meaningless document signed by Cox and Ibn Saud on December 26th, 1915 following Shakespear's death.

Gertrude spent Christmas 1916 with Philby at Amara on the Tigris. 'I'm going with the kind Revenue Commissioner Mr Philby.' In London the reverberations of the Dardanelles and Kut-al-Amara brought drastic changes to the Whitehall administration. Before leaving Gertrude wrote to her father: 'What a strange metamorphosis, isn't it, that Lloyd George should be leading a Cabinet which is practically a Unionist exponent of patriotism! His apotheosis and the complete collapse of Winston – who would have thought either possible.'

18
Iraq

A change of government gave a new complexion to the military and political institutions of Britain in the Middle East. The moment was opportune for a shake-up. Sir Archibald Murray's Egyptian Expeditionary force had pushed the Turks out of Sinai in the latter part of 1916. The Mesopotamian army, now under the fourth of its commanders, Lieutenant-General Sir Stanley Maude, 'Systematic Joe' as he was called by his men, had begun to advance with better planning and equipment than hitherto, along the road that had led to earlier disasters. The Sirdar, General Sir Reginald Wingate, had taken over as High Commissioner in Cairo. The carnage continued on the western front, but elsewhere there were gleams of hope. Gertrude received a C.B.E. in the honours list which marked the change to the war coalition.

The war inevitably brought its crop of personalities to Mesopotamia. As the retreat from Ctesiphon began, Philby, Hubert Young and D. L. R. Lorimer arrived as Assistant Political Officers. Captain A. T. Wilson was already there, a pre-war assistant to Cox in the Gulf and one of the most powerful personalities in the eastern administration. Even among the outstanding men and women around him, 'AT' was prominent. Hubert Young, who had already moved with Dawnay, Joyce and Lawrence among Faisal's warriors around Wadi Sirhan in the Syrian desert, and who was to play a part in the subsequent Arabian settlements, found Wilson too powerful a personality to work with. 'I admired him immensely,' he wrote, 'and I liked him personally, but he was a great centraliser, and I have always felt that actual physical separation is a great factor.' Cox was the first to agree that they should be kept apart. There was Bullard too, who responded to every observation with 'on the contrary', and Dobbs, both immensely able administrators with sharp wits and opinions of their own. When Young was sent to Nasiriyah as A.P.O. his nearest neighbour was a young officer named Captain H. R. P. Dickson who 'maintained British authority by sheer force of personality'. Others gradually came on the scene, often men of exceptional ability — Ronald Wingate, son of the Sirdar; Lionel Smith, Dean of Magdalen and tutor to Edward VII before the war; historians C. J. Edmonds, S. H. Longrigg, and many others. It is small wonder that there were differences of opinion about the future role of Britain in that country, differences which were to broaden into personal animosities and occasionally into lifelong feuds, though for the moment they were kept in check by the demands of administering vast territories inhabited by recalcitrant and sometimes hostile people, with few physical resources and little money. The two women of this fraternity, Gertrude and Mrs Lorimer, took it upon themselves to maintain order among so many disparate and opinionated men, lecturing them like schoolmistresses or surrogate mothers when the occasion arose. Perhaps Mrs Lorimer delivered the most telling reprimand when she wrote Philby a letter which, according to his biographer, he kept for the rest of his life. Following a quarrel he had had with her husband at Amara she remarked: 'When a young man without very wide experience finds himself differing about practical policy from an older man and senior official acting in circumstances of which the former knows nothing, it is sound for him to assume that there may be two sides to a question. This I think is an unimpeachable general principle ... ' Gertrude told the vituperative Philby, who was to become in the course of time one of the most brilliant of all Arabists, that he was 'too domineering and difficult' and 'too ready to come to blows with the military authorities'. Battle lines were drawn up early in the life of the British administration, but for the moment attitudes were tempered by the army's progress towards Baghdad.

By early March 1917 Gertrude was able to tell her father: 'That's the end of the German dream of domination in the Near East — Berlin — Baghdad and all the rest. Their place is not going to be in the sun; it would have been if they had left well alone and not tried to force the pace by war. We had, in my opinion, for all practical purposes resigned this country to them and they knew it well enough. Now they're out of it forever I hope, and they have no one but themselves to thank. We shall, I trust, make it a centre of Arab civilisation and prosperity ... ' She also told her father that after the war she would seek permission to 'do one bit of real Arabian exploration'. By now she was Cox's right arm, his trusted Oriental Secretary and confidante, and she was the hub of the Political Office's relationship with the tribes and the notables of the country. She described a visit to the military hospital at Basra, where the matron Miss Jones showed her round and took her to see wounded Turkish prisoners. 'I could have laughed and wept for them – from Konia, from Angora, from Caesarea, some from C'ple, and we talked of their homes and what fair country they lay in ... Among the officers was an Arab of Baghdad, dying poor boy ... [he] whispered painfully – the only question! News of the Sharif. Was it true that his rebellion prospered, and were we in agreement with him? ... '

Baghdad was captured on March 11th. Gertrude and other Political Officers moved in the wake of the army to the capital city. They travelled by troopship along the Tigris, setting out on April 5th. Cox was already in Baghdad, having entered with the army to hear General Maude read his proclamation of deliverance and of Britain's support for Iraqi aspirations. She was able to step ashore for an hour or two at Amara to meet Philby who was A.P.O. there. Three days later they looked out on the battlefields around Kut. 'We stood on the bridge and traced the terrible Sannaiyat lines which already are almost obliterated and will soon be overgrown – no battlefields will bear fewer marks of war than these Mesopotamian plains ... It seems almost incomprehensible that as one looked across the level peaceful land, scattered over with black Arab tents; for the Arabs are coming back to their accustomed pastures and the sheep cover the river banks along which the Turkish army fled a month ago.' She soon settled into her new office and home. She was disappointed with the first house that was allocated to her and went out to find a place for herself. With her undying love of flowers she was more concerned with the garden than the abode and she found a 'rose garden with three summer-houses' quite close to the Political Office. Within days of her arrival, London was asking for signed articles from her for propaganda purposes. Mesopotamia was in the news again, this time for the encouraging fact that the Indian army had provided the first significant victory after a nightmare of reverses. London intended to make the best of it and nobody was more able than Gertrude to meet their needs. In the past year she had contributed a flow of well-written, informative articles to Hogarth's *Arabian Report* and *Arab Bulletin*, and had maintained day by day an output of intelligence information based on her military and civil interrogations of Arabs and Turks. In October there was a treatise on 'The Basis of Government in Turkish Arabia', with a typically assertive early statement – 'And he who, without being guilty of incautious curiosity, was forced by circumstances to test the relations that existed between documentary evidence *à la turque* and the hard facts of the Ottoman Empire, was apt to find himself lost in bewildered annoyance, not unaccompanied by uncontrollable hilarity ... That the Turkish Empire should have run at all was, at a hasty appreciation, a matter for marvel ... '; followed by an appraisal of the Ottoman law. There followed a summary which should have been framed in every office of the British administration:

> ... men who have kept the tradition of a personal independence, which was limited only by their own customs, entirely ignorant of a world which lay outside their swamps and pastures, and as entirely indifferent to its interests as to the opportunities it offers, will not in a day fall into step with European ambitions, nor welcome European methods. Nor can they be hastened ... In our own history, from the Moot Court through Magna Charter to the Imperial Parliament was the work of centuries, yet the first contained the grain of all that came after.

There followed bulletins on subjects as diverse as the tribal authorities and backgrounds of the great shaikhs of Arabia; rivalries and rebellion in Muscat and Oman; and the tribal fights of the Shamiyah: 'Human nature being what it is – and at bottom the same in the Arab as in the European, pugnacious, ambitious and covetous, sometimes loyal but mainly treacherous, occasionally enlightened but always restless – the tribal fights in the Shamiyah desert may be expected to exhibit the same to and fro, change and interchange, of alliances, as may be found in the history of the relations between the various nations which compose Europe.' Even the Whitehall Treasury, sick as it was of Arabia and Arabs and the assumptions of the British who moved among them that the Chancellor had access to a bottomless [pit of money, looked forward to reading Gertrude's compositions. Along with Hogarth and Lawrence, she provided war-time reading which has

certainly never been equalled in intelligence documents, and seldom in any kind of official paper. Her reports sparkled with wit
and irony as well as fact, and they received fulsome praise from
the High Commissioner, Sir Henry McMahon. After his 'resignation' on December 20th, 1916 he wrote to the new Foreign
Secretary Balfour, enclosing a summary of the work of the Bureau
from its inception to 'the date on which I handed over its complete direction to the Sirdar'. 'The negotiations connected with
this question [the Sharif] have been lengthy and many complex
problems have arisen. It has appeared to me desirable ... that all
the main issues and salient documents (quoted verbatim where
necessary) should be incorporated into one memorandum, which
will serve as a complete record, readily available for future
reference. I welcome the opportunity thus afforded of recording
my high appreciation of the services of the members of the Arab
Bureau ... ' There follows his testimonial of the services of his
team: Brigadier-General G. F. Clayton, Commander D. G.
Hogarth, Major Kinahan Cornwallis, Captain T. E. Lawrence,
Captain the Hon. W. A. Ormsby-Gore, Lt-Colonel C. E. Wilson,
Mr Ronald Storrs, Lt-Colonel A. C. Parker, Mr A. B. Fforde
(forgotten in McMahon's first letter but remembered a few days
later) and 'Miss Gertrude Bell, who gave valuable assistance to me
in the early days of the Arab movement and is now, under the
direction of Sir Percy Cox, acting as correspondent of the Bureau
in Mesopotamia, thereby promoting co-ordination and the constant interchange of information. Her intimate knowledge of
Arabia, ability and energy, have rendered her services of great
value. The manner in which she has so long devoted herself to
the work of the Arab Bureau under the most trying conditions of
country and climate, is deserving of special notice.' On February
2nd, 1917 Austen Chamberlain wrote to the Viceroy:

My Lord, I forward for the information of Your Excellency in
Council a copy of a letter that has been received from the
Foreign Office regarding the staff of the Arab Bureau ... it
affords me particular pleasure to request Your Excellency – as
desired by the Secretary of State for Foreign Affairs – to express
to Miss Gertrude Bell the appreciation of His Majesty's Government for her valuable services. I have the honour to be My
Lord, Your Lordship's most obedient humble servant, Austen
Chamberlain.

o

The Viceroy was delighted to pass on this glowing tribute to Gertrude's work, but he was no more persuaded of the good of the Bureau's work under Wingate than his predecessor had been when McMahon was the unsuspecting instrument of Kitchener's and the Foreign Office's policies. One notion of which the Viceroy was uncomfortably aware was the desire of the Bureau to obtain the release from confinement in India of the prominent Basra citizen Sayid Talib, whom Cox had sent away at the beginning of the war. The Foreign Office had been warned before the outbreak of war that this man was a 'rogue' and 'murderer' who was in the pay of the Turks though he was prepared to sell his services to either side. In March 1916, while he was in Basra, Lawrence received an unsigned letter from a member of the Bureau which read: 'The Colonel has asked me to put you *au fait* with the situation as it stands ... The only difficulty that has been encountered so far is the refusal of the Indian Government to send Talib to Basra. However, we wrote a pretty strong telegram yesterday practically that Talib's co-operation was essential and added that at least he might be allowed to come to Cairo ... When Talib is in Cairo we shall work him into a good humour and then write the WO saying that we have seen him and we think he is quite safe and hope in this way to get him off as No. 3 party ... General MacMunn is going out as I.G.C. to Basra. We have had a talk with him and he has promised you all the support possible. He knows all about you ... The most important thing of all (at all events when we are getting into touch and buying people and so on) will be cash. Finally, the WO have asked us for the names of, and given permission for the going to Basra of any Turkish, Arab and Kurd officers at present in India who wish to co-operate with us ... ' It was not the kind of letter to instil confidence in the Indian Government or in Cox. It seems that the scheme at that time was to appoint Talib in the place of Farouki, the go-between in the Sharif negotiations, and send him with Nuri Said an ex-Turkish officer then working with the Bureau, and with Storrs's friend and Enver Pasha's rival for the leadership of the Young Turks, Aziz al Masri, to complete the negotiations with the Sharif. In an outgoing letter at the same time, Lawrence had written to Mark Sykes: 'Indian interests are secondary ... He [Cox] thinks that Lord Hardinge is very sound ... Cox is entirely ignorant of Arab societies and of Turkish politics ... '

Now, after the taking of Baghdad, the Indian Government was

in a stronger position. In May Ronald Storrs arrived in Baghdad full of *bonhomie*. 'It was mighty fun,' wrote Gertrude. 'Mr Storrs set the whole bazaar rocking with laughter and established my reputation for ever as a provider of good company. Unfortunately I am too busy to go around with him much, but such interludes are very reviving and the result is I've upped and outlined a reasonable scheme for the government of this country – *pas dégoûte*! which I really think may be useful as something to bite upon. There's nothing like a spice of audacity; but the truth is that the High and Mighty at home are ignorant of the most obvious things and every now and then it's well to reel off a string of platitudes. I've found before now that what should rightly be an immense yawn of boredom at one's obviousness is really a gape of semi-enlightened amazement. The delightful thing is when they write back and give you, in the deepest confidence, the news that after long consultation they have resolved on the following scheme – and behold it's what you wrote months ago.' It does not seem to have occurred to Gertrude that as the confidante of the civil head of the administration she should not be in communication with officials in Whitehall, or the Press, except perhaps on matters of a purely personal nature.

Storrs had arrived in the aftermath of the dispute with the Sharif over his title, and he was able to give Gertrude an amusing account of the proceedings. He had visited Jidda just before the bombshell of October 29th, 1916 when Abdullah, calling himself 'Minister for Foreign Affairs', had issued a statement to the world Press and to Colonel Wilson, Wingate's representative in Hijaz: 'According to the wish of the people and the assembly of the Ulema, the great master His Majesty our Lord and Lord of all, Al Husain ibn Ali, has been recognised as King of the Arab Nation ... ' On that occasion, when Storrs had conveyed a statement from Wingate that there would be no troops or aeroplanes for a projected attack on Rabegh, Abdullah had said with truth: 'Forgive me, it was your letter and your messages that began this thing with us, and you know it from the beginning and from before the beginning.' In December, with France and the French representative in the Hijaz Colonel Bremond breathing fire, Storrs had returned to Jidda. After that visit the Foreign Office noted: 'Mr Storrs writes amusingly, but did not get very much out of the Sharif.' He did, however, succeed in getting some good photographs of Husain and the excitable Sykes had issued memos in all

directions insisting that they be issued to the Press and announcing
that he wished to see them in 'the Arab Press, the *Times of India*
and the *Illustrated London News*'.

By the end of May Storrs had gone back to Cairo and Gertrude
returned to her shaikhs and to the routine of the Political Office
where already plans were being laid for the aftermath of hostilities.
Cox, the supreme diplomat of the East, towered over the proceedings by his very presence. Tall and slim, urbane in manner and
impeccable in dress, he was respected by everyone and so could
command the support of his divergent crew even when there
were disagreements on matters of policy. Even so, those disagreements existed and they were beginning to show themselves
if only over meals in the mess where headquarters staff and the
Political Officers in the field were able to meet and talk. Many of
the A.P.O.s were young men who administered territories as large
as Wales or Yorkshire, with neither police nor military assistance
in controlling their lawless tribes. It was they who came face to
face with the real problems. But unlike Cox and his Baghdad
assistants Philby and Gertrude, they were unaware of the grandi-
ose schemes of Whitehall and the Arab Bureau. When the
Bolsheviks came to power in 1917 and divulged the details of the
Sykes–Picot agreement to Husain in Mecca, everyone became
aware that Britain was intending to stay in Mesopotamia and that
the French would take over Damascus and most of Syria. Cox and
his principal assistants saw no immediate objection to the idea but
the men who had to maintain law and order in the marshes and
deserts and far-flung townships could see disaster clearly written
on the wall. Gertrude had herself seen the dangers inherent in the
idea of Arab nationalism and an externally imposed administration many years earlier. In *The Desert and the Sown* she had written:
'Of what value are the Pan-Arabic associations and inflammatory
leaflets that they issue from foreign printing presses? The answer
is easy: They are worth nothing at all. There is no nation of
Arabs; the Syrian merchant is separated by a wider gulf from the
badawin than he is from the Osmanli, the Syrian country is inhabited by Arabic speaking races all eager to be at each other's
throats, and only prevented from fulfilling their natural desires by
the rugged half-fed soldier who draws at rare intervals the Sultan's
pay.' In her later work, *Amurath to Amurath*, she recounted the
impressions she had formed in the Mosul region after the Young
Turks' revolution: ' ... nowhere will the Arab nationalist move-

ment, if it reaches the blossoming point, find a more congenial soil, and nowhere will it be watered by fuller streams of lawless vanity. Cruel and bloody as Ottoman rule has shown itself upon these remote frontiers, it is better than the untrammelled mastery of Arab Beg or Kurdish Agha, and if the half exterminated Christian sects, the persecuted Yezidis, the wretched fellahin of every creed, who sow in terror crops which they may never reap, are to win protection and prosperity, it is to the Turk that they must look.' It had always been the view of Hogarth, from whom Gertrude derived much of her philosophy of government in the East, that with all their faults, the Turks had half a millennium of experience in these territories which could not be thrown over-board with impunity. By the end of the year 1917, however, Cox and his Oriental Secretary were already looking to the implemen-tation of the plans of Whitehall and the Quai d'Orsay to administer these vast tracts of Arab-occupied land. In June Gertrude re-ceived from the Foreign Office a copy of the still secret agreement between Sykes and M. Georges Picot, with a request for her comments. She wrote a lengthy appraisal of the document and she made special reference to paragraph (2) which read: 'They [the Allies] propose to replace it [Ottoman sovereignty] by a dual control, half French and half British, each zone being further divided into two parts, the one completely under foreign ad-ministration, the other more or less autonomous under foreign guidance.' At the head of her report, Gertrude observed: 'A bold and decided policy previously agreed upon by all concerned in regard to Arab national aspirations.' And in the main body of her report she said: 'The policy implied by these aims is wholly in consonance with the fundamental principles to uphold which the Allies embarked upon war with the Central European powers; is one which commends itself to those who wish to see one of the great races of the world given scope to develop and use its special capacities in its own way, and to those who hold that civilisation is better served by the amicable co-operation of different racial units than by attempting to ignore or suppress essential diverg-ence.'

If there was contradiction in her observations over the decade which separated her first writings on the subject from those of 1917, it must be conceded that she was not alone in her inconsis-tency. Hogarth, Sykes, Lawrence and the others involved in this tight-rope walk of expediency, contradicted themselves time and time again. It has been said of them all that if they had a fault it was that they were over-articulate, that the world might have been a more peaceful place for future generations if they and their like had not been such 'able and persuasive' writers. In a way, though, they simply gave expression to a very common English belief that, when all is said and done, those who appear to wish to wander freely in the open spaces of the world and who despise governments of every kind, are in reality merely marking time, waiting to have conferred upon them the self-evident blessings of parliamentary democracy and the Stock Exchange.

Gertrude laboured on through the great heat of the summers of the last two war years, and the equally trying conditions of the wet and muddy winters, producing a massive output of work. By the middle of 1917 she was working on her sixth paper on Turkey; she had written another report on Ibn Saud running to twenty-five pages and setting out the complex relations between Britain, the Amir and that mercurial Iraqi Sayid Talib, who she said 'had tried to get Britain to engage his services in the event of war, through Shaikh Khazal (of Muhammerah), but his terms were too extravagant'. There were her weekly I.E.F. 'D' intelligence summaries; countless memos on the shaikhs and tribes in and around Mesopotamia; a note on the transliteration of Arabic for the London School of Oriental Studies; a translation and codification of the Shia Traditions; reports on Syria and Mesopotamia; several major contributions to Hogarth's *Bulletin*; a report on Ismail Bey, 'the most formidable figure in northern Mesopotamian politics in the last 10 years of Abdul Hamid's reign', who gave himself up to the British in December 1917; a report on Sadun Pasha, chief of the large and troublesome Muntafiq tribal confederation; a long paper on the situation in Hail. She also took on the editorship of the official Arabic newspaper *Al Arab*, with a roguish monk from Beirut as her deputy. And all the time she maintained a prodigious flow of letters to her parents, friends and officials of government. She seemed content with her life. She entertained extensively in her Baghdad home, her relationships with the young men of the military and civil authorities were pleasantly friendly, and with the women guarded. She had found a new home and a new life. She spoke of 'carrying on an existence' among people she loved. That was almost certainly the truth of the matter. A shrewd womanly comment was made by an earlier biographer:

> It is noteworthy that Gertrude knew herself to be merely 'carrying on an existence', in however worthwhile a manner. Nothing but the love of husband and children, for which she had always longed and which had always been denied, could enable her to live fully and completely; and at the age of forty-eight she was still alone.

By late 1917 the Secretary of State for India, Austen Chamberlain, had resigned, taking on himself an unfair burden of the blame for the scandal of Kut and the incompetence of generals and medical authorities which had resulted in the unnecessary deaths from wounds and starvation of so many British troops. Edwin Montagu, another of Gertrude's close acquaintances in power, took over at the India Office. General Allenby, fresh from the indecisive Arras offensive, had been appointed C.-in-C. of the Egyptian Expeditionary Force which, after the success of 1916 in Sinai under General Murray had met with determined opposition from the Turks at Gaza and so was held up in its bid to advance into Palestine. The 'Bull' as they called him in France was to roll up the Ottoman carpet over the long and difficult Syrian front during the coming year by patient, brilliant generalship which produced one of the great victories of the war with less loss of life than was incurred in any other campaign; and the credit was to go to others.

Gertrude seems to have required little but the affection of her family at this time, except for riding boots, and maps and dictionaries; 'I would so much like Roget's Thesaurus ... I have so often to dress up the same theme in new words,' she wrote to Lady Bell. In 1918 she had a brief holiday in Persia and contracted two bouts of malaria, which left her painfully thin but no less energetic than before. Only one event of the period roused her to anger, the Balfour Declaration which added another strand to Britain's web of promises. Three years earlier, after visiting a hospital for Indian troops at Le Touquet in France, she had written to Doughty-Wylie: 'I told you how Herbert Samuel wrote and asked me if I thought we could turn Palestine into a Jewish state under British protection? ... I told him I had always wanted to create a neutral belt, if Turkey broke up, between French Syria and the Egyptian frontier. Alliances are not imperishable ... Then I plotted out for

him Palestine Prima, under the guarantees of the Powers ... '
Now she wrote: 'By the way, I hate Mr Balfour's Zionist pro-
nouncement with regard to Syria [Palestine was then regarded by
the outside world as part of Ottoman Syria, over which the French
had assumed a watching brief on behalf of Christian Europe since
the last of the Crusades]. It's my belief that it can't be carried out,
the country is wholly unsuited to the ends the Jews have in view;
it is a poor land, incapable of great development and with a solid
two-thirds of its population Mohammedan Arabs who look on
Jews with contempt. To my mind it's a wholly artificial scheme
divorced from all relation to facts and I wish it the ill-success that
it deserves — and will get, I fancy.'

Her home mail was delivered by Sir Percy who had to make a
sudden dash to England at the behest of Lord Hardinge, who was
involved in the Foreign Office effort to formulate plans for settling
matters which had been arranged in the heat of the moment and
were about to be repented.

One of the letters carried by Cox, dated February 22nd, was
addressed to Lord Hardinge: 'I must send a word of greeting to
you by Sir Percy. It is an admirable plan to call him in to your
councils ... He will give you such a vivid impression of our conditions and his tale will help you to stand out for us. Things look
so black now that the fact that we cannot abandon this country
to its fate needs insisting upon ... I should like to tell you what
amazing strides have been made towards ordered government
since last March. Basra vilayet is ... under peace conditions; we
have had almost no trouble in Baghdad vilayet. The frontier tribes,
the people only half in Occupied Territory, have been a little tiresome, nothing to speak of ... and the rest have all come to heel
without a shot fired. There's no important element against us,
above all no religious feeling ... The stronger the hold we are
able to keep here the better the inhabitants will be pleased. What
they dread is any half measure ... ' There followed a detailed
analysis of the political and military requirements of British rule,
for the need to keep the two chief vilayets Basra and Baghdad together, and her assessment of public opinion. There were also
letters to her father and to Domnul. To the former she spoke of
her continuing sorrow. 'Oh Father, dearest, do you know that
tonight [February 22nd] is just three years since D. and I parted.
I can't think why the recurring date should bring back old memories so strongly, but it is so, and I've lived again through the

four days three years ago almost minute by minute ... this sorrow
at the back of everything deadens me in a way to all else, to
whether I go home or whether I stay here in the East, or what
happens. And yet in a curious way it quickens the inner life and
makes me live more on thought and memory ... '

To Chirol there was mention of another sadness, the death of
Sir Cecil Spring-Rice, husband of the Lascelles daughter, her
cousin Florence; 'My mind is full of Springy and of Florence and
her children – they are old enough to sorrow too – poor little
souls ... Dear Springy, kind and sympathetic friend! I grieve so
much for him, but it's always the living I think of most.'

In March 1918, as news came of the big German offensive on
the western front, which was only partially offset by General
Brooking's annihilation of the Turkish army on the Euphrates
and Allenby's progress in Syria, Gertrude learnt that she had been
awarded the Founder's Medal of the Royal Geographical Society
'Oh, dear, I wish I could feel that I really deserved such an
honour! How puffed up I should be ... I made two interesting
journeys down the Euphrates and compiled a tribal geography of
which I'll send you a copy ... ', she told the director. Her father
stood in for her at the presentation ceremony.

One result of Cox's visit to London was that he was asked to
take over as Chargé d'Affaires in Tehran in succession to Sir
Charles Marling, to negotiate an Anglo-Persian treaty to which
Curzon was committed. It was a bad time to leave Iraq (the
British began to drop the term Mesopotamia after the capture of
Baghdad), and for A. T. Wilson, his deputy, to have to take over.
A rising at Najaf in April, encouraged by the religious leaders of
the holy city of the Shia, was a portent of things to come.
Gertrude's optimism received an early rebuff. A Political Officer
was murdered. Writing home in April 1918 about the Najaf affair,
she told her father: 'Dry rot has set in among the rebels ... already
a good number of the murderers of Captain Marshall have been
handed over to us. I expect and hope we'll hang them. The whole
business has been very successfully managed thanks to Captain
Wilson and Captain Balfour.'

The latter had arrived in 1917, and he was followed by others.
'I like having these Egyptians – Sudanese rather,' she said of the
new Judicial Officer, Sir Edgar Bonham-Carter. Of Wilson, she
wrote: 'I don't think I've ever told you about Captain Wilson, a
very remarkable creature. He began by regarding me as "a born

intriguer" and I, not unnaturally, regarded him with some suspicion also ... We have ended by becoming firm friends and I
have the greatest respect for his amazing intelligence. I think I've
helped to educate him a little also, but he educates himself and
some day will be a very big man. He is getting so much more
tolerant and patient, such a statesman. I love working with him.'

19
The Mandate

The armistice of November 1918 found her recuperating from her last bout of malaria, which came on in October. Meanwhile the world's politicians buzzed around the hotels of Paris and prepared for the Peace Conferences at Versailles and Sèvres.

Much of her time was spent with the G.O.C., General MacMunn — the successor of General Maude who died from cholera in the previous year — and the C.-in-C., General Sir William Marshall. 'I spend most of my mornings in talk. The C.-in-C. has been a great help. He is very wise and moderate and I take his counsel not having Sir Percy. I am quite the politician at present!'

At the end of the year she had even gone so far as to tell her father, 'I'm second choice for High Commissioner here, so I'm told! what would all the Permanent Officials say if we suggested it?' She added: 'Had a delicious day out with Evelyn Howell (sent over from India to look into the country's finances) and Frank Balfour.' Gertrude had been instrumental in arranging a series of lectures by Professor George Margoliouth, the Oxford Arabist, to which all the Political Officers in the Baghdad vicinity were expected to go. 'It was an extraordinary *tour de force*,' she wrote, 'he lectured for fifty minutes on the ancient splendours of Baghdad, in classical Arabic and without a note.' Some of the young 'Politicals' were not so impressed. They mixed with the local Arabs who spoke a far from classical version of the tongue and they learnt to converse in the dialects of their own neighbourhoods. In such places life was still primitive and language had not caught up with the terms of the twentieth century. At one lecture an intrepid spirit interrupted the learned professor to ask, 'How do you say in Arabic — Do you drive a motor car?' Margoliouth was not amused.

Gertrude remarked at this time — 'I do wish they would drop the idea of an Arab Amir; it tires me to think of setting up a brand new court.'

The Anglo-French armistice declaration of November 8th had included the clause: 'Indigenous population should exercise the right of self-determination regarding the form of national government under which they should live.' It was reasonable enough as a statement of intention, and accorded with President Wilson's post-war doctrine of self-determination for the liberated nations. But it posed incalculable dangers for those territories which had been freed from the rule of the Turks and which had no interest in, or facility for, government as the western nations knew it. As time went on Cox and Gertrude — she following a sudden and almost inexplicable *volte face* — were prepared to try to form a national government from the rag-bag of merchants and ex-Turkish officials of Damascus and Baghdad who now flocked around them with ill-conceived plans and ambitions. Wilson was not. He believed, rightly or wrongly, that to seek the sanction of a people with no experience of government, who were divided between townsfolk who sought no greater freedom than that which allowed them to wrangle and double-deal to their heart's content, and tribesmen who asked nothing more than to be left alone to wage their feuds, was the extreme of folly. 'Govern or get out,' was the gist of his argument. Gertrude's friend Frank Balfour had been made Military Governor of Baghdad, so that she had another ally close to hand. 'If we get a permanent form of government established here by this time next year I think we shall be lucky; meanwhile we shall go on, I suppose, as we are, with the C-in-C at the head of the administration. As long as it is Sir William it doesn't matter how long he occupies that post, for he is so wise and liberal in his dealings with the administrative side ... ' Things were not so easy for Wilson, however. Tough and intellectually formidable, he was not easily by-passed in the civil councils over which he was supposed to preside. The military, however, had a stranglehold over any policy he wished to pursue. Questions of law and order were in their somewhat ineffectual hands; and he was, in army rank, a mere Captain, though in 1919 he was given the rank of Brevet Lt-Colonel. Gertrude in her civilian capacity was in a much better position than he to deal with them on a footing of personal equality, and she and they began to form a united front against Wilson and his policy.

In August 1918, Wilson had received a letter from Hirtzel of the India Office congratulating him on his appointment as Acting Civil Commissioner, and he was somewhat surprised to find in it a reference to 'a letter from Miss Gertrude Bell which contains a flaming testimonial to your qualities and to the success of your administration ... ' It was the first intimation to Wilson that his assistant was in touch with Whitehall on matters of government. Their relationship remained tenable, if occasionally strained, however. Meals in No. 1 Mess at the Political Office in Baghdad were memorable events for many visitors at this time. Bertram Thomas recalled the gatherings there of the 'good and the great', who made the mess their home, with AT, as Wilson was always called, taking the principal guests for a walk before dinner and conferring on them a monologue on some chosen topic which gave the impression that he had 'swotted' his subject 'in the Encyclopaedia Britannica' before they arrived. Meals with the brilliant chief and Miss Bell were much looked forward to by visitors of the period.

In February 1919 Wilson sent to the India Office via the Foreign Department at Delhi a memorandum by Gertrude entitled *Self-Determination in Mesopotamia*, together with a note on the views of the Naquib of Baghdad, an important figure in the community though aged and representative of the Sunni minority. It was a closely reasoned document and it showed that at this stage her views and Wilson's, though he expressed reservations in his covering note to the Foreign Department, were far from being irreconcilable. 'The publication of the Anglo-French declaration,' she wrote, 'whatever may have been its political significance elsewhere, was at best a regrettable necessity in the Iraq.' She went on:

Previous to its appearance the people of Mesopotamia, having witnessed the successful termination of the war, had taken it for granted that the country would remain under British control and were as a whole content to accept the decision of arms. The declaration opened up other possibilities which were regarded almost universally with anxiety, but gave opportunity for political intrigue to the less stable and more fanatical elements ... its publication occurred very shortly after the return to Baghdad under the terms of the Armistice of a number of persons undesirable in the interests of public tranquillity. Men of Arab race who had been in Turkish Civil or Military employment and had

thrown in their lot with the Turks after the occupation, active
members of the Committee of Union and Progress (the Party
to whom the entrance of Turkey into the War against Great
Britain was directly due) and others who had not ventured to
remain in Baghdad on account of their well-known Turkish
sympathies came back from Mosul early in November ... The
effect of the declaration was no doubt heightened by the news
that the Sharif Faisal had gone to the Peace Conference as the
representative of an independent Arab State.

There was reference to the difficulties of minorities in Syria and
Iraq and to the 'invidious position' of stable elements such as the
Naquib and the Darwesh, Sayid Muhammad Kadhim al Yazdi.

By the time her report had reached London, Gertrude was on
her way to Paris, her first visit 'home' for nearly four years. She
had gone at the instigation of Wilson who was anxious that she
should put the case for Iraq at the Peace Conference and believed
that she was as well qualified as anyone to do so. She stayed at the
Hotel Majestic, close by the residences of the main Foreign Office
delegation and of Lloyd George and President Wilson. The story
of the subsequent events has been told time and again: the
whispered conversations among the national clans, endless tea and
dinner parties; the famous statesmen of the world rushing to and
fro with breathless enthusiasm for their various causes; and at
the centre of it all, the diminutive figure of Lawrence in his silken
Arab robes with gold-threaded *agal*, and his charge the Amir
Faisal, or the Sharif Faisal as they now called him, son of Husain
of Mecca, come to pick up the rewards of the war-time alliance.
Sir Hubert Young had spent the latter part of the war in Syria
with Allenby after serving in Iraq, and now he was translated to
assisting Curzon who held the Foreign Office fort while Balfour
was away in Paris. He had met Lawrence during the latter's visit to
Basra in 1916 and was so confounded by his antics that he never
sought to renew their old friendship. Among the first documents
to meet Young's gaze when he went to the Foreign Office was a
petition from the so-called Committee of the Covenant, formed
by a group of Faisal's Syrian and Mesopotamian officers in the
aftermath of the victory at Aqaba on July 6th, 1917. Towards the
end of that year the officers had formed an offshoot of the organisation, the Covenant of Iraq, and on June 11th, 1918 they had
petitioned the British Government asking that areas in Arabia

which were free and independent before the war, and areas emancipated from Turkish rule by the action of Arabs themselves during the war, would be recognised as independent and supported in their struggle for freedom. 'When I saw this document for the first time in the FO, it at once became clear to me why the Arabs had made such superhuman efforts to win their race with the British cavalry into Deraa, Damascus and Aleppo ... ', he wrote. The promises to Husain, the demands of the Covenanters, the Sykes–Picot agreement and the Balfour Declaration combined to produce a pretty skein for the statesmen to unravel. 'It never entered anyone's mind that to make peace with Turkey would take almost exactly as long as it had taken to fight her, and that as far as Mesopotamia was concerned no less than seven years would pass before final agreement had been reached,' wrote Young.

Already many of the milling delegates and advisers in Paris had expressed their views forcibly to the *Interdepartmental Conference on Middle East Affairs*, formed by Lloyd George's coalition government to consider the 'whole question' in the last months of 1918. Lawrence, already filling the role of war hero for which the British public yearned, had made his view plain. There should be three independent Sharifian states, Syria and Upper and Lower Mesopotamia, under the three sons of Husain, while the old man ruled the Hijaz as King and Caliph. Wilson in Baghdad had replied that the time was not ripe for an Arab government in that country, and reiterated his response to the provisions of the Sykes–Picot agreement that 'Mesopotamia neither expected nor desired sweeping schemes of independence'. Nevertheless, in November 1918 he had been instructed to ask the people of the country three questions: Did they favour a single Arab state under British tutelage? If so did they consider that a titular Arab head should be placed over the new state? In that event whom would they prefer as head of State? Wilson's reply was that there was no adequate means of establishing public opinion in Iraq at that time. 'There was no conclusive reply,' said Young.

In March Gertrude wrote: 'I'm lunching tomorrow with Mr Balfour (Foreign Secretary) who, I fancy, really doesn't care. Ultimately I hope to catch Mr Lloyd George by the coat tails, and if I can manage to do so I believe I can enlist his sympathies. Meanwhile we've sent for Colonel Wilson from Baghdad.' The Civil Commissioner had been given his new rank of temporary Lt-Colonel in order to give him something like adequate status in a country under military occupation. She also said they had sent for Hogarth to help form a solid block with Lawrence, so as to present a united opinion of 'Near Easterns'. 'I'm filling up my time by getting into touch with the French ... The Mesopotamian settlement is so closely linked with the Syrian that we can't consider one without the other, and in the case of Syria it's the French attitude that counts.'

By the end of March Wilson had arrived and Gertrude was preparing to leave for a well-earned holiday with her father. They had dinner with Wickham Steed, the editor of *The Times*, 'I don't like him but he was very useful', and they were taken by Domnul and Lawrence to see French political journalists. 'After dinner TEL explained exactly the existing situations between Faisal and his Syrians on the one hand and France on the other ... He did it quite admirably. His charm, simplicity and sincerity made a deep personal impression and convinced his listeners ... ' Wilson was not so enchanted. In April, after Gertrude had gone on a motoring holiday through Europe with her father, he had lunched with Lloyd George and met Chaim Weizmann, and had tea with Balfour and Lord Robert Cecil, the 'moving spirit in the League of Nations movement'. He left Paris in May, 'having done all I could'. Before returning to Baghdad he wrote:

Miss Bell, who was in Paris when I arrived, left before I did and passed through Paris on April 22nd on her way to Algiers ... I saw a good deal of Colonel T E Lawrence whilst in Paris; he originally came with Sharif Faisal, but stayed on after the latter had left Paris and returned to Syria. He is about to retire into private life; he seems to have done immense harm and our difficulties with the French in Syria seem to me to be mainly due to his actions and advice. I also saw Sharif Faisal twice – at his house – a florid Louis XVI mansion, and once at the Majestic where he had tea with Miss Bell and I. He was the centre of a net of French intrigue ... as the self constituted champion of Syria ... The conflict of the ideals of Zionism with the hard facts of Muhammedan predominance in Palestine is another matter with which the proposed International Commission will have to deal and for which there is no obvious solution ... Curzon was enormously overworked, rather depressed and pessimistic... Lord Hardinge is at Paris but is now a nonentity ... I saw a good deal of Sir Arthur Hirtzel who is as good as ever, but

19 Women of the Howeitat at Tor al Tubaiq, northern Arabia

20 Shaikhs of Abu Tayya at the camp of the Howeitat

21, 22, 23 Tribesmen pose for Gertrude at Hail

24 At camp, Gertrude's servant Fattuh in the foreground

rather too anti Turk and anti Muhammedan to be quite a safe
guide for HMG in these matters I should think.

While Wilson and Gertrude moved around Paris putting their
somewhat divergent viewpoints to all and sundry, a separate cause
was being canvassed at the same hotel tables and in the same
chambers and lobbies: that of the Zionists and the demand of the
Jews for a national home in compliance with the Balfour Declaration. In 1917, at the start of his final campaign against the Turks
in Syria, Allenby had taken the precaution of appointing his own
military intelligence chief in Cairo, Colonel Richard Meinertzhagen, the nephew of Sidney Webb. He worked alongside
Wyndham Deedes, Wingate's right-hand man until then, who was
responsible for political intelligence under the new regime.
Meinertzhagen's first act was to appoint as his chief 'agent' in
Palestine the fair-haired, blue-eyed Jew Aaron Aaronsohn who
had hitherto been in Cairo as Chaim Weizmann's representative
among the intriguing factions of the British war administration.
Aaronsohn, who also kept in close touch with the Americans
through the U.S. Department of Agriculture, for whom he worked
as a botanist in pre-war Palestine, knew the Turks, Arabs,
Germans and Britons who roamed the region better than any man
alive, though few of them knew him as anything more than an
innocent among them. He proved one of the most brilliant spies
of the war, contributing vitally to the success of Allenby's campaign, only to be killed in a mysterious air accident over the
English Channel during the Peace Conference in 1919.

After the capture of Jerusalem Meinertzhagen was transferred
to the War Office as deputy to General 'Freddie' Maurice, the
Director of Military Operations, where he acted as a counterbalance
to what had come to be regarded as the 'Lawrence' or 'Sharifite'
lobby. His own political vacillations were just about comparable
with Lawrence's. When he first went to the Middle East he was a
convinced Zionist who was suspicious of the Jews. After he left
the area he became a Hebraphile who was suspicious of Zionism.
At Paris he was to be seen for the most part in the company of
Weizmann, and while Gertrude was present at the Conference he
brought Faisal, Lawrence and Weizmann together to compose
a famous letter to Felix Frankfurter, the head of the American
Zionist delegation. The letter was eventually signed by Faisal:
'Dear Mr Frankfurter—I want to take this opportunity of my

P

final contact with American Zionists to tell you what I have often been able to say to Dr Weizmann in the past. We feel that the Arabs and Jews are cousins in race, have suffered similar oppression at the hands of powers stronger than themselves ... We Arabs, especially the educated among us, look with the deepest sympathy on the Zionist movement ... We will wish the Jews a hearty welcome here ... People less informed and less responsible than our leaders and yours ignoring the need for co-operation of the Arabs and Zionists, have been trying to exploit the local difficulties that must necessarily arise in Palestine in the early stages of our movements ... Faisal.'

It was but one remarkable event in very strange and indeterminate proceedings. The representatives of the Allied Powers eventually decided to postpone decisions on matters of self-determination and appointed an International Commission instead. Wilson had returned to an Iraq which was dangerously disturbed and which had no adequate means to deal with large-scale violence. He held his job reluctantly, having insisted from the moment he took over that he was there in an 'acting' capacity only until Sir Percy could leave Tehran and resume his authority. Cox on the other hand was not too keen to return and in August 1919 wrote to Wilson: 'As I have told you the only reason which would tempt me back to Mespot would be the prospect of handing the job over to you.'

Gertrude made a leisurely way back accompanied by her maid Marie Delaere who had waited for her at Sloane Street and Rounton during the war years. She called on Clayton and Milne Cheetham, then in charge of the virtually defunct Arab Bureau. She also had another meeting with Meinertzhagen who had returned to Cairo from Paris, though Allenby was shortly to give him marching orders. Faisal – already called by his supporters 'King of Syria' – was at that moment in London. The Syrian question was still in the melting pot and France took up an increasingly equivocal position. All the pretenders to power in the Arab lands passed to and fro and Gertrude met many of them as she and Clayton made a tour of the Levant and Palestine. They talked to Storrs, Governor of Jerusalem after Allenby's occupation in direct succession to Pontius Pilate. And they met innumerable refugees, Galicians, Jews, Arabs, Iraqis, Turkish deserters. Perhaps the most important of these homeless wanderers from the point of view of post-war Iraq was the omnipresent Sayid Talib, finally released from captivity by the Indian Government and seeking support among the disaffected Iraqis in Syria. But there were others who were destined to play an important part in the political life of the region, among them Nuri Said Pasha, the leading figure in Faisal's army. She went through Syria to Damascus, then to Beirut and on to Aleppo where she saw Fattuh for the first time since the war started. He had fallen on hard times and she did her best to help him by approaching the authorities and lending him money. 'We have had such happy times together – my poor Fattuh!'

On October 8th Wilson wrote to Captain Geoffrey Stephenson who had been a Political Officer in Iraq and was now working at the India Office: 'I shall be interested to know what Miss Bell is going to do when she comes here. She will take some handling. I have abolished the Arab Bureau but I have no doubt she can find a place ... some sort of outlet must be found for her energies, and she is undoubtedly popular in Baghdad among the natives, with whom she keeps in close touch, to her advantage, though it is sometimes dangerous.' Wilson need not have worried about Gertrude's employment. Her first self-imposed task on arriving back in Baghdad was to compose another of her long and very readable essays, this time on the Syria she had just examined at first hand. It began with a conversation piece from an official report of the Peace Conference which pre-empted a good deal of argument about government in Arab countries:

1st Statesman: The country will be very badly governed.
2nd Statesman: Why should it not be badly governed?
3rd Statesman: It ought to be badly governed.

Entitled 'Syria in October 1919', it began: 'The fortnight which I spent in Syria (4th October to 20th October) fell at a time of acute political uncertainty and apprehension.' She went on to give another of her masterly summaries of the problems – the dismay caused by an agreement reached by the French and British Prime Ministers and Lord Allenby on September 16th, and the possible withdrawal of troops which that agreement foreshadowed; the difficulties posed by the geographical boundaries of the administrative territories, roughly according to the Sykes–Picot agreement, and a detailed account of the functions of the British and French officers working within those boundaries. There was a long section on the Zionist claim, concluding with the words:

> If both parties would exercise forbearance, it is conceivable that Zionists might obtain a good deal of what they want without forcing the Moslems to relinquish much of what they have got, but I could see no tendency towards moderation among the latter, and no intention among the former to go forward with caution. Dr Weizmann's representative in Jerusalem, Dr Eder, rejects the idea that Zionism can be allowed to proceed slowly ... The increase of material well-being he regards as the most persuasive of arguments, and no doubt up to a point he is right ...

She reviewed the activities of the returning agitators and the new power among the Turks, Mustafa Kamal; the view of Yasin Pasha, 'now one of the extreme exponents of Arab independence as against a French mandate or any other form of foreign control ... [and] the moving spirit of the Ahd al Iraq, The Mesopotamian League'. There were references to long conversations with Yasin and with other members of the League, with Jafar Pasha al Askari and Yusuf Beg Suwaidi, Governor and deputy Governor of Aleppo; and to the views of British officials. Finally:

> The oysters have been eaten and put down in the bill; it is useless to speculate by whom and in what proportions the bill will be met. A more profitable line of thought lies in the direction of considering how the twelve-month existence – even if it fail to exist longer – of an independent Arab State has affected and will affect Mesopotamia. It is true that the Arab administration has left much to be desired, and equally true that it has been artificially financed by our subsidy to the Sharif; but it has presented, nevertheless, the outward appearance of a national Government; public business has been kept going, tramways have run, streets have been lighted, people have bought and sold, and a normal world has been maintained ... and if it crumbles ... its failure will be attributed, not to inherent defects, but to British indifference and French ambition ... We have stated that it is our intention to assist and establish in Syria and in Mesopotamia indigenous governments and administrations ... I believe that events of the last year have left us no choice in Mesopotamia. Local conditions, the vast potential wealth of the country, the tribal character of its rural population, the lack of material from which to draw official personnel will make the problem harder to solve than elsewhere. I venture to think that the answer to such objections is that any alterna-

tive line of action would create problems the solution of which we are learning to be harder still. GLB, November 15, 1919.

Wilson admired the report for its thoroughness. But it contradicted everything he stood for in the administration, at any rate in its concluding sentences. He sent the report to the Secretary of State on the day he received it, with a covering note which said: 'Sir, I have the honour to enclose herewith an interesting and valuable note by Miss G. L. Bell CBE, entitled "Syria in 1919". A few comments thereon in so far as it directly affects these territories are perhaps called for from me.' He went on:

> The fundamental assumption throughout this note and, I should add, throughout recent correspondence which has reached me from London, is that an Arab State in Mesopotamia and elsewhere within a short period of years is a possibility, and that the recognition and creation of a logical scheme of Government on these lines, in supercession of those on which we are now working in Mesopotamia, would be practicable and popular; in other words the assumption is that the Anglo-French Declaration of November 18th, 1918 represents a practical line of policy to pursue in the near future. My observations in this country and elsewhere have forced me to the conclusion that this assumption is erroneous ... I venture, probably for the last time, in my present capacity, to lay before HMG the considerations which have led me to this conclusion.

He went on to argue, forcibly and with a good deal of historical evidence on his side, that it was impossible to create an artificial state, 'a new sovereign Mohammadan State', by diplomatic or administrative means out of the remnants of the Turkish Empire. The sentiments of the population were against such a belief, he said. The warlike Kurds 'numbering half a million will never accept an Arab ruler'. The Shia, numbering $1\frac{3}{4}$ million in Iraq, would not accept Sunni domination — 'and no form of Government has yet been envisaged, which does not involve Sunni domination.' A revived Turkish Government would, he said, have less difficulty in asserting itself. Then there were substantial Jewish and Christian minorities to be considered. Three-quarters of the population was tribal, he reminded Whitehall, 'with no previous tradition of obedience to any government'. He concluded:

> Finally, if I may be permitted to make a personal reference, I

beg leave to assure the Government that by birth, by training and by temperament, I am in sympathy with a democratic as opposed to a bureaucratic conception of Government, and if I find myself unable to advocate the immediate introduction of a logical scheme of Arab Government into Mesopotamia it is because I believe the result would be the antithesis of a democratic Government and that the creation and maintenance of an indigenous Arab Government is inconsistent with the changes which we are now endeavouring to introduce into the Governments of India and Egypt ... '

By now Wilson's replacement by Cox was agreed in principle, though the latter showed no particular anxiety to return. Meanwhile, growing personal animosity between the chief and his distinguished assistant complicated the day-to-day life of the Civil Commission. In December 1919, Wilson wired Cox: 'Current gossip that you are coming here, to be succeeded by Haig in Tehran.' And a month before Cox had wired to the effect that he would not return except as High Commissioner. But that appointment could not properly be made until the mandate had been settled and approved by the League of Nations. Clearly, however Cox and Wilson intended the changeover to take place early in the new year, for on December 20th AT asked Cox if he should order furniture for him. Two days later, following the intervention of Curzon, the return was postponed. By January 1920, Wilson seems to have been at his wits' end. On the 2nd he wrote a rambling, almost incoherent letter to Cox which referred over and over again to a nameless 'individual', and followed it with an even longer draft telegram: 'I do not think there will always be room in this office for activities of the kind which I suggest (in telegram). The telegram will serve to show how the land lies.' Correspondence went on for two months, both men referring to an 'individual' or to 'him' in the course of which Sir Percy tried to persuade AT to stay on as his deputy. On March 10th, 1920 Cox wired again:

When your draft telegram of June 4 reached me ... I was expecting order to proceed home at once and contemplated asking you to defer decision in regard to individual referred to until I got home ... I am now instructed to await my successor expected in the latter part of May. Previous to receipt of your letter and draft telegram I have received a letter from individual indicating that there was some rift in the lute. I took it to be a

passing cloud and in reply said that I hoped it would have
passed before my answer arrived. In these circumstances, were
I coming soon, I should have asked you to reconsider the idea
of dispensing with individual's services from April and letting
matter stand over until I came as I think I could find use for—.
As things are I stay here until late May and then run home as I
hope ... so I feel less justified in tying your hands.

Nevertheless Cox felt that it would be a terrible blow to the
'individual' and if relations were still strained he recommended
Wilson to give 'individual' leave for the hot season. In the meantime, he said, if Wilson approved, he would write 'to individual
and say that if correspondence with people in high places is indulged in over your head and possibly on lines opposed to your
views, misunderstandings are inevitable and only right course is
to observe complete loyalty to you ... I will wait for the sign
from you.' A letter from Cox to Gertrude, dated November 9th,
1919 and delivered on February 9th, 1920 read: 'Dear Khatun,
It is good to know that you are back; how I wish we could for-
gather and have a confab. What a lot you must know of the doings
of the mighty! ... Your welcome letter of August 7th took three
months to reach here ... ' On it Wilson had written: 'Miss Bell—
what an extraordinarily long time this has taken to come.' The
triangular dispute was perhaps not so very confidential.

On March 19th AT had written to Sir Percy in response to a
telegram from Tehran: 'I hope to meet *his* father shortly and I shall
then suggest to *him* the necessity for inducing his *son* to spend the
hot weather or part of it away from Mesopotamia. Apart from this
the situation has in other respects somewhat improved. Nevertheless, the correspondence continues. I regard it obviously with
suspicion and I care not whether it is well intentioned or in conformity with my views or not. I think therefore, that a communication from you along the lines suggested would be of use.'

This correspondence occurred at the worst possible time. Iraq
was on the point of revolt when it started. Rebellion had broken
out when it came to the boil. Meanwhile Sir Percy arrived in
London to advise the Cabinet in person on its Mesopotamian and
Arabian policies. On July 14th Wilson wrote to him at the India
Office and at last he came out into the open:

If you can find a job for Miss Bell at home I think you will be
well advised to do so. Her irresponsible activities are a source

of considerable concern to me here and are not a little resented
by the Political Officers. She will have finished the Blue Book
by the end of the month, after which there will really be nothing
for her to do.

There can be little doubt that Gertrude had set out to promote
her own policies, policies which had been discussed, formulated
and sharpened by her meetings with Hogarth, Lawrence, Faisal
and the rest of the Sharifite lobby at Paris. She had access to the
most important men of government and she saw no reason why
she should not use those contacts. It has been said in her defence
that it was 'a typically woman-like thing' to correspond over her
chief's head with his superiors. But it is not a defence that she
would have welcomed. She inhabited a man's world without
asking or giving quarter, and if indiscreet correspondence has
been characteristic of many women in history, so has it been of
men. Her letters were not malicious and were probably not intended to defy Wilson so much as to put her own point of view.
All the same, they were indiscreet and caused Wilson great annoyance at a time of peculiar difficulty in his temporary and unsought
job. One thing is certain, Gertrude helped to destroy her own
high standing among the 'Politicals' by her disloyalty to Wilson.
Much can be said on the other side. Opinions which Wilson came
to hold later hardly accorded with his description of himself as a
born democrat and liberal. His unbending religious orthodoxy
was laughable to many people, and offensive to others. His Latin
tags in the Political Office and the Mess, sometimes misquoted,
and his super-patriotism – Cromwell's 'We are a people with the
stamp of God upon us' was his favourite quotation – became
something of a joke. Yet he was, without a shadow of doubt, the
hero-figure of the young Political Officers who came to Iraq after
the war. They and many others in the community admired him
beyond measure for his unfailing support for the underdog and
his unwillingness to submit to the tyranny of Whitehall and the
military. Whenever a Political Officer was in difficulty or there
was fighting in his territory, Wilson was there within hours, often
using an aeroplane to get to the scene. By the same token,
Gertrude was ridiculed for what was often called her 'status
snobbery', her dislike of her own sex and her hob-nobbing with
the elite. On one occasion she wrote to Chirol: 'I really think I am
beginning to get hold of the women here, I mean the women of

the better classes. *Pas sans peine*, though they meet one more than half way ... I am now going to try a more ambitious scheme and get the leading ladies to form a committee to collect among rich families (themselves) funds for a small women's hospital for the better classes, about which some of them seem keen.' Her relations with the Arabs were based on much the same assumptions of worth. As the shaikhs and men of the desert filtered through her office, asking to see Cox or, later, Wilson, she would greet them according to status and with unfailing excitement. There would be a high-pitched greeting, the customary 'Peace be upon thee', and then endless enquiries as to the health and prosperity of the visitor and his family, accompanied by much gesticulation. If the visitor was important, goodbyes would be prolonged and accompanied by many utterances of *Fi aman illah!* Go in the peace of the Lord. If they were of lesser importance they would be sent on their way with a mere *rihlah muwaffaqah* – bon voyage. When the visitor had departed, the young Political Officers within earshot would look out of the office doors leading on to the balconies and repeat the performance to each other, simulating the gestures of Al Khatun, like Ibn Saud entertaining his desert warriors.

On December 18th, 1919 Gertrude had written to her father to tell him that she looked forward to a visit from him early in the new year, that she had entertained thirty ladies to tea, was riding a lot and generally enjoying life. There was, she said, no news of demobilisation, but she hoped that they would get some of the men out of the country before the hot weather came, though 'I shall miss all the nice people bitterly when they go'. She had been to tea with one of her closest Arab friends, Hajji Naji, 'the farmer who takes no interest in politics as long as he is assured that we won't go'. Then came an aside which, in the light of what was to happen in the months ahead, was to prove as prophetic as it was contradictory:

The provincial magnates are going strongly against an Arab Amir, I think, and even against an Arab Govt. They say they don't want to be rid of one tyranny in order to fall into the clutches of another. I hope that is the way things will go, for I don't want a Court here and all the fuss and trouble. It could not fail to be an impediment. However, that prospect is fading. It's a compliment to us isn't it?

There was a final paragraph that helps to establish the somewhat compromising position of Gertrude in the aftermath of the war. 'Would you please glance at the enclosed ... published by the Intelligence Branch here,' she asked her father. 'I should be very glad if you would enter a protest against any official body so un-qualified issuing things of this sort ... Let them draw up proper propaganda written by competent persons, but this stuff does nothing but harm.'

The atmosphere of the time and the qualities of Britain's administrators are summed up by the Van Esses. They were es-pecially fond of Wilson and Gertrude, and she spent some of her happiest moments in Iraq with them. Mrs Van Ess wrote:

A.T. was a great friend of John's; they saw eye to eye on the problems of the current situation and their solutions would have been nearly identical. John considered Colonel Wilson the brains of Sir Percy Cox's administration; he recognised that Sir Percy had an impressive façade and was an imposing figurehead, but he often exclaimed in private, 'He is just a rubber stamp for Lord Curzon!'

Of Gertrude:

During those lovely spring days Gertrude sat with her feet tucked under her in true Arab style, on a settee in John's study, smoking his cigarettes and arguing with him interminably, but always amicably. 'But Gertrude!' he would exclaim. 'You are flying in the face of four millenniums of history if you try to draw a line around Iraq and call it a political entity! Assyria always looked to the west and east and north, and Babylonia to the south. They have never been an independent unit. You've got to take time to get them integrated, it must be done gradually. They have no conception of nationhood yet.'

But those joyous days of spring sunshine were flanked by the cold, wet months of winter and by the unendurable heat of summer. Problems of day-to-day government and international politics were interspersed with long periods of concern for the archaeological treasures of the country and Gertrude made many arduous journeys to the great mounds near Hillah where ancient Babylon lay partly bared, and to those other mounds of Akkad and Sumer, Babylonia and Chaldea at Sippar, Kish, Birs (ancient Borsippa), Erech, Lagash, Larsa, Eridu and Ur – where so much remained to be discovered and where she kept a keen vigil lest robbers or thoughtless troops should disturb the debris or the hidden tombs in which were buried the earliest known records of mankind. And she made frequent journeys to Ctesiphon where the great Roman-inspired arch, damaged in war-time fighting, was in danger of collapse. Gertrude and the Director of Public Works, J. M. Wilson, an able and sensitive architect, had taken it on themselves to preserve for posterity a structure of which she had written: 'It is the most remarkable of all known Sassanian buildings, and one of the most imposing ruins in the world.' When in Baghdad she would often trudge through dusty lanes or slither through mud and slime to the central bazaars of the city, protected at their entrance by the splendid Saracenic hall of Khan Aurtmah, in order to rescue from unscrupulous salesmen priceless cuneiform tablets and other precious objects stolen from the archaeological sites. This was the period of the British Museum's and the University of Pennsylvania's interest in Ur and of the visit of the redoubtable Dr H. R. Hall who later spoke of the great help Gertrude rendered him and of her 'devotion to her self-imposed mission'.

In February 1920 Gertrude received news of the death of her uncle Sir Frank Lascelles. 'I did love him so much,' she wrote to Chirol. 'Domnul, please take care of yourself. There's no one to replace people like you – I mean to replace them in my own life.' In March her father arrived in Baghdad, 'looking extremely well – it's impossible to say what a joy it is to see him'. She took him on a tour of the country, staying with the Political Officers stationed along their route and meeting Arab notables as they went. Fattuh arrived too from Aleppo to help raise her spirits. But it was altogether a depressing time. Trouble was in the air throughout the country and her long and bitter battle with Wilson had taken its toll of her. And despite his genial manner, her father was suffering the early pangs of financial trouble, something that was unique in his experience. As the post-war depression began to take a grip on the economy, the ordinary share-values of the Dorman Long Company, in which Sir Hugh and Sir Arthur Dorman were by far the largest stockholders, began to fall. In the hope of boosting their quoted price the two old men began to buy them up and in the end they competed with each other as much out of vanity as of tactical necessity. Their buying spree did nothing to improve things, however. Neither was reduced to poverty but the decline of the company's fortunes, along with those of the rest of the steel industry, worsened over the years until the watershed of 1926; and for the first time in her life Gertrude became aware of the need for some financial stringency, as opposed to the care which she usually exercised.

Soon after her father's departure, in June 1920, Gertrude received a call from one of Baghdad's most sensible and respected political figures, Sulaiman Faidhi. Not only her office but her home too attracted a constant procession of visitors intent on staking their claims to influence and office under the new dispensation. But Sulaiman was different. He had no personal ambitions other than to see an Arab government composed of honest men working within the framework of a British mandate. Gertrude recorded the conversation which took place on the evening of Saturday June 12th, for the benefit of the Secretary of State and the Viceroy.

Sulaiman told her: 'Since you took Baghdad you have been talking about an Arab government, but three years and more have elapsed and nothing materializes. You say that you can do nothing until peace with Turkey has been signed, but so far as we know that may be months or even years ahead. You say that you can't do anything until the mandate had been granted you. But that explanation does not carry conviction because we have seen an Arab government set up in Syria before any western power had received the mandate ... You said in your declaration that you would set up a native government drawing its authority from the initiative and free choice of the people concerned, yet you proceed to draw up a scheme without consulting anyone. It would have been easy for you to take one or two leading men into your councils and this would have removed the reproach which is levelled against your scheme ... Your scheme is already in everyone's hands ... practically everyone in Baghdad who cares to have a copy has got one ... We do not like it at all ... I will give you one example since you ask for one. We should not agree to the President of the Council being appointed by the Government. We hold it essential that he should be chosen by the Council ... ' Sulaiman ended with a plea: 'You would be well advised to give us a long rope. We cannot possibly run the country without your assistance and advice and we shall come to you at once for both if you don't try to force us to do so. It is my belief that you cannot force us, but if you act now with care and consideration you will never need to try.' Sulaiman's was a salutary warning, but little heed was taken of moderate opinion in the spring of 1920. In April Britain's mandate was confirmed at San Remo and the British administration pursued its plan to govern provisionally with an Arab leader of its own choice, the Naqib, as President of the Council. Wilson had warned, and so had well-intentioned Iraqis. The dam was about to burst.

In the summer of 1920 rebellion broke out, beginning with tribal conflicts on the middle Euphrates and spreading quickly as religious leaders fanned the hatred of centuries among Shia and Sunni. It was the districts around the holy cities of Najaf and Karbala that suffered most. A British peace-keeping force, consisting mostly of raw recruits since the seasoned soldiers of the British army had been demobilised, finally put down the rebellion. But there were many casualties, particularly in the Manchester Regiment which was sent up to the Hillah region on the Euphrates. The Tigris tribes and the main cities were not greatly affected, but the outburst cost the British exchequer an estimated £40 million and the public at home was becoming heartily sick of the Arabian adventure. It was in this atmosphere of disillusion, with constant cries from the British Press for the Government to cut its losses, that the most inspired and persistent public relations scheme in the country's history was conceived – 'Lawrence of Arabia'. Obligingly, an American journalist named Lowell Thomas, who had seen Lawrence in Syria and had a passing acquaintance-ship with him, decided to tour the world with the story of the desert adventure which was largely a figment of his own imagination and which extended by a good distance Lawrence's own somewhat romanticised version of war-time events. Thomas filled lecture halls and theatres with his dramatic story, crowds waited for hours to obtain tickets for his performances at the Royal Opera House and the Royal Albert Hall only to find that every seat was taken. He attracted an audience of more than a million in a few months. Up to this time, Gertrude Bell was by common consent the most famous of contemporary English people in Arabia. Within a year, all previous history, all fact and sense had been swamped by the Lawrence myth, though Lawrence was the victim rather than the instigator of the deceit.

The rebellion in Iraq was shortlived, but its consequences were far-reaching. The British Government determined to find a way out of its dilemma at the least possible expense to the taxpayer.

But Lawrence had written a letter to the *Sunday Times* on August 22nd, 1920 suggesting that the rebellion was a spontaneous rising against British oppression in the country. It was just one of a series of letters to the Press from the old Arab Bureau brigade which incensed Wilson at a time when he was coping with insurrection, along with the Kurdish problem where an early attempt at autonomy had been abandoned by the administration. The military authority was unwilling to support him, especially since General Sir Aylmer Haldane had taken over from MacMunn as G.O.C. in March, and soon another problem came to the fore – the rising strength and insistence of Ibn Saud. Wilson's was not a light burden and he was at no great pains to conceal his irritation from the India Office. According to his biographer he comforted himself at the time by putting a new Latin motto over his desk, *Aequam memento rebus in arduis servare mentem,* which he rendered rather freely – 'All men, when prosperity is at its height, should consider within themselves in what way they would endure disaster'. He beseeched the India Office, in the words of Cromwell, 'in the bowels of Christ, consider it possible that ye may be mistaken'. The quarrel between Wilson and Gertrude came to its unfortunate climax at the height of the revolt.

Gertrude seems to have known that she was in danger of being dismissed. In June she wrote in explanation of her admitted indiscretions, 'I had an appalling scene last week with AT ... I gave one of our Arab friends here a bit of information I ought not technically to have given. It wasn't of much importance, and it didn't occur to me I had done wrong until I mentioned it casually ... He told me my indiscretions were intolerable and that I should never see another paper in the office. I apologised for that particular indiscretion ... but he continued: "You've done more harm here than anyone. If I hadn't been going away myself I should have asked for your dismissal months ago – you and your Amir." I know really what's at the bottom of it – I've been right and he has been wrong.'

She was certainly stretching her chief's patience to an extreme limit when, at the start of the rebellion in July, she wrote a letter to Haldane the G.O.C. which expressed her belief that the bottom had dropped out of the agitation, an impression gained from 'many heart-to-heart interviews'. Haldane took her word for it and delayed military action, and afterwards cited Gertrude's letter to Wilson as an excuse. Wilson deserves the last word: '... it was,

to say the least, imprudent of him to prefer [her] private mis-
calculations to the measured misgivings ... of her official superior'.

Gertrude was by now an unashamed Sharifian. On July 10th
she wrote to Lawrence: 'Beloved Boy, I've been reading with
amusement your articles in the papers; what curious organs you
choose for self expression! However, whatever the organs I'm
largely in agreement with what you say. I have for some time past
been bringing up very forcibly the contention that the argument
to the effect that we can't put up an Arab Government here before
signing the peace with Turkey is quite obvious nonsense. I took
the example of Syria; Palestine is even better but we hadn't
appointed a King of the Jews when I first began the campaign
here. We've paid for our failure to make good our promises ...
If you knew what an infernal time I've had here! however I
suppose I shall tell you some day ... '

Then she admonished Lawrence for his remarks in the Press on
Ibn Saud. 'Now about your treatment of the Ibn Saud question.
It's all very well for you to talk as if the protection of the Hijaz
against Ibn Saud were an easy matter. It isn't. I repeat what I told
you in Paris that I.S. is much the stronger of the two. It is only
the fact that he has acted in accordance with our wishes which has
prevented him from gobbling up the Hijaz any time during the
past twelve months ... '

Whitehall, having more or less ignored Ibn Saud since the days
of the Shakespear mission, now saw in him a threat to its entire
Sharifian commitment. Philby had been sent from Iraq to Riyadh
to meet the Amir of Najd in the spring of 1917, as the princes of
Mecca were gaining in prominence and self-esteem. At the time
Ibn Saud was engaged in a desultory campaign against his constant rivals, the Shammar of Ibn Rashid. The Amir of Hail, in
alliance with the Turks, was harrying the Sharifian force around
the Hijaz railway at Madayin Saleh. Philby's mission was intended
to gain Ibn Saud's wholehearted support for Britain's war effort
and to induce him to attack Hail. Philby gave him £20,000 from
a purse in his own keeping and left the warrior to his own devices,
going on to meet the Sharif at Mecca. In the meantime, Ibn Saud
had received appeals from the people of the oasis town of Khurma,
between Najd and the Hijaz, for protection from the Sharif's
attacks. Hogarth was at Mecca at the same time on behalf of
Wingate, the new High Commissioner. 'The King occasionally
burst into full-throated badawin accents,' said Philby, 'but he was

usually polished and quiet, more like a Turkish *Mufti*.' Philby
asked him if he could make his return journey by land through the
Hijaz. The king refused, remarking that 'People were saying that
he had sold his country to the English'. As Philby went to take his
leave the old man said to the English party that 'they would come
in due course to accept his view of Ibn Saud's unworthiness'.
Philby replied: 'I was sent to Najd by the British Government to
see things with my own eyes, and it is my misfortune that I have
arrived at conclusions widely differing from those of Your
Majesty.' Hogarth, said Philby, averted his eyes. Now, in 1920, a
desert force called the Ikhwan, the Brotherhood, reviving the old
religious fanaticism of the Wahhabi kingdom, was on the rampage
and had already opened Ibn Saud's pathway to Mecca. Three times
in 1918, Husain's forces attacked the Saudi sympathisers of the
oasis of Khurma. In August of that year Philby wrote a memorandum to the Government in which he said: 'Ibn Saud most undoubtedly claims Khurma as being within his jurisdiction—he
does so not only on religious and territorial grounds but also on
historical, administrative and tribal grounds. He therefore considers the Sharif's action as aggressive and hostile to himself.' In
August, Wilson Pasha, Wingate's representative in the Hijaz,
declared: 'Khurma belongs to Husain.' Backed by British words,
if not deeds, Husain decided to try again in 1919. His army was
annihilated. In 1920 the House of Rashid, Ibn Saud's bitter rivals
in Najd, succumbed to the last of a long series of royal homicides.
Saud ibn Rashid, the young ruler who had been in the care of the
Sharif in his youth and had been the ally, however unreliable, of
the Turks, became the last victim of a bloody history of murder
and dishonour. By that time Britain, encouraged by Hogarth and
Lawrence, had begun to toy with the idea of an alliance between
the Rashids and Husain to bolster the tottering power of its Arab
protégés. But it was too late. Early in 1921 Ibn Saud took Hail.

In August 1920 the Iraqi insurrectionists claimed their most distinguished victim, Colonel Leachman, explorer and soldier of
fortune. In March, Leachman had been posted to Dulaim on the
Upper Euphrates, following an operation for appendicitis. He
occupied a district which for four years had been the centre of
looting and murder, but he gave as good as he got among the
wild men who surrounded him. Several officers had been killed
but the intrepid Leachman was not perturbed. On August 12th

25 A water well on the Hail route

26 Turkiyyeh, 'chatterbox' of
the Rashid court at Hail

27 A woman companion at Hail during Gertrude's house arrest

28 A view of Hail with Jabal Shammar in the background

29 The last camp in the Nafud desert on the way to Mesopotamia

30 Shammar tribesmen outside the gates of Hail

31 A playful tribesman at Al Juwarib

32 Gertrude's caravan leaving Hail

33 Shaikh Abdullah bin Haiya and one of his sons at Hail

34 Gertrude on her camel in Baghdad at the end of her central Arabian journey

he told a group of Iraqis to mend a culvert at Kadhimain near Fallujah. One of the Iraqis, Shaikh Dhari, turned to his friends and said that Leachman was strong and might do them harm if they refused. Leachman strode out to show them the way and as he went he was shot in the back. He was buried near the site of his murder but his body was later exhumed and taken to Baghdad where he was re-buried with full military honours at the North Gate cemetery on March 1st, 1921.

'He always used extremely unmeasured language to the Arabs and Shaikh Dhari had many grudges against him,' wrote Gertrude. 'He was a wild soldier of fortune but a very gallant officer and his name was known all over Arabia.' He was also capable of straight talking with Gertrude. 'Colonel Leachman told me the other day that my unbounded conceit was the talk of Iraq,' she admitted to Philby.

Another soldier of fortune, Sayid Talib, was back in Iraq and now saw himself as a suitable Head of State. 'The Lord knows what is going to happen here – the best suggestion I can make is that now Faisal is in England Sir Percy should crown him King of Mesopotamia in Westminster Abbey (if it hasn't tumbled down) and then come back hand in hand with him ... I don't see S. Talib as King, however, and I fancy that he had some doubts about it himself ... ' In September they were holding farewell parties for AT. 'The night before he left he came in to say good-bye. I told him that I was feeling more deeply discouraged than I could well say and that I regretted acutely that we had not made a better job of our relations. He replied that he had come to apologise and I stopped him and said I felt sure it was as much my fault as his and that I hoped he would carry away no ill-feelings, a sentiment to which he cordially responded.'

But she still thought he was wrong. 'What has happened here will always be remembered against him ... It may be my point of view that is wrong, in which case I certainly ought not to remain here. That will be for Sir Percy to judge.'

Sir Percy arrived in Basra in October 1920 to a popular welcome and a 17-gun salute. He had recently signed the Anglo-Persian agreement which was heralded as a triumph for Curzon's policy of barring the Bolsheviks' route to India, as earlier British policies had barred the same route to their imperial predecessors, but the euphoria did not last long. The Bolshevik army advanced through northern Persia and the country's administrative centre was

Q

moved from Tehran to Isfahan. By February 1921 Reza Khan the
Persian Minister of War had staged a *coup d'état* and repudiated the
Anglo-Persian treaty to the accompaniment of international pro-
tests that Cox had bribed three members of the Tehran government in an effort to gain majority support for Britain's plans in the
area. Such events did not bode well for Iraq. Nationalist politicians in many parts of the Middle East were beginning to take an
interest in the oil resources of the region, as were foreign countries and international companies. Though the subject was hardly
ever mentioned officially it certainly played a part in many of the
angry disputes which accompanied Britain's intervention in
Persia and Iraq, and in the semi-independent Gulf states which
flanked them. Cox was succeeded in Tehran first by Herman
Norman and then by Gertrude's old friend Sir Percy Loraine. She
was soon giving him friendly advice on the conduct of Persian
affairs.

The year 1921 belonged to Winston Churchill however. Whatever the consequences which might flow from his actions, nobody
would be able to complain of inertia. As soon as he became
Colonial Secretary at the start of the year he appointed Lawrence
his adviser on Arabian matters. But he took the precaution of
appointing a second adviser to an adjoining office, Colonel
Meinertzhagen the pro-Israelite.

20
Faisal's Kingdom

The situation that confronted H.M. Government in Iraq at the beginning of 1921 was a most unsatisfactory one.

Sir Winston Churchill,
The World Crisis: The Aftermath

In the aftermath of the rebellion and the intrigues of the year 1920, Gertrude sat down and calmly wrote her finest political work, *Review of the Civil Administration of Mesopotamia*. It was a monumental document and if Churchill, when he took over the responsibility for the territory, sought inside guidance, he found it in her brilliant summary of events. Made up of ten chapters, it was in effect a résumé of Britain's role in the Persian Gulf and Eastern Arabia and of the events which led from the appearance of the Indian Expeditionary Forces at the Shatt al Arab under cover of naval guns on November 6th, 1914 to the return of Sir Percy Cox in October 1920 as High Commissioner. She began:

In the spring of 1910, Ottoman rule in Mesopotamia was epitomised by a singularly competent observer, Mr J. G. Lorimer, British Resident in Baghdad, in words which cannot be bettered. 'The universal Turkish system of administration,' he wrote in the Political Diary for the month of March, 'is in almost every respect unsuitable to Iraq. The Turks themselves must recognise that it is a failure here, but probably few of them appreciate the cause, though it is sufficiently obvious. Iraq is not an integral part of the Ottoman Empire, but a foreign dependency ... I had no idea before coming to Baghdad of the extent to which Turkey is a country of red tape and blind and dumb officialdom, or of the degree in which the Turkish

position in Iraq is unsupported by physical force. One cannot
but admire, however, the dogged and uncomplaining resolution with which the Turkish civil bureaucracy and skeleton
army persist in their impossible tasks ... '

Such a survey of the past would seem to hold signal warnings for
those who came in succession to the Turks.

'No sooner had Sayid Talib left to meet Sir Percy than all the
undercurrent of hostility to him began to come to the surface,'
she wrote on October 10th, 1920. 'Sir Percy is bringing S. Talib
back with him and Baghdad is muttering grimly at the joint
arrival.' She went on to attack criticisms of British policy in the
home Press; criticisms which arose primarily from the vast and
increasing cost of the occupation to the taxpayer, over £20 million
a year at a time of grave economic difficulty. 'On the whole the
English papers write egregious nonsense in detail – such as, for
instance, that the management of Arab affairs has gone wrong
ever since the death of Maude! – Maude! anyone more totally removed from the remotest idea of self-government in Asia it would
be impossible to conceive ... One of the papers says, quite rightly,
that we had promised an Arab Government with British advisers.
Let us now turn to another mandated province – Palestine. The
same general principles should apply there as here, it seems to me;
yet within the last two months Herbert Samuel has established in
Palestine proper, exactly what has borne sway here, a British
Government with native advisers. He does it because any sort of
native institution of a really independent kind ... would reject
Zionism – but isn't that a sufficient condemnation of Zionism?'

Cox had brought with him Sir Colin Garbett as his chief secretary and Philby who was to act as adviser to the Minister of the
Interior in a provisional government. Sir Percy lost no time in
putting the plans formulated in Whitehall to the Administrative
Council. An Arab government under the presidency of the Naqib,
and the withdrawal of practically all land forces and their replacement by Air Force reinforcements with Air Vice-Marshal Sir
John Salmond taking over the command of defence forces, was
the gist of the plan. At this point Gertrude and Philby took virtual
charge of the proceedings. 'Sir Percy was interviewing Evelyn
Howell and Colonel Slater who are wholly concerned with
British ... personnel, matters which seem to me to be quite unimportant compared with the future of Mesopotamia ... ' She and

Philby sat down and arranged for the High Commissioner to go to Mosul to inform the local chiefs of his plans, to arrange for meetings with the leading Shaikhs of the Euphrates, particularly the Anaiza chief Fahad Beg, and wrote out a list of over a hundred notables he should interview. They formed a dynamic secretariat.

But such tasks were a small part of Gertrude's work at this time. Presented with a positive if by no means comprehensive plan of action, she found a new lease of life. Having completed her review of the administration, which was published as a Government Paper and earned the applause of both Houses of Parliament, she started again to produce a weekly intelligence summary and to invite all the leading figures of Iraq society to her office for informal talks. Her intelligence summaries resumed their old flavour of informative commentary which kept Whitehall abreast of events in a most unaccustomed way. The first edition to reach the Colonial Office was number 4, dated January 14th, 1921 (the first three went to the India Office) and Under-Secretary Shuckburgh noted: 'There is a lot of meat in this ... I should very much like to get hold of earlier numbers ... Will this be possible?' It gave an account of events up to the end of the year. Under the heading 'Electoral Law' Gertrude wrote that it had been amended to provide for tribal representation. 'The suggestion met with considerable opposition at the bottom of which lay the rooted objection of the propertied and conservative classes to admit the tribesmen who are regarded as little removed from savages, to share in the councils of State. The HC explained the reasons and held sway.' December 15th: 'Council decided that Congress should consist of 100 members, of whom 20 should be elected by the shaikhs of tribes.' There would also be four Jewish and five Christian representatives. Iraq was defined. The wholly Kurdish division of Sulaimanya and the Kurdish districts in the Mosul and Kirkuk divisions of the old Ottoman regime were to be included within the state. The country was to be divided into 10 Liwahs each with a Mutassarif, 35 Qadhas with Kaimakams, and 85 Nahiyahs with Mudirs in charge of them. The new Secretary of State for the Colonies could hardly have asked for a more detailed account of events in the mandated territory. Of Sayid Talib, Minister for the Interior in the first Provisional Government and the chief contender for power under the regime which would follow from the promised elections, she wrote: 'Sayid Talib Pasha has been unflagging in his efforts to win over men of all shades of political opinion. He has done his best to ingratiate himself with the Shias and Nationalists but few have confidence in him and none trust his intentions.' The newspaper *Istiqlal*, 'Independent', was meanwhile propagating the cause of Faisal or alternatively of his brother Abdullah. 'Sayid Talib now urges its suppression on the grounds of Bolshevik and Kemalist tendencies, but he was anxious that the order should come from anyone but the Ministry of the Interior.'

For five years her weekly reports were to summarise the course of events in the country in remarkable detail, and they were fitted in between countless other tasks. She resumed her old position of Oriental Secretary which, though it had not, like the Iraq branch of the Arab Bureau, been abolished by Wilson, had become nothing more than a formal title. Together with Philby she went energetically about the arrangements for a Provisional Assembly and the setting up of an Arab Government with British advisers, and for the time being they worked in close harmony. On January 3rd, 1921 she wrote: 'I really think you might search over history from end to end without finding poorer masters of it than Lloyd George and Winston Churchill.'

According to Churchill, his first step on taking over the Colonial Office was to summon the Cairo Conference. That is not quite true. On January 8th, 1921 the Council of State met in Baghdad under its President the Naqib. The chief ministers were Sayid Talib, Interior; Sasun Effendi Haskail, Finance; Sayid Mustafa Effendi Alusi, Justice; Izzat Pasha, Education. Their British counterparts were Philby, Interior; Sir Edgar Bonham Carter, Justice; General Atkinson, Commerce; Colonel Slater, Finance. They discussed plans for an election. Outside, the walls of Baghdad were decorated with the graffiti of the people.

'Woe betide you O Ministers – rotten O prisoners.'
'Does your conscience not trouble you?'
'O you Muhammadan Indian military brethren who are ignor-
ant of the events of the world' – written in Urdu.
'O countrymen Muhammadan and Hindu warrior brethren ...
You know that all the pomp and power of the British is due
to India ... They have treated you like beasts in Transvaal,
Egypt, Persia, Afghanistan, China ... '

On January 10th, 1921 Gertrude wrote to her father: 'Shortly after I got to the office this morning, Sir Percy sent me a note

asking me to come and speak to him in his house, which is next
door ... [he] handed me a telegram from Winston Churchill saying
that HMG had placed the decisions as to their policy in Mesopotamia in the hands of the Secretary of State for War and he
therefore informed the High Commissioner and the Commander
in Chief that he could not burden the British public with the expenditure necessary to carry out the programme suggested i.e. Sir
Percy Cox's recent suggestion that he should bring about the
selection of Faisal as Amir of Iraq, that being, in his view, the only
way of establishing speedily a stable Arab Government and reduc-
ing the British army of occupation ... ' British troops were to
evacuate the Mosul area as soon as General Ironside could safely
get his men out of Persia (by June 1921) and the mandate should
be retained and imposed by a strong police force. Meanwhile,
they, the British administrators, would clear out of Baghdad and
establish their headquarters in Basra. 'Sir Percy and I agreed that
this scheme had no sense or meaning,' she wrote. Indeed, it was
an impossible plan, and wiser counsels prevailed in Whitehall, for
Churchill was soon in the throes of planning his Cairo Conference.
A mere two months before Sir Percy and Lady Cox, with Gertrude,
Captain Clayton (Iltyd, the General's brother) and Sayid Talib and
the notables of Baghdad jostling around him, had stood on the
station platform at Baghdad to the strains of 'God Save the King'
and the cheers of the multitude. 'I thought as he [Cox] stood there
in his white and gold lace, with his air of fine and simple dignity,
that there had never been an arrival more momentous – never anyone on whom more conflicting emotions were centred, hopes and
doubts and fears, but above all confidence in his personal integrity
and wisdom. It was all I could do not to cry.' Now, it looked as
though Sir Percy was playing at the very least an oblique game
with the Iraqis. Even as they prepared to form an elected Assembly,
he had in mind the imposition of Faisal by Britain, presumably in
the fairly certain knowledge that the French would eject him
from Syria the moment they received the mandate, which they
did.

The important role of Gertrude in the negotiations taking place
at this time is suggested by the fact that Councils of State were
often held at her home. She entertained there a great deal in the
latter part of 1920 and in 1921, trying to bring together the disparate forces from which Britain hoped to produce a provisional
government and an elected assembly. She and Philby laboured

mightily at their tasks, he working close to Talib, she canvassing the opinions and support of all and sundry. But there was still considerable confusion in the minds of those who worked so hard for a stable government. In October 1920 Gertrude had written: 'But I also think that Sayid Talib will go under.' In December, 'Today ... Talib came and I must confess that he made a favourable impression on me. He told me frankly that he wished to be Amir of Iraq ... I thought he showed wisdom and good sense ... ' By the end of the year he had resigned and wanted to go to England with his children. A few days later he was back. The effort to find a suitable ruler resulted in the canvassing of strange names. Two pro-Turkish notables, Hikmat Beg and Sasun Effendi, were invited to lunch and asked what they thought of a son of the Sultan of Turkey as ruler. They thought it a bad idea. The Aga Khan was considered. The Naqib was a favoured choice but he was old and weak and Gertrude's main concern was that he should survive until an election could be fixed. Even Ibn Saud was thought of and as quickly dismissed.

Gertrude was far from well at this time. In October 1920 she had written to her father: 'I mentioned bronchitis last week – well it's won.' The effects of malaria, a constant chesty cold, the climate and overwork were beginning to tell on her. She was not easily oppressed by illness, however, and even as she lay in bed with bronchitis her room swarmed with Arab shaikhs and political aspirants. By the new year she seemed fully recovered.

She left for Churchill's Cairo Conference late in February 1921, aboard H.M.S. *Hardinge*. The Colonial Secretary had gathered together anyone who might have a contribution to make to the proceedings. With Cox's contingent from Iraq were Sir Aylmer Haldane the G.O.C., Sasun Effendi the Minister of Finance in the Provisional Government, Jafar Pasha the Minister of Defence, Major-General E. H. Atkinson adviser to the Ministry of Works, Lt-Colonel S. Slater the financial adviser, Major-General Sir Edmund Ironside commander of the British army in Persia, Sir Edgar Bonham Carter the judicial adviser, and Gertrude. Churchill took Sir Reginald Wingate, Hogarth, Young, Storrs, Clayton, George Lloyd and Lawrence with him.

She wrote from Cairo on 12th March: 'We arrived yesterday. I got Father's telegram at Aden saying he is coming – it really is splendid of him ... T. E. Lawrence and others met us at the station

—I was glad to see him. We retired at once to my bedroom ... and had an hour's talk, after which I had a long talk with Clementine [Churchill] while Sir Percy was cosseted with Mr Churchill. A.T. is here!—not at the Conference but as Managing Director of the Anglo-Persian Oil Company. We had a cordial meeting but I've not seen him to talk to and don't much want to.' The main decisions of the Conference amounted to a nearly complete affirmation of Britain's war-time promises to Husain of Mecca. Faisal was invited to proceed to Baghdad as a candidate for the throne of Iraq, and his brother Abdullah, who had already declared himself King of Iraq and who was conveniently in Jerusalem when Churchill went on there, was invited to become sovereign of the artificially created state of Transjordan. 'Faisal,' said Churchill, 'was an ideal candidate.' He had 'very special qualifications for the post ... He had himself fought gallantly on our side and had taken part in the various exploits of desert warfare with which the name of Colonel Lawrence will always be associated.'

Gertrude described the conference to Frank Balfour who had left his job as Military Governor of Baghdad to marry and was now in England:

> My beloved Frank, I'll tell you about our Conference. It has been wonderful. We covered more work in a fortnight than has ever been got through in a year. Mr Churchill was admirable, most ready to meet everyone halfway and masterly alike in guiding a big political meeting and in conducting the small committees into which we broke up. Not the least favourable circumstance was that Sir Percy and I, coming out with a definite programme, found when we came to open our packet that it coincided exactly with that which the Secretary of State had brought with him. We are now going back to Baghdad to square the Naqib and to convince Sayid Talib, if he is convincible, that his hopes are doomed to disappointment ...

She returned after a brief holiday in Egypt with her father and the taking of a photograph with Churchill, Clementine and Lawrence on camels in the shade of the Pyramids, the occasion on which the Secretary of State fell from his steed to provide the world with its most vivid picture of the Cairo gathering. The first of the 'Politicals' encountered by Gertrude on arriving back in Iraq was Ronald Wingate and she greeted him with the words: 'We've pulled it off!' She proceeded to tell him that Churchill had agreed that Faisal should be offered the throne of Iraq. On April 11th Cox wired to Churchill: 'Long interview with the Naqib of Baghdad in the presence of Talib.' He reported a conversation regarding the need to cut military expenditure and the decision to invite Faisal to the country. The Naqib 'could not agree that the Sharif or his family had the slightest claim to concern themselves with Iraq and he was confident that HMG, with its well-known sense of justice, would be of his opinion'.

'I replied,' said Cox, 'that I could not agree with him there; the Sharif and his family had rendered HMG valuable services ... and HMG would not be justified in standing in the way of one of the Sharif's sons, if the Mesopotamian people expressed a desire for him.' There was a final reference to the claim of another candidate, the Shaikh of Muhammerah, who was openly canvassing for the throne. Cox and the Naqib agreed that he had no chance of candidature. Sayid Talib announced that he would continue to serve his country but that he had no further interest in the rulership. Churchill, taking a Machiavellian view, suggested several candidates so as to split the vote in Faisal's favour. A few days later, on April 16th, Percival Landon, the *Daily Telegraph* correspondent, was invited to dinner by Talib to meet the French Consul and his wife. Among the other guests were Mr and Mrs Tod, he being a director of the Lynch company which ran the Tigris ferries and had many other commercial interests; and two distinguished Arabs, the Amir al Rabiah, a tribal leader from the region of Kut, and Shaikh Salim al Khaiyun. After the ladies had retired, Talib made a speech in Arabic. Sayid Husain, Secretary to the Council of Ministers, sat next to the *Daily Telegraph* correspondent and translated for him. Talib said that he wanted an assurance that Britain would remain neutral in the matter of selecting a ruler and that he had reason to believe that certain British officials were predisposed to the Sharif and were trying to exert an improper influence. He turned to Landon and asked: 'Do you confirm what I say?' Landon is said to have replied that he had the word of the High Commissioner that no improper influence was being brought to bear. Talib is alleged to have declared that he would appeal to King George V, with a view to biased officials being removed. Landon then said that he should address his appeal to the High Commissioner, and added: 'Many British officials favour the Naqib.' Sayid Husain turned to Talib and said: 'He's got us there.' Talib is said to have blustered and then remarked:

'If the British do not faithfully carry out their pledges, there is the Amir Rabiah with 20,000 tribesmen, and Shaikh Salim and all his tribesmen, to ask the reason why.' He added: 'If there is any sign of the British taking sides, the Naqib is prepared to appeal to the Islamic world.'

Cox heard about the discourse within a few hours. Gertrude, in a letter to her parents, tends to give the impression that she was present. In fact, she was not. She commented: 'It was an incitement to rebellion as bad as anything which was said by the men who roused the country last year, and not far from a declaration of *jihad*.' And she added: 'It's not beyond the bounds of possibility that Talib may prosecute the electoral campaign so hotly as to find himself in gaol.' Gertrude wrote the letter containing those observations the day after Talib's party, the 17th. That morning Cox had consulted Haldane who agreed to arrest Talib. Gertrude described how Talib had called on Lady Cox at 4.30 in the afternoon and had tea with her. Afterwards, when Talib had said farewell to his hostess, Major Bovill who was also a guest left before the Iraqi and waited for him near the Tigris bridge by Cox's house. 'I regret that I have orders to arrest you,' he said. 'I feel a load off my mind,' observed Gertrude. 'Talib was capable of anything. He was already gathering round him the band of cutthroats he used to employ in Turkish times at Basra ... It was an item added to my report yesterday because I wanted to warn Sir Percy that he was almost certain to attempt the assassination of Faisal if the latter came here,' she wrote. The arrest was an act of social and political insensibility, and Gertrude's part in it cannot escape criticism any more than can Sir Percy's or Lady Cox's. Many observers at the time, and not a few of the British on the spot, thought it an unseemly end to an unseemly career; for murderer and rogue Talib certainly was, but Cox had been prepared to use him for his own ends when there were no other leaders of his stature close at hand. Cox later reported to Churchill in London: 'He was arrested in a public thoroughfare this afternoon and is being sent down river to Fao. I do not anticipate any trouble as I think the great majority of people are relieved. I trust you will be able to support me in my action and authorise me to send him to Ceylon.' Churchill replied that Talib's speech was seditious and that he must be exiled. The Iraqi spent most of his remaining days wandering from one part of Europe to another, subsidised by Britain but always threatened with the withdrawal of that subsidy if he ever went near Iraq. He finally took up residence in Munich. Britain, meanwhile, turned to Faisal. As Churchill remarked to Cox, he represented the last opportunity for *beau geste* on Britain's part. On June 23rd, 1921 Gertrude wrote: 'Faisal arrives in Basra today ... ' and on the 26th: 'Yesterday we had news of Faisal's arrival in Basra and an excellent reception, heaven be praised. The news came from Mr Philby whom by a master stroke of policy Sir Percy sent down to Basra to meet Faisal. I can't help hoping that Faisal will make a conquest and that Mr Philby will come back an ardent Sharifian.'

It was a master stroke that was to lead to Philby's dismissal within a matter of days. Faisal's reception was hardly enthusiastic. The Arab leader of the welcoming procession cried to the crowd, 'For the sake of Allah, cheer!'

After Faisal's arrival at Baghdad, with Kinahan Cornwallis, who had accompanied him from Jidda, Cox learnt that already the Sharif's son had been angered by being told that he (Cox) was indifferent to his claim to the throne and that Philby wanted a republic in the country. Philby, according to Cornwallis, had 'stood back' from the reception committee at Basra and had been altogether discourteous.

On July 7th Gertrude wrote: 'Mr Philby came back on Sunday night [he had gone straight to Hillah where he stayed with the Political Officer Major Dickson, allegedly suffering from fever] and interviewed Sir Percy the following morning. Sir Percy told him to hand over to Mr Thompson. It's a real tragedy his dismissal but he has himself to thank. Sir Percy has given him a very long rope. He sent him down to Basra to meet Faisal in the hope that the two would come to terms. Mr Philby did nothing but insist on the merits of Ibn Saud and on his own conviction that a republic was what Iraq needed.' Philby had told Dickson to carry on with a tour that he had arranged in the district, so that the Political Officer was not at his post when, soon after arrival, Faisal went through Hillah on his journey to Baghdad. The Major's wife had arrived in the country as a newly wed a year earlier, and was invited to one of the Khatun's dinner parties. She recalled: 'The other guests were five senior Arab officials, and most of the conversation in Arabic, but Miss Bell did make one loud remark in English to the effect that it was *such* a pity that promising young Englishmen went and married such fools of women.' Violet Dickson never quite forgave Gertrude, but her husband made his peace with Faisal for not being present at the ceremonial visit.

While the charade of parading Faisal through Iraq to seek the approval of the people went on during the two months following his arrival in the country, Churchill drove a carriage and pair through the war-time agreements with France and the Sharif. The old man of Mecca was being repaid by the appointment of Abdullah to the throne of Transjordan and of Faisal to that of Iraq. Meanwhile Churchill confirmed that Palestine was to remain a British mandate open to Jewish settlement, listening first to Lawrence then to Meinertzhagen among his counsellors in Whitehall, each claiming in turn that Britain was turning its back on solemn promises. Lawrence was still publicly proclaiming the rights of the Sharif and representing himself as the fountainhead of all that happened in the war in Arabia, and all that followed from it. 'He told me,' wrote Meinertzhagen, 'that he craved to be famous and had a horror of being known to like being known ... ' Again according to Meinertzhagen, TEL wondered if all established reputations were 'founded like mine, on fraud'. 'I'm terribly sorry for the little man. He has such charm and has got himself into a deplorable mess.' While Cox and Gertrude worked to gain public support for Faisal in Iraq, Churchill was discussing their efforts at dinner with Shuckburgh and Freddie Guest, Secretary to the Air Council, and with his advisers. 'I was much struck by the attitude of Winston towards Lawrence, which almost amounted to hero worship,' wrote Meinertzhagen. 'Winston asked him question after question ... Lawrence, who is as quick as a monkey in conversation, took full advantage of this and took care not to say anything which would be unpleasant hearing, interlarding his remarks with a suitable amount of flattery. Winston revelled in it, but to Shuckburgh and me it was nothing but nauseating. He ... spoke eulogistically of Faisal and Abdullah. The latter worthless Arab has proved his worthlessness in Transjordan, but Lawrence still sees advantages to us in keeping him there, drawing a huge salary for doing nothing ... It is clear that Lawrence, with his mad, self-seeking pan-Arab policy, pays no account to what the policy is costing the country, and Winston is quite prepared to spend hundreds of thousands on bolstering the effete House of Husain, and in paying subsidies to Husain's enemies to keep quiet. Heaven knows where this mad policy is going to lead us.' Meinertzhagen told Churchill

that in his efforts to implement McMahon's pledges to the Sharif
he was tearing up the Balfour Declaration by degrees, and that he
should put a time limit of seven years on Abdullah's kingship.
Churchill thought the idea 'might work'. Gertrude meanwhile got
on with the business of seeking public approval for Faisal in Iraq
and preparing for his coronation on the assumption that such
support was a foregone conclusion—which it was. On July 17th
she wrote to Frank Balfour again, giving him an amusing account
of the procession of suppliants and sycophants, doers and dream-
ers, to the ante-chamber of Faisal's palace where they waited for
hours on end for a chance to declare their loyalty 'in the name of
the people'. And she remarked: 'My reports will give you a
general idea of how things are going—it has been most skilfully
managed by Sir Percy, no less so by Faisal, and the Naqib has
contributed ... like the old gentleman he is. I haven't a shadow
of doubt that we are on the right track. The only cloud has been
the Philby episode ... He has been out of focus ever since the
deportation of Talib, and he adhered obstinately to his conception
of a republic—surely the most complete reduction to the absurd
in this country—even after HMG had declared against it. I hope
he may not be lost to us ... He may find a job later in land settlement work ... ' In fact, the disgraced Philby was sent to Abdullah
in Transjordan to help control that corner of the growing
Hashemite empire, where he spent much of his time in correspondence with Ibn Saud until, after three years, an R.A.F. censor
unsuspectingly intercepted a letter and informed the authorities
that he was in touch with the Saudi Amir, whereupon he turned
his back on all the mandates and went to serve the only Arab
leader he genuinely admired at the Saudi capital of Riyadh.

The so-called election of Faisal was no more than a referendum
in the event, though even with a single candidate standing, the
claim of the High Commission that 96 per cent of the people
voted for Britain's nominee for the throne must be viewed with
some suspicion, especially since the majority of the population
was illiterate. Faisal was eventually crowned on August 23rd,
1921. The ceremony at the *sarai* on the bank of the Tigris was the
stuff of which Gertrude's most descriptive letters were made, but
on this occasion she wrote in a relatively low key.

... we've got our King crowned and Sir Percy and I agree that
we're now half seas over, the remaining half is the Congress and

the Organic Law ... The enthronement took place at 6am on Tuesday, admirably arranged. A dais about 2ft 6ins. high was set up in the middle of the big sarai courtyard; behind it are the quarters Faisal is occupying, the big Government reception rooms; in front were seated in blocks, English and Arab officials, townsmen, Ministers, local deputations ... Exactly at 6 we saw Faisal in uniform, Sir Percy in white diplomatic uniform with all his ribbons and stars, Sir Aylmer, Mr Cornwallis, and a following of ADCs ... We all stood up while they came in and sat when they had taken their places on the dais. Faisal looked very dignified but much strung up – it was an agitating moment. He looked along the front row and caught my eye and I gave him a tiny salute. Then Sayid Husain stood up and read Sir Percy's proclamation in which he announced that Faisal had been elected King by 96 per cent of the people of Mesopotamia, long live the King! With that we stood up and saluted him. The national flag was broken on the flagstaff by his side and the band played 'God Save the King' – they have no national anthem yet. There followed a salute of 21 guns ... It was an amazing thing to see all Iraq, from North to South gathered together. It is the first time it has happened in history ...

The King was hardly returned to his palace before Gertrude was taking tea with him and advising him on his domestic arrangements. 'When we had made Mesopotamia a model Arab state there was not an Arab of Syria and Palestine who wouldn't want to be part of it, and before I died I looked to see Faisal ruling from the Persian frontier to the Mediterranean ... ' she told the King.

A few days before the Coronation she had written to J. E. Shuckburgh, who had been seconded by the India Office to the Colonial Office during Churchill's tenure, complaining bitterly about a letter to *The Times* which, she said, was so provoking that the Under-Secretary would have to forgive her scribbled handwriting. She sent him some of her own photographs of life in Baghdad for publicity purposes, together with an article for *Blackwood's Magazine*, addressed to her mother. 'I wish we could reach a far larger public ... What we want is cinematographic films. I feel certain we could get something, with Faisal a central figure, which would draw our gaping noodles – who, after all,

pay the price,' she wrote, adding: 'I do not wish – nor could I –
to emulate Miss Rosita Forbes. In the matter of trumpet blowing
she is unique; but I have a feeling that we might at any rate be
loud enough to drown the penny whistles of people like Stanley
Reed [the letter-writer to *The Times*] ...' On October 13th, having
presumably given the matter mature thought, Shuckburgh replied:
'Dear Miss Bell, ... I quite agree with what you say as to the need
for more propaganda ... We have now got here an officer (Mr
Caird) who acts as our publicity agent, and who serves up to the
press in suitable form such material as we are able to give him.
We would like to have further notes from you. Your *magnum opus*
which we published as a Blue Book last year covers a great deal
of the ground but it is rather difficult to get people to read Blue
Books ... I am afraid I have been very bad at answering your
letters on general political matters in Iraq, but it is not because I
do not appreciate them ... '

Gertrude's work was increasingly concerned with the King's
comfort and with propaganda designed to counter criticism of the
new regime at home. Her output of articles and reports was enormous and would have taxed the resources of many a person half
her age. But her role in the affairs of the High Commission
diminished. By October 1922 Bonar Law's brief ministry had
taken over from Lloyd George's, and Churchill was replaced at
the Colonial Office by the Duke of Devonshire. In London,
Meinertzhagen breathed a sigh of relief. On October 29th he
wrote: 'So Winston is gone. He acts almost entirely by instinct
and is usually right, though easily led astray by some enthusiast.
A hard master to serve, works like a Trojan himself and expects
equally hard work from his staff ... CO will be restful after the
fulminations of Winston.' Gertrude's Intelligence Summary No.
24 arrived at the Colonial Office in late December. 'It would have
impressed Churchill greatly,' wrote Shuckburgh. Gertrude's own
reaction to the change was predictable. 'The news of the Cabinet
appointments reached us last night,' she wrote on October 25th.
'I'm so enchanted to have the Duke as our Minister that I've
written to tell him so ... '

In February 1922 Cox had told the government that he proposed
to send to London the antiquities of Samarra which the German
archaeologists under Dr Hertzfeld had found before the war
during the excavations on the banks of the Tigris above Baghdad.
He was anxious to send them as 'spoils of war' he said before the

35 Churchill's Cairo Conference, 1921. On the Colonial Secretary's left (*front row*) is Sir Percy Cox, and on his right Sir Herbert Samuel; in the second front row, Gertrude is second from the left, T. E. Lawrence is fourth from the right and Sir Hubert Young is extreme right

36 King Faisal with Lord (George) and Lady Lloyd; Gertrude and Sir Ronald Storrs stand behind

37 A drawing of Gertrude by John Sargent, 1923

native government took over in the country. To discuss them with the Iraq authorities would, he thought, be unnecessary. However, Faisal was anxious to protect the country's archaeological heritage and in October the Cabinet appointed Gertrude honorary Director of Archaeology. The department of Antiquities was part of the Ministry of Works under her friend Sabih Bey, and so she was able to work amicably with the Iraqi side in what was in some ways the most apposite task of her entire life, though it was perhaps a comedown from her role of kingmaker. To her credit, Gertrude stood by the German claim to a share of the treasures, while T. E. Lawrence advised the Foreign Office that they should all go to the British Museum. As the archaeological expeditions of Europe and America returned to the country, and her Carchemish acquaintance of pre-war days Sir Leonard Woolley came to excavate the mounds of Ur, she assumed the responsibility for ensuring that the old methods of haphazard and competitive digging for treasures and the unfair apportionment of the finds was replaced by an orderly approach in which Iraq received its proper share of the spoils.

There was still strength and physical endurance in her slender frame and every day she went riding and swimming. Al Khatun remained the most familiar sight in Baghdad, loved by the Arabs and increasingly estranged from her own people. During 1922, at a time when Cox was preparing his last major diplomatic act in the East – a conference at Ujair on the Al Hasa coast to fix the boundaries of Iraq, Syria, Transjordan, Kuwait and Saudi Arabia – the Syrian writer Ameen Rihani turned up in Baghdad. He was travelling around the peninsula in the hope of meeting Ibn Saud. But his first call was on Faisal, established in his temporary palace on the east bank of the Tigris. He found the King of Iraq in a sour mood as far as Britain and Gertrude were concerned. He did not like the terms of the proposed Anglo-Iraq treaty and he blamed her for allowing it to be imposed on him. Afterwards, Rihani crossed the river to the High Commission where he was received by Gertrude.

The Iraqis call her Khatun, that is a lady of the court who keeps an open eye and ear for the benefit of the State. I found Miss Bell had two other loyal troopers – her tongue and her mind – and the manner of being quite at home in Baghdad. Her figure is quite English – tall and lank; her face is aristocratic – rather long and

R

sharp; and her silver hair is not inharmonious with the persistent pink in her delicate complexion ... She keeps the reins of conversation in her own hand. She speaks Arabic almost without an accent, often mixing it with her English, and emphasising it with a dogmatic though graceful gesture. Her energy and agility amazed me.

The Syrian, who lived in America at the time, enjoyed the one-sided conversation and seemed to take to Gertrude, especially when she agreed to help him join Sir Percy's expedition to Ujair where he would be able to meet the acknowledged king of the desert. He noted that Khatun chain-smoked and paced up and down her office, opening a casement window, flouncing on her divan, puffing and talking and calling him 'Ameen Effendi'. And he wrote: 'I was pleased. I was relieved. The Khatun, I said to myself, is still a woman, Allah be praised. I admired what she exhibited of her mind at the first meeting; and when she unveiled a corner of her heart I was surprised.' She told him: 'I am an Iraqi, and I want to see the people of Iraq achieve their freedom and independence ... ' Rihani was 'enlightened and amused' by her. 'But my admiration of her as a woman could hardly vie with my doubt in her ability to manage the affairs of her new Kingdom, let alone its turbulent tribes.' He was entertained by her at her home and in the Salaam Library, Iraq's first public library, of which she was president, and he spoke of her 'thoughtfulness and kindly disposition'. In the end he went ahead of Cox to Bahrain, whence he joined Ibn Saud.

As formal government became established the British advisers to Faisal's Cabinet took over more of the work that had once belonged to the High Commission and the Political Office before it. Sir Percy Cox and his successor Sir Henry Dobbs, loyally assisted by Gertrude, concerned themselves increasingly with government in London and with countering the criticism of the cost of propping up the Hashemite kings in Iraq, Transjordan and the Hijaz. It was chiefly Gertrude, however, who to the bitter end fought the critics of the King and the regime; her pen never lost its power or her intellect its cutting edge. The Department of Antiquities became her refuge from the disappointments of office and from private sadness as the years went by. 'She slipped back,' said Janet Courtney, 'to the quiet ways of history and archaeology.' At first she was indispensable to the King, looking after his young son Ghazi, organising receptions, advising him privately, accompanying him on tours, always curtsying to him and referring to him with studied deference as 'Your Majesty'. It is said that when she bathed with members of the High Commission staff on one occasion, she spotted the royal launch approaching and immediately left the river and stood to attention in her swimming costume, water dripping from her, as it went by. Shades of that day at Oxford many years before when she hurriedly changed her dress on hearing of the death of the Emperor! She even went so far as to suggest magisterially that the other women of Baghdad, wives of government officials and High Commission staff, should curtsy to the King, but some of them adamantly refused to do so, insisting that he was an Arab chief unaccustomed to receiving women in audience much less to having them curtsy to him.

Gertrude's inconsistencies in matters of status and preferment are not easily rationalised. She was not a conventional woman; indeed, throughout her life she had mixed with the great and the famous on a footing of social equality and, in the main, of intellectual superiority. In girlhood she had expressed disappointment at her grandfather's acceptance of a baronetcy, wishing that he could have the honour without the title. Then there were those quips with emperors and queens. Few ever read more widely or with less constraint. She was as familiar with Stuart Mill and Morris and Marx as with Sir Joshua Stamp or Sir Ernest Benn, or Sir Edward Grey on fly fishing. Her outspoken atheism and her habit of smoking in public hardly point to a woman hidebound by the conventions of her day. Yet in her deference to position and status she sometimes exhibited a formality, an almost affected admiration, which made nonsense of her own convictions and attitudes. She was of course the daughter of one of the leading capitalists of the age, but the Bells were unusually articulate capitalists. Grandfather Lowthian was essentially an academic among industrialists, one of the first in a country where it was not unusual for leaders of industry to be illiterate, and where high intelligence was deemed anything but a virtue among the very rich. Unlike many of their neighbours, the Bells mixed easily with the 'gentry', yet even to some of their relatives they were 'trade'. Perhaps in childhood Gertrude had subconsciously acquired that almost ostentatious awareness of status which was so at variance with her catholicity of mind, her habits, and above

all with her ability to move among those most defiant and class-
less of human beings, the Arabs of the desert. It ill becomes our
own age to look on her actions with censure or ridicule, however.
An age which readily exchanges cloth caps for coronets, in which
Maharajas become tax collectors for socialist governments without a moment's hesitation, should not try too hard to find
psychological explanations for such things. Inconsistency cuts
across time and class, and those who are without it are the duller
for being so.

Two years after the coronation of Faisal she wrote to her father:
'Darling, I want to tell you, just you who know and understand
everything, that I am acutely conscious of how much life has
given me. I've gone back now to the old feeling of joy in existence
and I'm happy feeling that I've got the love and confidence of an
entire nation; it's a very wonderful and absorbing thing – almost
too absorbing perhaps ... I don't for a moment suppose that I can
make much difference to our ultimate relations with the Arabs and
with Asia, but for the time I'm one of the factors in the game. I
can't think why all the people here turn to me for comfort and
encouragement ... ' Her father was now turned eighty and he,
with the family to whom she was so devoted, seemed ever more
remote. But the aged Sir Hugh Bell maintained a regular and
affectionate correspondence with his daughter while continuing to
travel up and down Britain delivering his Free Trade lectures. In
1923 Asquith called on uncle Lyulph, Lord Sheffield, at Alderley
and found Gertrude's father there, 'a strippling of 80 ... the only
man in England who could talk Lord Sheffield down'.

Anxious to see her family again, Gertrude returned home in
May of that year, along with Sir Percy who was retiring after
forty years' service in the East. It was a brief visit and the occasion
was marked by the drawing of the best-known portrait of her by
John Sargent, an artist whom she had known and admired since
her youth. It showed her as a fit and alert-looking woman,
certainly no older than her fifty-five years. While in England, she
corresponded with Lawrence who sought her advice on the publication of his *Seven Pillars of Wisdom*. Otherwise it was a quiet,
mainly domestic stay.

The grip of the new Iraq was irresistible by now. For the
moment it had become the family she longed for throughout her
adult life, and like any other family it soon began to grow apart
from its devoted and watchful parent. If, as Rihani and others

had noticed, Faisal was sometimes angry with her when he could not have his own way, she had good cause to feel aggrieved by her protégé's conduct. Early in his reign Faisal dismissed five of his Cabinet ministers in a fit of pique. Cox, who had admitted to Churchill before the coronation that he could not properly lay down the law to the king once he was enthroned, laid it down firmly with Gertrude's blessing, and the ministers were reinstated. There were, of course, vociferous Arab opponents of the regime, especially among the Shia majority who were virtually unrepresented in the government. Internal differences were never far from eruption. Kurds would not live contentedly alongside Arabs, Armenians and Turks. Sunni and Shia could never be reconciled. Tribesmen wanted nothing whatever to do with government of any kind. Gertrude and her colleagues had taken on an unenviable task, but as they had been told, indeed as she herself had recognised when she first came to the Arabian peninsula, they flew in the face of millennia of history in their attempt to make a kingdom out of a few vilayets of the Ottoman Empire; with, at that, an alien king as their instrument. But by now there was no other way, except the coward's course of simple retreat. Gertrude's view of Faisal became in the end a romantic vision:

> I send you a little puff about HM's farm which I published in the Baghdad Times. I hear that the cinema man was a great success ... He photographed all the farm, with the King picking cotton and the tractors working etc. and we shall have it in Baghdad shortly. I had an immense talk with HM yesterday afternoon about his household arrangements and Syria and everything ...

But as she toiled to convince the world of the justice of the Hashemite cause, Faisal and his father and brothers continued to plot against the powers that had sustained them. In a moment of exasperation she described the old man of Mecca as 'That old rogue King Husain'. Then, putting on her rose-tinted spectacles: 'I was having tea with HM this afternoon, it was the loveliest Oriental scene. He was sitting in the garden near a fountain in full Arab dress, the white and gold of the Meccan princes ... ' In February 1924 there were rumours that Mustafa Kamal's Turks and the French were plotting with Husain to make Ali, the eldest of the Hashemite princes, king of Syria in an effort to undermine the British position in Iraq. While Lord Milner was admitting to the Cabinet in London that British policy was designed to 'diddle' France out of Syria, the French demonstrated that they were no strangers to political perfidy. Nuri as-Said had gone to Damascus for talks with the French governor General Weygand. Ali was in Amman, also talking to the French and to agents of Mustafa Kamal. While these intrigues were taking place, Dobbs was touring the Iraq countryside with a leading moderate politician, Taufiq al Khalid, who had been Minister of Agriculture in the Naqib's provisional government. He was the uncle of Husain's representative in London, Dr Naji al Asil, 'deep in the secrets of those who are buzzing around Amman' according to an intelligence report. When Taufiq returned from his tour with the High Commissioner, he was asked by Faisal what he had talked about. 'Agriculture,' he replied. Faisal did not believe him. A few days later the Iraqi went to see the British chief of the C.I.D. in Baghdad, shaking with fear and convinced that his life was in danger. On February 23rd he was shot in the back outside his house. Dobbs wrote a personal letter to the Secretary of State. 'There is little likelihood that the murderer will be traced,' he said. 'I am sorry to say that many of those with inner knowledge of Baghdad affairs strongly suspect that the murder was done by order of King Faisal, and with the cognizance of Nuri Pasha the Minister of Defence.'

Most of the politicians of the new regime were the old-guard pashas experienced in the perfidious ways of their Turkish ex-masters. They needed little instruction in their craft. But there were good men among them and, considering the frailty of the structure on which they rested, many enjoyed lengthy periods of office. Jafar Pasha was assassinated in the military coup of 1936; Abdul Mehsin Beg al Sadun, son of Ajaimi the Muntafiq leader, committed suicide. Others, including the most powerful personality of them all, Nuri Said, who had fought on both sides in the war and was doubly respected, were murdered in the revolution of 1958, along with surviving members of Faisal's family then in Iraq.

Perhaps if Gertrude had been able to foresee the end to it all, she would have had second thoughts about the regime to which she was so attached and whose ambitions she supported so loyally. But hindsight is the prerogative of the observers of life, not of the players. Lawrence said of her: ' ... she was not a good judge of men or situations: and was always the slave of some momentary power: at one time Hogarth, at another Wilson, at another me, at last Sir Percy Cox. She changed her direction each time like a weathercock: because she had no great depth of mind. But depth and strength of emotion – Oh Lord yes. Her life had crisis after crisis ... A wonderful person.' Coming from a man who freely admitted the fraudulence of his own claims and promises it was an impudent judgment. But Lawrence was a highly intelligent and perceptive man and he had seen in Gertrude that fatal, essentially feminine fault, an inclination to believe the men she liked, and to cease to believe them when she stopped liking them.

She went home to England again in 1925. Her trip less than two years before had been official and she had had little time to see friends and relatives. This time she went on well-earned leave, arriving in the hottest days of June. Janet Courtney, with whom she spent several days in London, was staggered by her appearance, by her 'white hair' and 'skeleton-like' body. But it must be remembered that Janet had not seen her friend for five years. Gertrude had gone through many an ordeal in that time and her blood had been thinned by the terrible heat of the Iraq summers. Her niece Pauline Trevelyan, daughter of her sister Molly, was nineteen years old when Gertrude arrived home in July and she was to recall her aunt's appearance in London with affection and no sense of shock. 'She had become so acclimatised to the great heat of the East that even in that London summer weather she needed a roaring fire and wore a fur coat all day – a beautiful fox-skin full length coat, echoing the colour of her hair. She would stand with her back to the fire smoking a Turkish cigarette in a long holder, and discoursing on such a wide range of subjects – people past and present, history, letters, art and architecture, her travels, archaeology, our family – and how devoted she was to all at home, above all to her father ... ' Gertrude's generosity, her willingness to spend so much of her precious time at home with her niece, taking her to see the Assyrian exhibits at the British Museum, the Constable paintings at the Victoria and Albert, all the time explaining and conveying her own excitements and knowledge, made a lasting impression on her young companion. Mrs Dower, as Pauline Trevelyan became, remembered her aunt as the Hogarths and others remembered her, for her immense capacity for enjoying life, and for imparting her exhilaration to others. 'Gertrude's greatest interest was people, and wherever she went she made friends, lifelong friends who never forgot her,'

Mrs Dower remarked in later life. And that quality of identifying herself with the people among whom she moved, ordinary and extraordinary people, was Gertrude's great strength as a traveller and as a lone woman in what was still a man's world. Nothing is more indicative of her genuine interest in people than her marvellous collection of photographs, some 6,000 plates which cover the entire period of her travels in the Middle East and make a unique record of the architectural and archaeological features of the region. But most importantly she captured the spirit and character of the people she moved among, portraying their faces and demeanours with infinite care and immense professionalism. In her photography, as in almost everything she did, heart and mind weighed equally in the scales.

The fact remains, however, that Gertrude could be an uncomfortable companion for those who did not stand up to her in argument. She returned to Iraq by way of Cairo and Damascus in the company of her cousin Sylvia Stanley, or Mrs Anthony Henley as she had become, though sadly her husband had died just before. The assured, defiant Gertrude found her match in her travelling companion. Perhaps, as they passed through Syria, the vision of Faisal as King of all the Arab lands came to mind again. At any rate she turned to Mrs Henley and said: 'The French will be thrown out of here within a year.' Surprised by the certainty of Gertrude's conviction, her cousin replied, 'Surely not, Gertrude, the French are much too strong and proud to allow themselves to be pushed around by Faisal.' Gertrude was emphatic. 'Sylvia, you must allow that I know best.' Her cousin, a true Stanley, replied, 'In that case, Gertrude, there can be no further rational conversation between us.' Gertrude was always impressed by people who fought back.

Perhaps Husain of Mecca had perceived early in his negotiations with Britain that Baghdad was the logical axis of the Hashemite empire he envisaged for himself and his sons. If so, he was not alone. Sir Mark Sykes, a sick man as the war drew to a close and unable to play a very active part in the proceedings which followed from his impetuous war-time acts (he died at the Paris Peace Conference in 1919), had realised that the capital of the Abbassids was more representative than its predecessor Damascus of 'the other peoples who had been swept into the folds of the mantle of the Prophet'; more cosmopolitan and more geographically suited to become the hub of an Asiatic empire. Hogarth, 'father confessor' of the Arab Bureau, had taken up the argument in the *Arab Bulletin*:

> The compelling cause [of Baghdad's ascendency] was rather the force of economic gravity in the great plain-land of South-West Asia. Its centre shifted as inevitably from Damascus to Iraq as it had shifted from Mecca to Damascus ... Should Empire be there again, the centre of gravity will swing round the same arc. Mecca will not keep it, nor can Damascus long; its swing may be more slow, since Iraq is not now what it was before Haluga ruined its canals; but eventually it must gravitate to the old point of rest, and Semitic Empire will cease as before to be purely Arab or purely Semitic, or anything more than West Asian. There are Arabs who know this tradition and hope of the Hashemite Caliphate of Baghdad was doubtless in the minds of the Emir of Mecca when he claimed the style and title of Hashemite King.

From the moment he arrived in Baghdad, Faisal had fulminated against the French and their mandate in Syria, and had talked openly to Gertrude of extending his empire to the bordering lands. He and his British advisers had reckoned without the most potent force in Arabia, however, Ibn Saud. Gertrude had begun, as did most people who set eyes on that imposing ruler of Najd and 'all its tribes', with admiration. She finished by loathing him; a woman scorned, she hoped profoundly that he would be put in his place. In 1914 Britain had signed a treaty with the Turks designed to restrict Ibn Saud to his homeland and to guarantee his rival Ibn Rashid against attack. In 1917 Philby had been sent to Riyadh in the company of Lt-Colonel Cunliffe Owen as representative of the C.-in-C., and Colonel Hamilton of Kuwait, to reverse that policy by offering Ibn Saud money and arms with which to attack Hail. But Ibn Saud had waited on Britain for six years by then. Now he saw which way the wind was blowing and he decided to bide his time.

In November 1921, when Ibn Saud finally took Hail, the Shammar tribesmen sought refuge in Iraq. Just before the event, Gertrude wrote: 'The problem is that the Shammar, harried by Ibn Saud, have fled in large numbers from the vicinity of Hail and taken refuge with our own Anaiza ... Faisal was most wise about it and concocted schemes for restraining the Shammar, even though he ardently desires (and so do we all) to see Ibn Saud frustrated in his attempt to capture Hail.' It is hard to see anything more than a pathetic attempt to wriggle out of the consequences of their own folly in the attitudes of Britain and Faisal at this time, and there is a quality of sadness in Gertrude's acceptance of their dishonour. At the last they tried to bring about a compact between Ibn Rashid and the Sharif to bolster Husain's implausible regime. Now they refused protection to the unfortunate tribesmen who fled for their lives in the face of Ibn Saud's fanatical Ikhwan warriors.

While these military events unfolded, one government after another came and went in the turmoil of Iraqi politics, the Kurdish problem grew in complexity and insolubility, the religious leaders of Najaf and Karbala continued to preach hatred of the infidel intruders. Order of a kind was maintained in the country by the R.A.F. which found that bombing from the air was a cheaper and easier way than the sending of land troops to deal with recalcitrant tribes.

On May 3rd, 1922 Churchill had written a note to Hubert Young, then gravitated to the Colonial Office, which needed no signature to prove its authorship:

> I cannot understand why it is not possible to come to an agreement. What is the outstanding clash on the Treaty? Be ready to show it to me tomorrow morning ... The Mandate does not depend on the preamble of the Treaty but has a wholly different and persisting authority. Nor do I see any reason why we should not say that when Iraq is ready to stand by itself we shall have discharged the condition of our Mandate.

Under the sleepy stewardship of the Duke of Devonshire, things took a little longer to happen. But a treaty was eventually signed at Baghdad between Britain and Faisal's Government, on October 10th 1922. Its protocol was signed on April 30th, 1923, just before Sir Percy Cox retired (in May) and Sir Henry Dobbs, to Gertrude's great pleasure, took over as High Commissioner. She could not have asked for a better succession, for next to Cox among the men around her she admired most the intelligent, sophisticated Dobbs, though she found her mental stimulus at this time, and the last of those intellectual attachments which for her amounted almost to passions, in a new arrival, Vyvyan Holland, who rivalled her as a linguist and shared her Spartan qualities of mind. It was said of

Holland that he learnt languages as a mental exercise, one after another, like an intellectual gymnast in training.

Though she felt deeply her gradual exclusion from political affairs, she seemed happy among the antiquities of Iraq and in the company of her devoted friend Hajji Naji, an old man on whose ground her own home was situated and who delighted to share with her the simple pleasures of his blossoming trees and shrubs and the chorus of his nightingales, and who each year took the first of his fruit to her. As director of antiquities she supervised the activities of the new generation of British and American archaeologists who came to dig and she had many an argument with her old colleagues Campbell Thompson, Hall, Woolley and members of the American team from the University of Pennsylvania, but she held the balance between them and their rival claims, and with her great knowledge and emphatic manner usually won them over to her way of thinking whenever there was a dispute regarding the allocation of finds. Baghdad, rightly, became the world's chief storehouse of the treasures of Babylon, Assyria, Sumer and Chaldea under her aegis. Up to this time her office had consisted of a single room in the *serai* of the royal palace. Now she was promised a more suitable building.

A peace treaty with Turkey was signed in October 1922 and confirmed at Lausanne in July 1923 in the wake of Mustafa Kamal's spectacular revival of Turkish ambition and virility. The protocol which governed Britain's alliance with Faisal cut down the period of the treaty from twenty years to four from the ratification of Lausanne, and provided that if Iraq was meanwhile elected to the League of Nations, Britain's responsibility would end immediately. The Iraqi Assembly proceeded to attack the treaty as being ungenerous and inadequate, and there were riots and murders in consequence during 1923 and 1924. The treaty and its subsidiary agreements were put by Britain before the League of Nations on September 20th, 1924 and they were accepted as giving effect to the provisions of the Covenant of the League. King George V and Faisal I of Iraq ratified them on December 12th, 1924.

Though Gertrude had less and less to do with the British administration and the Iraqi court, she continued to keep an eye on the King's young son Ghazi, the heir to the throne, and to help him with his English lessons. She was still busy with her weekly intelligence reports, articles for the Colonial Office's home

19. 2. 2.5

My dear miss Bell,
    How are you?
I am sending
Hamid and Faress in
the motor - car for the
box. Thank you
very much.

Ghazi

Letter to Gertrude from Crown Prince Ghazi

propaganda machine and the annual reports which summarised events with unfailing regularity and authority and implanted the famous initials GLB indelibly on the minds of those few ministers and officials of Whitehall who did not already know her. She still worked for long hours in the Victorian Colonial-style High Commission on the right bank of the Tigris with its six rooms up and down facing the river and shuttered windows, its wrought-iron gates and balconies and handsomely laid-out gardens, and at her cottage home. She was described, *in situ* as it were, by Vita Sackville-West who went to Baghdad early in 1926 with her husband Harold Nicolson and wrote of the journey in *Passenger to Tehran*.

Baghdad ... is a dusty jumble of mean buildings connected by atrocious streets, quagmires of mud in rainy weather, and in dry weather a series of pits and holes over which an English farmer might well hesitate to drive a wagon. I confess that I was startled by the roads of Baghdad, especially after we had turned out of the main street ... Then a door in a blank wall ... a broadly smiling servant, a rush of dogs, a vista of a garden-path edged with carnations in pots, a little verandah and a little low house at the end of the path, an English voice — Gertrude Bell. I had known her first in Constantinople, where she had arrived straight out of the desert, with all the evening dresses and cutlery and napery that she insisted on taking with her on her wanderings; and then in England; but here she was in her right place ... would I like to see her museum, wouldn't I? Did I know she was Director of Antiquities in Iraq? wasn't that a joke? and would I like to come to tea with the king? ... I limped after her as she led me down the path, talking all the time, now in English to me, now in Arabic to the eager servants. She had the gift of making everyone feel suddenly eager ... Then she was back in her chair, pouring out information: the state of Iraq, the excavations of Ur, the need for a decent museum, what new books had come out? and what was happening in England? The doctors had told her that she ought not to go through another summer in Baghdad, but what should she do in England? ...

While Miss Sackville-West was on her travels she received a letter from Virginia Woolf who knew Gertrude well from bygone days in London, one of those skittish, opinionated letters in which the writer specialized. In it she asked: 'Now where are you? With Miss Gertrude Bell, I suppose. I suppose you are very happy, seeing things, lovely things. I don't know what Baghdad is like so I won't tell you. Miss Bell has a very long nose: she is like an Aberdeen terrier; she is a masterful woman, has everyone under her thumb, and makes you feel a little inefficient. Still, she is extremely kind, and asks so and so to meet you, and you are very grateful to her ... '

Early in 1925 Gertrude wrote to her stepmother: 'Darling, this isn't going to be a very bright letter for I am suffering from the shock of a double domestic tragedy with which I am sure you will sympathise – the death of my darling little spaniel, Peter, and of his mother, Sally ... My whole household was affected to tears – they all loved them ... ' In February 1926, when she returned from a visit to the excavations at Ur, she found a telegram awaiting her to tell her that her brother Hugo had died. He had been married for just three years (to Frances Morkill) and was returning from his living in South Africa when he was taken seriously ill on the ship with typhoid fever. He died in hospital in England. 'My darling Father and Mother, I am writing to you with the heaviest of hearts. It is so dreadful to think of what you have gone through and of your sorrow now ... I can't find words to write ... Poor, poor, Frances. I don't yet realise it all clearly, it has been such a sudden shock.' To Hugo's wife she wrote: 'I know exactly what you mean when you write of the world loving his beautiful sweetness and goodness.' Gertrude herself had just recovered from a severe chill which verged on pneumonia, and she had been rushed to hospital at the end of 1925. Her parents wanted her to return home. Strikes and bitter industrial disputes during the Twenties, culminating in the General Strike of 1926 had further reduced the family fortunes. She was determined to establish her museum, however. 'I can't leave it now,' she told them. She completed a report on Iraq for the League of Nations, and in April reported in her weekly summary of events that conscription was being considered in Iraq in order to deal with the troubles in the Mosul area. In that month too, she reported that the Tigris had burst its banks and the whole city was flooded; 'the greatest losses have been sustained at the King's Palace and at the Baghdad North railway station.' At the end of the month the King opened the Chamber of Deputies and the President, Rashid Ali Beg, resigned. On June 5th Iraq signed a treaty of non-aggression with Turkey.

On July 6th Faisal left for Europe, to take the waters of Vichy and then to proceed to London, stating that he would like to stay at Buckingham Palace. Faisal's tailor and perfumier, when they got wind of the visit, promptly asked the Colonial Office if it could underwrite the Arab King's credit as he had not paid his bills for previous calls on them. The C.O. replied that it could not. King George's secretary told the Colonial Office: 'HM desires me to say that the only day on which he can receive King Faisal is Tuesday 10th August. HM only returns from Cowes on 9th ... ' By then Sir Gilbert Clayton had signed a treaty with Ibn Saud recognising him as the legitimate King of all central Arabia including the Hijaz. Husain, unwelcome even in the lands of his sons, had gone into exile in Cyprus. Ali, his eldest son, had reigned briefly for a year in Jidda as the Sharif of the Holy Cities. Now in July 1926 he was Faisal's Regent in Iraq. Gertrude had told her parents a few weeks earlier that she had found a new 'place' for her museum. 'It is an excellent building which will give me ample space ... and an office for myself.

At some time in her Iraq years Gertrude wrote an undated essay which she called 'Romance'. It was meant for the *Arab Bulletin* but was never used. In it she captured the essence of her adopted land and some of that joy which ran through the letters and literature of her youth.

> I have written of politics and of commerce, of steamships and locomotive engines, but I have not pronounced the word which is the keynote of the 'Iraq. It is *romance*. Wherever you may look for it you shall find it. The great twin rivers, gloriously named; the huge Babylonian plains, now desert, which were once a garden of the world, their story stretching back into the dark recesses of time – they shout romance. No less insistent on the imagination, and no less brilliantly coloured, are the later chapters in the history of the 'Iraq. The echoing name of Alexander haunts them, the jewelled splendour of the Sassanian King of Kings, the changing face of the Muhammadan Khalifates, and last (to English ears not least), the enterprise, the rigours, the courage of our seamen and merchants who forced their path through the gates of the 'Iraq and brought the Pax Britannica into the torrid seas of the Persian Gulf ...

And then she took a nostalgic journey through the country she had known under its Turkish rulers and under the monarchy she had helped to create. 'I have never returned to the 'Iraq without returning to Babylon,' she writes in recollection of the great German archaeologist Koldewey and his colleagues digging at the mound of Nebuchadnezzar ... 'all pomp and glory paraded before their eyes and fallen into dust ... ' She had written of Dr Koldewey in a letter home in 1918: 'It's no good trying to think of him as an alien enemy and my heart ached when I stood in the empty dusty little room where Fattuh used to put up my camp furniture and the Germans and I held eager conversations over plans of Babylon or Ukhaidir. What a dreadful world of broken friendships we have created between us.' In her 'Romance', she recalled him excavating to the heart of one of the great ziggurats, to an inner core of sun-dried bricks, all that remained from the depredations of robbers over thousands of years. ' "I call that old," said Dr Koldewey as he examined the bricks. "How old?" I asked. "Ten thousand, twenty thousand years," he answered. "How can I tell? We can't date the pre-historic period in Babylon." ' There was a concluding story of her Arab friend who was known as the Lord of the Merchants, who on a visit to Paris sought a gift for his liege, Shaikh Khazal of Muhammerah. In the end he purchased two life-size wax images of European women. They had wooden hands which he replaced with wax ones at a cost of 250 francs per lady. ' "Why," asked his English companion, "did he not put a gramophone within each of the images, that the Shaikh might hear the voice of the women of Paris as well as their form?" Deploring, all too late, his own lack of imagination, he answered: "Allahi! *Khursh fikar*! that by God, that's a sweet thought." '

There in a brief pen-picture was *her* Iraq, in its antiquity and novelty, its perversity and levity, the adopted family which she protected with motherly devotion and affection and portrayed with unsurpassed powers of description. It was, in a way, her valedictory essay.

On July 7th, the day after the King's departure for Europe, she wrote to her father to say that her 'faithful friend' Sir Percy Loraine had arrived from Tehran in the aftermath of Reza Khan's accession to the ancient throne of Persia and the inception of the Pahlavi dynasty. Sir Henry Dobbs gave a dinner party for the ambassador and of course Gertrude was present. They ate in the large cool ballroom of the High Commission and were entertained by Russian dancers. On the night of July 11th she went to bed after her customary evening swim and told Marie to call her at six the next morning. She kept by her bedside a phial of proprietary barbiturates known as 'Dial' and she took a fatal dose during the night.

Her death was certified by Dr W. Dunlop, director of the Royal Hospital Baghdad, as having occurred from Dial poisoning in the early morning of July 12th, 1926, two days before her fifty-eighth birthday.

S

Epilogue

We wither away but they wane not,
the stars that above us rise;
the mountains remain after us,
and the strong towers when we are gone.

Labid ibn Rabi'ah
quoted in *Amurath to Amurath*

Gertrude was buried in the British cemetery at Baghdad on the
evening of Monday July 12th. Troops and mourners lined the
street, and all the notables of Iraq, except the King who was represented in his absence by the Regent Ali, were there to mourn
her as were the High Commissioner and his staff and the British
advisers.

An official statement from Sir Henry Dobbs spoke of the 'bitter
personal and official loss through the sudden death on the early
morning of 12 July' of his Oriental Secretary and the Director of
Antiquities of the Government of Iraq. 'No word of mine,' said
Dobbs, 'can add to the lustre of her name in this country and
among this nation which she served with her last breath, as few
countries and nations have been served by their own sons and
daughters; nor can any record faithfully represent the grief which
has swept over the land at the news of her death and the gratitude
with which the people of Iraq will ever remember her wonderful
work among them. Miss Bell had abandoned a family in which
she was worshipped, a luxurious home, an immense circle of
devoted friends, a wide field of the most varied intellectual and
artistic interests and had for the last ten years of her life consecrated all the indomitable fervour of her spirit and all the astounding
gifts of her mind to the service of the Arab cause and especially of
Iraq.'

The nationalist newspaper *Al Alam al Arabi* wrote: 'The true sincerity of her patriotism, free from all desire for personal gain, and the zeal for the interests of her country which illuminated the service of this noble and incomparable woman makes her an example to all men of Iraq; especially at this time when Iraq is so sorely in need of serving hands ... We pray from our hearts that the sons of our country will follow her great example by serving their country as she served hers.'

The Times wrote in a leader on July 13th: 'Some power in her linked her love of the East with a practical aim that became a dominating purpose ... That she endured drudgery, was never dismayed by continual disappointment and never allowed her idealism to turn to bitterness, shows a strength of character rare indeed among those of the English for whom the East has become a passion. She was the one distinguished woman among them and her quality was of the purest English mettle ... Miss Bell has left the memory of a great Englishwoman.'

King George V wrote to Sir Hugh and Lady Bell: 'The Queen and I are grieved to hear of the death of your distinguished and gifted daughter, whom we held in high regard. The nation will with us mourn one who by her intellectual powers, force of character and personal courage rendered important and what I trust will prove lasting benefit to the country and to those regions where she worked with such devotion and self-sacrifice ... '

There were tributes from the new Colonial Secretary Leo Amery, from distinguished archaeologists the world over, from Chirol, Wilson, Cox and almost all who had served with her, whether in amity or discord. All made handsome acknowledgment of her part in the creation of the Kingdom of Iraq. More than twenty years were to pass before that monarchy was drowned in blood and the corpses of its political masters dragged through the streets of Baghdad by republican mobs as a warning to others who might be tempted to engage in the dangerous business of king-making. At the moment of his early triumph in 1927, King Faisal suggested that one of the principal rooms in the Baghdad Museum which Gertrude created should be dedicated to her memory. A plaque was placed in it which read:

GERTRUDE BELL

Whose memory the Arabs will ever hold in reverence and affection
Created this Museum in 1923
Being the Honorary Director of Antiquities for the Iraq
With wonderful knowledge and devotion
She assembled the most precious objects in it
And through the heat of the Summer
Worked on them until the day of her death
On 12th July, 1926
King Faisal and the Government of Iraq
In gratitude for her great deeds in this country
Have ordered that the Principal Wing shall bear her name
And with their permission
Her friends have erected this Tablet.

Looking back from the turmoil of Faisal's Iraq, from a world torn asunder by war and the efforts of the peace-makers, there is danger of losing sight of the achievements of so few years past; of the mountaineer who won the admiration of the finest climbers of her age, of the translator of Hafiz and the chronicler of the early churches of Asia Minor, of that solid body of writing at the pinnacle of which stands *The Desert and the Sown*, of the dutiful and loving daughter and sister. Her fame has faded with the years, but it will not die. Her real work will remain an inspiration to generations of archaeologists and other scholars, and her example will be quoted by those who seek adventure in deserts and on mountains, long after that disastrous experiment in Arab king-making has been forgotten. When, a year after her death, David Hogarth gave a presidential lecture on the 1913 journey to Hail at the Royal Geographical Society, he said:

She had all the charm of a woman combined with very many of the qualities that we associate with men. She was known in the East for those manly qualities. Fattuh, her servant ... was also my servant for one journey ... I remember an awful week in the north of Syria when it rained day after day, and day after day I told him we could not start because the weather had not lifted. Once he did not ask, but merely said, 'I suppose we don't start today?' I said 'No.' He said, 'No, *we* shan't start, but the *sitt*' — with an expressive gesture — 'she went through mud and water to her waist.'

He added most truthfully that 'if ever anyone did, Gertrude warmed herself through and through at the fires of life!' But it was Dr Hogarth's sister Janet who bridged the years. In 1928, just before their own deaths, Gertrude's parents went to represent her at Oxford when Dame Elizabeth Wordsworth received the D.B.E. from the Duchess of York. Janet Courtney was there too and she recalled the carefree days when the two young women walked together 'in that Oxford garden among the roses and the scarlet robes ... Gertrude was gone but two years before in that blazing Iraq summer ... Time couldn't touch her, though she made so little effort to escape him.'

Notes

Biographical Note

Gertrude Bell seldom dated her letters, apart from reference to the day of the week on which they were written. Fortunately her parents, sisters and brothers kept many of their envelopes so that in the selected correspondence published by members of the family accurate chronology was possible. Many hundreds of letters in the possession of the University libraries at Newcastle upon Tyne and Durham cannot be dated with certainty, however, though in 1966 Winifred Cotterill Donkin catalogued the correspondence at the former institution with considerable ingenuity so that it is possible to use previously unpublished letters in the context of Gertrude's known journeys and activities with reasonable assurance. Even so, months and years are often in doubt and in the following notes no attempt is made to date the correspondence except where necessary for identification. The letters published over the years by Lady Bell, Lady Richmond and Miss Elizabeth Burgoyne are given in date order and are readily accessible, and those in the University library of Newcastle upon Tyne can be traced with reference to Miss Donkin's list. Correspondence with Sir Valentine Chirol and Colonel Frank and Lady Frances Balfour is kept in the Oriental Section of the Durham University Library, as are the papers of Sir Gilbert Clayton.

Abbreviations

FAMILY
FB   Florence Bell
GLB Gertrude Bell
HB   Hugh Bell

PERSONAL CORRESPONDENCE
BL   letters published by Lady Bell in *The Letters of Gertrude Bell*, second one-volume edition, 1974.

CEB correspondence in Elizabeth Burgoyne's *Gertrude Bell: from her Personal Papers* (two volumes).
EBL letters in Lady Richmond's *The Earlier Letters of Gertrude Bell*.
UBL unpublished or part-published correspondence in the University Library, Newcastle upon Tyne.
VC letters to Valentine Chirol in the Oriental Section, Durham University Library (Boxes 303/4, 303/4/1 and 303/4/2).
XBL Balfour correspondence, Durham (Box 303/1/1).

OFFICIAL DOCUMENTS
CO Colonial Office
DMI Director of Military Intelligence
DMO Director of Military Operations
DNI Director of Naval Intelligence
DNO Director of Naval Operations
FO Foreign and Commonwealth Office
IO India Office (L/P&S: Political and Secret Department records)
PRO Public Record Office, London
WO War Office

SOCIETIES
CASJ Central Asiatic Society Journal (now *Journal of the Royal Society for Asian Affairs*)
GJ Journal of the Royal Geographical Society
RGS Royal Geographical Society

Other references are given in full. In the case of manuscript or rare works the British Library shelf-mark is given.

In other studies works by Janet Hogarth are sometimes listed under her married name, Mrs W. L. Courtney; here the former is used throughout.

For full bibliographical details of publications mentioned in the Notes see Bibliography.

1 Early Days

page
1   See *Washington*, ed. W. R. Arbuckle. A pictorial guide to the district.
1   See also *A History of the County of Durham*, University of London Institute of Historical Research, original edition,

1905. Includes the *Boldan Book* of 1180 compiled for Bishop Pudsey, *vide* Washington, tenure which pre-dates Norman Conquest. 'William of Hertburn holds Wessington except the church and the land belonging to the church ... ' He changed his name to de Wessington.

1   *Bygone Durham*, ed. W. Andrews. History of the county from Roman times to the end of the nineteenth century.

1   Washington Hall. Inscription indicates that the architect was A. B. Higham.

1   Sir Isaac Lowthian Bell, J.P., D.L., Ll.D., F.R.S. Listed in *Dictionary of National Biography* (Supplement) 1901–1950, and *Who's Who*, 1890. b. 1816, son of Thomas L. Bell. m. Margaret, daughter of Hugh Lee Pattinson, 1842. Educated Bruce's Academy and Napier College, Edinburgh. Studied chemistry and physics in Germany, Denmark, and Paris. Joined father's ironworks, Losh, Wilson and Bell, at Walker, Tyneside, 1836. Started chemical works at Washington near Gateshead with father-in-law Hugh Pattinson in 1852. Meanwhile, in 1844, with brothers Thomas and John, formed firm of Bell Brothers, leasing blast-furnace at Wylam-on-Tyne. Assumed direction of Walker works on death of father in 1845. 1854 started Clarence works on Tees, opposite Middlesbrough. Helped built Cleveland Railway to convey ironstone. Also acquired quarries and collieries. Cleveland Railway purchased by N.E. Railway in 1865 and Lowthian Bell made life director. Ultimately employed 6,000 people. Owned 3,000 acres of land, including valuable salt bed found in 1874 near Clarence. President Iron and Steel Institute 1873–5; Bessemer Gold Medallist 1874; F.R.S. 1875; President Institution of Mechanical Engineers 1884; President Society of Chemical Industry 1889; Albert Medal of Royal Society of Arts 1895; Mayor of Newcastle upon Tyne 1854–5 and 1862–3. Liberal Member of Parliament for Hartlepool 1875–80. Baronet 1885.

2   'Child of fortune', Tabor, *Pioneer Women*.

2   Hugh Bell. Sir Thomas Hugh, second baronet. *Who's Who*, 1902 *et seq.* H.M. Lord Lieutenant of N. Riding of Yorkshire from 1906. J.P., D.L. (Durham), Hon. D.C.L. Leeds. Deputy Lieutenant and Sheriff 1895. b. Walker-on-Tyne Feb. 10th, 1844, eldest son of Sir Isaac L. Bell, F.R.S. and Margaret, daughter of Hugh L. Pattinson, F.R.S. Educated Merchiston Castle, Edinburgh, Paris and Göttingen. Director Brunner Mond & Co. Ltd, Dorman Long & Co.

Ltd, Horden Collieries, Pearson and Dorman Long (chairman), L.N.E. Railway, Yorkshire Insurance Company.

2   Shield family. *Ward's Directory of Northumberland*, 1850 *et seq*. Also General Register of births, marriages and deaths, London. Maria Shield b. Aug. 24th, 1843 at States Hall, Jesmond. Daughter of John Shield, merchant, and Catherine (*née* Barnett).

2   Marriage April 23rd, 1867 at St Paul's Episcopal Church, Rothesay, Isle of Bute. Register of Marriages for Burgh of Rothesay, County of Bute.

3   Gertrude's infancy and death of Maria Bell. Diaries of Elizabeth Bell, in possession of Mr John Bell Dixon. *UBL*, *BL*, *EBL*. *General Register*, London, *vide* Mary Bell. In the turmoil which followed her death the birth of Gertrude's brother Maurice was never officially recorded.

3   Letter to grandmother, March 26th, 1874, *UBL*. Lady Bell (Gertrude's stepmother) gives first letter in Gertrude's hand as Sept. 1874, written to her; and Lady Richmond as spring 1876, also to her mother.

5   Mrs Thomas Marshall and Horace Marshall, *EBL* pp. 1–3. *BL* p. 19 *et seq*.

6   Florence Olliffe (second Lady Bell), *EBL*, *BL*.

6   Letter to *FB*, Sept. 25th, 1874, *BL*.

6   Lyulph, Baron Stanley of Alderley (later Lord Sheffield) and Aunt Maisie, *BL* p. 28 *et seq*. Also see *Autobiography* of Bertrand Russell p. 27 *et seq*.

7   Marriage of Hugh Bell to Florence Olliffe, *EBL* p. 3. General Registry, London.

7   Letter from Dulverton, *UBL*.

7   Letter from Rounton, August 1878, *EBL*.

8   Letter from 'Highfield', *UBL*.

2 Society and Oxford

10   Florence, Lady Bell, *née* Olliffe. See Janet Hogarth, *An Oxford Portrait Gallery*. Also *EBL*, *BL*, *CEB*.

10   Sir I. L. Bell, *Dictionary of National Biography*, *EBL*.

10   Bell family at Rounton, Redcar and Saltburn, *EBL*, *BL*, Diaries of Elizabeth Bell.

10   Olliffes in Paris and London, see Una Pope-Hennessy, *Charles Dickens*, pp. 24, 374, 426, 435. Also *BL* and *EBL*.

11   Views of Lady Bell, Janet Hogarth, *op. cit.*

11   Lascelles family, Janet Hogarth, *op. cit.*, BL, EBL, CEB.
11   Holidays and early education, *EBL*.
12   Letters, *EBL*.
12   Hugo Bell (Hugh Lowthian), *EBL, BL, CEB*.
12   Elsa Bell (Lady Richmond), *EBL, BL, CEB*.
12   Molly Bell (Lady Trevelyan), *EBL, BL, CEB*.
12   Letter about Mr Gladstone, *EBL*.
13   Letter to Horace Marshall, *EBL*.
13   Tuition and Queen's College, *BL* p. 19, *EBL* p. 17 *et seq.*
14   Gertrude in London, *EBL, UBL, BL*.
14   Mrs Richmond Ritchie (Anne Thackeray), *EBL*.
14   Letters, *EBL*.
14   Work at Queen's College, *EBL, UBL*.
15   Lady Margaret Hall, Oxford, *EBL* p. 95 *et seq.*, *BL* pp. 19–21. Janet Hogarth, *op. cit.* Also see *BL* p. 18, *Recollected in Tranquillity* by same author and article in *North American Review*.
16   Gertrude's appearance, *BL*, p. 20, *EBL* p. 99 *et seq.*, Janet Hogarth, *An Oxford Portrait Gallery*.
17   Oxford activities, *EBL, UBL*.
18   Letter about O'Connor, *EBL*.
19   Weilheim, *EBL*.
19   Viva voce. According to Janet Hogarth, *op. cit.*, Gertrude's parents were present at the examination, but FB (*BL* p. 21) quotes Mr Hassall in citing the Gardiner version of the story.
19   Commemoration Ball, Janet Hogarth, *op. cit.*
20   Tommy Olliffe, *EBL*, p. 125.
20   Margaret (first Lady Bell), *EBL* p. 117.
20   *Washington*, ed. W. R. Arbuckle.
20   Hugh Lee Pattinson, *Dictionary of National Biography* (Supplement) 1901–50. He was chased from America by angry gold speculators in 1840.
20   Thomas L. Bell. In *Ward's Directory of Northumberland 1850* he is described as an iron manufacturer, merchant and coalfitter of Gloucester House, N. Elswick.
20   Losh. Barrister and classical scholar. At this time Vice-Consul for Prussia, Sweden, Norway, and Turkey, among his many other activities. See also *Diaries* of James Losh, Surtees Society Vol. CLXXI, 1956, British Library Ac. 8045/119.
20   Courtenay Bodley. Mr John Bell Dixon in interview with author, Feb. 2nd, 1977. Also Sir John Leslie, *Memoir of J.E.C. Bodley* (British Library mark 10824 c. 11).

21   Lady Stanley and Dover Street circle, *EBL* p. 174, Bertrand
            Russell, *Autobiography* and Nancy Mitford, *The Ladies of
            Alderley.*

3   Europe and London

22   Gertrude in London, *EBL, BL, UBL.*
22   Lady Lascelles, quoted, *BL.* In affirmation of her remark,
            an unpublished letter from *GLB* dated July 17th, 1889 from
            the Marshalls' home, Highfield, Leeds, to *FB* says of other
            guests: 'Rather amusing – though they have none of them
            heard of Morris, so to speak!'
22   Bucharest, *EBL, BL, UBL.*
23   Letter to Elsa, *EBL.*
23   Letter to *FB, EBL.*
23   'Domnul' a Rumanian nickname meaning 'the Gentleman'.
23   Letters to Horace Marshall, *EBL* p. 193 *et seq.*
24   *GLB*'s attitude, *BL* p. 21.
24   Queen of Rumania, *EBL, UBL.*
25   Constantinople, *EBL, UBL.*
25   Quotation from an earlier biographer, Miss Elizabeth
            Burgoyne, *CEB* Vol. 1, p. 21.
26   Billy Lascelles, *BL, EBL.*
26   London and Redcar, *BL, EBL, UBL.*
26   Hugo's musical development. See *Hugh Lowthian Bell*, a
            posthumous appreciation by *FB* and Elsa (Lady Richmond)
            for private circulation, printed by Appleyard of Middles-
            brough, 1928.
27   Life at Red Barns. See *Hugh Lowthian Bell*, part 2.
27   Hugo at school, ibid.
28   Development of the iron and steel industry in North-east
            England. *At the Works* by Florence Bell, published 1907.
            A remarkable and much-neglected sociological work. In
            order to achieve continuity in the story of the Bells' con-
            tribution to the industrial development of the area, a few
            details derived from other sources have been interpolated
            here. See *The Industrial Resources of Tyne and Wear*, ed. Sir
            W. G. Armstrong, I. L. Bell *et al.*; *The Industrial North in the
            Last Decade of the Nineteenth Century*, Talbot Baines, with
            preface by Sir Hugh Bell; *The Economic History of the British
            Iron and Steel Industry*, Alan Birch (Mr Birch quotes C.
            Wilson in *Steel Review* No. 6, April 1957); *British Industrial-
            ists 1850–1950*, Miss C. Erickson, p. 35 *et seq.*

28   *A History of the County of Durham.* Also *Durham County and City*, British Association for the Advancement of Science, Durham, 1970, containing Sir Lowthian Bell's evidence to Royal Commission in the 1880s. And, *Diaries* of James Losh, Surtees Society, Vol. CLXXI, 1956.

28   Losh notes: 'May 1798 entered into partnership with Thomas Bell and Captain Thain in Alkali business.'

29   Mallets and dinner at Russells, *UBL* Feb. 14th and 15th, 1890, *CEB.*

30   Gertrude and smoking, *BL.*

30   *A Doll's House, UBL* to *HB* 1890, no date.

31   Henry James at Audley Square, *BL, UBL* dated March 8th, 1890, and *CEB* p. 23.

4 Persian Pictures

32   All references to the Persian journey in this chapter are taken from published correspondence, *BL, EBL,* and *CEB.*

36   Engagement to Cadogan, *VC* July 1892. Gertrude remarks that the marriage was unlikely because of his 'financial prospects'.

37   Death of Henry Cadogan, August 1893, *EBL* p. 341.

37   Hafiz. She would have had access to several translations of the poet's works in the British Museum Library, which she visited frequently during the years 1894–7 (see following chapters), notably the Calcutta version of 1791 with an account of the life of Hafiz by Abu Talib Khan Isfahani, and an English version by H. Wilberforce Clarke published in Calcutta in 1891. There was also a German edition by J. von Hammer published in Stuttgart in 1812. A manuscript in the Chetham Library, Manchester, contains a number of poems from the *Divan.* There were many translations of scattered stanzas from 1875 onward.

38   Quotation: ' ... compounded almost equally of head and heart', Storrs, *Orientations.* Arberry, *CEB,* Vol. 1, p. 26.

5 Family Matters

39   Billy Lascelles. *GLB*'s diary, April 12th–13th, 1895. She resumed her habit of keeping a diary of events at this point after a lapse of some fifteen years. At any rate, the surviving diaries end at Dec. 31st, 1878 and resume on April 12th,

1893 and continue with a few interruptions until October 1919. They are often scribbled and illegible.

39   *GLB* in England, *BL*, *CEB*.

39   Letter from Canterbury, *BL*, is dated Aug. 13th, 1892, which cannot be correct since she was in Persia then. Probably 1893.

39   In London, *BL*, *CEB*.

40   Hugo. See *Hugh Lowthian Bell*, by *FB* and Elsa Richmond, part 2, and *EBL*.

40   Journey to Algiers, *CEB* and *UBL*, from Avignon, Basle, Geneva, Potsdam, Berlin and Weimar, April–May 1893.

41   Stepmother's play, *Alan's Wife*. See Theatre notes by Archer and Grein and other material in British Library, listed under *Alan's Wife* (shelf-mark 2303 e9). See also contemporary reviews. Play published by Henry & Co., Bouverie Street, London, 1893.

41   Works by Lady Bell. Florence's literary output was considerable between the years 1890 and 1917. Over forty works are listed by the British Library, several for children, in French, English and German, and a four-act play *The Dean of St Patrick's*, in addition to *Alan's Wife*.

42   Bernard Shaw, *Collected Letters,* 1898–1910, ed. Dan H. Laurence.

42   Shaw to Archer, Jan. 24th, 1900: 'What I supplied is not what you wanted: well, follow up Alan's Wife: even if you fail, it will freshen you for other successes. There that's my advice to you and Miss Elizabeth ... ' And another letter, Jan. 27th, 1900: ' ... Alan's Wife is the only seed that has come up as you wanted it.'

43   Letter, July 5th, 1889, *BL*.

43   Hugh Bell's writings and speeches. He was a prolific writer of pamphlets, letters and articles to the Press (his letters to *The Times* and other newspapers between the 1880s and 1930 are too numerous to list), and speech-maker. Characteristic viewpoints are to be found in his Preface to Baines, *Industrial North*, and an address to the National Association of Merchants and Manufacturers, reprinted in the *Contemporary Review* for December 1920, on *High Wages: their cause and effect*. A favourite quotation was from Herbert Spencer: 'Any arrangements which in a considerable degree prevent superiority from profiting by the rewards of superiority, or shield inferiority from the evils it entails – any arrangements which tend to make it as well to be inferior as to be superior,

are arrangements diametrically opposed to the progress of organisation and the reaching of a higher life.'

44   Description of Hugh Bell. Letter from Mr John Dorman Bolckow to author, Feb. 2nd, 1977. Conversations with Mr John Bell Dixon. Diaries of Elizabeth Bell.

6 Round the World

45   Journey 1894, *GLB* Diary (April 1893–Sept. 1894). See *CEB* pp. 34–6.

46   Redcar 1894, *BL.*

46   Switzerland, 1895, *CEB.*

47   London. 1896, *BL.*

47   Italy, 1896, *BL.*

47–8   Letters about London, Beckenham and Ascot, *BL, UBL.*

48   Mary Talbot, *BL, CEB.* See also Janet Hogarth, *An Oxford Portrait Gallery* and *The Women of My Time.*

49   Berlin, 1897, *UBL.* Letters dated Feb. 2nd and Feb. 17th from British Embassy. Also *BL* and *CEB* and *GLB* Diary (March 1896–Aug. 1897) and *HB.*

50   Mary, Lady Lascelles, *BL.*

50   Round-the-world cruise, *BL* and *UBL* postmarked Dec. 29th, *City of Rio de Janeiro.* Also *UBL,* Tokyo, March 8th.

7 Jerusalem

53   Journey to Middle East, *BL.*

53   Smyrna, *UBL* to *FB* dated Dec. 5th.

53   s.s. *Rossia, BL.*

53   Jerusalem, *BL* to *FB, HB* and Elsa. *UBL* to Elsa dated Wed. 20th, to *FB* Feb. 6th and *HB* Feb. 11th. See also Diary (Dec. 1898–April 1900).

56   Dicksons, *UBL* to *FB,* Thursday 12th.

56   Arabic lessons, *BL, UBL.*

57   Aunt Ada and Maurice, *BL.*

57   Elsa and Molly. See *Flight of the Mind*; Letters of Virginia Woolf, Vol. 1, p. 34.

57   *Monthly Cousin.* Copies in University Library, Newcastle upon Tyne, *CEB.*

59   Desert journey, *BL, CEB.* Route described in letter-diary to *HB* from Ayun Musa, March 20th, 1900, *BL* pp. 64–75.

62   Russian consulate, *BL* April 22nd, 1900.

63   Journey to Jabal Druse, *BL*, *CEB*.
65   Palmyra, *BL*.

8   Courage and Determination

66   In the Alps 1897, *BL*, *CEB*.
66   Greece, *UBL* from Athens, March 1899, to *FB*.   Also to same from Athens April 11th, 1899.
67   Vatican and Arcadia, *UBL* April 1899.
67   Bayreuth, *BL*, *UBL* Aug. 1899 to *FB*.
67   Ascent of Meije, *UBL* Monday (probably Aug. 28th) to *HB*. Also *BL* and *CEB*, and *UBL* Aug. 31st to Elsa.
68   Bodley correspondence, *UBL* to *HB* (August).
69   Return to French Alps 1900, *BL*, *CEB*, and *UBL* to *HB* (Aug. 2nd) and 21st from Chamonix and to *FB* Aug. 6th.
70   With Hugo at Redcar, *CEB* and Gertrude's Diaries (April 1900–Aug. 1902).
70   Cedars of Lebanon. One grew on the lawn at Rounton (the estate was abolished between the wars) and another was planted at the Trevelyan family home at Wallington, *BL* p. 105.
70   At the Bell factories, Middlesbrough, *CEB* to *HB* Aug. 21st.
70   Chirol, *VC*.
71   Queen Victoria's death, *CEB*, *GLB* Diaries (1900–1902).
71   Redcar and Rounton, *CEB*.
72   Bernese Oberland, *CEB* and *UBL* Aug. 1901 to *FB* from Rosenlaui, and Sept. 1901 to *FB* from Grindelwald. *UBL* September to *HB* also from Grindelwald.
73   Mediterranean journey. Algiers, Malta, Sicily, *CEB* and *GLB* Diaries. Letter to *FB* from Malcajik, March 1902, *UBL*, *CEB*.
76   Smyrna and visit to Colophon. 'Her notes and photographs cannot be found,' Hill, *Antiquities*, Vol. L, 1976.
76   To Haifa on s.s. *Cleopatra*, *UBL* to *FB* March 1902. *CEB*.
76   Palestine, *CEB* and Diaries.
78   Return to Bernese Oberland, *BL*.
78   Chirol, *VC* undated.
79   Letter to *HB*, *BL*.
80   Mountaineering, *BL*. Summary of achievements by Colonel Strutt and others, pp. 128–9.
80   Letter to *HB*, *UBL* dated 'Friday'.

9 Durbar

81   For Gertrude's views on the women's suffrage movement and women's rights, see Janet Hogarth, *An Oxford Portrait Gallery* and *The Women of My Time*, *BL* and *CEB*. Elizabeth Burgoyne in Vol. I of *Gertrude Bell: from her Personal Papers*, p. 274, states: 'Much later, so her friend Janet Courtney told me, she was amused by her own attitude.' *GLB* joined the Women's Anti-Suffrage League in 1908.

81   Letter to Chirol, *VC*, *CEB* p. 90.

82   Queen Victoria and Edward VII, *CEB* pp. 54, 95.

82   Bishop Michael Furse, *BL* p. 131 *et seq.*

83   World voyage. Gertrude's letters home, *BL* p. 131 *et seq.*, and *CEB* p. 137 *et seq.* give a somewhat different account of the voyage from that conveyed by the diaries of brother and sister. For extracts from Hugo's diary see *Hugh Lowthian Bell* by *FB* and Elsa Richmond. Also *GLB* Diary 1902. *UBL* dated 'Tuesday 16 in the train' and 'Delhi Durbar Dec. 21' give ecstatic accounts of the early stages of journey.

10 Inheritance

91   Bertrand Russell's recollection. See Clark, *The Life of Bertrand Russell*, p. 78.

91   After publishing *Persian Pictures* anonymously, she put her name to her writings, though often reluctantly. See *BL*, and Janet Hogarth, *An Oxford Portrait Gallery*.

91   Family business. Mr John Bell Dixon, conversation with author Feb. 11th, 1977, and letter from Mr John Dorman Bolckow, C.B.E., to author March 2nd, 1977. See also sources quoted in Chapter 3.

91   Quoted description of Isaac Lowthian Bell, Birch, *An Economic History of the British Iron and Steel Industry*.

92   Arrangement with Dorman Long. Letter from Mr John Dorman Bolckow, see above.

93   Letter about her grandfather, *UBL* Nov. 5th from 95 Sloane Street. See *BL* p. 143.

93   Mary Katherine (Molly) Bell married Charles Trevelyan, the Labour M.P. and noted pacifist on Jan. 6th, 1904.

11 Asia Minor

94   Letter to Edward Stanley, *BL*.

95   Visit to Paris, *BL* pp. 146–8.

T

95 Hugo, *BL* and *Hugh Lowthian Bell* by *FB* and Elsa Richmond.
95 Letters from s.s. *Ortona* and Syria, *BL*, *UBL* of Jan/March, April to *HB*, *FB* and Elsa.
96 Mark Sykes, *BL* p. 152. Gertrude adds: 'I've seen a great deal of the Sykeses and I like them very much.' For Sykes's view of Gertrude at this time, see *Mark Sykes: Portrait of an Amateur* by Roger Adelson, in particular footnote 5, Chapter 6. Gorst succeeded Cromer in 1907.
97 *Bint Aarab*. The literal meaning is 'girl' or 'daughter of the Arab'. Gertrude's translation, *BL* p. 156, is liberal.
97–9 Letters from Jabal Druse, Damascus, Baalbek, Homs, Hama, Konia etc., *BL*, *CEB*. Also Gertrude's Diary (Jan. to May 1905).
98 Anatolian churches, meetings with Sir William Ramsay and Mr George Lloyd, see *BL* pp. 176–87.
99 Tributes to Gertrude's archaeological work in Asia Minor from Sir William Ramsay, *BL* p. 188. See also *A Thousand and One Churches*, and Hill, *Antiquity*.
99 Rounton and Paris 1906, *CEB* p. 227 *et seq.*
100 Visit to Anatolia 1906–7, *BL* pp. 191–209.
100 Letters from Cairo, Jan. 1907, *BL*, *CEB*, *UBL*.
100 Dinner with Cromers, *BL* p. 190.
100 Elsa, marriage to Commander Herbert Richmond, *UBL*. Gertrude's reaction to news of the impending wedding is probably explained by letter to *FB* April 20th, *CEB*: 'The trouble is I don't think anyone good enough for her; still I suppose she can't remain single for that reason ... ' They were married on July 8th, 1907.
101 Conversation with Fattuh, *BL* p. 209.
103 Sir William Ramsay, *UBL* to Hugo, June 14th, and *BL*.
104 Fattuh's illness, *UBL* to *FB* July 18th, 1907.
104 Letter to Chirol about Ramsay, *VC*.
104 Captain Doughty-Wylie, *VC* letter from s.s. *Ophir*, following Morocco Conference. Expresses their shared elation at result of conference.
105 Constantinople, *UBL* July 27th, 'On board the *Imogen*'.
105 Return to England, *BL* and *CEB*.

12 Mesopotamia

106 Rounton, Cambo and London, *BL* and Robins, broadcast.
107 Euphrates journey, *GLB* Diary (Jan. to July 1909). *GJ* Vol. 36, 1910, p. 513 *et seq.* Also, *CEB* and *UBL*, post-marked

Alexandria, Baalbek, Aleppo and Euphrates (Jan. 27th to July 4th, 1909). Rakka to Ana, see Hogarth, *GJ* Vol. 68, 1926, p. 365, and *BL*.

108   Deutsche-Orient Gesellschaft, Samarra, Babylon, etc., *CEB* Vol. 1, pp. 267–8, and *GLB*, *Amurath to Amurath*.

108   Palace and castle at Ukhaidir, see Lloyd, *Ruined Cities of Iraq*.

110   Anti-Suffrage movement, *VC* and *BL* p. 215.
       Britons in Middle East. Hogarth, see *Memoir* by C. R. L. Fletcher, *GJ* Vol. 71, April 1928; Sykes, see his *The Caliph's Last Heritage* p. 504 *et seq.*, Leslie, *Mark Sykes: His Life and Letters*, and Adelson, *Mark Sykes: Portrait of an Amateur*. Lawrence and others, see own writings and biographies in Bibliography and Kedourie, 'Young Turks, Freemasons and Jews', *Middle East Studies* (London), Vol. vii. Also Stewart, *T. E. Lawrence* and *The Middle East: Temple of Janus*.

112   Journey, 1911, *BL*, *CEB*. Also *UBL* to *HB* from Babylon, March 18th; Diyarbakir, May 7th; Constantinople, June 15th.

113   Lorimer, *BL* p. 242.

113   Early travellers and archaeological discovery in Mesopotamia. See Lloyd, *Foundations in the Dust*, with introduction by Sir Leonard Woolley.

115   *Gazetteer of the Persian Gulf*, Government of India Press, Bombay 1913.

115   Baghdad and Carchemish, *BL*, *CEB*.

116   An interesting account of Lawrence at Carchemish is provided by Alfred Ehrentreich in *Neuphilologische Monatsschrift*, ed. Walter Huebner, Leipzig, March 1936. He had access to reports of German intelligence officer von Oppenheim, and recorded: 'Er war ein Traumer, ein Mensch der Phantasie, ein stiller Gelehrter.' Von Oppenheim reported that Woolley was the Englishman most feared by the Turks. See also Stewart, *T. E. Lawrence*.

116   TEL on Gertrude, March 20th, 1911, *The Home Letters of TEL to His Brothers*.

116   TEL to Hogarth and Mrs Lawrence, *The Letters of TEL*.

13 Encounter

117   Shakespeare's reference is, of course, to the early Sultans, the first of whom, captor of Adrianople and organiser of the Janissaries, is better known as Murad, Sultan from 1319–39.

117   Coronation of King George V, *VC*, *CEB*.
117   Chirol, *VC*, *CEB*, *Who's Who*.
118   Florence Lascelles, *CEB*.
118   Maurice Bell, *CEB*.
118   Hugo, see *Hugh Lowthian Bell* by *FB* and Elsa Richmond.
118   Women's movement, *VC*.
118   Turkey, *VC*.
118   Doughty-Wylie, *Army List*, *Who's Who*.
119   Armenian massacres. First occurred in 1895. See Kinross, *The Ottoman Centuries*. Also see article 'Gertrude Bell' by Seton Dearden, *Cornhill Magazine*, Winter 1969–70.
120   Gertrude in London, *UBL* May 1912.
121   Doughty-Wylie/*GLB* correspondence. University Library, N. upon T. This correspondence is separate from the main body of *GLB* letters. There are some 90 letters from him to her in typescript, from 1913 to 1915, the first dated Aug. 15th 1913; and nine from her to him. They are marked in her hand 'D's letters'. The correspondence is summarised in the article by Mr Seton Dearden, *op. cit.*

14   Hail

126   Cox's views, *BL* p. 409 *et seq*. See also Winstone, *Captain Shakespear*, about restrictions on travel in central Arabia.
127   Voyage to Alexandria on s.s. *Lotus*, *UBL* to *FB* dated Nov. 14th, contains remark: 'I had a girl in my sleeper who is going to be married to a man called Shakespear in Calcutta. I know about his brother; he is a very able man in the Persian Gulf.' Wording suggests that she did not at that time know that Captain Shakespear had been given permission to cross Arabia at almost the same time.
128   Correspondence with Doughty-Wylie, *UBL*, and 'Gertrude Bell' by Seton Dearden.
129   Chirol, *VC*, *CEB*.
129   Journey to Hail. See Gertrude's brief account in *GJ* Vol. 44, July 1914, pp. 76–7, and detailed description by Hogarth, *GJ* Vol. 70, No. 1, July 1927.
130–3 Letters, *BL*, *VC*.
132   Doughty-Wylie, *loc. cit.*
133   Mallet, *CEB*.
133   Desert routes, earlier travellers. See Lloyd, *Ruined Cities of Iraq* and preface by Woolley. Also, Freeth and Winstone, *Explorers of Arabia*.

135   Shaikh Auda abu Tayya and Howeitat, *BL* p. 271. Gertrude seems to have had an easier time with this colourful shaikh than either Lawrence or Shakespear. See Lawrence, *Seven Pillars of Wisdom* and Winstone, *op. cit.*

135   Gertrude's map of her route together with field notes, *RGS* archives and map room. Map contains her own annotations.

136   Hail. See Palgrave, Doughty, Blunts and subsequent travellers (Bibliography), *BL* pp. 279–81, *CEB*. Several guest houses established by Abdullah of Hail and Tallal ibn Rashid, *vide* Palgrave and Guarmani. Description of Hail, *GLB* Diary (Nov. 1913 to April 1914), and unpublished document at N. upon T., used in Gertrude Bell Exhibition assembled by Department of Archaeology at Newcastle upon Tyne, London and Oxford, 1976–77.

140   Doughty-Wylie letters, *loc. cit.*

15 War

143   Letter, Baghdad, to Doughty-Wylie, *UBL*, *VC*.

143   Mallet, dispatch 355 Constantinople to Sir Edward Grey, May 20th, 1914.

144   Letter to Chirol, *VC*.

145   *HB* and *FB* to America. See Bertrand Russell, *Autobiography*, p. 219.

146   Letter to *The Times*, June 13th, 1914. 'An Englishwoman's Desert Journey. Arab Intrigues.'

147   For background to Britain's policies from Palmerston to First World War, see Kedourie, *England and the Middle East*, *vide* p. 11, 'The Ottoman Empire was to remain inviolate, and yet the Ottoman Empire was not able to defend itself,' *et seq*. See also Temperley, *Cambridge Historical Journal*, 1933, p. 166; Gooch and Temperley, *British Documents on the Origin of the War*; Stewart, *The Middle East – Temple of Janus*.

147   Government of India, attitude of Cox and Shakespear, restiveness in central Arabia, L/P&S/10/384.

147   Asiatic policy. Above file. Correspondence between Holderness (*IO*) and Louis Mallet (*FO*). Government of India telegram to Cox, June 10th, 1913, repeated July 1st and 8th.

148   Suffragettes, *CEB*. Also see *The Times* correspondence columns throughout month of June 1914.

148   *RGS* award. Gill Memorial prize for 1913-14 journey to

Hail. She accepted theodolite used on her travels in lieu of monetary award.

149   Clandon Park. Letter to Dr Keltie Nov. 19th, 1914, *GLB* correspondence, *RGS* archive.

149   Boulogne, *BL, CEB, UBL.*

149   London office of Red Cross, *BL,* and author's conversations with Hon. Mrs Sylvia Henley.

150   Report on Syria, *WO*(MO2) doc. 48014.

151   Letter from Shakespear. Mr Seton Dearden to author.

152   Shakespear's maps and notes, *RGS* to *GLB* Nov. 11th, 1915.

152   British policy towards Turkey's eastern empire. On July 30th, 1913 Lord Cromer, then resident in London, wrote to Kitchener: 'It may very well be that before any long time has elapsed we should be in the presence of a situation which will practically involve the dismemberment of the Ottoman dominions in Asia.' *Kitchener Papers,* PRO 30/57–44.

16 The Arab Bureau

154   Doughty-Wylie, Feb. 1915. *WO* 157, Intelligence Summaries, 687–9.

154   Troop movements, Mesopotamia, Suez and Dardanelles, *WO* 157/776.

154   Armenian abductions, *WO* 33. First report from M.I. agent in American 'Gotchnag' Aug. 14th, 1915.

154–7 Doughty-Wylie correspondence. N. upon T.

154–8 Gallipoli. See Bush, *Gallipoli* and other published works (Bibliography). Also, Raynfield, *The Dardanelles Campaign* (unpublished), Imperial War Museum.

154   Appointment of Doughty-Wylie as Chief Intelligence Officer confirmed by *WO* to C.-in-C., March 8th, message 199 (*WO* 33/731).

157   D.-W. Obituary. *The Times, Manchester Guardian* and other newspapers, May 4th to May 24th.

157   Gertrude's reaction, *CEB* and author's conversations with family.

157   Lilian Doughty-Wylie. Bush, *op. cit.* He states she was the woman who 'landed at Sedd al Bahr on Nov. 17th, 1915' and laid a wreath on his grave, but admits that there was no official confirmation. Perhaps it was a dream, he suggests.

158   Kitchener. See Magnus, *Kitchener, vide* outbreak of war,

p. 277, Dardanelles p. 308 *et seq.* Also Kitchener Papers, *PRO* 30/57–44.

158 Meetings and correspondence with Abdullah ibn Husain of Mecca and with Husain, Grand Sharif, L/P&S/18(B215/ 222) and *FO* 882.

158 Simla residence. Malcolm Muggeridge in *The Greenstick*, part 1 of his autobiography, says: 'Wildflower Hall, built by Lord Kitchener when he was Commander-in-Chief, some little distance away from Simla, just far enough to make a pleasant ride and feel like a rival seat of authority.'

158 Fitzgerald, Storrs. See Magnus, *op. cit.* and Adelson, *Mark Sykes: Portrait of an Amateur.* Also Storrs, *Orientations.*

159 Kitchener/Abdullah, document B222, telegrams 219 and 233. B22, telegram 303, L/P&S/18.

160 Freya Stark. See Stark, *Letters*, vol. 3.

161 Sykes. Adelson, *op. cit.* and *BL* p. 295. 'Bundle of prejudices', Lawrence, *Seven Pillars of Wisdom.*

161 Letter to *HB* marked 'Sunday', *UBL.*

161 Letter to *HB*, Sat. Nov. 20th, P&O *Arabia, UBL.*

161 Arrival in Cairo, Nov. 30th, *BL.*

162 Personnel and activities in Cairo, *BL, CEB* and *UBL.*

163 Clayton, Sykes, *FO* 882 (Arab Bureau) Vol. ii, Dec. 13th and 20th, 1915.

163 Formation of Bureau. Telegrams *FO*, High Commissioner, *Intrusive* Cairo, Jan. 1st–4th, 1916. *FO* 882.

164 Interdepartmental Committee, Jan. 7th, 1916, *FO* 882, and L/P&S/10/576.

164 Fitzgerald to Clayton, *FO* 882. See also McMahon to Nicolson. Private letter regarding control of Bureau and counter-espionage, Feb. 2nd, 1916, *FO* 882, and document P4744/15, L/P&S/10/576, Dec. 30th, 1915: 'Mr Chamberlain understands that the Bureau will be under supervision of CID and that Intelligence will be co-ordinated with DMI and disseminated by news department FO.'

164 *IO* viewpoint, L/P&S/10/576 minute Jan. 14th, 1916.

164 Sykes–Picot negotiation, Petrograd and Declaration of London, *FO* 822.

164 Letter from *GLB* Jan. 16th, *BL.*

164 Letter from *GLB* Jan. 24th, *BL.*

165–6 Letter to Lord Robert Cecil, from Court Hotel Cairo, *FO* 371 and *CEB.*

166 Arab nationalism. See quotations from *GLB* and TEL in Kedourie, *England and the Middle East, vide* TEL 'a doctrinaire without a doctrine'.

166   *Arab Report* and *Arab Bulletin*, L/P&S/10/657–8.
167   Dardanelles withdrawal. CAB/19 Dardanelles and Meso-
      potamia Committee. *WO* Series C (secret telegrams), and
      Kitchener Papers. Also Magnus, *op. cit.*, p. 370.
167   Letter to *FB* Jan. 1st, *CEB*.
167   Letter about Gallipoli, Jan. 10th, *CEB*.
167   Journey to India, *CEB*, *BL* and *UBL*.

17 Oriental Secretary

168   Kitchener, Robertson. Magnus, *Kitchener*.
168   War in Mesopotamia and elsewhere. See *History of the Great
      War: Principal Events*, HMSO, 1922. For an account of the
      early battles in Mesopotamia, together with the inside story
      of British, German and Turkish intelligence in the area,
      there is no better guide than Lt-Col. C. C. R. Murphy, see
      especially *Soldiers of the Prophet*, told with the aid of Turkish
      intelligence records. Also Wilson, *Loyalties, Mesopotamia*.
169   Townshend. See Maj.-General Sir Charles V. F. Town-
      shend, *My Campaign in Mesopotamia*, based on own diaries.
      cf. Moberly, *The Campaign in Mesopotamia*, and other
      accounts.
169   Gertrude's arrival in India, *BL* to *FB* Feb. 1st, *et seq*, *CEB*.
170   Hardinge's attitude to Bureau, L/P&S/10/576. Telegram
      Feb. 15th, *et seq*, FO 882 (HRG/15/1).
170   Visit of Wemyss, Herbert, Lawrence. See Herbert, *Mons,
      Anzac and Kut*, Wilson, *op. cit.* Also Townshend, *op. cit.*, and
      Murphy, *op. cit.*
170   Al Masri, Lawrence, *Seven Pillars of Wisdom*, Storrs,
      Orientations, *WO* 33 (Nov. 27th, 1915) Maxwell to
      Kitchener.
170   India's Muslims. Concern of Viceroy, L/P&S/597.
171   Herbert to Clayton, FO 882, Nov. 7th, 1915.
171   Hardinge to Wingate, FO 882, Nov. 28th, 1915.
172   'Westerners' and 'Easterners', views of generals and poli-
      ticians, see Terraine, *Douglas Haig*, and *Private Papers* ed.
      Robert Blake.
172   Appointment of A. B. Fforde, L/P&S/10/576.
173   Note to Captain Hall, *BL*.
173   Gertrude to Basra, *BL*, *CEB*. See also *VC*. Gertrude's
      approval of Lady Cox diminished after 1918.
173   Impressions of Basra and personnel, *BL*, *CEB*.
174   April, to *FB*, *CEB*. Also *BL* April 9th ' ... This week has

been greatly enlivened by the appearance of Mr Lawrence, sent out as liaison officer from Egypt ... '

174   Hirtzel to Viceroy, L/P&S/10/576.

174   Viceroy to IO, *ibid.*

174   Kut-al-Amara. Townshend and Murphy, *op. cit.*

176   Lawrence and Herbert. Viceroy to London, conveys message from G.O.C. Force 'D' May 22nd. L/P&S/10/576. Also see Wilson *op. cit.* and Herbert *op. cit.* and Moberly, *The Campaign in Mesopotamia,* which recites events without comment. According to latter, move had Cabinet approval.

176   Viceroy to London, L/P&S/10/576.

177   Hirtzel minute, *ibid.*

177   General Lake's telegram, *ibid.*

177   Hirtzel's comment, *ibid.*

177   Chamberlain. Dec. 29th, 1915, see Robbins, *Sir Edward Grey.*

177   Lloyd to Wingate, FO 882: Hijaz Rising, document HRG 16/9.

178   Letter to *FB, UBL.*

178   Nasiriyah and Basra, May 1916, *UBL, VC, CEB.*

178   Edmonds, author of *Kurds, Turks and Arabs.*

179   *GLB* Correspondent of Bureau and *Arab Bulletin.* L/P&S/ 10/576 and L/P&S/10/657–8.

179   Communication with Ibn Rashid, *BL, GLB* to *HB,* May 4th.

179   Lorimer, Shakespear, Leachman. L/P&S/10/515–17 (Personnel), L/P&S/18, L/P&S/10/506–11.

180   Abdul Aziz bin Abdurrahman bin Faisal al Saud, *Ibn Saud.* A highly unreliable intelligence report from Basra to *DMI* Cairo, week ending March 1st, 1916 (L/P&S/10/585) and included in *Arabian Report,* March 12th, 1916, based on information supplied by Political Agent Bahrain, source Dr Harrison, American Mission.

181   Hogarth, L/P&S/10/586.

181   Van Esses, *CEB,* pp. 36–9, Vol. 2. See also Van Ess, *Pioneers in the Arab World.*

182   Al Khatun. See review by Cox of Rihani's *Ibn Sa'ood, GJ* Vol. 71, 594 (1928). Cox did not speak Arabic, however, and Rihani's translation is the more accurate.

183   Philby, see own works and Monroe, *Philby of Arabia.*

183   Reader Bullard, *BL, CEB.*

183   Armenians, L/P&S/10/586 document 4121/16.

184   Arab Revolt. FO 882, and L/P&S/10/586 *vide* Holderness, Feb. 25th, 1916. 'I have never seen any evidence that a strong Arab state ... is within the bounds of possibility ... '

184   Sharif's proclamation, *FO* 882.

185   French view of Anglo-Arab negotiations. M. Paul Cambon to Lord Grey of Fallodon, Nov. 27th, 1916, *FO* 882.

185   Lawrence. See Aldington, *Lawrence of Arabia*; Kedourie, *England and the Middle East* and *In the Anglo-Arab Labyrinth*; Stewart, *The Middle East: the Temple of Janus*.

185   War Committee. Proceedings July 6th, 1916, L/P&S/10/598 document 2793, and CAB/42/16.

186   Sykes and India Office. L/P&S/10/586, minute to S. of S., 3543/16.

187   Sirdar, Simla, *ibid*.

187   Durbar in Kuwait, BL, *CEB*. *FO* 371/395, and L/P&S/10/657. Basra, *Arab Bulletin* No. 38, Jan. 12th, 1917.

188   Relations with Bin Saud, L/P&S/10/576–586, 657, 658. See Wilson, *op. cit.* and Philby, *Arabian Days*, p. 140 *et seq.*

190   Letters, BL, *CEB*.

18 Iraq

191   War. See Official History.

191   Maude, *BL*. Also Wilson, *Loyalties* and Murphy, *Soldiers of the Prophet*.

191   Personalities, *BL*, *CEB*. Also Monroe, *Philby of Arabia*.

192–3   Letters, *BL*, *CEB*.

193   Baghdad, *BL*, *CEB*. For roles of Mark Sykes, Austen Chamberlain, Curzon, Hardinge and Milner in drafting Baghdad proclamation, see Adelson, *Mark Sykes: Portrait of an Amateur*, p. 223–4.

194   *Arab Bulletin*. Foreign Office Library and *IO*. Gertrude's major contributions collected in Cornwallis, *The Arab War*.

194   Treasury attitude and amounts of money involved, *FO* 882 and L/P&S/576 which show payments of £50,000 and £150,000 per month. *WO* 33/969 (secret report from military intelligence) says £250,000 a month.

195   McMahon testimonials, *FO* 371.

196   Sayid Talib. Note from Shakespear to Hirtzel, June 26th, 1916, L/P&S/10/385: 'The man is a strong, wilful, utterly unscrupulous character usually heavily in debt and therefore importunate.'

196   Lawrence and Talib, *FO* 882. Also the *Letters of TEL*, p. 265, Britain engaged in secret talks with Talib and al Masri before Kitchener's contact with Sharif, in pursuance of policy of 'division of Islam'.

196   Unsigned letter to TEL. Probably from George Lloyd.
197   Storrs, *BL*, May 11th, 1917.
197   Storrs at Jidda and Abdullah's statement, *FO* 882.
197   Sykes's memos, *ibid*.
198   Sharifian solution. See Kedourie, *England and the Middle East*. Also Marlowe, Monroe, Philby and Wilson in works already quoted.
198   Conflicting views on policy. See Marlowe, *Life of Sir Arnold Wilson*; Philby, *Arabian Days*; Wilson, *Loyalties*.
198   Sykes–Picot agreement and revelation by Bolsheviks, *WO* 33/696. See also Katz, *Battleground*, pp. 49–52, and Lloyd George, *The Truth about the Peace Treaties*.
199   Gertrude on Sykes–Picot agreement, *FO* 882, document X/LO 3951, June 1917.
200   'Able and persuasive writers.' John Connell, *The 'Office'*, p. 32.
200   *GLB*'s work. Political documentation too voluminous to list, but much of it to be found in *FO* 882 and L/P&S/10/586. Intelligence reports filed under *WO* 33/905 Series C, Vol. 5. Correspondence with *RGS* about work on maps. December 1918, *RGS* archive.
200   *Al Arab, BL, CEB*.
201   Quotation from 'an earlier biographer', Elizabeth Burgoyne, *CEB* p. 60, Vol. 2.
201   Austen Chamberlain and Mesopotamian setbacks. Report of Parliamentary Commission on Mesopotamia, 1917. Cmd. 8610.
201   Allenby, see Official History of the War. Also, Wavell, *Allenby: Soldier and Statesman*, and War Cabinet C1/137/391.
201   Letter to *FB, UBL* Feb. 24th.
201   Balfour Declaration, *GLB*'s views on, *CEB*, p. 74, Vol. 2. Letter to Doughty-Wylie, *UBL*, Le Touquet, January 1915.
202   Cox in London. Letters to Hardinge, Chirol etc., *CEB, VC*.
203   Founder's Medal, *RGS*. Presented to Sir Hugh Bell by President, Sir Thomas Holdich, May 27th, 1918.
203   Letters, *BL, CEB*.

19   The Mandate

205   Letters from *GLB, BL, CEB*. From Civil Commission, Dec. 7th, 1917, *BL*: 'I haven't seen Gen. Marshall since I came back but he gives signs of being sympathetic towards our side of the game.'

205   *GLB* letter mentioning Howell, Margoliouth, etc., Dec. 5th, 1918, *CEB*.

206   Armistice declaration, see Official History.

206   Cox, Wilson and *GLB*, views on post-war government. See Cox, Notes to *BL*, p. 409 *et seq.*, and Graves, *Life of Sir Percy Cox*; Marlowe, *Life of Sir Arnold Wilson*; Wilson Papers, British Museum, MSS (52455–59); Wilson, *Loyalties*; and, for view from within Whitehall, Young, *The Independent Arab*.

206   Wilson's appointment, discussions in Baghdad etc., see Marlowe, *op. cit.* and Young, *op. cit.* Also *BL*, *CEB*.

207   *GLB*'s memo and report, *Self-Determination in Mesopotamia*. File 4722/18, L/P&S/10/755–64.

208   Peace Conference, letter to *FB* (dated Sunday, March 16th), 'Lord Robert [Cecil] is, I think, the salient figure of the Conference and T. E. Lawrence the most picturesque ...' See also Wilson, *op. cit.* and BM MSS (52455–59), Young, *op. cit.*, *BL*, *CEB*, *UBL*, *TEL Letters*, p. 282 *et seq.*

209   Wilson on self-government, BM MSS (52455–59).

209   Gertrude in Paris, *BL*, *CEB*, *UBL*.

210   Wilson in Paris, *op. cit.* and BM MSS (52455–59).

210   Wilson about Gertrude, BM MSS (52455–59).

211   Meinertzhagen and Aaronsohn, see Aaronsohn, *Yoman 1916–18* and Meinertzhagen, *Middle East Diary*. Also U.S. Department of Agriculture *Bulletin* 180, 1910. For details of other 'agents' of same family see Engle, *The Nili Spies*.

211   Letter to Frankfurter. Its provenance seems connected with an almost incoherent essay by Sykes (*FO 882*) filed by the *FO* before Sykes left for Paris in January 1919. Sykes had carefully cut his signature from the original document.

212   International Commission. The King-Crane Commission, set up at the request of President Wilson. British representatives were McMahon and Hogarth.

212   Wilson/Cox discussions, BM MSS (52455–59) and Marlowe, *op. cit.*

212   Gertrude's return, *BL*, *CEB*.

212   Dismissal of Meinertzhagen, see his *Middle East Diary*, also Wavell, *Allenby: Soldier and Statesman*.

212   Syrian question. Secret agreement between Clemenceau and Faisal. See TEL, *Letters*, p. 671.

212   Storrs in Jerusalem, see his *Orientations*.

213   Arab politicians in Syria, *BL*, *CEB*.

213   Fattuh, *CEB*.

213   Wilson to Stephenson, BM MSS (52455–59).

213–16   *GLB*'s report 'Syria in October 1919' and Wilson's note L/P&S/18 (B337).

216   Cox/Wilson about *GLB*, BM MSS (25455–59) and Marlowe, *op. cit.*

216–19   Wilson and *GLB* in Baghdad, Marlowe, *op. cit.*, and author's correspondence with Brigadier Longrigg and Mr Lionel Jardine.

219   Letter to *HB* Dec. 18th, *BL*, *CEB*.

220   The Van Esses. See Mrs Van Ess, *Pioneers in the Arab World*.

220   Gertrude and archaeological work, see H. R. Hall, *A Season's Work at Ur*, Methuen, 1930.

221   Bell fortunes. Conversations with Mr J. Bell Dixon, and letter March 2nd, 1977 from Mr John Dorman Bolckow to author, *vide* 'Protection for steel was a political issue in 1925/35. My grandfather [Sir Arthur Dorman] was a Conservative and Protectionist, Sir Hugh Bell was a Liberal Free Trader ... '

222   Interview with Sulaiman Faidhi. Report June 4th, 1920 to S. of S., *IO*. Box 303/1/2 Durham.

223   Iraq rebellion. For supplementary accounts see Wilson, *op. cit.* (1917–20) and Haldane, *The Insurrection in Mesopotamia*.

223   Lawrence's version, see Thomas, *With Lawrence in Arabia* and Marlowe, *op. cit.*

224   *GLB* letters, *BL*, *CEB*, *UBL*. Also *VC* July 19th, 1920, 'Personally, as I daresay my Father will have told you, I've had the most difficult months which have ever fallen to my lot.'

224–5   Haldane/Wilson. See *Loyalties* and Wilson Papers, London Library, *GLB* to Lawrence. See Lawrence, *Letters from his Friends*, cf. *CEB* pp. 162–3, 'The thing isn't made any easier by the tosh T. E. Lawrence is writing in the papers,' and, 'Again I'm up against T. E. Lawrence.' L/P&S/11/175 (*WO* and *IO* views).

225   Ibn Saud. See Philby, *Heart of Arabia* p. 229 *et seq.* and *Arabian Jubilee* p. 55 *et seq.* For history of dispute between Sharif and Ibn Saud, *FO* 882. Ikhwan, see Philby, *op. cit.* and Dickson, *Kuwait and Her Neighbours*.

226   Philby and Khurma dispute, L/P&S/18 (B308) and *FO* 882 (IS/18/37) and Monroe, *Philby of Arabia*.

226   Death of Leachman, L/P&S/11/175 (file 5890). *GLB*'s views, *CEB* and Monroe, *op. cit.*

227   *GLB* on Wilson, *BL*, *CEB*, *UBL*.

227   Arrival of Cox in Basra, *UBL* Sunday Oct. 17th to *HB*.

228   Churchill. See *The World Crisis* – Vol. 4, *The Aftermath*.

20   Faisal's Kingdom

229   *Review of the Civil Administration of Mesopotamia*, IO Parliamentary Papers C. Vol. 51 Cmd. 1061.

230   Letters, *BL*, *CEB*.

230–4   Provisional government. A detailed and authoritative account of the setting up of government in post-war Iraq and the constitutional problems involved is given in Longrigg, *Iraq 1900 to 1950*. For summary of events see chapter by Dobbs, *BL* p. 439 *et seq*.

231   Colonial Office. The *CO* took 'Arabian' matters out of the hands of the *IO* and *FO* in January 1921 and events from that date are recorded in the Colonial Office Register *CO* 781. Many of the most important documents of the period were destroyed under statute after Churchill's departure in 1922. Where there is no document, the Register summary is given here. A detailed account of the 'Sharifian solution' in Syria and Iraq and of the effect on British policy of Bolshevik plans and the rise of Mustafa Kamal (Ataturk) is given in Intelligence Report *WO* 33/969.

231   Intelligence Summaries, no. 4 onwards, *CO* 730/1.

231   Sayid Talib, *CEB* Vol. 2, p. 60. *UBL*. See also Monroe, *Philby of Arabia*, p. 105, quotes *GLB*, 'a succès de crime', and Philby 'an accomplished villain'. And Intelligence Report No. 4, *ibid*.

232   *GLB* on Lloyd George and Churchill, *CEB*.

232   Churchill, *The World Crisis: The Aftermath*. Meeting of Naqib's Council, Intelligence Report 5, Jan. 15th, 1921. *CO* 730/1.

232   Wall slogans. Intelligence Report 6, Jan. 31st, 1921. *CO* 730/1.

233   Message from Churchill, *UBL* Jan. 10th. Letter forms part of diary of events sent to *HB* at this time. Headed 'Extremist Opposition'.

233   Meetings with Iraqis, *BL*, *CEB*. Also Intelligence Reports 6–9 about candidates for Amirate, *CO* 730/1.

234   *GLB* to *HB*, *CEB*.

234   Cairo Conference. See Churchill *op. cit.* Cox in *BL*, *CEB*.

234   Letter from Cairo, March 12th, *CEB*. Wilson was not managing director of Anglo-Persian Oil Company. He became M.D. of its managing agency in the Gulf, after a brief spell as Acting Resident at Bushire.

235   Churchill, *op. cit.*

235   Letter from *GLB* to Frank Balfour, *XBL* (Box 301/1/1).

235   Conversation with Wingate. See Wingate, *Not in the
       Limelight*, p. 95.

236   Cox to Churchill, April 1921. *CO* 730 (messages *CO* 17766
       and 17873).

237   Arrest of Talib. *CO* 730/1 (April 16th). See also *CEB*, and
       Haldane, *The Insurrection in Mesopotamia*.

238   Churchill's remark to Cox, *CO* 730/1 (April 21st).

238   Arrival of Faisal, *BL*, *CEB*. Also see Dorothy Van Ess,
       Pioneers in the Arab World.

238   Philby, see Monroe, *Philby of Arabia*.

238   Letter July 7th, *CEB*.

238   Mrs Dickson (Dame Violet). See *Forty Years in Kuwait*,
       pp. 23–4. Also Stark, *Letters*.

239   Churchill and Palestine/Syria, *CO* 730/17: messages between
       Samuel, Curzon, Lawrence, Allenby, Cox and Churchill,
       March–August 1921.

239   Meinertzhagen, *Middle East Diary*.

240   Faisal in Iraq, *BL*, *CEB*. Also *CO* 730/17, article by *GLB*
       for Intelligence Report, *The Amir Faisal in Mesopotamia*.
       Young in *The Independent Arab* asserts he had 'almost
       universal approval'.

240   Letter to Frank Balfour, July 17th, 1921, *XLB*.

240   Philby in Transjordan. Monroe, *op. cit.*, quotes Philby to
       GLB p. 119, 'Of course nobody here or in Syria wants him
       [Abdullah] or any member of the Sharifian family, but what
       matter?'

240   Philby correspondence with Ibn Saud, *CO* 730 (Air Staff
       Intelligence Summaries) and *CO* 730/44 (Censorship) March
       26th, 1924, Dobbs to S. of S. Thomas: 'No doubt as to
       authenticity, Bourdillon recognises Arab handwriting.'

240   Referendum. Gertrude wrote to *HB* Aug. 14th, *BL*: 'The
       referendum is finished ... With one exception he has been
       elected unanimously.' She did not question the 96 per cent.
       Everyone else did.

240   *GLB* letter, *BL*.

241   *GLB* to Shuckburgh, *IO*, *CO* 730/17.

242   Duke of Devonshire. Meinertzhagen *op. cit.* and *CO*
       730/35.

242   Samarra antiquities, L/P&S/10/689 and *CO* 781 (Register)
       1922.

243   Rihani. See *Ibn Sa'ood*, p. 6 *et seq.*

243   Gertrude from 1922 to 1925. *BL*, *CEB*, and *UBL* to *HB*

Feb. (?) 10th, 1922, Jan. 30th, 1924, Feb. 11th, 1925. These letters show dramatic changes of mood and often deep depression.

245   Gertrude's attitude to King and British officials, *BL*, *CEB*, and author's conversations with ex-officials. Letter from Mr C. J. Edmonds to author, May 17th, 1976.

245   Gertrude's reading. Her library, presented to King's College, Newcastle upon Tyne, after her death, comprises more than 2,000 volumes.

246   Asquith. See Earl of Oxford and Asquith, *Memoirs and Reflections*, p. 207.

246   Gertrude in England, 1923, *CEB* and *The Letters of TEL*, p. 543, October 4th, 1927.

246   Publication of *Seven Pillars of Wisdom*, see Liddell Hart, *TEL in Arabia and After*, p. 402, 'The decisive impulse came from Gertrude Bell who, having read the book, craved to possess a copy.'

247   Administration. See Longrigg, *Iraq 1900 to 1950*.

247   Nationality problems. See Edmonds, *Kurds, Turks and Arabs*. Also *CO* 781 (Reg.) Vols 2–6. Most relevant documents destroyed under statute.

247   Lord Milner. See Lloyd George, *The Truth about the Peace Treaties*.

248   Renewed violence and murder of Taufiq al Khalid *CO* 730/54–71. Also Meinertzhagen, *op. cit.* and *VC* letter no. 55 (incorrectly dated February 4th, 1916) about peace with Turkey, religious conflicts in Iraq and attitude of 'Meine Wenigkeit', presumably Lawrence.

248   Arab politicians, *IO* memo C131. See also Longrigg and Edmonds, *op. cit.*

248   Nuri Said Pasha. See Stark, *Dust in the Lion's Paw*, footnote p. 141.

249–50   Gertrude in England, 1925. See Janet Hogarth, *An Oxford Portrait Gallery*. Also, address by Mrs Pauline Dower at opening of Gertrude Bell Exhibition, University of Newcastle upon Tyne, May 1976. Hon. Mrs Sylvia Henley, interview with author, Aug. 25th, 1976.

251   Ibn Saud, L/P&S/10/38.

252   Churchill to Young, *CO* 730/21.

252   Treaty of Alliance, *CO* 730/43.

253   GLB's exclusion from political matters, see Edmonds, address to Royal Central Asian Society. June 25th, 1969.

253   Gertrude and antiquities, *BL*, *CEB*. See also Lloyd, *Foundations in the Dust*. Also Hill, *Antiquities*.

253   Treaties and Iraq Assembly. See Longrigg and Edmonds, *op. cit.* Cox and Dobbs, *BL*, pp. 409–53.

255   Virginia Woolf to Vita Sackville-West, *A Change of Perspective.*

256   Letter to *FB*, Feb. 11th, *UBL.*

256   Death of Hugo. *Hugh Lowthian Bell* by *FB* and Elsa Richmond, British Library MSS and *The Times*, Feb. 3rd, 1926. He was forty-seven.

256   Letters, *BL*, *CEB.*

256   Baghdad floods, *CO* 730/106, Intelligence Report No. 8, April 15th.

256   Events in Baghdad and Faisal's visit to Vichy and London, *CO* 730 (105–7).

257   Clayton and Treaty with Ibn Saud, *FO* 882 and Clayton Papers, Box 471/11 (1927) Durham.

257   'Romance' of Iraq. *The Arab War*, Introduction by Sir Kinahan Cornwallis.

258   Letters, *BL*, *CEB.*

259   Death. Registrar General's Overseas Records, London. *CO* 730/105/107. Intelligence Report No. 15, July 1926.

259   'Dial'. Normal dose is 20–40 milligrammes; a fatal dose for a normally healthy person would be in excess of 100 milligrammes (National Poison Information Centre, London).

Epilogue

261   Dobbs, *CO* 730/105.

262   *Al Alam al Arabi*, July 14th, 1926.

262   King and Queen and other messages, *BL* p. 624.

263   David Hogarth, *GJ.*

264   Janet Hogarth, *An Oxford Portrait Gallery.*

264   Lady Bell died May 16th, 1930 at 5 Lennox Gardens, London. Sir Hugh Bell died June 29th, 1931 at 95 Sloane Street, effects £264,909.2.2, save and except settled land.

Bibliography

Gertrude Bell's own library of more than 2,000 books, presented to the University Library of Newcastle upon Tyne after her death, along with some 6,000 photographic negatives, manuscripts of published and unpublished articles, letters to her family, periodicals, press cuttings and other material, are listed in a catalogue compiled by Winifred Cotterill Donkin and published by the University in 1960. Books from the GLB collection listed here are marked with an asterisk. In addition, the archives of the Royal Geographical Society of London contain twelve of Gertrude's field notebooks with plans of churches and other buildings, and copies of inscriptions, from Anatolia, Syria, Iraq and Arabia, covering the period 1905–14, along with over 200 photographic negatives from the 1913–14 journey and a notebook containing astronomical observations and altitudes.

Published works by Gertrude Bell

Safar Nameh, Persian Pictures, published anonymously, Bentley, London, 1894. Subsequent editions with title *Persian Pictures* (1) with foreword by Sr E. Denison Ross, Benn, 1928, and (2) published by Cape, 1937.

Poems from the Divan of Hafiz, Heinemann, 1897. Reprinted with foreword by Sir E. Denison Ross, 1928.

'Islam in India', *Nineteenth Century and After*, Vol. 60, 1906.

'Notes on a Journey through Cilicia and Lycaonia', *Revue Archéologique*, VII, 1906–7.

The Desert and the Sown, Heinemann, 1907. (Subsequent editions.)

The Thousand and One Churches (with Sir William Ramsay), Hodder and Stoughton, 1909.

'The Vaulting System at Ukhaidir', *Journal of Hellenic Studies*, XXX, 1910.

'Churches and Monasteries of the Tûr Abdîn and Neighbouring Districts', *Amida*, Heidelberg, 1910 (see Berchem and Strzygowski);

included in *Zeitschrift für Geschichte der Architektur*, No. 9, Heidelberg, 1913.

Amurath to Amurath, Heinemann, 1911. (Subsequent editions.)

'Damascus', *Blackwood's Magazine*, Vol. 189, 1911.

'Asiatic Turkey under the Constitution', *Blackwood's Magazine*, Vol. 190, 1911.

'Postroad through the Syrian Desert', *Blackwood's Magazine*, Vol. 190, 1911.

Palace and Mosque at Ukhaidir, Clarendon Press, 1914.

The Arabs of Mesopotamia, published anonymously, Government Press, Basra, 1918.

Review of the Civil Administration of Mesopotamia, Cmd. 1061, HMSO, 1920.

'Great Britain and Iraq: An Experiment in Anglo-Asiatic Relations', published anonymously, *The Round Table*, London, 1924.

The Arab War. Confidential information for GHQ Cairo from Gertrude L. Bell. Dispatches for the *Arab Bulletin*. Introduction by Sir Kinahan Cornwallis. Golden Cockerel Press, London, 1940.

Iraq in *Encyclopaedia Britannica* (14th edition).

General

Aaronsohn, Aaron, *Yoman 1916–18*, Karni, Tel Aviv, 1970.

Aaronsohn, Alex, *With the Turks in Palestine*, Bümplitz-Bern, 1916.

Abdullah ibn Husain. King of Transjordan, *Memoirs*, ed. Philip Graves, Cape, 1950.

Adelson, R., *Mark Sykes: Portrait of an Amateur*, Cape, 1975.

Ahmed, Jamal Muhammad, *The Intellectual Origins of Arab Nationalism*, O.U.P., 1960.

Ainsworth, W. F., *Travels and Researches in Asia Minor*, 2 vols, London, 1842.*

—— *A Personal Narrative of the Euphrates Expedition*, 2 vols, London, 1888.*

Alderson, Frank, *View North: A long look at Northern England*, David and Charles, 1968.

Aldington, Richard, *Lawrence of Arabia*, Collins, 1955.

Alexander, C., *Baghdad in Bygone Days*, London, 1928.

Ali Bey, *Travels of Ali al Abbassi, alias Domingo Badia y Lieblich of Cadiz, 1803–1807*, London, 1816.

Anderson, M. S., *The Eastern Question, 1774–1923*, Macmillan, 1966.

Andrae, W., *Der Anu-Adad-Tempel in Assur*, Leipzig, 1909.*

—— *Hatra: der Assur-Expedition der Deutschen Orient-Gesellschaft*, Leipzig, 1908–12.*

Andrae, W., *Die Festungswerke von Assur*, Leipzig, 1913.*

—— *Die Stelenreihen in Assur*, Leipzig, 1913.*

Andrews, W., ed., *Bygone Durham*, London, 1898.

Antonius, George, *The Arab Awakening*, Hamish Hamilton, 1938.

Arberry, A. J., *The Koran Interpreted*, Allen and Unwin, 1955.

—— with Landau, R., eds, *Islam Today*, Faber, 1943.

Arbuckle, W. R., ed., *Washington, A Pictorial History*, Durham, 1969.

Argyll, Duke of, *Our Responsibilities for Turkey*, London, 1896.

Armstrong, H. C., *Lord of Arabia*, Arthur Barker, 1934.

Arniz, G. and van Berchem, M., *Mémoire sur les antiquités musulmanes de Ts' Ivan-Tcheon*, Leyden, 1911.*

Arthur, Sir G., *Life of Lord Kitchener*, 3 vols, London, 1920.

Asquith, Lord, *Memories and Reflections*, Cassell, 1928.

Atiyah, E., *The Arabs*, Penguin, 1955.

—— *Palestine Essays*, Copenhagen, 1972.

Babinger, Franz, *Hans Dernschwams Tagebuch einer Reise nach Konstantinopol und Kleinasien, 1553–55*, Berlin, 1923.

—— *Sonderdruck aus Islam*, *vide* Gertrude Bell, Ch. 16, Vol. 1, Berlin, 1923.

Badger, G. P., *The Nestorians and their Rituals*, London, 1852.*

Baillie-Fraser, J., *Travels in Koordistan, Mesopotamia* etc., London, 1840.

Baines, Talbot, *The Industrial North in the Last Decade of the Nineteenth Century*, reprinted from *The Times* with Preface by Sir Hugh Bell, London, 1928.

Balfour, Lord, *Speeches on Zionism*, Arrowsmith, London, 1928.

Ballu, A., *Le Monastère byzantin de Tébessa*, Paris, 1897.*

Barber, C. H., *Besieged in Kut and After*, London, 1917.

Barbour, N., *Nisi Dominus, A Survey of the Palestine Controversy*, Harrap, 1946.

Baring, E. (1st Earl of Cromer), *Modern Egypt*, 2 vols, London, 1908.

—— *Ancient and Modern Imperialism*, London, 1910.

—— *Political and Literary Essays*, London, 1914.

—— *Abbas II*, London, 1915.*

Batūtah, ibn, *Voyages d'ibn Batoutah*, Arabic text with French translation by Defrémery and Sanguinetti, Paris, 1893–9.*

Bayet, C., *L'Art byzantin*, Paris, 1904.*

Beale, T. W., *An Oriental Biographical Dictionary*, revised by H. G. Keene, London, 1894.*

Bean, C. E. W., *The Story of Anzac*, Angus and Robertson, Sydney, 1921.

Beauchamp, L'Abbé de, *Journal*, Paris, 1791.

Bein, Alex, *Theodore Herzl*, translation by Samuel, East and West Library, 1957.

Bell, Elsa, see Richmond, Lady.

Bell, Gertrude, see Published Works of, also Bell, Lady and Richmond, Lady.

Bell, Sir Hugh, *High Wages: their cause and effect*, address to National Association of Merchants and Manufacturers, reprinted in *Contemporary Review*, December 1920.

—— '*Safeguarding*' *and the Iron and Steel Industries*, address to Free Trade Union, London, 1925. (BM mark 8245 e75).

—— Preface to *The Industrial North*, see Baines, 1928.

—— with Sir Swire Smith and Walter Runciman, *Protection and Industry*, Methuen, 1904.

Bell, Sir Isaac Lowthian, *Chemical Phenomena of Iron Smelting*, Routledge, 1872.

—— *Principles of the Manufacture of Iron and Steel*, Routledge, 1884.

—— *The Iron Trade of Britain*, British Iron Trade Association, 1886.

—— *Report on Iron Manufacture in the United States*, HMSO, 1887.

—— with Baron Armstrong *et al.*, *The Industrial Resources of Tyne and Wear*, address to British Association, Longman, Green, 1864.

Bell, Lady (Mrs Hugh), principal works:

—— *Chamber Comedies*, London, 1890.

—— *Alan's Wife*, Henry & Co., London, 1893.

—— *Conversational Openings*, London, 1899.

—— *At the Works*, London, 1907. Re-published with an introduction by Frederick Alderson, David and Charles, 1969.

—— *The Good Ship Brompton Castle* (a novel), Mills and Boon, London, 1915.

—— *Letters of Gertrude Bell*, selected and edited, 2 vols, Benn, 1927. (Subsequent impressions and editions.)

—— with Elsa Bell (Lady Richmond), *Hugh Lowthian Bell* (Hugo), private circulation, printed by Appleyard, Middlesbrough, 1928, British Library X203/453.

Belloc, H., *The Jews*, London, 1922.

Benndorf, O., and Niemann, G., *Reisen in Lykien and Karien*, Vienna, 1884.*

Bérard, V., *La Révolution turque*, Paris, 1909.*

Berchem, M. van, and Strzygowski, J., *Amida: matériaux pour l'épigraphie et l'histoire musulmans du Diyar-Bekr*, Heidelberg, 1919.*

Berchem, M. van, and Fatio, E., *Voyage en Syrie*, Cairo, 1913–14.*

Birch, Alan, *An Economic History of the British Iron and Steel Industry*, Frank Cass, 1967.

Birch-Reynardson, H., *Mesopotamia 1914-15*, London, 1919.

Birdwood, General Lord, *Nuri as-Said, a Study in Arab Leadership*, Cassell, 1959.

Blunt, Lady Anne, *Bedouin Tribes of the Euphrates*, London, 1879.*

—— *A Pilgrimage to Nejd*, London, 1881.*

Blunt, W. S., *The Future of Islam*, London, 1882.
—— *My Diaries, 1888–1914*, 2 vols, London, 1919.
Boyle, Clara, *A Servant of Empire*, Methuen, 1938.
—— *Boyle of Cairo*, T. Wilson, 1965.
Bremond, E., *Le Hedjaz dans la Guerre Mondiale*, Payot, Paris, 1931.
Brydges, Sir H. Jones, *A Brief History of the Wahauby*, London, 1834.
Buckingham, J. S., *Travels in Palestine*, London, 1822.*
—— *Travel among the Arab Tribes*, London, 1825.*
—— *Travels in Mesopotamia*, London, 1827.*
—— *Travels in Assyria, Media and Persia*, London, 1829.*
Burckhardt, J. L., *Travels in Syria and the Holy Land*, London, 1822.*
Burgoyne, Elizabeth, *Gertrude Bell: from her Personal Papers*, Benn, 2 vols, 1958–1961.
Burne, A. H., *Mesopotamia, the Last Phase*, Aldershot, 1936.
Burton, Sir Richard, *Personal Narrative of a Pilgrimage to Al-Madinah and Meccah*, London, 1906.*
Busch, Briton Cooper, *Britain, India and the Arabs*, University of California Press, 1971.
Bush, Eric W., *Gallipoli*, Allen and Unwin, 1975.
Caetani, L., *Annali dell'Islam*, 6 vols, Milan, 1905–13.*
Callwell, Sir C. E., *The Life of Sir Stanley Maude*, Constable, 1920.
Campbell Thompson, R., *The Epic of Gilgamesh*, London, 1928.
Canning, Stratford, Viscount de Redcliffe, *The Eastern Question*, London, 1881.
Carne, J., *Syria, the Holy Land, Asia Minor*, illustrated, 3 vols, London. 1836–8.*
Carruthers, A. D. M., *Arabian Adventure to the Great Nafud*, London, 1935.
Chandler, R., *Travels in Asia Minor*, London, 1776.*
Chapot, V., *La Frontière de l'Euphrate*, Paris, 1907.*
Chardin, J., *Voyages du Chevalier Chardin en Perse, et autres lieux de l'Orient*, 10 vols, ed. L. Langlès, Paris, 1811.*
Cheesman, R. E., *In Unknown Arabia*, Macmillan, 1926.
Chesney, F. R., *The Expedition for the Survey of the Rivers Euphrates and Tigris*, 2 vols, London, 1850.*
Chiera, E., *They Wrote on Clay*, Chicago, 1938.
Chirol, Sir V. I., *Indian Unrest*, London, 1910.
—— with Lord Eversley, *The Turkish Empire*, London, 1923.
Churchill, Sir Winston, *The World Crisis*, 4 vols, Thornton Butterworth, 1923–6.
Clark, R. W., *The Life of Bertrand Russell*, Cape, 1975.
Clarke, H. Wilberforce, *Hafiz*, translation from Calcutta Edition of 1791, 3 vols, Calcutta, 1891.

Clermont-Ganneau, C., *et al.*, *Les Travaux archéologiques en Syrie de 1920 à 1922*, Paris, 1923.*

Conder, C. R., *Heth and Moab: Explorations in Syria, 1881 and 1882*, London, 1892.*

Connell, John, *The 'Office'*, Allan Wingate, 1958.

Courtney, Janet E., see Hogarth, Janet.

Cowlin, Dorothy, *A Woman in the Desert* (Gertrude Bell), Frederick Muller, 1967.

Cunliffe Owen, F., 'The Assyrian Adventure of 1920', *CASJ*, 1922.

—— 'A Note on the Iraq Treaty and Alliance 1930', *CASJ*, Vol. XVII (iv), 1930.

Curtis, Michael, ed., *People and Politics in the Middle East*, Transaction Books, New Jersey, U.S.A., 1971.

Curzon, R., Baron Zouche, *Visits to the Monasteries of the Levant*, 5th edition, London, 1865.*

—— *Tales of Travel*, London, 1923.

Dalman, G., *Petra und seine Felsheiligümer*, Leipzig, 1908.*

—— *Neue Petra-Forschungen und der Heilige Felsen von Jerusalem*, Leipzig, 1912.*

Dalton, O. M., *Byzantine Art and Archaeology*, Oxford, 1911.*

Dane, E., *British Campaigns in the Near East*, 2 vols, London, 1918.

Davidson, Sir John H., *Political Strategy, Mesopotamia*, London, 1922.

Davidson, Sir Nigel, 'Iraq: The New State', *CASJ*, Vol. XIX (ii), 1932.

De Bode, C. A., *Travels in Luristan and Arabistan*, 2 vols, London, 1845.*

Deedes, Sir Wyndham, 'Palestine', *CASJ*, Vol. X (iv), 1923.

De Gaury, Gerald, *Rulers of Mecca*, Harrap, 1951.

—— *Three Kings of Baghdad*, Hutchinson, 1961.

Delitzsch, F., *Babel und Bibel*, Leipzig, 1903.*

Della Valle, Pietro, *The Travels of P. della Valle in East India and Arabia Deserta*, Paris, 1663, translated by G. Havers, London, 1665.

Dickson, H. R. P., *The Arab of the Desert*, Allen and Unwin, 1949.

—— *Kuwait and Her Neighbours*, Allen and Unwin, 1956.

Dickson, Violet, *Forty Years in Kuwait*, Allen and Unwin, 1971.

Diehl, C., *Manuel d' Art byzantin*, Paris, 1910.*

Djemal Pasha, *Memories of a Turkish Statesman 1913–1919*, Doran, New York, 1922.

Dorys, G., *Abdul-Hamid intime*, Paris, 1909.*

Doughty, Charles, *Travels in Arabia Deserta*, C.U.P., 1888; Cape, 1921.

Dussaud, R., *Voyage archéologique au Safa et dans le Djebel ed-Drûz*, Paris, 1901.*

—— *Missions dans les régions désertiques de la Syrie moyenne*, Paris, 1903.*

—— *Les Arabes en Syrie avant l'Islam*, Paris, 1907.*

Edmonds, C. J., *Kurds, Turks and Arabs*, O.U.P., 1957.

Edmonds, C. J., 'The Kurdish War in Iraq: A Plan for Peace', *CASJ*, Vol. LVI (i), 1967.

—— 'Gertrude Bell, in the Near and Middle East', *CASJ*, Vol. LVI (iii), 1969.

Ehrentreich, A., *Lawrence of Arabia*, Leipzig, 1936.

Eldred, J., *The Voyages of J. Eldred to Trypolis, Babylon etc.*, 1583, Hakluyt, Vol. vi, Glasgow, 1904.

Engle, Anita, *The Nili Spies*, Hogarth Press, 1958.

Erickson, C., *British Industrialists: Steel and Hosiery, 1850–1950*, C.U.P., 1959.

Euting, J., *Nabatäische Inschriften an Arabien*, Berlin, 1885.*

—— *Tagbuch einer Reise in Inner-Arabien*, 2 vols, Leyden, 1914.*

Evans, R., *Brief Outline of the Mesopotamian Campaign*, London, 1926.

Ewing, W., *Arab and Druze at Home*, London, 1907.*

Fakhri Bey Nashashibi, 'The Arab Position in Palestine', *CASJ*, Vol. XXIII (iii), 1936.

Fergusson, J., *History of Indian and Eastern Architecture*, London, 1899.*

Ferrier, A., and Dunsterville, J. H., *Voyage pittoresque de la Syrie, de la Phoenicie et de la Palestine*, 2 vols, Paris, 1798–9.*

Fletcher, C. L. R., Memoir of D. G. Hogarth, with references to Gertrude Bell, *G.J.*, Vol. 71, 1928.

Fraser, D., *The Short Cut to India*, Edinburgh, 1909.*

Fraser, Lovat, *India Under Lord Curzon and After*, London, 1921.

Garstang, J., *The Land of the Hittites: An Account of Recent Explorations and Discoveries in Asia Minor*, London, 1910.*

Ghanima, J. R., *The Trade of Iraq in Ancient and Modern Times*, Baghdad, 1922.*

Gibb, H. A. R., *Travels of Ibn Battuta, 1325–54*, translation, London, 1929.

—— with Bowen, H., *Islamic Society and the West*, O.U.P., 1950.

Gillard, David, *The Struggle for Asia*, Methuen, 1977.

Gleich, Major-General Franz von, *Von Balken nach Baghdad*, Berlin, 1921.

Glubb, Sir John, *A Soldier with the Arabs*, Hodder and Stoughton, 1957.

—— *Britain and the Arabs*, Hodder and Stoughton, 1959.

Goldziher, I., *Vorlesungen über den Islam*, Heidelberg, 1910.*

Gooch, G. D. and Temperley, H. W. V., eds, *British Documents on the Origin of the War*, 1926–38, Vol. X, Part II.

Grant, A. J. and Temperley, H. W. V., *Europe in the 19th and 20th Centuries*, 6th edn, Longmans, 1963.

Graves, Philip, *The Life of Sir Percy Cox*, Hutchinson, 1941.

Graves, Robert, *Lawrence and the Arabs*, Cape, 1935.

Graves, R. W., *Storm Centres of the Middle East, 1879–1929*, London. 1933.

Grey, Viscount Edward of Fallodon, *Twenty-Five Years*, London, 1928.

Grothe, H., *Meine Vorderasienexpedition, 1906 und 1907*, Leipzig, 1911–12.*

Groves, A. N., *Journal of Mr. Anthony Groves, Missionary*, London. 1831.

Hafiz (Shīrāīz), *Der Diwan des grossen lyrischen Dichters Hafis im Persischen etc.*, ed. Vincenz Ritter, Ronenzweig-Schwannau, 3 vols, Vienna, 1858–64.*

—— *Twenty Poems*, ed. and translated by A. J. Arberry, C.U.P., 1948.

Haig, Earl, *The Private Papers of Douglas Haig*, ed. Robert Blake, Eyre and Spottiswoode, 1952.

Haldane, Lt-General Sir Aylmer, 'Despatch on operations in Mesopotamia', *London Gazette*, 3rd supplement, July 1st, 1921.

—— *The Insurrection in Mesopotamia, 1920*, London, 1922.

—— *A Soldier's Saga*, Blackwood, 1948.

Hall, Dr H. R., 'The British Museum Archaeological Mission in Mesopotamia in 1919', *CASJ*, Vol. IX (iii), 1922.

—— *A Season's Work at Ur*, Methuen, 1930.

Haslip, J., *Lady Hester Stanhope*, London, 1934.

Heidel, A., *The Gilgamesh Epic and Old Testament Parallels*, Chicago, 1946.

Herbert, Aubrey, M.P., *Mons, Anzac and Kut*, London, 1930.

Herzfeld, E., *Samarra: Aufnahmen und Untersuchungen zur Islamischen Archaeologie*, Berlin, 1907.

—— *Erster Vorläufiger Bericht über die Ausgrabungen von Samarra*, Berlin, 1912.

—— *Die Aufnahme des Sasanidischen Denkmals von Paikūli*, Berlin, 1914.*

Heyd, W., *Histoire du Commerce du Levant au Moyen Age*, Leipzig, 1885.

Hill, G., *With the Beduins*: a narrative of journeys and adventures in Syria, London, 1891.*

Hill, Stephen, articles on Gertrude Bell, *Antiquity*, Vol. L, 1976, and *Observer*, Colour Supplement, May 9th, 1976 (illustrated).

Hilprecht, H. V., *Explorations in Bible Lands during the 19th Century*, Edinburgh, 1903.*

—— *The Excavations in Assyria and Babylon*, Philadelphia, 1904.

Hirschfeld, G., *Paphlagonische Felsengräber: ein Beitrag zur Kunstgeschichte Kleinasiens*, Berlin, 1885.*

Hitti, Philip K., *History of the Arabs*, Macmillan, 1937.

——*History of Syria*, Macmillan, 1951.

Hogarth, David, *A Wandering Scholar in the Levant*, London, 1896.

—— *The Nearer East*, London, 1905.

—— *The Penetration of Arabia*, Clarendon Press, 1922.

Hogarth, David, Obituary of Gertrude Bell, *G.J.*, Vol. 68, 1926.
—— Paper on journey to Hail, with remarks by Sir Hugh Bell, *G.J.*, Vol. 70, 1927.
—— Review of *Letters of Gertrude Bell*, ed. Lady Bell, *G.J.*, Vol. 70, 1927.
Hogarth, Janet (Mrs J. E. Courtney), *Freethinkers of the 19th Century*, London, 1920.
—— *Recollected in Tranquillity*, London, 1926.
—— *An Oxford Portrait Gallery*, London, 1931.
—— *The Women of My Time*, London, 1934.
—— with Courtney, W. L.; *Pillars of Empire*, London, 1918.
Hornby, E., *Sinai and Petra: Journals 1899 and 1901*, London, 1901.
Hourani, A., *Arabic Thought in the Liberal Age, 1798–1939*, O.U.P., 1962.
Howard, H. N., *The King-Crane Commission*, Beirut, 1963.
Howell, Sir Evelyn B., 'Links with the Past', *CASJ*, Vol. L (iii), 1963.
Huber, C., *Voyage dans l'Arabie centrale*, Paris, 1885.*
—— *Journal d'un Voyage en Arabie*, Paris, 1891.*
Humann, K., and Puchstein, O., *Reisen in Kleinasien und Nordsyrien*, Berlin, 1890.*
Hunter, F. Fraser, 'Mapping Arabia', *GJ*, Vol. 54, 1919.
Hurgronje, C. Snouck, *Mekka*, The Hague, 1888.
Husaini, Ishak Musa, *The Moslem Brethren*, Beirut, 1956.
Hutchinson, E. H., *Violent Truce*, New York, 1956.
Hutton, W. H., *Constantinople: The Story of the Old Capital of the Empire*, London, 1900.*
Ihsan al-Jabiri, 'La Syrie du 8 mars au 26 juillet 1920', *La Nation Arabe*, April, 1930.
Inchbold, A. C., *Under the Syrian Sun: The Lebanon, Baalbek, Galilee and Judaea*, London, 1906.*
Ireland, P. W., *Iraq: A Study in Political Development*, Cape, 1937.
Issawi, Charles, *Egypt in Revolution*. O.U.P., 1963.
Jafar Pasha el Askeri, 'Five Years' Progress in Iraq', *CASJ*, Vol. XIV (i), 1927.
Jaussen, A., and Savignac, R., *Mission archéologique en Arabie (1907)* etc., Paris, 1909.*
Jeffries, J. M. N., *Palestine: the Reality*, Longmans, 1939.
Jerphanion, G. de, *Inscriptions byzantines de la région d'Urgub en Cappadoce*, Beirut, 1913.*
Jerusalem, Elisabeth, *Gertrude Bells Anteil an der Englischen Politik in Mesopotamia, 1916–26.* A doctoral thesis for the Philosophy Faculty of the University of Vienna c. 1935. Copies in British Library and Royal Geographical Society Library.

Jomard, Edmé F., *Études géographiques et historiques sur l'Arabie*, Paris, 1839.

Jones, J. F., *Memoirs connected with Baghdad etc.*, Bombay, 1857.*

Joseph, Bernard, *British Rule in Palestine*, Public Affairs Press, Washington D.C., 1948.

Jubayr, ibn, *Rihlat ibn Jubayr*, Twelfth-century travels in Palestine, Mesopotamia, Arabia etc., translated into Italian by C. Schiaparelli, Rome, 1906. Translated into English and ed. from MS at Leyden by W. Wright and revised by M. J. de Goeje, London, 1907.*

Judeich, W., *Kleinasiatische Studien: Untersuchungen zur Griechisch-Persischen Geschichte des IV Jahrhunderts*, Marburg, 1892.*

Jung, Eugène, *La Révolte arabe I. De 1906 à la révolte de 1916*, Paris, 1924.

—— *L'Islam et l'Asie devant l'Imperialisme*, Paris, 1927.

Kamil, Mustafa, *Egyptiens et Anglais*, Paris, 1906.

Kamm, Josephine, *Gertrude Bell, Daughter of the Desert*, Preface by Sir John Glubb and foreword by Lady Richmond, Bodley Head, 1956.

Kampffmeyer, G., *Urkunden und Berichte zur Gegenwärts-geschichte des Arabischen Orients*, Mitteilungen des Seminars für Orientalische Sprachen, Berlin, 1924.

Katz, Samuel, *Battleground: Fact and Fantasy in Palestine*, W. H. Allen, 1973.

Kearsey, A., *Notes on the Mesopotamian Campaign*, London, 1927.

Kedourie, Elie, *England and the Middle East*, Bowes and Bowes, 1956.

—— *The Chatham House Version*, Weidenfeld and Nicolson, 1970.

—— *In the Anglo-Arab Labyrinth*, C.U.P., 1976.

Kelly, J. B., *Britain and the Persian Gulf, 1788–1880*, O.U.P., 1968.

Khadduri, Majid, *Independent Iraq, 1832–1958*, O.U.P., 1960.

Khairallah, K. T., *Les Régions arabes libérées*, Paris, 1919.

Kiernan, R. H., *The Unveiling of Arabia*, Harrap, 1937.

Kiesling, Oberstleutnant Hans von, *Mit Feldmarschall Von der Goltz Pasha in Mesopotamia und Persia*, Berlin, 1926.

Kimche, Jon, *Seven Fallen Pillars*, Secker and Warburg, 1950.

—— *The Unromantics: The Great Powers and the Balfour Declaration*, Weidenfeld and Nicolson, 1968.

Kinnier Wilson, J. V., *Documents from the Old Testament*, ed. D. Winton Thomas, London, 1958.

Kinross, Lord, *Ataturk, the Rebirth of a Nation*, Weidenfeld and Nicolson, 1964.

—— *The Ottoman Centuries*, Cape, 1977.

Kirk, G. E., *A Short History of the Middle East*, Methuen, 1948.

Kitchener, Lt Horatio (Lord Kitchener), and Lt C. R. Conder, *The Survey of Western Palestine*, Palestine Exploration Fund, London, 1831.

Knight, E. F., *The Awakening of Turkey, a history of the revolution of 1908*, London, 1909.*

Knightley, Philip, and Simpson, Colin, *The Secret Lives of Lawrence of Arabia*, Nelson, 1969.

Koldewey, R., *Die Tempel von Babylon und Borsippa*. Leipzig, 1911.*

—— *Das Wieder erstehende Babylon*, Leipzig, 1913.*

—— *The Excavations at Babylon*, London, 1914.

Kramer, S. N., *Sumerian Mythology*, Philadelphia, 1944.

—— *The Sumerians*, Chicago and London, 1964.

—— *Cradle of Civilization*, Time Life Books, New York, 1967.

—— *Ancient Near Eastern Texts Relating to the Old Testament*, ed. Pritchard, Princeton, 1969.

Laemmens, H., *Le Berceau de l'Islam, l'Arabie occidentale à la veille de l'Hégire*, Rome, 1914.

Lambert, W. G., and Millard, A. R., *Atra-Lasīs. The Babylonian Story of the Flood*, O.U.P., 1969.

Lane-Poole, Stanley, *Life of Stratford Canning*, London, 1888.

—— *The Story of Cairo: history, monuments and social life*, London, 1893.*

—— *The Mohammadan Dynasties*, Constable, 1894.*

—— *Saladin and the Fall of the Kingdom of Jerusalem*, New York, 1898.*

Lawley, Sir Arthur, *A Message from Mesopotamia*, London, 1917.

Lawrence, T. E., *The Seven Pillars of Wisdom*, Cape, 1935, Penguin, 1962.

—— *T. E. Lawrence by his Friends*, ed. A. W. Lawrence, London, 1937.

—— *The Letters of TEL*, ed. D. Garnett, Cape, 1938.

—— *Secret Despatches from Arabia*, ed. A. W. Lawrence, Golden Cockerel Press, London, 1939.

—— *The Home Letters of TEL to his Brothers*, Blackwell, 1954.

—— *Letters to T. E. Lawrence*, ed. A. W. Lawrence, Cape, 1962.

Layard, A. H. (Sir Henry), *Nineveh and its Remains*, London, 1849.*

—— *The Monuments of Nineveh*, London, 1853.

—— *Nineveh and Babylon*, London, 1853.

—— *Early Adventures in Persia, Susiana etc.*, 1887.

—— *Autobiography and Letters*, London, 1903.

Leaf, W., *Versions from Hafiz: an essay in Persian metre*, London, 1898.*

Lee, D. Fitzgerald, *'D' Force (Mesopotamia) in the Great War*, London, 1927.

Leslie, Sir John, *Memoir of J. E. C. Bodley*, London, 1930.

Leslie, Sir Shane, *Mark Sykes: His Life and Letters*, London, 1929.

Lewis, Bernard, *Notes and Documents from the Turkish Archives*, Israel Oriental Society, 1952.

—— *The Emergence of Modern Turkey*, O.U.P., 1961.

Libbey, W., and F. E. Hoskins, *The Jordan Valley and Petra*, New York, 1905.*

Liddell Hart, B. H., *T. E. Lawrence*, Cape, 1935.

—— with Graves, R., *T. E. Lawrence to his Biographer*, Faber, 1939.

Littmann, E., *Arabische Beduin Anerzählungen*, Arabic and German texts, Strasburg, 1908.*

Lloyd, Seton, *Mesopotamia. Excavations on Sumerian Sites*, London, 1936.

—— *Ruined Cities of Iraq*, O.U.P., 1942.

—— *Foundations in the Dust*, O.U.P., 1947.

Lloyd George, David, *The Truth about the Peace Treaties*, Gollancz, 1936.

Loder, J. de V., *The Truth about Mesopotamia, Palestine and Syria*, London, 1923.

Loftus, W. K., *Travels and Researches in Chaldaea and Susiana*, London, 1857.

Longrigg, S. H., *Four Centuries of Modern Iraq*, Clarendon Press, 1925.

—— *Iraq 1900 to 1950*, Royal Institute of International Affairs, O.U.P., 1953.

Lorimer, J. G., *Gazetteer of the Persian Gulf*, Government Press, Bombay, 1913.

Losh, James, *Diaries*, in publications of the Surtees Society, Vol. CLXXI, 1956. (British Library mark Ac 8045/119).

Lufti as-Sayyid, Afaf, *Egypt and Cromer: A Study in Anglo-Egyptian Relations*, John Murray, 1968.

Lyautey, P., *Le Drame oriental*, Paris, 1924.

McCallum, D., Major 'The French in Syria 1919–1924', *CASJ*, Vol. XII (i), 1925.

Mack, John E., *A Prince of our Disorder: the Life of T. E. Lawrence*, Weidenfeld and Nicolson, 1976.

MacMunn, Lt-General Sir G. F., see Official Publications; also 'Gertrude Bell and T. E. Lawrence: the other side of their stories', *The World Today*, Nov./Dec. 1927.

Magnus, Sir Philip, *Kitchener – Portrait of an Imperialist*, John Murray, 1958.

Majmu'ah, *A Persian Anthology*, in Persian, Tehran, 1890.*

Mandeville, Sir J., *The Voiage and Travayle of Sir John Maundeville, Knight*, ed. J. Ashton, London, 1887.*

Margoliouth, D. S., *Mohammad and the Rise of Islam* ('Heroes of the Nation'), New York, 1905.*

Marlowe, John, *The Seat of Pilate*, Cresset Press, 1959.

—— 'Arab–Persian Rivalry in the Persian Gulf', *CASJ*, Vol. LI (i), 1964.

—— *Late Victorian: The Life of Sir Arnold Wilson*, Cresset Press, 1967.

Marshall, Sir William, *Memories of Four Fronts*, Benn, 1929.

Masad, Paulus, *Libnan wa Suriya qabl al-intidab wa ba'duhn* (The Lebanon and Syria before and after the Mandate), Cairo, 1929.

Massey, W. T., *Allenby's Final Triumph*, London, 1920.

Massignon, L., *Mission en Mésopotamie*, Cairo, 1910–12.

Maundrell, H., *A Journey from Aleppo to Jerusalem at Easter 1697*, Oxford, 1749.*

Meinertzhagen, R. M., *Middle East Diary, 1917–56*, Cresset Press, London, 1959.

—— *Army Diary, 1899–1926*, Oliver and Boyd, 1960.

Mitford, Nancy, ed., *The Ladies of Alderley*, Chapman and Hall, 1938.

Monroe, Elizabeth, *Britain's Moment in the Middle East, 1914–1956*, Chatto and Windus, 1963.

—— *Philby of Arabia*, Faber, 1973.

Morris, James, *Pax Britannica, the Climax of an Empire*, Faber, 1968.

Mueller, D. H., *Epigraphische Denkmäler aus Arabien*, Vienna, 1889.*

Muggeridge, Malcolm, *Chronicles of Wasted Time*, Vol. I *The Greenstick*, Collins, 1972.

Muir, Sir William, *The Caliphate, its Rise, Decline and Fall*, ed. T. W. Weir, Grant, London, 1924.

Murphy, C. C. R., *Soldiers of the Prophet*, London, 1921.

Musil, A., *Kusejr 'Amra*, 2 vols, Vienna, 1907.*

—— *Arabia Petraea*, 4 vols, Vienna, 1907–8.*

—— *The Middle Euphrates*, New York, 1927.

Newton, C. T., *Travels and Discoveries in the Levant*, 2 vols, London, 1865.*

Nicholson, R. A., *A Literary History of the Arabs*, C.U.P., 1907.*

Nicolson, Harold, *Peacemaking 1919*, London, 1933.

Niebuhr, Carsten, *Description de l'Arabie* etc., Amsterdam, 1774.*

—— *Reise-Beschreibung nach Arabien und anderen umliegenden Ländern*, Copenhagen, 1774–1837.*

—— *Voyage en Arabie* etc., Amsterdam, 1776–80.*

Nolde, Baron E., *Reise nach Innerarabien, Kurdistan und Armenien*, Brunswick, 1895.*

Nutting, Anthony, *The Arabs*, Hollis, 1964.

—— *No End of a Lesson*, Hollis, 1967.

O'Leary, de Lacy, *Arabia before Muhammad*, Kegan Paul, 1923.

Olmstead, A. T., *et al.*, *Travel and Studies in the Near East*, Vol. I, Hittite inscriptions. (Cornell Expedition to Asia Minor and Assyro-Babylonian Orient), New York, 1911.*

Oppenheim, Max Freiherr von, *Von Mittelmeer zum Persischen Golf, durch den Hauran, die Syrische Wüste und Mesopotamien*, Berlin, 1900.*

—— *Griechische und lateinische Inschriften aus Syrien, Mesopotamien und Kleinasien*, Leipzig, 1905.

Ormsby-Gore, W., 'Great Britain, Mesopotamia and the Arabs', *The Nineteenth Century and After*, August, 1920.

Palgrave, W. G., *Central and Eastern Arabia*, Macmillan, 1865.

Palgrave, W. G., *Essays on Eastern Questions*, London, 1872.

Parfit, Canon J. T., *Twenty Years in Baghdad and Syria*, London, 1916.

Parrot, A., *The Flood and Noah's Ark*, London, 1955.

Pears, Sir Edwin, *The Fall of Constantinople* (4th Crusade), London, 1885.*

—— *Turkey and its People*, London, 1911.*

—— *Forty Years in Constantinople*, London, 1916.

Percy, H. A. G., Earl, *Notes from a Diary in Asiatic Turkey*, London, 1898.*

—— *Highlands of Asiatic Turkey*, London, 1901.*

Perlmann, M., *Arab–Jewish Diplomacy 1918–1922*, New York, 1944.

Peters, J. P., *Nippur, or Excavations and Adventures on the Euphrates* (narrative of University of Pennsylvania expedition to Babylonia 1888–1890), 2 vols, New York, 1897–8.

Petrie, Sir W. M. Flinders, *Heliopolis, Kafr Ammar and Shurafa*, London, 1915.*

Philby, H. St J., *The Heart of Arabia*, Constable, 1922.

—— 'Trans-Jordan', Vol. XI (iv), 1924.

—— *Arabia of the Wahhabis*, Constable 1928.

—— *Arabia*, Benn, 1930.

—— *Arabian Days*, Hale, 1948.

—— *Arabian Jubilee*, Hale, 1952.

Pingaud, A., *Histoire diplomatique de la France pendant la Grande Guerre*, Paris, 1938.

Place, Victor, *Ninive et l'Assyrie*, Paris, 1869.

Pognon, H., *Inscriptions sémitiques de la Syrie, de la Mésopotamie et de la région de Mossoul*, Paris, 1907.*

Ponsonby, Viscount, *Private Letters on the Eastern Question*, Brighton, 1854.

Pope-Hennessy, Una, *Charles Dickens*, Chatto and Windus, 1945.

Porter, J. L., *Five Years in Damascus*, 2 vols, London, 1885.*

Porter, Sir R. K., *Travels in Georgia, Persia, Armenia, ancient Babylonia, 1817–1820*, 2 vols, London, 1821.*

Ramsay, Sir W. M., *The Historical Geography of Asia Minor* (R.G.S. Supplementary Papers IV), London, 1890.*

—— *Studies in the History and Art of the Eastern Provinces of the Roman Empire*, London, 1906.*

Rassam, H., *Asshur and the Land of Nimrod*, New York, 1897.

Rawlinson, A., *Adventures in the Near East, 1918–22*, London, 1923.

Rawlinson, George, *The Five Great Monarchies of the Ancient Eastern World* (Chaldea, Assyria, Babylon, Media and Persia), 3 vols, London, 1871.*

—— *Memoir of Sir Henry Creswicke Rawlinson*, London, 1898.

Rawlinson, Sir Henry C., see Official and Institutional Publications,

British Museum, below; also *The Persian Cuneiform Inscription at Behistun*, London, 1846–51.

Rawlinson, Sir Henry C., *A Commentary on the Cuneiform Inscriptions of Babylon and Assyria*, London, 1850.

—— *Outline of the History of Assyria*, London, 1852.

—— *Notes on the Early History of Babylonia*, 1854.

—— *England and Russia in the East*, 1875.

Raynfield, F. A., *The Dardanelles Campaign* (unpublished), Imperial War Museum, London.

Renan, E., ed., *Histoire générale des langues sémitiques*, Paris, 1878.*

Reuther, O., *Das Wohnhaus in Baghdad und anderen Städten des Irak*, Berlin, 1910.*

—— *Ocheïdir nach aufnahmen von Mitgliedern der Babylon-Expedition der Deutschen Orient-Gesellschaft*, Leipzig, 1912.*

Rich, Claudius J., *Memoir on the Ruins of Babylon*, London, 1818.

—— *Narrative of a Residence in Koordistan and on the Site of Ancient Nineveh* etc., ed. by his widow, 2 vols, London, 1836.*

—— *Narrative of a Journey to the Site of Babylon*, London, 1839.

Richmond, Lady, *The Earlier Letters of Gertrude Bell*, collected and edited by Elsa Richmond, Benn, 1937.

—— *The Letters of Gertrude Bell*, selected from Lady Bell's standard edition by Lady Richmond, Penguin, 1953.

Riddell, Lord, *Intimate Diary of the Peace Conference and After*, London, 1933.

Ridley, M. R., *Gertrude Bell*, Blackie, 1941.

Rihani, Ameen, *Ibn Sa'ood*, Constable, 1928.

—— *Around the Coasts of Arabia*, London, 1930.

Robbins, Keith, *Sir Edward Grey*, Cassell, 1971.

Robins, Elizabeth, *Gertrude Bell*, typescript of a broadcast, 1926 (University Library, Newcastle upon Tyne).

Robinson, R. D., *The First Turkish Republic*, Harvard, U.S.A., 1963.

Ronaldshay, Earl of, *The Life of Lord Curzon*, 3 vols, London, 1928.

Rousan, Mahmoud, *Palestine and the Internationalization of Jerusalem*, Ministry of Culture, Baghdad, 1965.

Russell, Bertrand, *The Amberley Papers*, Hogarth Press, 1937.

—— *Autobiography*, Allen and Unwin, 1967.

Rutter, E., *The Holy Cities of Arabia*, Putnam, 1928.

Sackville-West, Vita, *Passenger to Tehran*, Penguin, 1943.

Sadleir, G. F., *Diary of a Journey Across Arabia*, Bombay, 1866.

Saleh, Zaki, *Mesopotamia 1600–1914, A Study in British Foreign Affairs*, Baghdad, 1957.

Samuel, Viscount, *Memoirs*, Cresset Press, 1945.

Sandes, E. W. G., *In Kut and Captivity with the 6th Indian Division*, London, 1924.

Sarre, F., *Reise in Kleinasien, Sommer 1895*, Berlin, 1896.*
—— with Herzfeld, E., *Archaeologische Reise im Euphrat-und-Tigris Gebiet*, 4 vols, Berlin, 1911–20.
Schweinitz, H. H., Graf von, *In Kleinasien*, etc., 1905, Berlin, 1906.*
Seetzen, U. J., *Reisen durch Syrien* etc., 4 vols, Berlin, 1854–9.*
Shaw's Collected Letters 1874–97, ed. D. H. Laurence, Reinhardt, 1965.
Sherson, E., *Townshend of Chitral and Kut*, London, 1928.
Smith, W. R., *Kinship and Marriage in Early Arabia*, London, 1907.*
Soane, E. B., *To Mesopotamia and Kurdistan in Disguise*, London, 1912.
Sokolow, N., *History of Zionism*, with introduction by A. J. Balfour, Longmans, 1919.
Stark, Freya, *Dust in the Lion's Paw*, Autobiography, John Murray, 1961.
—— *Turkey: A Sketch of Turkish History*, Thames and Hudson, 1971.
—— *Letters*, ed. Lucy Moorehead, Vol. 3, 1935–9, Compton Russell, 1976.
Stein, Leonard, *The Balfour Declaration*, Vallentine, Mitchell, 1961.
Stewart, Desmond, *The Middle East – Temple of Janus*, Hamish Hamilton, 1972.
—— *Theodore Herzl, Artist and Politician*, Hamish Hamilton, 1974.
—— *T. E. Lawrence*, Hamish Hamilton, 1977.
—— with John Haylock, *New Babylon, A Portrait of Iraq*, Collins, 1956.
Stitt, G. M. S., *A Prince of Arabia*, Allen and Unwin, 1948.
Storrs, Sir Ronald, *Orientations*, Nicholson and Watson, 1937.
Streck, M., *Die alte Landschaft Babylonien nach den Arabischen Geographen*, 2 vols, Leyden, 1900–1.*
Strzygowski, J., *Kleinasien: ein Neuland der Kunstgeschichte* (Churches described by J. W. Crowfoot and J. I. Smirnov), Leipzig, 1903.*
Sykes, Christopher, *Two Studies in Virtue*, Collins, 1953.
—— *Cross Roads to Israel; Palestine from Balfour to Berlin*, Collins, 1965.
Sykes, Sir Mark, *Through Five Turkish Provinces*, London, 1900.
—— *Dar ul Islam*, London, 1904.
—— 'Asiatic Turkey and the New Regime', *CASJ*, 1908.
—— *The Caliph's Last Heritage*, London, 1915.
Tabor, M. E., *Pioneer Women*, Gertrude Bell and others, 4 vols, Sheldon Press, 1930.
Tavernier, J. B., *The Six Voyages of John Baptista Tavernier, through Turkey into Persia and the East Indies, finished in the year 1670*. Made into English by J. P(hillips), London, 1678.
—— *Travels in India*, translated from French edn of 1676 by V. Ball, 2 vols, London, 1889.*
Temperley, H. W. V., *History of the Peace Conference*. British Institute of International Affairs, 1920–4. 'British Policy towards Parliamentary Rule and Constitutionalism in Turkey, 1830–1914', *Cambridge Historical Journal*, 1933.

Temperley, H. W. V., *England and the Near East: The Crimea*, Longmans, 1936 and Frank Cass, 1964.

Terraine, John, *Douglas Haig: The Educated Soldier*, Hutchinson, 1963.

Thomas, B., *Alarms and Excursions in Arabia*, London, 1930.

Thomas, Lowell, *With Lawrence of Arabia*, Hutchinson, 1925.

—— *The Boy's Life of Colonel Lawrence*, New York, 1927.

Thompson, R. Campbell, *A New Decipherment of the Hittite Hieroglyphics*, Oxford, 1913.*

—— *A Century of Exploration at Nineveh*, London, 1929.

Tibble, Anne, *Gertrude Bell*, A. & C. Black, 1958.

Townshend, General C. V., *My Captain in Mesopotamia*, Thornton Butterworth, 1920.

Trevelyan, Humphrey (Baron Trevelyan), 'Postscript to Asian Empire', *CASJ*, Vol. LV (iii), 1968.

—— *Worlds Apart*, Macmillan, 1971.

—— *The India We Left*, Macmillan, 1972.

—— *Diplomatic Channels*, Macmillan, 1973.

Tudela, Benjamin of, *Itinerarium Beniamini Tudelensis*, Antwerp, 1575. *The Itinerary of Benjamin of Tudela*, translated by Adler, London, 1907.

Urquhart, D., *The Spirit of the East*, London, 1838.

Van Ess, Dorothy, *Pioneers in the Arab World* (Gertrude Bell), No. 3, Historical Series of Reformed Church in America, W. B. Erdmans, Michigan, U.S.A., 1974.

Van Ess, John, *Meet the Arab*, Museum Press, 1947.

Van Lennep, H. J., *Asia Minor*, London, 1870.

Van Milligen, A., *Byzantine Constantinople*, London, 1899.*

—— *Byzantine Churches in Constantinople, their History and Architecture*, London, 1912.*

Vickery, C. E., 'Arabia and the Hedjaz', *CASJ*, 1923.

Villars, J. B., *T. E. Lawrence; or the Search for the Absolute*, translated from French by P. Dawney, Sidgwick and Jackson, 1958.

Vincenzo Maria di S. Caterina di Siena, *I Viaggi all'Indie Orientali*, Venice, 1683.

Viollet, H., *Un Palais musulman du IXème siècle*, Paris, 1911.*

—— and Flury, S., *Un Monument des premiers siècles de l'Hégire en Perse*, Paris, 1921.*

Wallin, G. A., 'Report on a Journey to Hail and Najd', *GJ*, Vol. 24, 1854.

Waterfield, Gordon, *Sir Percy Loraine, Professional Diplomat*, John Murray, 1973.

Wavell, A. J. B., *A Modern Pilgrim in Mecca*, London, 1912.*

Wavell, Field-Marshal Viscount, *Allenby: Soldier and Statesman*, Harrap, 1946.

Webster, C. K., *The Foreign Policy of Palmerston*, Bell, 1951.

Weizmann, Chaim, 'The Jewish Position in Palestine', *CASJ*, Vol. XXIII (iii), 1936.

—— *Trial and Error*, Hamish Hamilton, 1949.

Wellsted, J. R., *Travels in Arabia*, 2 vols, London, 1838.*

Wigram, W. A., *The Assyrian Settlement*, London, 1922.

—— with E. T. A. Wigram, *The Cradle of Mankind*, London, 1914.*

Willcocks, Sir W., *The Irrigation of Mesopotamia*, 2 vols, London, 1911.

Willson, B., 'Our Amazing Syrian Adventure', *National Review*, 1920.

Wilson, Sir Arnold T., *Loyalties, Mesopotamia*, 2 vols, O.U.P., 1930–1.

—— 'Mesopotamia 1914–21', *CASJ*, Vol. VIII (iii), 1921.

Wingate, Sir Ronald, *Not in the Limelight*, Hutchinson, 1959.

Winstone, H. V. F., *Captain Shakespear*, Cape, 1976.

—— with Freeth, Zahra, *Kuwait: Prospect and Reality*, Allen and Unwin, 1972.

—— *Explorers of Arabia*, Allen and Unwin, 1977.

Wittlin, Alma, *Abdul Hamid, the Shadow of God*, translated from German by N. Denny, J. Lane, 1940.

Woodward, E. L. and Butler, R., *Documents on British Foreign Policy, 1919–39*, Vol. I 1947, Vol. IV 1952.

Woolf, Virginia, *Flight of the Mind*, Letters 1888–1912 ed. Nigel Nicolson, Vol. 1, Hogarth Press, 1975.

—— *A Change of Perspective, Letters of Virginia Woolf, 1923–28*, ed. Nigel Nicolson, Hogarth Press, 1977.

Woolley, Sir C. L., 'The Excavations at Ur of the Chaldees, 1922–23', *CASJ*, Vol. X (iv), 1923.

—— 'Ur and Tel el Obeid', *CASJ*, Vol. XI (iv), 1924.

—— 'The Excavations at Ur, 1924–25', *CAJS*, Vol. XII (iv), 1925.

—— *Ur of the Chaldees*, London, 1929.

—— *Ur Excavations*, 3 vols, Kegan Paul, 1934–9.

—— *The Development of Sumerian Art*, London, 1935.

Wright, Denis, *The English Among the Persians*, Heinemann, 1977.

Wüstenfeld, F., *Genealogische Tabellen der Arabischen Stämme und Familien*, 2 vols, Göttingen, 1852–3.*

—— *Chroniken der Stadt Mekka*, Leipzig, 1857.

Young, Sir G., *Corps de droit ottoman*, 7 vols, Clarendon Press, 1905–6.

Young, Sir H., *The Independent Arab*, John Murray, 1933.

Young, Kenneth, *Arthur James Balfour*, Bell, 1963.

Younghusband, Lt-General Sir G. J., *Forty Years a Soldier*, London, 1923.

Zeine, Z. N., *The Struggle for Arab Independence*, Beirut, 1960.

Zetland, Marquess of, *Lord Cromer*, London, 1932.

Zwemer, Rev. S. M., *Arabia: the Cradle of Islam*, Revell, New York, 1900, and London, 1912.*

Official and Institutional Publications

British Museum:
The Babylonian Story of the Deluge and the Epic of Gilgamesh, E. A. W. Budge, 1920.
The Cuneiform Inscriptions, translated by Sir H. C. Rawlinson, 4 vols, 1861–91. Shelf marks 1705 C12 and 1706 C27.
The Flood, Edmond Sollberger, with brief history of Sumerian, Babylonian and Assyrian legends and bibliography, 1962.
A Guide to Babylonian and Assyrian Antiquities, 1908.*
A Guide to the Early Christian and Byzantine Antiquities, 1903.*
Carnegie Endowment, *Report of the International Commission of Inquiry into the Balkan Wars*, Washington, 1914.*
Central Asiatic Society Journal (CASJ) miscellaneous items:
'The Early Days of the Arab Government in Iraq', 'A Correspondent in Baghdad', Vol. IX (iv), 1922.
'Three Difficult Months in Iraq', 'A Correspondent in Baghdad', Vol. X (i), 1922..
'Current Affairs in Iraq', 'A Correspondent in Baghdad', Vol. X, 1923.
'Gertrude Bell', review of E. Burgoyne's work by D.C., Vol. XLIX (i), 1962.
See also in General section under Cunliffe Owen, Davidson (Sir Nigel), Deedes, Edwards, Fakhri Bey Nashashibi, Hall, Howell, Jafar Pasha el Askeri, Marlowe, McCallum, Philby, Sykes, Trevelyan, Vickery, Weizmann, Wilson and Woolley.
Committee of Imperial Defence, Historical Division, Official History of the War, 1920–33:
Military Operations Gallipoli, Aspinall-Oglander.
The Campaign in Mesopotamia, F. T. Moberly.
Australian Contingent BEF, 1914–18, C. E. W. Bean.
Military Operations in Egypt and Palestine from Outbreak of War to June 1917, G. MacMunn and Cyril Falls.
Military Operations in Egypt and Palestine from June 1917 to End of War, Cyril Falls.
Naval Operations, Vol. 3 *The Dardanelles Campaign, The Mesopotamian Campaign*, Sir Julian Corbett.
Correspondence between Sir Henry McMahon and The Sharif Husain of Mecca, Cmd. 1061, HMSO, 1939.
Report of Committee set up to consider certain correspondence between Sir Henry McMahon and the Sharif of Mecca in 1915 and 1916, Cmd. 6974, HMSO, 1939.

Geographical Journal, miscellaneous items:
  Vol. 72, 1928, p. 283. Review of *Persian Pictures* re-issued.
  Vol. 73, 1929, p. 498. Bell and Herzfeld on Samarra antiquities and
    ruins.
  See also in General section under Fletcher, Hogarth (David), Hunter
    and Wallin.
Mesopotamian Commission. Report of Commission appointed by Act
  of Parliament, 1917, Cmd. 8610.
Ottoman Archives, Programme du Ministère des Travaux Publics,
  Constantinople, 1909.*
Palestine Exploration Fund, Summary 1865–95, London, 1895.
Palestine Royal Commission, minutes of public sessions, Cmd. 5479,
  CO 134, 1937.
Princeton University Archaeological Expedition to Syria, 1904–5 and
  1909, 16 vols, Leyden, 1907–22.*
Turkey, Cmd. 8304, HMSO, 1897.
University of London Institute of Historical Research, *A History of the
  County of Durham,* from the first edition of 1905, London, 1968.

Index